The Sopherim and Scripture

INTRODUCTION TO THE TEXT OF THE OLD TESTAMENT

FROM THE AUTHORS AND SCRIBES TO THE MODERN CRITICAL TEXT

Edward D. Andrews

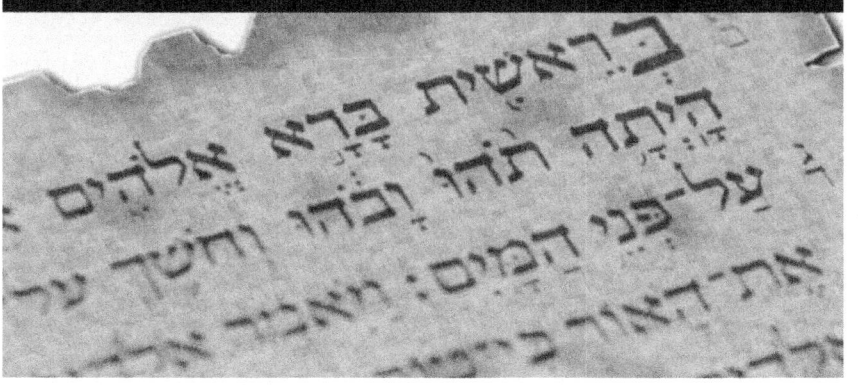

INTRODUCTION TO THE TEXT OF THE OLD TESTAMENT

From the Authors and Scribes to the Modern Critical Text

Edward D. Andrews

Christian Publishing House
Cambridge, Ohio

Copyright © 2023 Edward D. Andrews

All rights reserved. Except for brief quotations in articles, other publications, book reviews, and blogs, no part of this book may be reproduced in any manner without prior written permission from the publishers. For information, write, support@christianpublishers.org

Unless otherwise stated, Scripture quotations are from Updated American Standard Version (UASV) Copyright © 2022 by Christian Publishing House

INTRODUCTION TO THE TEXT OF THE OLD TESTAMENT: From the Authors and Scribes to the Modern Critical Text by Edward D. Andrews

ISBN-13: **9798375131528**

Table of Contents

Preface 6

Introduction... 7

CHAPTER 1 The Hebrew Old Testament from the Days of Ezra to the Biblia Hebraica Stuttgartensia 9

CHAPTER 2 Writing After the Flood in the Ancient Near East 25

CHAPTER 2 Transmission of the Old Testament Text............72

CAHPTER 3 The Dead Sea Scrolls 115

CHAPTER 4 The Samaritan Pentateuch 156

CHAPTER 5 The Greek Septuagint...................................... 177

CHAPTER 6 The Aramaic Targums 205

CHAPTER 7 The Syriac Peshitta 214

CHAPTER 8 The Latin Vulgate 225

CHAPTER 9 The Goal and Task of Textual Criticism 235

CHAPTER 10 Scribal Changes in the Hebrew Old Testament Text..248

CHAPTER 11 Old Testament Textual Commentary on the Book of Genesis 257

CHAPTER 12 The Importance of Textual Criticism................292

GLOSSARY OF TECHNICAL TERMS 296

BIBLIOGRAPHY 311

Edward D. Andrews

Preface

The Old Testament is a treasure trove of history, culture, and spiritual wisdom. Its texts have shaped the beliefs and practices of countless individuals and communities throughout the centuries. In this book, we will embark on a journey through the text of the Old Testament, exploring its origins and development from the perspectives of the authors and scribes who created it to the modern critical text that we have today. As we delve deeper into the meaning and significance of these ancient texts, we will gain a deeper understanding of the rich cultural and religious heritage that they represent. Whether you are a student of theology, a historian, or a pastor or churchgoer who is interested in learning more about this important aspect of human history, this book will provide you with a wealth of knowledge and inspiration. So, let us begin this journey together and discover the true depth and beauty of the Old Testament.

Old Testament textual criticism is important for a number of reasons.

First, the Old Testament is a central text in Judaism and Christianity, and a reliable and accurate text is important for understanding and interpreting the teachings and beliefs of these religions.

Second, the Old Testament is a significant historical document that provides insight into the history and culture of the ancient Near East. A reliable and accurate text is important for understanding the events and people described in the Old Testament and for reconstructing the history of the region.

Third, the Old Testament is an important source of literature and has had a significant influence on Western culture. A reliable and accurate text is important for understanding the literature and its place in the cultural tradition.

Finally, textual criticism is an important tool for scholars and researchers studying the Old Testament and other ancient texts. It helps to establish the most accurate and reliable version of the text, which can then be used as the basis for further study and interpretation. The goal is the process of attempting to ascertain the original wording of an original text.

Introduction

Welcome to the world of the Old Testament! This ancient collection of texts has played a significant role in shaping human history, culture, and spiritual beliefs. From the earliest authors and scribes to the modern critical text, the Old Testament has undergone a fascinating journey of development and interpretation.

In this book, we will dive into the rich history and cultural context of the Old Testament, examining the texts from the perspectives of the authors and scribes who created them. We will explore the various literary genres and styles found within the Old Testament and gain a deeper understanding of their meanings and significance. We will also delve into the modern critical text and discover how scholars have approached the study of the Old Testament throughout the centuries.

This journey will not only deepen your knowledge and understanding of the Old Testament, but it will also inspire you to think more critically and creatively about the world around you. It will open your eyes to the rich cultural and religious heritage of the past and help you appreciate the legacy of the Old Testament in shaping the present and the future.

So, whether you are a student of theology, a historian, or simply someone who is interested in learning more about this important aspect of human history, this book is for you. I invite you to come along with me on this journey and discover the true depth and beauty of the Old Testament.

Insights Into

Old Testament textual criticism is the study of the texts of the Old Testament, the Hebrew Bible, with the goal of identifying and reconstructing the original text. This involves examining the various manuscripts and versions of the Old Testament that have been preserved over the centuries in order to determine the most accurate representation of the original text.

Textual criticism is a method of studying the transmission of texts over time and involves examining the various manuscripts and versions of a text to identify errors and inconsistencies and to establish the most accurate version of the text. In the case of the Old Testament, this involves looking at the Hebrew manuscripts as well as translations into other languages, such as Greek, Latin, and English.

Textual critics use a variety of tools and methods to study the texts, including paleography, which is the study of ancient writing systems and scripts; linguistics, which is the study of language and its structure; and comparative literature, which involves comparing texts to one another in order to identify similarities and differences.

The goal of Old Testament textual criticism is to establish the most accurate and reliable text of the Old Testament, which can then be used as the basis for translations and other scholarly studies. The goal is the process of attempting to ascertain the original wording of an original text.

CHAPTER 1 The Hebrew Old Testament from the Days of Ezra to the Biblia Hebraica Stuttgartensia

A Brief Overview

The Hebrew Old Testament, also known as the Tanakh or Hebrew Bible, is the collection of thirty-nine sacred texts that are central to Judaism and are also accepted by many Christian denominations as part of their canon of scripture. The Hebrew Old Testament includes the Torah (also known as the Pentateuch or the Five Books of Moses), the Prophets, and the Writings. It is the authoritative text of the Old Testament by Jews and many Christian scholars.

The Hebrew Old Testament was transmitted orally and in written form throughout ancient Israel and beyond. It originated in the second millennium BC and was based on earlier oral and written records when considering the information in Genesis. The books once produced were transmitted orally and in written form in ancient Israel.

Over time, the Hebrew Old Testament was copied and preserved by a number of different groups of scribes and scholars, including the Sopherim (also spelled Soferim or Sopherin), who was responsible for establishing the system of vocalization and cantillation that is used in the Masoretic Text, the traditional Hebrew text of the Jewish Bible. The Masoretic Text is named after the Masoretes, Jewish scholars who worked to preserve and standardize the text of the Hebrew Bible between the 6th and 10th centuries AD.

The Masoretic Text is considered to be a reliable representation of the original Hebrew text of the Bible, and it is often used as the basis for translations of the Old Testament into other languages. It is also an important part of Jewish religious tradition and is used in Jewish worship and study.

Overall, the Hebrew Old Testament has been transmitted and preserved through a combination of oral and written tradition. It has been carefully preserved and studied by a number of different groups of scribes and scholars over the centuries. It is an important source for scholars studying the history and development of the Hebrew Bible and the cultural and historical context in which it was produced.

The Sopherim, the Men Who Copied the Hebrew Scriptures Starting in the Days of Ezra

The Sopherim (also spelled Soferim or Sopherin) were a group of Jewish scribes and scholars who were responsible for copying and preserving the Hebrew Scriptures (also known as the Tanakh or Old Testament) starting in the days of Ezra, a Jewish priest and scribe who lived in the 5th century BC.

According to tradition, the Sopherim were responsible for establishing the system of vocalization and cantillation that is used in the Masoretic Text, the traditional Hebrew text of the Jewish Bible. They also played a role in the development of the Jewish system of biblical interpretation known as midrash, which involves the careful study and interpretation of the Hebrew Bible.

The Sopherim were important figures in Jewish history and played a crucial role in preserving and transmitting the Hebrew Scriptures. They were responsible for ensuring the accuracy and integrity of the text and for passing it down from one generation to the next. Their work was instrumental in the development of the Masoretic Text, which is considered to be the authoritative text of the Hebrew Bible by Jews and many Christian scholars.

Overall, the Sopherim were a group of dedicated and skilled scribes and scholars who played a crucial role in preserving and transmitting the Hebrew Scriptures. Their work continues to be important for scholars studying the Hebrew Bible and for those who use the Masoretic Text in Jewish worship and study. Even so, some sopherim between the days of Ezra and the time of Jesus took liberties with the Hebrew text, making textual changes. The scribal successors of the Sopherim a few centuries after Jesus Christ were

INTRODUCTION TO THE TEXT OF THE OLD TESTAMENT

known as the Masoretes. These detected the scribal changes made by the earlier Sopherim. So, they documented them in the margin or at the end of the Hebrew text.

The Consonantal Hebrew Text of the First and Second Centuries CE

The consonantal Hebrew text of the first and second centuries CE refers to the form of the Hebrew Bible that was used in ancient Israel during this time period. This text consisted only of the consonants of the Hebrew words, without any vowel points or other marks to indicate pronunciation or grammatical structure.

The consonantal Hebrew text was used during a time when the oral tradition of the Hebrew Bible was still strong, and many people were familiar with the correct pronunciation and interpretation of the text. However, as the oral tradition began to decline and the Hebrew language changed over time, it became increasingly important to preserve the correct pronunciation and interpretation of the text in written form. This led to the development of the Masoretic Text, a version of the Hebrew Bible that included vowel points and other marks to help preserve the correct pronunciation and interpretation of the text.

The consonantal Hebrew text of the first and second centuries CE is an important source for scholars studying the history and development of the Hebrew Bible. It provides valuable insights into the form and content of the Hebrew text during this time period and helps scholars understand how the text may have changed over time. However, it is generally not used as the basis for modern translations of the Old Testament into other languages, as the Masoretic Text is generally considered to be a more accurate and reliable representation of the original Hebrew text.

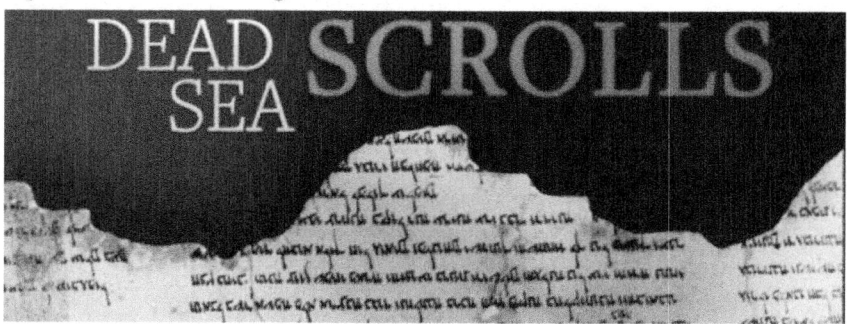

Image 1 The Dead Sea Scrolls are ancient Jewish and Hebrew religious manuscripts discovered between 1946 and 1956 at the Qumran Caves

11

Dead Sea Scrolls

The Dead Sea Scrolls are a collection of Jewish texts that were discovered in the 1940s in the vicinity of the Dead Sea in Israel. The texts are written in Hebrew, with some fragments written in Greek and Aramaic. They are believed to have been written between the 2nd century BC and the 1st century AD, and include fragments from every book of the Hebrew Bible, as well as other Jewish texts such as hymns, prayers, and legal texts.

The Dead Sea Scrolls are significant because they are some of the oldest surviving copies of the Hebrew Bible, and they provide valuable insights into the history and development of the text. They contain many variations and differences from the traditional Masoretic Text, the version of the Hebrew Bible that is used by Jews and many Christian scholars today. These differences have allowed scholars to study how the text of the Hebrew Bible may have changed over time and how different copies of the text may have influenced each other.

The Dead Sea Scrolls are also significant because they provide a window into the religious and cultural life of the ancient Jewish community that produced them. They contain many texts that are not found in the Masoretic Text, including hymns, prayers, and legal texts, which help scholars understand the beliefs and practices of the ancient Jewish community.

Overall, the Dead Sea Scrolls are an important source for scholars studying the Hebrew Bible and the history and culture of ancient Judaism. They are a valuable resource for understanding the text of the Hebrew Bible and the religious and cultural context in which it was produced.

The Masoretic Text

The Masoretic Text is the traditional Hebrew text of the Jewish Bible (also known as the Tanakh or Old Testament). It is named after the Masoretes, Jewish scholars who worked to preserve and standardize the text of the Hebrew Bible between the 6th and 10th centuries CE.

The Masoretic Text is considered to be the authoritative text of the Hebrew Bible by Jews and many Christian scholars. It is based on the text of the Hebrew Bible as it was transmitted orally and in written form in ancient Israel and is considered to be a reliable representation of the original text.

The Masoretic Text is written in Hebrew and consists of the Torah (the first five books of the Old Testament), the Nevi'im (the prophets), and the Ketuvim (the writings). It is written in consonantal text, with vowel points and other marks added to indicate pronunciation and grammatical structure. The vowel points and other marks are known as the Masorah and were added by the Masoretes to help preserve the correct pronunciation and interpretation of the text.

The Masoretic Text has a long and complex history, with many different versions and manuscripts being produced over the centuries. The most well-known version of the Masoretic Text is the one produced by the Masorete Aaron ben Moses ben Asher in the 9th century CE, which is considered to be the most accurate and reliable version.

In addition to preserving and standardizing the text of the Hebrew Bible, the Masoretes also played a crucial role in the development of the Jewish system of biblical interpretation known as Midrash. They believed that the text of the Hebrew Bible contained many layers of meaning and that it was important to study and interpret it carefully in order to understand its full significance.

The Masoretic Text continues to be an important source for scholars studying the Hebrew Bible, and it is often used as the basis for translations of the Old Testament into other languages. It is also an important part of Jewish religious tradition and is used in Jewish worship and study.

Who Were the Masoretes?

The Masoretes were Jewish scholars who worked to preserve and standardize the text of the Hebrew Bible (also known as the Tanakh or Old Testament) between the 6th and 10th centuries CE. The Masoretic Text is named after them.

The Masoretes were based in Palestine and Babylonia, and they worked to ensure the accuracy and integrity of the Hebrew text of the Bible by adding vowel points and other marks to the consonantal text. These marks, known as the Masorah, helped to preserve the correct pronunciation and interpretation of the text.

The Masoretes were also responsible for the development of the Jewish system of biblical interpretation known as midrash, which involves the careful study and interpretation of the Hebrew Bible. They believed that the text of the Hebrew Bible contained many layers of meaning and that it was important to study and interpret it carefully in order to understand its full significance.

The most well-known Masorete was Aaron ben Moses ben Asher, who produced a version of the Masoretic Text in the 9th century CE that is considered to be the most accurate and reliable version. Other important Masoretes include his father Moses ben Asher and his brother Aharon ben Asher.

The work of the Masoretes was crucial in preserving the Hebrew text of the Bible and ensuring its accuracy and integrity. Their work continues to be important for scholars studying the Hebrew Bible, and the Masoretic Text is often used as the basis for translations of the Old Testament into other languages. It is also an important part of Jewish religious tradition and is used in Jewish worship and study.

Image 2 'Text of the Tradition') is the authoritative Hebrew and Aramaic text of the 24 books of the Hebrew Bible (Tanakh) in Rabbinic Judaism

INTRODUCTION TO THE TEXT OF THE OLD TESTAMENT

The Masorah

The Masorah is a set of marks and annotations added to the Masoretic Text, the traditional Hebrew text of the Jewish Bible (also known as the Tanakh or Old Testament). The Masorah was added by the Masoretes, Jewish scholars who worked to preserve and standardize the text of the Hebrew Bible between the 6th and 10th centuries CE.

The Masorah consists of vowel points and other marks added to the consonantal text of the Hebrew Bible in order to indicate pronunciation and grammatical structure. It also includes annotations and comments on the text, such as notes on word usage and spelling and lists of synonyms and variant readings.

The Masorah was added by the Masoretes in order to help preserve the correct pronunciation and interpretation of the text. It is an important part of the Masoretic Text and is often used by scholars studying the Hebrew Bible to help understand the text and its context.

The Masorah is divided into two main categories: the larger Masorah, which is found in the margins of the text, and the smaller Masorah, which is found in the text itself. The larger Masorah includes lists of synonyms and variant readings, as well as other annotations and comments on the text, while the smaller Masorah consists primarily of vowel points and other marks added to the consonantal text.

Overall, the Masorah is an important feature of the Masoretic Text and is a valuable resource for scholars studying the Hebrew Bible. It helps to preserve the accuracy and integrity of the text and provides important insights into the history and context of the Hebrew Bible.

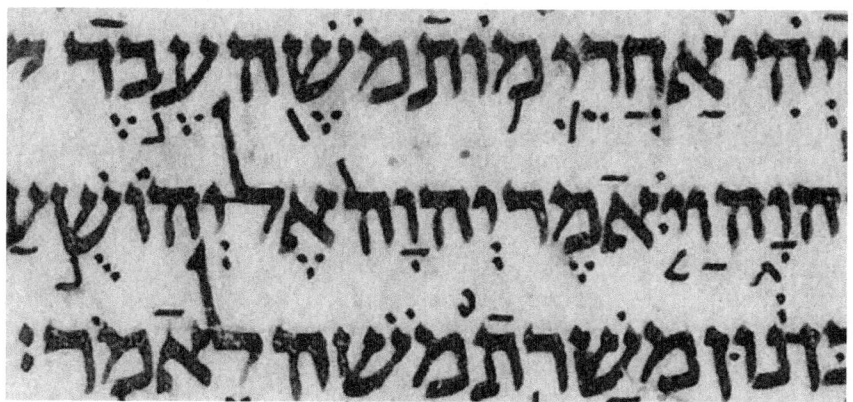

Image 3 'Crown of Aleppo') is a medieval bound manuscript of the Hebrew Bible. The codex was written in the city of Tiberias in the tenth century CE (circa 920)

The Aleppo Codex

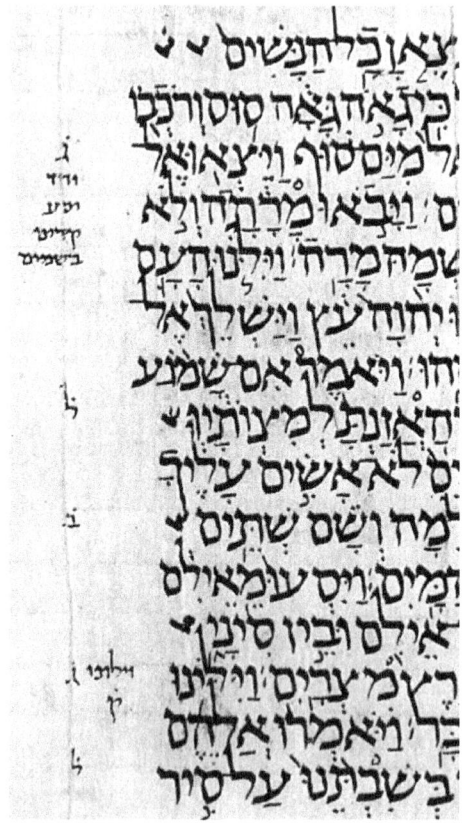

Image 4 Leningrad Codex text sample, portions of Exodus 15:21-16:3

The Aleppo Codex is a medieval Hebrew Bible manuscript that is considered to be one of the most important and reliable copies of the Masoretic Text, the traditional Hebrew text of the Jewish Bible (also known as the Tanakh or Old Testament). It was produced in the 10th century CE in the city of Tiberias, Israel, and is named after the city of Aleppo in Syria, where it was housed for many centuries.

The Aleppo Codex is a parchment manuscript that contains the complete text of the Hebrew Bible, including the Torah (the first five books of the Old Testament), the Nevi'im (the prophets), and the ketuvim (the writings). It is written in consonantal text, with vowel points and other marks added to indicate pronunciation and grammatical structure. These marks are known as the Masorah, and were added by the Masoretes, Jewish scholars who worked to preserve and standardize the text of the Hebrew Bible.

The Aleppo Codex is considered to be one of the most accurate and reliable copies of the Masoretic Text, and it is often used as the basis for translations of the Old Testament into other languages. It is also an important part of Jewish religious tradition and is used in Jewish worship and study.

The Aleppo Codex has a long and complex history, and it has suffered many trials and tribulations over the centuries. It was damaged in a fire in the synagogue where it was housed in Aleppo in the late 19th century, and many of its pages were lost or stolen. However, the remaining pages were rescued and brought to Jerusalem, where they are now housed in the National Library

INTRODUCTION TO THE TEXT OF THE OLD TESTAMENT

of Israel. Despite its damaged condition, the Aleppo Codex remains an important and valuable source for scholars studying the Hebrew Bible.

Leningrad Codex Leningrad B 19A

The Leningrad Codex (also known as Codex Leningrad B 19A) is a medieval Hebrew Bible manuscript that is considered to be one of the most important and reliable copies of the Masoretic Text, the traditional Hebrew text of the Jewish Bible (also known as the Tanakh or Old Testament). It was produced in the 11th century CE in the city of Leningrad (now known as St. Petersburg) in Russia and is named after the city where it was produced.

The Leningrad Codex is a parchment manuscript that contains the complete text of the Hebrew Bible, including the Torah (the first five books of the Old Testament), the Nevi'im (the prophets), and the ketuvim (the writings). It is written in consonantal text, with vowel points and other marks added to indicate pronunciation and grammatical structure. These marks are known as the Masorah and were added by the Masoretes, Jewish scholars who worked to preserve and standardize the text of the Hebrew Bible.

The Leningrad Codex is considered to be one of the most accurate and reliable copies of the Masoretic Text, and it is often used as the basis for translations of the Old Testament into other languages. It is also an important part of Jewish religious tradition and is used in Jewish worship and study.

The Leningrad Codex is currently housed in the National Library of Russia in St. Petersburg, where it is designated as Codex Leningrad B 19A. It is an important source for scholars studying the Hebrew Bible and is widely regarded as one of the most important and reliable copies of the Masoretic Text.

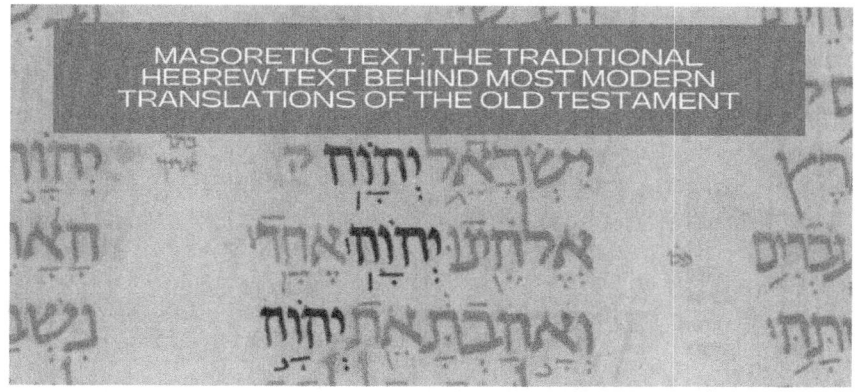

Image 5 Masoretic text, (from Hebrew masoreth, "tradition"), traditional Hebrew text of the Jewish Bible

The Trustworthiness of the Masoretic Text

The Masoretic Text is generally considered to be a highly trustworthy representation of the original Hebrew text of the Jewish Bible (also known as the Tanakh or Old Testament). It is based on the text of the Hebrew Bible as it was transmitted orally and in written form in ancient Israel and is considered to be a reliable representation of the original text.

The Masoretic Text has a long and complex history, with many different versions and manuscripts being produced over the centuries. However, the version produced by the Masorete Aaron ben Moses ben Asher in the 9th century CE is considered to be the most accurate and reliable version, and it is often used as the basis for translations of the Old Testament into other languages.

In addition to being based on the original Hebrew text of the Bible, the Masoretic Text is also highly reliable because it was carefully preserved and transmitted by the Masoretes, who were dedicated to ensuring the accuracy and integrity of the text. They added vowel points and other marks to the consonantal text in order to preserve the correct pronunciation and interpretation of the text, and they worked to ensure that the text was transmitted accurately from one generation to the next.

While there are some differences between the Masoretic Text and other ancient versions of the Hebrew Bible, such as the Septuagint and the Dead Sea Scrolls, these differences are generally minor and do not affect the overall reliability of the Masoretic Text. Overall, the Masoretic Text is considered to be a highly trustworthy representation of the original Hebrew text of the Bible.

The primary weight of external evidence generally goes to the original language manuscripts, and the **Codex Leningrad B 19A** and the **Aleppo Codex** are almost always preferred. In Old Testament Textual Criticism, the Masoretic text is our starting point and should only be abandoned as a last resort. While it is true that the Masoretic Text is not perfect, there needs to be a heavy burden of proof in we are to go with an alternative reading. All of the evidence needs to be examined before concluding that a reading in the Masoretic Text is corrupt. The Septuagint continues to be very much important today and is used by textual scholars to help uncover copyists' errors that **might have** crept into the Hebrew manuscripts either intentionally or unintentionally. However, it cannot do it alone without the support of other sources. There are a number of times when you might have the Syriac, Septuagint, Dead Sea Scrolls, Aramaic Targums, and the Vulgate

INTRODUCTION TO THE TEXT OF THE OLD TESTAMENT

that are at odds with the Masoretic Text the preferred choice should not be the MT.

Initially, the Septuagint (LXX) was viewed by the Jews as inspired by God, equal to the Hebrew Scriptures. However, in the first century C.E., the Christians adopted the Septuagint in their churches. It was used by the Christians in their evangelism to make disciples and to debate the Jews on Jesus being the long-awaited Messiah. Soon, the Jews began to look at the Septuagint with suspicion. This resulted in the Jews of the second century C.E. abandoning the Septuagint and returning to the Hebrew Scriptures. This has proved to be beneficial for the textual scholar and translator. In the second century C.E., other Greek translations of the Septuagint were produced. We have, for example, **LXX**[Aq] Aquila, **LXX**[Sym] Symmachus, and **LXX**[Th] Theodotion. The consonantal text of the Hebrew Scriptures became the standard text between the first and second centuries C.E. However, textual variants still continued until the Masoretes and the Masoretic text. However, scribes taking liberties by altering the text was no longer the case, as was true of the previous period of the Sopherim. The scribes who copied the Hebrew Scriptures from the time of Ezra down to the time of Jesus were called Sopherim, i.e., scribes.

From the 6th century C.E. to the 10th century C.E., we have the Masoretes, groups of extraordinary Jewish scribe-scholars. The Masoretes were very much concerned with the accurate transmission of each word, even each letter, of the text they were copying. Accuracy was of supreme importance; therefore, the Masoretes use the side margins of each page to inform others of deliberate or inadvertent changes in the text by past copyists. The Masoretes also use these marginal notes for other reasons as well, such as unusual word forms and combinations. They even marked how frequently they occurred within a book or even the whole Hebrew Old Testament. Of course, marginal spaces were very limited, so they used abbreviated code. They also formed a cross-checking tool where they would mark the middle word and letter of certain books. Their push for accuracy moved them to go so far as to count every letter of the Hebrew Old Testament.

In the Masoretic text, we find notes in the side margins, which are known as the Small Masora. There are also notes in the top margin, which are referred to as the Large Masora. Any other notes placed elsewhere within the text are called the Final Masora. The Masoretes used the notes in the top and bottom margins to record more extensive notes, comments concerning the abbreviated notes in the side margins. This enabled them to be able to cross-check their work. We must remember that there were no numbered verses at this time, and they had no Bible concordances. Well, one might wonder how the Masoretes could refer to different parts of the Hebrew text to have an effective cross-checking system. They would list part of a parallel verse in the top and bottom margins to remind them of where the word(s) indicated were found. Because they were dealing with limited space, they often could only list one word to remind them where each parallel verse could be found. To have an effective cross-reference system by way of these marginal notes, the Masoretes would literally have to have memorized the entire Hebrew Bible.

The Second Rabbinic Bible of Jacob ben Chayyim Published in 1524-25

The Second Rabbinic Bible (also known as the Second Rabbinic Edition or the Ben Chayyim Bible) is a Hebrew Bible that was published in 1524-25 by Jacob ben Chayyim, a Jewish rabbi and scholar. It is considered to be an important and influential edition of the Masoretic Text, the traditional Hebrew text of the Jewish Bible (also known as the Tanakh or Old Testament).

The Second Rabbinic Bible is notable for its accuracy and thoroughness. It is based on a number of manuscripts and includes a detailed Masorah (a set of marks and annotations added to the Masoretic Text to indicate pronunciation and grammatical structure) that was carefully checked and verified by Jacob ben Chayyim and other scholars. The Masorah includes a large number of variant readings and annotations, as well as lists of synonyms and other information that is useful for understanding the text.

The Second Rabbinic Bible is also notable for its introduction, which was written by Jacob ben Chayyim and provides valuable insights into the history and development of the Masoretic Text. It is considered to be an important source for scholars studying the Hebrew Bible and the history of the Masoretic Text.

Overall, the Second Rabbinic Bible is an important and influential edition of the Masoretic Text that is widely respected for its accuracy and thoroughness. It is an important resource for scholars studying the Hebrew Bible and is often used as the basis for translations of the Old Testament into other languages.

Oxford, Benjamin Kennicott Published Variant Readings from Over 600 Hebrew Manuscripts

Yes, that is correct. Benjamin Kennicott (1718-1783) was an English theologian and biblical scholar who is known for his work on the Hebrew Bible. In the late 18th century, he published a two-volume work called "Vetus Testamentum Hebraicum cum Variis Lectionibus" (The Hebrew Old Testament with Various Readings), which included variant readings from over 600 Hebrew manuscripts of the Bible.

Kennicott's work was an important contribution to the study of the Hebrew Bible and helped to establish the importance of examining a wide range of manuscripts in order to understand the text of the Bible. He collected and studied a large number of manuscripts from various sources, including the British Museum, the Vatican Library, and other libraries and collections around Europe.

Kennicott's work was also significant because it was one of the first scholarly efforts to systematically compare and analyze variant readings from different Hebrew manuscripts of the Bible. He carefully examined the manuscripts and recorded the differences between them, providing valuable insights into the history and development of the text.

Overall, Kennicott's work was an important contribution to the study of the Hebrew Bible and helped to establish the importance of examining a wide range of manuscripts in order to understand the text of the Bible. It is still highly regarded by scholars today and is an important resource for those studying the Hebrew Bible.

In 1784-98, at Parma, the Italian scholar J. B. de Rossi Published Variant Readings of Over 800 More Manuscripts

In the late 18th century, the Italian scholar J. B. de Rossi (1742-1831) published a two-volume work called "Variarum Lectionum in Vetus Testamentum Collectio Nova" (A New Collection of Variant Readings in the Old Testament), which included variant readings from over 800 Hebrew manuscripts of the Bible.

De Rossi's work was an important contribution to the study of the Hebrew Bible and helped to establish the importance of examining a wide range of manuscripts in order to understand the text of the Bible. He collected and studied a large number of manuscripts from various sources, including the Vatican Library and other libraries and collections in Europe.

De Rossi's work was also significant because it was one of the first scholarly efforts to systematically compare and analyze variant readings from different Hebrew manuscripts of the Bible. He carefully examined the manuscripts and recorded the differences between them, providing valuable insights into the history and development of the text.

Overall, de Rossi's work was an important contribution to the study of the Hebrew Bible and helped to establish the importance of examining a wide range of manuscripts in order to understand the text of the Bible. It is still highly regarded by scholars today and is an important resource for those studying the Hebrew Bible.

Hebrew Scholar S. Baer of Germany Produced a Master Text

S. Baer (also known as Solomon Baer) was a German Hebrew scholar who was active in the 19th century. He is known for his work on the Hebrew Bible and is credited with producing a "master text" of the Masoretic Text, the traditional Hebrew text of the Jewish Bible (also known as the Tanakh or Old Testament).

Baer's work on the Masoretic Text was an important contribution to the study of the Hebrew Bible and helped to establish the importance of examining a wide range of manuscripts in order to understand the text of the Bible. He collected and studied a large number of manuscripts from various sources, including the British Museum, the Vatican Library, and other libraries and collections around Europe.

Baer's master text of the Masoretic Text was based on a careful analysis of these manuscripts and was intended to provide a reliable and accurate representation of the original Hebrew text. It was widely respected by scholars and was often used as the basis for translations of the Old Testament into other languages.

Overall, Baer's work on the Masoretic Text was an important contribution to the study of the Hebrew Bible and helped to establish the importance of examining a wide range of manuscripts in order to understand the text of the Bible. It is still highly regarded by scholars today and is an important resource for those studying the Hebrew Bible.

C. D. Ginsburg Produced a Critical Master Text of the Hebrew Bible

C. D. Ginsburg (also known as Christian David Ginsburg) was a 19th-century British scholar who is known for his work on the Hebrew Bible. He is credited with producing a "critical master text" of the Hebrew Bible, which was based on a careful analysis of a wide range of manuscripts and was intended to provide a reliable and accurate representation of the original Hebrew text.

Ginsburg's critical master text of the Hebrew Bible was an important contribution to the study of the Hebrew Bible and helped to establish the importance of examining a wide range of manuscripts in order to understand the text of the Bible. He collected and studied a large number of manuscripts from various sources, including the British Museum, the Vatican Library, and other libraries and collections around Europe.

Ginsburg's critical master text of the Hebrew Bible was widely respected by scholars and was often used as the basis for translations of the Old Testament into other languages. It is still highly regarded by scholars today and is an important resource for those studying the Hebrew Bible.

Overall, Ginsburg's work on the Hebrew Bible was an important contribution to the study of the text and helped to establish the importance of examining a wide range of manuscripts in order to understand the text of the Bible. His critical master text of the Hebrew Bible is still highly regarded by scholars today and is an important resource for those studying the Hebrew Bible.

Rudolf Kittel Produced the Hebrew Text Entitled Biblia Hebraica, or "The Hebrew Bible"

Rudolf Kittel (1853-1929) was a German theologian and biblical scholar who is known for his work on the Hebrew Bible. He is credited with producing a Hebrew text of the Bible called Biblia Hebraica, or "The Hebrew Bible," which is widely considered to be one of the most accurate and reliable editions of the Masoretic Text, the traditional Hebrew text of the Jewish Bible (also known as the Tanakh or Old Testament).

Kittel's Biblia Hebraica was based on a careful analysis of a wide range of manuscripts and was intended to provide a reliable and accurate representation of the original Hebrew text. It includes a detailed Masorah (a set of marks and annotations added to the Masoretic Text to indicate pronunciation and grammatical structure) that was carefully checked and verified by Kittel and other scholars. The Masorah includes a large number of variant readings and annotations, as well as lists of synonyms and other information that is useful for understanding the text.

Kittel's Biblia Hebraica is widely respected by scholars and is often used as the basis for translations of the Old Testament into other languages. It is still highly regarded by scholars today and is an important resource for those studying the Hebrew Bible.

Overall, Kittel's work on the Hebrew Bible was an important contribution to the study of the text and helped to establish the importance of examining a wide range of manuscripts in order to understand the text of the Bible. His Biblia Hebraica is still highly regarded by scholars today and is an important resource for those studying the Hebrew Bible.

Biblia Hebraica Stuttgartensia

The Biblia Hebraica Stuttgartensia (BHS) is a modern critical edition of the Masoretic Text, the traditional Hebrew text of the Jewish Bible (also known as the Tanakh or Old Testament). It is widely considered to be one of the most accurate and reliable editions of the Masoretic Text and is often used as the basis for translations of the Old Testament into other languages.

The BHS was published by the Deutsche Bibelgesellschaft (German Bible Society) in Stuttgart, Germany, in the 1970s and 1980s. It is based on a thorough analysis of a wide range of manuscripts and includes a detailed Masorah (a set of marks and annotations added to the Masoretic Text to indicate pronunciation and grammatical structure) that was carefully checked and verified by scholars. The Masorah includes a large number of variant readings and annotations, as well as lists of synonyms and other information that is useful for understanding the text.

The BHS is an important resource for scholars studying the Hebrew Bible and is widely respected for its accuracy and thoroughness. It is often used as the standard text for scholarly work on the Hebrew Bible and is also used in Jewish worship and study.

Overall, the Biblia Hebraica Stuttgartensia is a modern critical edition of the Masoretic Text that is widely considered to be one of the most accurate and reliable editions of the text. It is an important resource for scholars studying the Hebrew Bible and is often used as the basis for translations of the Old Testament into other languages.

INTRODUCTION TO THE TEXT OF THE OLD TESTAMENT

CHAPTER 2 Writing After the Flood in the Ancient Near East

Writing Before the Worldwide Flood of Noah

It is uncertain whether any of the historical accounts recorded in the book of Genesis were documented in writing prior to the Flood, as there are no explicit references to pre-Flood writing in the Bible. Nevertheless, it is worth noting that various advancements such as the construction of cities, the creation of musical instruments, and the manufacture of iron and copper tools, were present well before the Flood, as stated in Genesis 4:17, 21, 22. Thus, it is logical to infer that the development of a method of writing would have been within the capabilities of humanity at that time. Additionally, it is known that the original language spoken by humanity, later known as Hebrew, and the Israelites, who continued to speak that language, utilized an alphabet. This lends credibility to the possibility that alphabetic writing existed before the Flood.

Assyrian King Ashurbanipal[1] spoke of reading "inscriptions on stone from the time before the flood." (*Light From the Ancient Past*, by J. Finegan, 1959, pp. 216, 217) However, it is just as likely that those were simply inscribed before some local flood of considerable proportions. Yet, it is just as possible that they were recounting events prior to the Flood. For example, what is termed "The Sumerian King List," after mentioning that eight kings ruled for 241,000 years, states: "(Then) the Flood swept over (the earth)." (*Ancient Near Eastern Texts*, edited by J. Pritchard, 1974, p. 265) Such a record, plainly, is not authentic.

According to Bible chronology, the global Flood of Noah's day occurred around 2348 BCE (Before Common Era). The Bible states that the Flood occurred in the 600th year of Noah's life, and according to the genealogy in Genesis, this would place the Flood around 2348 BCE. Many clay tablets that have been excavated by archaeologists have been assigned dates earlier than 2348 BCE, but these dates are based on conjecture and are not verified by dated documents. The artifacts excavated by archaeologists are not definitively known to date from pre-Flood times, and any assignment of items to the pre-Flood period is based on the interpretation of findings that may only provide evidence of a great local flood, not a global one as described in the Bible. It is important to note that the dating of artifacts is a complex and ongoing process, and there is ongoing debate among scholars about the accuracy of these dates and their relationship to biblical chronology.

Writing After the Worldwide Flood of Noah

We need to discuss the different writing systems that developed after the confusion of languages at the Tower of Babel as mentioned in the Bible. Historians have explained that various peoples, such as the Babylonians and Assyrians, used cuneiform script, which is believed to have been developed

---

[1] Ashurbanipal (also spelled Ashurbanipal or Assurbanipal) was an Assyrian king who ruled from 668 BCE to 627 BCE. He was the last strong king of the Assyrian Empire and was known for his military conquests, building projects, and cultural achievements. Ashurbanipal is most famous for his role in the preservation of Mesopotamian literature and culture. He built a library at his palace in Nineveh, which contained tens of thousands of clay tablets covering a wide range of subjects, including literature, law, medicine, and astronomy. Many of the texts from this library are now housed in the British Museum and other institutions, and they have provided invaluable insights into the history and culture of ancient Mesopotamia. Ashurbanipal's reign also saw the empire reach its greatest territorial extent, but it was also the beginning of the end for the Assyrian Empire, as it was sacked and destroyed by a coalition of Babylonians, Medes, and Persians just a few years after Ashurbanipal's death.

INTRODUCTION TO THE TEXT OF THE OLD TESTAMENT

by the Sumerians from their earlier pictographic writing. They have also noted that there is evidence that more than one writing system was used at the same time. They have provided an example of an ancient Assyrian wall painting depicting two scribes, one using cuneiform script to write in Akkadian, and the other using a brush to write on papyrus or skin, possibly in Aramaic. They have also discovered what is known as the Egyptian hieroglyphic writing, which consisted of distinct pictorial representations and geometric forms. Scholars also explain that although hieroglyphic writing continued to be used for inscriptions on monuments and wall paintings, other forms of writing such as hieratic and demotic came into use. They have described those non-alphabetic systems, such as hieroglyphic, used pictorial representation or its linear or cursive form to represent the depicted object, an idea, another word or syllable with the same pronunciation. We can use an example of a simple drawing of an eye to illustrate how this could be used to represent different words or syllables with the same pronunciation in English.

The Israelites used an alphabetic writing system in which each written consonant symbol represented a specific consonant sound. However, the vowel sounds had to be inferred by the reader, with the context determining the intended word in cases where the spelling was the same, but the vowel sounds were different. This was not a significant issue, as even contemporary Hebrew publications, such as magazines and newspapers, frequently leave out vowel points altogether.

Israelite priests and notable figures such as Moses, Joshua, Samuel, David, and Jehu possessed knowledge of reading and writing, and it is likely that the general population was literate as well. The command for the Israelites to write on the doorposts of their houses suggests that they were literate. Additionally, the Law required that the king, upon being crowned, make a copy of the Law and read it daily.

Although written Hebrew material was prevalent, few Israelite inscriptions have been discovered. This is likely due to the Israelites not constructing many monuments to commemorate their achievements. Most writing, including the books of the Bible, were likely done with ink on perishable materials such as papyrus or parchment, and would not have survived in the moist soil of Palestine. However, the message of the Bible was preserved through centuries of careful copying and recopying. The Bible's history encompasses the beginning of humanity and even beyond. While ancient inscriptions on stone and clay tablets, prisms, and cylinders may be older than the oldest surviving Bible manuscript, they have little relevance to modern life and in some cases contain inaccuracies. The Bible stands out among ancient writings for its meaningful message, which merits more than casual attention.

Origin of the Hebrew Language

The origin of Hebrew, along with other ancient languages such as Sumerian, Akkadian, Aramaic, and Egyptian, is not documented in secular history. These languages are already fully developed in the earliest written records that have been discovered. Theories about the origin and development of Hebrew, such as the idea that it derived from Aramaic or a Canaanite dialect, are speculative. The same is true for attempts to explain the origin of many words found in the Hebrew Scriptures, as scholars often assign an Akkadian or Aramaic origin to these words. However, as Dr. Edward Horowitz notes, "there are wide differences of opinion among scholars" in the field of etymology, and even among the most respected authorities, there are ongoing disagreements.

The Bible is the only reliable historical source for the origin of Hebrew language. According to the Bible, Hebrew was spoken by the Israelite descendants of Abram, who was a descendant of Shem, one of Noah's sons. Given the prophetic blessing on Shem, it is plausible to believe that Shem's language was not affected by the confusion of languages at the Tower of Babel. This would mean that the language that came to be known as Hebrew was the original language spoken by all mankind from Adam onwards. Secular history provides no other explanation for the origin of Hebrew.

From Abraham Onward

The Bible suggests that Abraham, who was known as "the Hebrew," was able to communicate with the Hamitic people of Canaan without the use of interpreters. It is possible that he spoke Akkadian, as he had lived in Ur of the Chaldeans, where Akkadian was an international language. It could also be that the people of Canaan, who lived near the Semitic peoples of Syria and Arabia, were bilingual. Additionally, the alphabet has clear Semitic origins, which could have influenced the use of Semitic languages by people of other language groups, particularly those in positions of power or official roles.

In the Ancient Near East

Writing in the ancient Near East refers to the various writing systems and scripts used in the region during ancient times. The ancient Near East

INTRODUCTION TO THE TEXT OF THE OLD TESTAMENT

was home to a number of civilizations that developed their own writing systems, including the Sumerians, the Akkadians, the Hittites, and the Egyptians.

The earliest known writing system in the ancient Near East was developed by the Sumerians, who lived in what is now southern Iraq. This writing system, known as cuneiform, was invented around the 4th millennium BCE and was used to record a variety of information, including legal documents, religious texts, and accounts of daily life. Cuneiform was written on clay tablets using a stylus, and the tablets were then baked to preserve the writing.

The Akkadians, who lived in what is now northern Iraq and Syria, also used cuneiform to write their language, which was a Semitic language related to Hebrew and Arabic. The Hittites, who lived in what is now modern-day Turkey, used a script known as hieroglyphic Hittite, which was a combination of cuneiform and hieroglyphics.

The ancient Egyptians developed their own writing system, known as hieroglyphics, which was used to write the Egyptian language. Hieroglyphics were written on papyrus, stone tablets, and other materials, and were used to record a wide range of information, including religious texts, legal documents, and accounts of daily life.

Writing in the ancient Near East played a vital role in the development of civilization and the preservation of knowledge and culture. It allowed people to record and transmit information, ideas, and beliefs, and has provided a wealth of information about the history and culture of the region.

Jacob was able to communicate with his Aramaean relatives, despite some differences in language. Joseph, who was enslaved by Potiphar, used an interpreter when speaking with his Hebrew brothers when they came to Egypt. Moses, who was raised in the courts of Pharaoh, likely knew multiple languages, including Hebrew, Egyptian, and possibly Akkadian, among others.—Ge 31:46-47; 39:1; 42:6, 23; Ex 2:10. 15-22.

Image 6 The first known Sumerian-Akkadian bilingual tablet dates from the reign of Rimush. Louvre Museum AO 5477. The top half is in Sumerian, the bottom half is its translation in Akkadian

INTRODUCTION TO THE TEXT OF THE OLD TESTAMENT

Sumerian Writing

Sumerian writing is the earliest known writing system in the world, developed by the Sumerians, who lived in what is now southern Iraq. This writing system, known as cuneiform, was invented around the 4th millennium BCE and was used to record a variety of information, including legal documents, religious texts, and accounts of daily life.

Cuneiform was written on clay tablets using a stylus, and the tablets were then baked to preserve the writing. The tablets were inscribed with characters that represented sounds, words, and ideas. The characters were made up of combinations of lines and wedges, and could be written in different directions, depending on the orientation of the tablet.

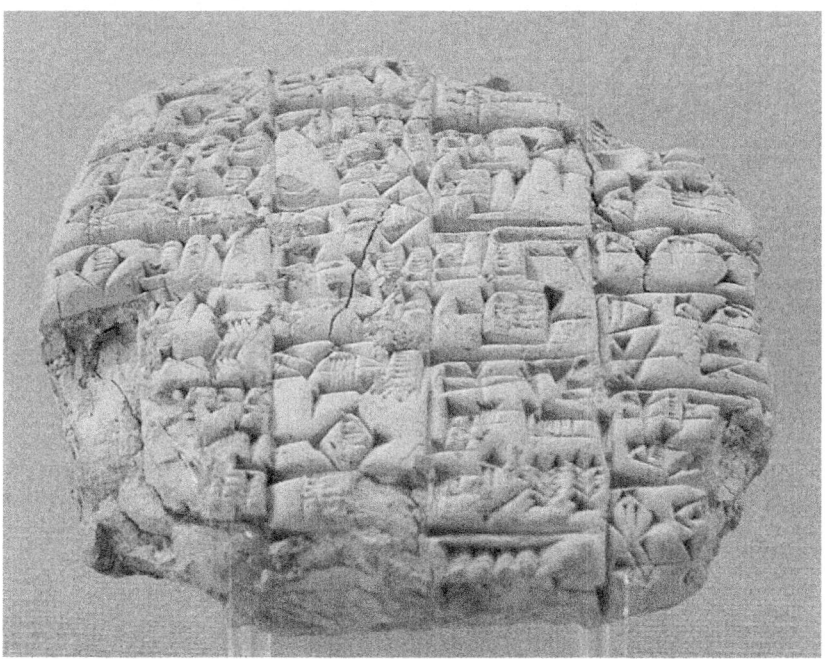

Image 7 Letter sent by the high-priest Lu'enna to the king of Lagash (maybe Urukagina), informing him of his son's death in combat, c. 2400 BC, found in Telloh (ancient Girsu)

Sumerian cuneiform was used to write a variety of languages, including Sumerian, Akkadian, and Hittite. It was used in ancient Mesopotamia for over 3,000 years and played a crucial role in the development of civilization and the preservation of knowledge and culture.

Sumerian cuneiform is an important source of information about the history and culture of the ancient Near East and has provided a wealth of information about the beliefs, customs, and daily life of the Sumerians. It is also an important resource for scholars and researchers studying the history of writing and the development of civilization.

Image 8 Akkadian language inscription on the obelisk of Manishtushu

Akkadian Writing

Ancient Akkadian writing refers to the cuneiform writing system used by the Akkadians, who lived in what is now northern Iraq and Syria. The Akkadians were a Semitic people who spoke a language related to Hebrew and Arabic, and they adopted the cuneiform writing system developed by the Sumerians to write their own language.

Cuneiform was written on clay tablets using a stylus, and the tablets were then baked to preserve the writing. The tablets were inscribed with characters that represented sounds, words, and ideas. The characters were made up of combinations of lines and wedges, and could be written in different directions, depending on the orientation of the tablet.

INTRODUCTION TO THE TEXT OF THE OLD TESTAMENT

Akkadian cuneiform was used in ancient Mesopotamia for over 3,000 years and played a crucial role in the development of civilization and the preservation of knowledge and culture. It was used to record a wide range of information, including legal documents, religious texts, and accounts of daily life.

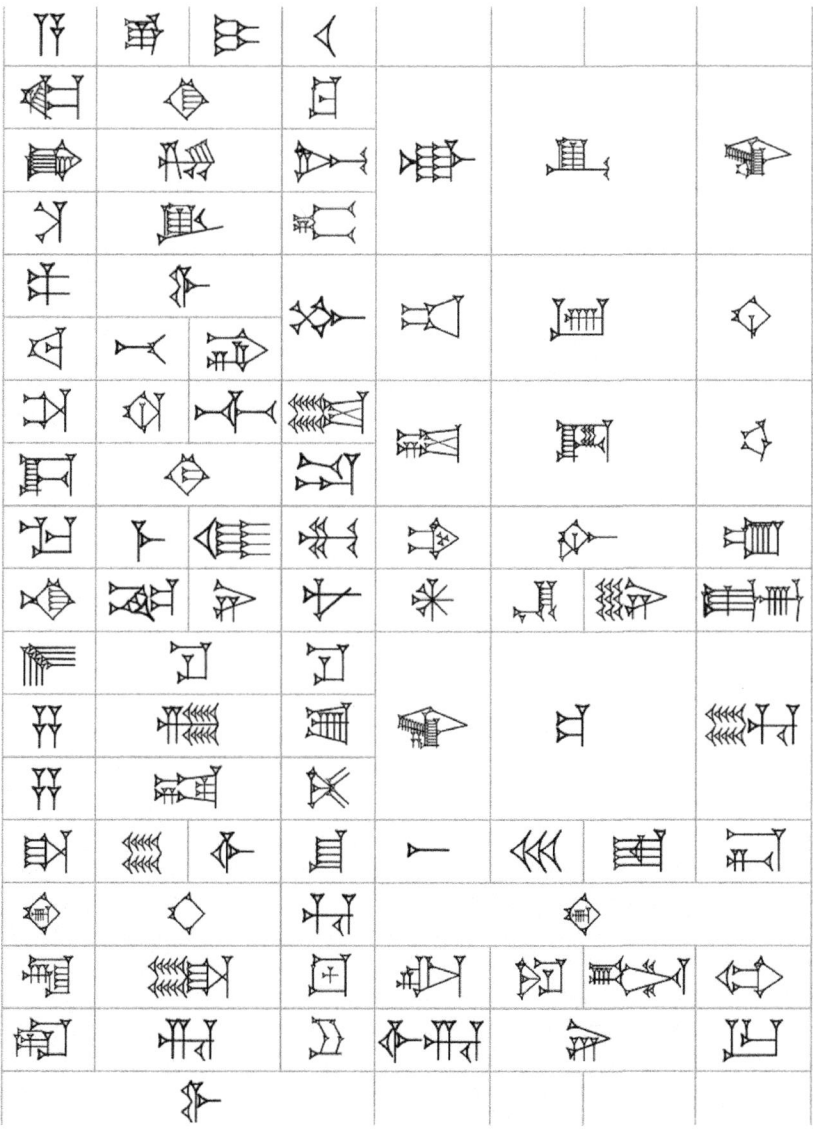

Image 9 Sumero-Akkadian cuneiform syllabary, used by early Akkadian rulers

Akkadian cuneiform is an important source of information about the history and culture of the ancient Near East and has provided a wealth of information about the beliefs, customs, and daily life of the Akkadians. It is also an important resource for scholars and researchers studying the history of writing and the development of civilization.

The Akkadian civilization, a Semitic-speaking people, adopted and adapted the Sumerian system of cuneiform writing during the middle of the third millennium BCE. This is noteworthy as the Sumerians, who created the script, were not of Semitic descent. The Akkadians utilized cuneiform, a system of wedge-shaped marks made by pressing a triangular-shaped stylus into clay tablets, to express their own language. A key alteration made by the Akkadians was the increased utilization of syllabic signs. Although, it is important to note that their writing system was not solely composed of syllabic signs. The six hundred to seven hundred signs present in the system included six signs for vowels, ninety-seven signs for open syllables, more than two hundred signs for closed syllables, and about three hundred ideograms. The ideograms inherited from the Sumerians were like a set of building blocks, which the Akkadians took and used to construct their own language, just as a child might use the same set of building blocks to make different structures. In the same way that a child might give different names to the structures they build, the Akkadians likely assigned their own pronunciations to the ideograms they inherited from the Sumerians. This would be similar to "2 km" being read as "two kilometers" by an English speaker, while a French speaker would read it as "deux kilomètres." The numerical symbols remain the same, but the pronunciation and meaning may change based on the language of the reader.

The Akkadian language plays a significant role in biblical studies for several reasons. Firstly, it is the oldest known Semitic language and its decipherment and study in the 19th century has greatly aided in understanding the Hebrew language. The Akkadian writing system, which dates back to the middle of the 3rd millennium BCE, provides a historical and linguistic context for the writing activities of various figures in the Old Testament. Additionally, creation and flood accounts in the Babylonian dialect of Akkadian can be compared and contrasted with their biblical counterparts, providing valuable insight into the similarities and differences between the two. Furthermore, Akkadian legal documents, royal annals, and correspondence offer important historical and cultural information that helps to further our understanding of the time period in which these texts were written. In summary, the Akkadian language plays a crucial role in biblical studies, providing valuable historical, linguistic, and cultural context that helps to deepen our understanding of the Old Testament.

INTRODUCTION TO THE TEXT OF THE OLD TESTAMENT

Image 10 Ancient Egyptian writing, Egyptian hieroglyphs, wall inscriptions

Egyptian Writing

The ancient Egyptians developed one of the earliest writing systems in the Near East. This writing system, known as hieroglyphics, was used for religious texts, monumental inscriptions, and other official documents. The hieroglyphic script consisted of a combination of logographic and alphabetic elements, and it was used to write the ancient Egyptian language.

Origins and Evolution of Egyptian Writing

The origins of Egyptian writing can be traced back to the Early Dynastic Period (ca. 3150-2613 BCE). The earliest known examples of hieroglyphics are found on pottery vessels and ivory labels from this period. Over time, the script evolved and became more sophisticated, with the development of new forms of signs, such as ligatures and determinatives. By the Old Kingdom (ca. 2613-2181 BCE), hieroglyphics had become the dominant script for monumental inscriptions and religious texts.

Uses of Egyptian Writing

Egyptian writing was used for a wide range of purposes, including religious texts, monumental inscriptions, and official documents. Religious texts, such as the Book of the Dead, were written on funerary objects and tomb walls. Monuments such as obelisks and statues were inscribed with hieroglyphics to commemorate important events, such as the coronation of a pharaoh. Official documents, such as royal decrees, were written on papyrus and stored in the archives of the royal palace.

Decipherment of Egyptian Writing

The decipherment of hieroglyphics was a slow process that took centuries. The first step was the realization that hieroglyphics was a writing system, and not just a form of art. In the 18th century, the French scholar Jean-Francois Champollion made the crucial breakthrough by realizing that the hieroglyphic script was a combination of logographic and alphabetic elements. He was able to decipher the hieroglyphics of the Rosetta Stone, which was a key to unlocking the secrets of Egyptian writing.

In conclusion, Egyptian writing, known as hieroglyphics, was a complex and sophisticated writing system used in ancient Egypt for religious texts, monumental inscriptions, and official documents. The origins of hieroglyphics can be traced back to the Early Dynastic Period and it was used throughout ancient Egyptian history. The decipherment of hieroglyphics was a gradual process that took centuries, but it was crucial in unlocking the secrets of ancient Egyptian culture and history.

Egyptian Writing and Biblical Hebrew and Certain other Semitic Languages

The Egyptian writing system, hieroglyphics, can help with the textual issues of Biblical Hebrew and certain other Semitic languages in several ways.

Firstly, the existence of hieroglyphics from the Early Dynastic period (ca. 3150-2613 BCE) provides a historical context for the development of other writing systems in the ancient Near East, including those of the Semitic languages. By studying hieroglyphics, scholars can gain a better understanding of the linguistic and cultural influences on the development of writing systems in other ancient Near Eastern cultures.

Secondly, the decipherment of hieroglyphics in the 19th century by Jean-Francois Champollion provided important insight into the workings of other writing systems in the ancient Near East. Champollion's realization that hieroglyphics was a combination of logographic and alphabetic elements helped scholars to understand that other writing systems, such as cuneiform and the Hebrew alphabet, were likely also a combination of these elements.

Thirdly, the comparison between the religious texts, monumental inscriptions and official documents written in hieroglyphics and the ones in biblical Hebrew can provide valuable insight into the similarities and differences between the two cultures and languages. For example, the creation and flood accounts in the Egyptian religious texts can be compared and contrasted with the biblical analogs, providing valuable insight into the similarities and differences between the two.

In summary, the study of hieroglyphics can provide important context for understanding the development of writing systems in the ancient Near East, including those of the Semitic languages. It can also provide valuable insights into the similarities and differences between the cultures and languages of ancient Egypt and the ancient Near East, including biblical Hebrew.

Demotic script is a script that was used in ancient Egypt for writing the Egyptian language. It was developed as a simplified form of hieroglyphics and was used primarily for administrative and private texts. Demotic script was used in Egypt from the 7th century BCE until the end of the 4th century CE and was mainly used for the day-to-day writing.

Like hieroglyphics, Demotic can also help with the textual issues of Biblical Hebrew and certain other Semitic languages. For instance, the study of Demotic can provide important context for understanding the evolution of writing systems in ancient Egypt and the Near East. By comparing Demotic with hieroglyphics and other writing systems, scholars can gain a better understanding of the linguistic and cultural influences on the development of writing systems in the ancient world.

Additionally, the comparison between texts written in Demotic and the ones in biblical Hebrew can provide valuable insight into the similarities and differences between the two cultures and languages. For example, the legal documents, letters, and private texts written in Demotic can be compared and contrasted with the biblical texts, providing valuable insight into the similarities and differences between the cultures and languages of ancient Egypt and the ancient Near East, including biblical Hebrew. Furthermore, Demotic script provides a unique perspective on the evolution of the Egyptian language and how it was written and used in everyday life, which can be useful for comparative studies and understanding the linguistic features of other Semitic languages.

Alphabetic Writing

The development of a true alphabetic script is considered the final stage in the history of writing. An alphabetic script is a writing system that uses a set of symbols or characters to represent the sounds of a language. Unlike logographic writing systems, such as hieroglyphics or cuneiform, an alphabetic script uses a small number of symbols to represent the sounds of a language, making it more efficient and easier to learn.

Origins and Evolution of Alphabetic Writing

The prevailing view among scholars today is that the alphabet, one of the most significant inventions in human history, was created by the Canaanites during the first half of the second millennium BCE. The earliest known examples of alphabetic inscriptions have been found in southern Egypt, specifically in the Wadi el-Hol, and in the Sinai Peninsula at Serabit el-Hadem. These inscriptions provide evidence that the invention of the alphabet likely occurred in the context of the turquoise mines of the Sinai Peninsula. The theory is that Canaanite workers, who were unable to read the Egyptian hieroglyphs and texts, were prompted to create a new script in which each letter represented a single sound. This new script, the alphabet, would have been more suitable for their needs of communication and record-keeping, and it's believed that the invention was not made by elite scribes, but by illiterate laborers.

Egyptologist Orly Goldwasser has argued that the Canaanites came to Egypt to work in the turquoise mines and that this context provided the necessary inspiration for the invention of the alphabet. The fact that the turquoise mines required the manual labor of foreign workers, and the presence of a temple to the goddess Hathor at Serabit el-Hadem suggest that the area was a melting pot of different cultures and languages. The need to communicate and record information in a more efficient way may have led to the creation of the alphabet.

The Proto-Canaanite script, also known as the proto-Sinaitic script, was developed according to the "acrophonic" principle, which means that the shape of the letter resembled an object that began with that sound. For example, a letter that looks like flowing water is used to represent the sound [m] in the word "mym" (water). Similarly, a letter with a long downstroke or tail represents the sound [n] as in the word "nhsh" (snake). Furthermore, the letter that sounds like [k] looks a bit like a "kp" (hand).

This early script, which is considered a precursor of the Phoenician alphabet, consisted of twenty-eight signs which could be written in different directions. The letters could be written upwards, downwards, right, left, backwards, or forwards. Additionally, letters might face different directions or have different orientations (rotation), which made the script more versatile.

The Proto-Canaanite script is considered an important step in the development of writing systems, as it represents the transition from a logographic system to a true alphabetic system. The development of this script and the acrophonic principle enabled the creation of a more efficient and adaptable writing system. The Proto-Canaanite script would eventually give rise to the Phoenician alphabet, which would be adopted by other cultures and evolve into the Greek, Latin, and other alphabets that are used today.

As the Proto-Canaanite script continued to evolve, it became more widely used and its direction became fixed in a right-to-left direction around 1000 BCE. At the same time, the Greeks adopted the script, but used it in a left-to-right direction and added vowel letters. This process of adaptation and evolution of the script would eventually lead to the creation of other writing systems such as the Phoenician, Paleo-Hebrew and Aramaic scripts.

It's important to remember that a script is different from a language. For example, French and English both use the Latin script (or alphabet), but they are different languages. Similarly, the various scripts that developed from Proto-Canaanite were used with different languages and dialects, such as Hebrew, Aramaic and others. In the case of Hebrew, the script was changed from the Paleo-Hebrew to the Aramaic script during its history.

The Phoenician script is considered one of the most important developments in the history of writing systems. The script is believed to have developed around 1000 BCE, with a reduced set of twenty-two consonants and a fixed right-to-left direction. The Phoenician script was widely used in commerce around the Mediterranean Sea, and several inscriptions have been found in this script in Israel from the biblical period.

The Phoenician script was used for writing the Phoenician language and it was widely used by the Phoenician people, who were a maritime civilization known for their seafaring and trading abilities. The Phoenicians spread their script and their language throughout the Mediterranean, influencing the development of writing systems in other cultures. The Phoenician script was the basis for the development of the Greek, the Etruscan, and the Roman alphabets, and it played a key role in the spread of literacy in the ancient world.

The Phoenician script is also significant for the study of biblical studies as several inscriptions in this script have been found in Israel from the biblical period. These inscriptions provide valuable historical and linguistic information about the societies and cultures of the ancient Near East. They also help scholars to understand the development of the Hebrew script and the historical context of the Hebrew Bible.

In conclusion, The Phoenician script is considered one of the most important developments in the history of writing systems. It developed around 1000 BCE, with a reduced set of twenty-two consonants and a fixed right-to-left direction. It was widely used in commerce around the Mediterranean Sea and several inscriptions have been found in this script in Israel from the biblical period. The Phoenician script was the basis for the development of several other alphabets, and it played a key role in the spread of literacy in the ancient world. It also provides important information for the study of biblical studies.

The Paleo-Hebrew and Aramaic scripts are believed to have developed from the Phoenician script. The Paleo-Hebrew script is first documented in the ninth century BCE in Israel and nearby Moab. It kept the same number of signs as the Phoenician script, but the shape of a few letters differed slightly. The Israelites used the Paleo-Hebrew script for writing until the early sixth century BCE. At that time, Aramaic began to be widely used as a common language in the region, and the Aramaic script began to be used for official correspondence throughout the area.

As a result of their exile to Babylon, the Jews began to speak and write Aramaic in order to conduct business and communicate with their neighbors. They then adopted the Aramaic script for writing and copying Scripture. This process led to the development of a new Jewish variant of the Aramaic script, which came to be called the Jewish or square script. This script was used for copying the books of the Old Testament during its transmission. By the third century BCE, the Jewish variant of the Aramaic script had developed its own characteristics.

In summary, The Paleo-Hebrew and Aramaic scripts developed from the Phoenician script. The Paleo-Hebrew script is first documented in the ninth century BCE in Israel and nearby Moab. It kept the same number of signs as the Phoenician script, but the shape of a few letters differed slightly. The Israelites used the Paleo-Hebrew script for writing until the early sixth century BCE, at which point the Aramaic script began to be widely used. As a result of their exile to Babylon, the Jews began to speak and write Aramaic and adopted the script for writing and copying scripture, which led to the development of a new Jewish variant of the Aramaic script, which came to be called the Jewish or square script. This script was used for copying the books of the Old Testament during its transmission.

INTRODUCTION TO THE TEXT OF THE OLD TESTAMENT

In looking at the ancient writing systems you've mentioned, the total number of signs and the number of syllabic signs can vary depending on the specific writing system being studied and the source of information. Here is an approximate breakdown of the total number of signs and the number of syllabic signs for each writing system:

Sumerian/Akkadian:

- Total signs: ca. 600
- Syllabic signs: ca. 100-150

Egyptian:

- Total signs: ca. 700
- Syllabic signs: ca. 100

Ugaritic:

- Total signs: 30
- Syllabic signs: —

Proto-Canaanite:

- Total signs: 28
- Syllabic signs: —

Paleo-Hebrew/Aramaic:

- Total signs: 22
- Syllabic signs: —

Latin:

- Total signs: 26
- Syllabic signs: —

It's worth mentioning that the above numbers are approximate, and some sources may present different numbers. Additionally, it's important to note that the numbers of syllabic signs are not always clearly defined or agreed upon by scholars.

Advantages of Alphabetic Writing

One of the main advantages of alphabetic writing is its efficiency. An alphabetic script uses a small number of symbols to represent the sounds of a language, making it easier to learn and use. This efficiency is particularly beneficial for writing languages with a large number of words, such as English or Spanish. Additionally, alphabetic writing is more adaptable to different languages, as it can be easily modified to fit the sounds of a new language. This adaptability has allowed the alphabet to be adopted and used by many cultures throughout history.

Impact of Alphabetic Writing

The development of alphabetic writing has had a significant impact on human history. Alphabetic writing has allowed for the spread of knowledge and the preservation of history, culture, and literature. It has also facilitated communication and commerce, making it easier to spread ideas and trade goods. Furthermore, the widespread use of alphabetic writing has made education more accessible, as it is easier to learn and use than logographic writing systems.

In conclusion, the development of a true alphabetic script is considered the final stage in the history of writing. An alphabetic script is a writing system that uses a set of symbols or characters to represent the sounds of a language. The Phoenician alphabet is the oldest known true alphabetic script, which was developed around the 12th century BCE. Alphabetic writing is more efficient and adaptable than logographic writing systems, it has allowed for the spread of knowledge and the preservation of history, culture, and literature. Additionally, it has facilitated communication and commerce and made education more accessible.

Writing the Hebrew Old Testament

The Hebrew language played a significant role in the writing of the majority of the inspired Scriptures, which include 39 books in total, composing around three-quarters of the content of the Bible. However, it's worth noting that a small portion of these books were written in Aramaic.

In the Hebrew Scriptures, the name Hebrew is not applied to the language. Instead, it is used to refer to individuals or to the people of Israel as a whole. The language is referred to as "the Jews' language" (2Ki 18:26, 28), "Jewish" (Ne 13:24), and "the language of Canaan" (Isa 19:18). These references were made in the eighth century BCE, during which time Hebrew was primarily spoken. In contrast, in the Christian Greek Scriptures, the name Hebrew is regularly applied to the language spoken by the Jews.

INTRODUCTION TO THE TEXT OF THE OLD TESTAMENT

Origin of the Hebrew Language

The origin of the Hebrew language is not clearly revealed in secular history. This is true for many ancient languages, such as Sumerian, Akkadian, Aramaean, and Egyptian, as these tongues appear already fully developed in the earliest written records found. Scholars have put forward various views concerning the origin and development of Hebrew, such as the idea that it derived from Aramaic or from some Canaanite dialect, but these views are largely speculative and unverified.

The same can be said for attempts to explain the derivation of many words found in the Hebrew Scriptures. Scholars often assign an Akkadian or an Aramaic source for many of these words. However, as Dr. Edward Horowitz notes, "In the field of etymology [the study of word origins] there are wide differences of opinion among scholars, even among the very best of them." He cites examples of explanations by renowned scholars of the etymology of certain Hebrew words, in each case showing that other prominent scholars disagree. He concludes that "we have these never-ending differences between equally highly respected authorities." —How the Hebrew Language Grew, 1960, pp. xix, xx.

The Bible is the primary and most reliable source for understanding the origin of the Hebrew language. According to the Bible, the Hebrew language was spoken by the Israelite descendants of Abram, who was also known as "Abram the Hebrew" (Genesis 14:13). Abram was a descendant of Shem, one of the sons of Noah (Genesis 11:10-26). In light of God's prophetic blessing on Shem (Genesis 9:26), it is reasonable to believe that Shem's language was not affected when God confused the language of the disapproved people at Babel (Genesis 11:5-9). This would mean that Shem's language remained the same as it had been previously, which is the "one language" that existed from Adam onward (Genesis 11:1). Therefore, it can be inferred that the language that eventually came to be known as Hebrew was the original language of mankind. Secular history does not provide any other explanation.

Question of the Language's Stability

The question of the stability of the Hebrew language over time is a valid concern, as history has shown that languages can change significantly over long periods. For example, the English spoken in the time of Alfred the Great (9th century CE) would be difficult for most English speakers today to understand. It may seem likely that the language originally spoken by Adam would have undergone substantial changes by the time the writing of the Hebrew Scriptures began with Moses. However, there are factors that suggest otherwise.

One important factor is the long life spans enjoyed by people during this time period. The Bible states that people such as Methuselah and Shem lived for over 900 years, which would have provided ample time for language to change. However, the long life spans would also have served as a factor in maintaining the stability of language. With only one human link being needed to connect Adam with the Flood survivors and Shem living well into the lifetime of Isaac and less than 150 years elapsed from the death of Isaac (1738 BCE) until the birth of Moses (1593 BCE), this overlapping of the lives of individuals several generations apart would have helped to maintain uniformity of speech.

It is evident that not all of Shem's descendants continued to speak the "one language" of pre-Flood times in its pure form, as seen in the development of differences among the Semitic languages, including Hebrew, Aramaic, Akkadian, and the various Arabic dialects. For example, in the 18th century BCE (around 1761 BCE), Abraham's grandson and grandnephew used different terms in naming the heap of stones they had set up as a memorial or witness between them. Jacob, the father of the Israelites, called it "Galeed," while Laban, a resident in Syria or Aram (though not himself a descendant of Aram), used the Aramaean term "Jegar-sahadutha." (Genesis 31:47)

The dissimilarity of these two terms, however, does not necessarily indicate a major difference between Aramaean and Hebrew at this point, as Jacob seems to have faced no particular problem in communication there in Syria. As new circumstances and situations arose, and new artifacts were produced, certain words would be coined to describe such developments. These terms might differ from place to place among geographically separated groups of the same language family, even while the actual structure of their language remained very much the same.

Among the Israelites themselves, some small variation in pronunciation developed, as seen in the different pronunciation of the word "Shibboleth" by the Ephraimites during the period of the Judges (1473 to 1117 BCE). (Judges 12:4-6) However, this is not a basis for claiming that the Israelites spoke separate dialects at that time.

In the 8th century BCE, the linguistic differences between Hebrew and Aramaic were significant enough for them to be considered separate languages. This can be observed in the historical account of King Hezekiah's representatives requesting that the spokesmen of Assyrian King Sennacherib communicate with them in Aramaic, as they were not fluent in Hebrew and did not want to be understood by the people listening in. Despite Aramaic being widely spoken in the Middle East and used in international diplomatic communication at the time, the majority of the Judeans were not able to understand it. The earliest known written documents in Aramaic from this period further confirm the distinction between the two languages.

The question arises as to whether Hebrew and Aramaic both diverged from a single original language or if one of them preserved the purity of the primary language. The Bible does not provide a definitive answer, but it can be inferred from the fact that Moses wrote the inspired Sacred Record in the same language spoken by the first man, that this language is the Hebrew.

The idea that history was recorded in writing prior to the Flood, and that this written history would have played a significant role in preserving the purity of the original language, is a belief held by some. The idea is that even if the history was passed down through oral tradition, it would still have served to maintain the stability of the original speech. This is exemplified by the extreme care that the Jews of later times showed in endeavoring to conserve the true form of the Sacred Record. This illustrates the concern that would have been shown in patriarchal times to transmit accurately the earliest record of God's dealings with men.

Another reason for believing that the Hebrew of the Bible accurately represents the "one language" of pre-Babel times is the remarkable stability of the Hebrew language during the thousand-year period in which the Hebrew Scriptures were written. *The International Standard Bible Encyclopedia* states that "One of the most remarkable facts connected with the Hebrew of the O[ld] T[estament] is that, although its literature covers a period of over a thousand years, the language (grammar and vocabulary) of the oldest parts differs little from that of the latest."—Edited by G. W. Bromiley, 1982, Vol. 2, p. 659.

This stability of the language over such a long period of time lends credibility to the belief that it was passed down with great care, and that it accurately represents the original language spoken before the confusion of tongues at the Tower of Babel.

Knowledge of the Language Incomplete

The knowledge of ancient Hebrew is not entirely complete. This is because there are very few other contemporaneous writings in the Hebrew language that have been found that could contribute to an understanding of the word usage. Some examples of such writings include the Gezer calendar, ostraca from Samaria, the Siloam inscription, and the Lachish ostraca. Additionally, there is a Phoenician inscription on the sarcophagus of King Ahiram in Byblos and the Moabite Stone which are closely resembling Hebrew and thought to be from the start of the first millennium B.C.E. However, the total amount of information provided by these inscriptions is only a small fraction of that found in the Hebrew Scriptures. Professor Burton L. Goddard states that: "In large measure, the Old Testament Hebrew must be self-explanatory." (*The Zondervan Pictorial Bible Dictionary*, edited by M. Tenney, 1963, p. 345) This means that due to the limited amount of additional information from contemporaneous Hebrew writings, the Old Testament Hebrew text must be able to explain itself to a certain degree.

The Hebrew Scriptures, also known as the Old Testament, are a collection of texts that cover a variety of subjects and utilize a wide range of vocabulary. However, it is important to note that the Hebrew Scriptures do not encompass all of the words and expressions used in ancient Hebrew. This is evident in other historical documents such as the Siloam inscription and the Lachish ostraca, which contain certain words and grammatical constructions that are not found in the Hebrew Scriptures yet are clearly of Hebrew origin. This suggests that the ancient vocabulary of the Hebrew-speaking people was much more extensive and included many more "root" words, as well as thousands of words derived from these root words, than what is currently known today.

The Old Testament contains a significant number of words and expressions that have unknown "roots" or origins. These words are commonly referred to as "loanwords" by lexicographers, who suggest that they were borrowed from other Semitic languages such as Aramaic, Akkadian, or Arabic. However, it is important to note that this is speculative and not a definitive conclusion. As stated by Edward Horowitz, "sometimes the borrowing is so ancient that scholars do not know which language did the borrowing and which was the original owner." This raises the possibility that these questioned terms are actually of Hebrew origin and serve as further evidence of the limitations of current knowledge about the ancient Hebrew language. It is important to consider that our understanding of historical languages is constantly evolving and there may be a discovery in future that could shed more light on the origins of these words.

The ancient Hebrew language is believed to have had a rich vocabulary due to various evidences found in writings from the start of the Common Era. These include non-Biblical religious texts, such as the Dead Sea Scrolls and the Mishnah. The Mishnah is a collection of rabbinic writings in Hebrew that discuss Jewish tradition and it was written during the early part of the Common Era. Professor Meyer Waxman, in his article for The Encyclopedia Americana (1956, Vol. XIV, p. 57a), highlights this point by stating that "Biblical Hebrew...does not exhaust the entire stock of words, as is proved by the Mishnah, which employs hundreds of Hebrew words not found in the Bible." This suggests that while some of the words found in the Mishnah may have been later additions or newly coined expressions, a significant number of them were likely part of the Hebrew vocabulary during the period when the Hebrew Scriptures were written.

It is important to note that the Mishnah is considered as one of the earliest examples of Hebrew literature after the Bible, hence it could provide evidence of the Hebrew vocabulary used in that era. It is also considered as one of the major texts in Jewish tradition, Mishnah is an important primary source for understanding the development of Rabbinic Judaism and the Oral Law. The Mishnah also provides insight into the social, political, and economic conditions of the time. Additionally, the Dead Sea Scrolls, which were written around the same time as the Mishnah, also provide evidence of a rich Hebrew vocabulary. These scrolls, which were discovered in the 1940s, contain texts from the Hebrew Bible as well as non-biblical texts and they provide insight into the beliefs and practices of the Jewish community that lived in the area of the Dead Sea during the Second Temple period.

When Did Hebrew Begin to Wane?

The question of when Hebrew began to wane is a topic of debate among scholars. Some argue that the Jews began to adopt Aramaic as their primary language during their exile in Babylon. However, this theory is not widely accepted as there is little concrete evidence to support it. Additionally, modern examples have shown that subjugated groups or immigrants often retain their native language for much longer than 70 years. Given that the Jews had the promise of returning to their homeland, it would not be expected that they would readily abandon the use of Hebrew in favor of Aramaic or Akkadian, which were the primary languages spoken in Babylon at the time.

It is true that Aramaic passages and words can be found in exilic and postexilic books such as Daniel, Ezra, and Esther. However, this is not unusual as these books include accounts of events that took place in Aramaic-speaking lands, as well as official correspondence. Additionally, the people described in these books were subject to domination by foreign powers who used Aramaic as a diplomatic language.

One passage of scripture, Nehemiah 8:8, describes the "putting of meaning" into and "giving understanding" in the reading of the Law. Some scholars have suggested that this implies that Hebrew was not perfectly understood by the returned exiles and that some Aramaic paraphrasing was done. However, the text places emphasis on the exposition of the sense and application of the teachings of the Law, rather than suggesting a lack of understanding of Hebrew.

In conclusion, the question of when Hebrew began to wane is a complex one and there is not a clear consensus among scholars. While it is true that Aramaic passages and words can be found in exilic and postexilic books, this does not necessarily indicate a widespread adoption of Aramaic as the primary language among the Jews. Additionally, the lack of concrete evidence and the presence of other explanations for the presence of Aramaic in these texts make it difficult to say for certain that Hebrew began to wane during the exile in Babylon.

Contrary to popular belief, there is no clear evidence in the Bible of any widespread abandonment of Hebrew as the daily language of the Jewish people. The Bible does mention instances in which certain Jews were found to have wives of Ashdodite, Ammonite, and Moabite descent, and their children did not know "how to speak Jewish." However, this is presented in the context of Nehemiah's indignation at the Jews for engaging in marriages with non-Israelites, indicating that such a slighting of Hebrew was strongly disapproved. This is consistent with the importance placed on the reading and understanding of God's Word, which was primarily written in Hebrew at the time.

The period between the close of the Hebrew canon, likely in the time of Ezra and Malachi in the 5th century BCE, and the start of the Common Era is not dealt with extensively in the Bible. Secular records from this time period are also scarce. However, even these sources provide little support for a widespread changeover from Hebrew to Aramaic among the Jewish people. The evidence suggests that many of the Apocryphal books, such as Judith, Ecclesiasticus (not Ecclesiastes), Baruch, and First Maccabees, were written in Hebrew. These works are generally believed to date from the last three centuries before the Common Era. Additionally, some of the non-Biblical writings found among the Dead Sea Scrolls were also in Hebrew, and Hebrew was used in compiling the Jewish Mishnah after the beginning of the Common Era. This further supports the idea that Hebrew continued to be widely used and understood among the Jewish people during this time period.

The idea that Aramaic completely replaced Hebrew as the primary language of the Jewish people has been a topic of debate among scholars.

INTRODUCTION TO THE TEXT OF THE OLD TESTAMENT

However, many experts, including Dr. William Chomsky, argue that this theory is without foundation and has been effectively disproved. Instead, it is likely that the Jews became a bilingual people, with Hebrew remaining the preferred tongue.

Dr. Chomsky notes that the Mishnaic Hebrew found in texts dating from this period, such as the Mishnah, bears all the characteristics of a typical vernacular spoken by peasants, merchants, and artisans. This suggests that Hebrew was still a widely used and understood language among the Jewish people during the Second Commonwealth, which is the period between the return from exile in Babylon and the Roman conquest of Jerusalem in 63 BCE.

Additionally, Dr. Chomsky suggests that the available evidence indicates that the Jews were generally conversant with both Hebrew and Aramaic during this period, and that they would sometimes use one language and sometimes the other depending on the context. This supports the idea that the Jewish people were bilingual, with Hebrew remaining the preferred tongue.

The idea that Hebrew continued as a living language well into the first century of the Common Era is supported by references to the Hebrew language in the Christian Greek Scriptures, also known as the New Testament. These references include John 5:2; 19:13, 17, 20; 20:16; and Revelation 9:11; 16:16. While some scholars argue that these references should be understood as references to Aramaic, rather than Hebrew, there is evidence to suggest that the term "Hebrew" is being used to refer to the Hebrew language.

For example, when the physician Luke states that Paul spoke to the people of Jerusalem in "the Hebrew language" (Acts 21:40; 22:2), it seems unlikely that he meant to imply that Paul was speaking in Aramaic or Syrian. Additionally, the Hebrew Scriptures distinguish between Aramaic (or Syrian) and "the Jews' language" (2 Kings 18:26), and the first-century Jewish historian Josephus also makes a distinction between Aramaic and Hebrew as distinct languages.

It is acknowledged that Aramaic was widely used throughout Palestine at this time. The use of Aramaic "Bar" (son), rather than Hebrew "Ben," in several names, such as Bartholomew and Simon Bar-Jonah, is one indication of familiarity with Aramaic. However, just because some Jews had Greek names, such as Andrew and Philip, it does not necessarily mean that Greek was their common language. It is likely that four languages were current in

Palestine during the first century of the Common Era: Hebrew, Latin, Greek, and Aramaic. Of these, Latin was likely the least common.

The question of what language Jesus primarily spoke is a topic of debate among scholars. While it is possible that Jesus may have used Aramaic on occasion, such as when speaking to the Syrophoenician woman (Mark 7:24-30), there is evidence to suggest that he primarily spoke Hebrew. Certain expressions recorded as spoken by Jesus are generally considered to be of Aramaic origin, but there is some uncertainty about this classification. For example, the words spoken by Jesus while he was being crucified, "Eli, Eli, lama sabachthani?" (Matthew 27:46; Mark 15:34), are usually considered to be Aramaic, possibly in a Galilean dialect. However, The Interpreter's Dictionary of the Bible notes that "opinion is divided in regard to the original language of the saying and as to whether Jesus himself would more naturally have used Hebrew or Aramaic." It's also noted that a form of Hebrew, somewhat influenced by Aramaic, may have been in use in Palestine during the first century CE.

One further evidence for the continued use of Hebrew in apostolic times is the testimony that Matthew's Gospel was originally written by him in Hebrew. This suggests that Hebrew was still a widely understood language among the Jewish people during the time of Jesus and the early Christian church, and that it was used for religious and literary purposes.

What Language Did Jesus Speak?

The question of what language Jesus primarily spoke is a topic of debate among scholars. Concerning the languages used in Palestine during the time Jesus was on earth, Professor G. Ernest Wright states that various languages were undoubtedly to be heard on the streets of the major cities, with Greek and Aramaic being the most common tongues. Most urban peoples could probably understand both, even in cities like Caesarea and Samaria where Greek was more common. Roman soldiers and officials might be heard conversing in Latin, and orthodox Jews may have spoken a late variety of Hebrew with one another, a language that is neither classical Hebrew nor Aramaic, despite its similarities to both.

Commenting further on the language spoken by Jesus, Professor Wright says that the language spoken by Jesus has been much debated. While it is unknown if he could speak Greek or Latin, in his teaching ministry, he regularly used either Aramaic or the highly Aramaicized popular Hebrew. When Paul addressed the mob in the Temple, it is said that he spoke Hebrew (Acts 21:40) Scholars generally have taken this to mean Aramaic, but it is quite possible that a popular Hebrew was then the common tongue among the Jews.

It is possible that Jesus and his early disciples, such as the apostle Peter, at least at times spoke Galilean Aramaic, as Peter was told on the night Christ was taken into custody: "Certainly you also are one of them, for, in fact, your dialect gives you away" (Mt 26:73). This may have been said because the apostle was using Galilean Aramaic at the time, though that is not certain, or he may have been speaking a Galilean Hebrew that differed dialectally from that employed in Jerusalem or elsewhere in Judea.

Additionally, when Jesus came to Nazareth in Galilee and entered the synagogue there, he read from the prophecy of Isaiah, evidently as written in Hebrew, and then said: "Today this scripture that you just heard is fulfilled" (Luke 4:16-21), which suggests that those present could understand Biblical Hebrew. Nothing is said about Jesus' translating this passage into Aramaic. So, again, this suggests that persons present on that occasion could readily understand Biblical Hebrew.

Furthermore, early indications suggest that the apostle Matthew first wrote his Gospel account in Hebrew. Eusebius of the third and fourth centuries CE, for example, stated that "the evangelist Matthew delivered his Gospel in the Hebrew tongue" (Patrologia Graeca, Vol. XXII, col. 941). Additionally, Jerome of the fourth and fifth centuries CE wrote that the "Hebrew Gospel" was translated into Greek by Matthew himself. Furthermore, Acts 6:1, referring to a time shortly after Pentecost 33 CE, mentions Greek-speaking Jews and Hebrew-speaking Jews in Jerusalem.

In conclusion, while it is not certain what language Jesus spoke, it is likely that he used a combination of Aramaic and a highly Aramaized popular Hebrew, as well as being able to speak Galilean Aramaic, Greek, and Latin. Additionally, it is possible that he primarily spoke a form of Hebrew, with occasional use of Aramaic expressions.

So, returning to the question of when Hebrew began to wane, it seems, then, the decline of the Hebrew language appears to have been primarily caused by the destruction of Jerusalem and its temple in 70 CE and the subsequent scattering of its remaining inhabitants. Despite this, the language continued to be used in synagogues among Jewish communities that had spread to other regions. From around the 6th century CE, Jewish scholars known as the Masoretes made significant efforts to preserve the purity of the Hebrew text of the Scriptures. Beginning in the 16th century, there was renewed interest in the study of ancient Hebrew, and the following century saw a surge in the study of other Semitic languages as well. This renewed interest and study has led to a greater understanding of the ancient Hebrew language and has resulted in improved translations of the Hebrew Scriptures.

Hebrew Alphabet and Script

The Hebrew alphabet, which is believed to have originated in the second millennium BCE, is composed of 22 consonants. Some of these consonants have the ability to represent two different sounds, resulting in a total of 28 sounds. In contrast, the vowel sounds were not represented by any specific characters in the written script and were instead left for the reader to interpret based on context, similar to how English speakers fill in the vowels in abbreviations such as "bldg." (building), "blvd." (boulevard), and "hgt." (height). It is believed that the traditional pronunciation of the Hebrew Scriptures was kept alive and passed down by those who specialized in reading the Law, Prophets, and Psalms for the instruction of the people.

In the second half of the first millennium CE, the Masoretes developed a system of dots and dashes known as vowel points, which were inserted into the consonantal text to indicate vowel sounds. Additionally, certain accent marks were added to indicate stress, pauses, connections between words and clauses, and musical notation.

The earliest known Hebrew inscriptions were recorded in an ancient script that was considerably different in form from the square-shaped Hebrew letters used in later documents from the early centuries of the Common Era. The square-shaped style is often referred to as "Aramaic" or "Assyrian." It is believed that the transition from ancient Hebrew characters to square Hebrew characters took place during the Babylonian exile. However, it should be noted that the old Hebrew script remained in use alongside the square script for some time. Coins from the period of Bar Kochba's revolt (132-135 CE) feature old Hebrew letters, and texts found in the Dead Sea caves were also written in the old Hebrew script.

INTRODUCTION TO THE TEXT OF THE OLD TESTAMENT

עברית

𐤏𐤁𐤓𐤉𐤕

Image 11 The word HEBREW written in modern Hebrew language (top) and in Paleo-Hebrew alphabet (bottom)

Origen, a Christian writer of the second and third centuries CE, stated that in the more accurate copies of the Greek translations of the Hebrew Scriptures, the Tetragrammaton (the sacred name of Jehovah) was written in ancient Hebrew letters. This claim has been confirmed by the discovery of fragmentary leather scrolls from the first century CE that contain the "minor" prophets in Greek, in which the Tetragrammaton appears in ancient Hebrew characters. Similarly, fragments from the late fifth or early sixth century CE of Aquila's Greek version also contain the divine name written in ancient Hebrew characters.

Dr. Horowitz argues that the old Hebrew alphabet was borrowed by the Greeks and passed on to Latin, and that the Greek alphabet bears a close resemblance to the old Hebrew alphabet.—*How the Hebrew Language Grew*, p. 18.

How Does the Father Feel About His Own Personal Name?

Isaiah 42:8 American Standard Version (ASV)

[8] I am Jehovah, that is my name; and my glory will I not give to another, neither my praise unto graven images.

Malachi 3:16 American Standard Version (ASV)

[16] Then they that feared Jehovah spake one with another; and Jehovah hearkened, and heard, and a book of remembrance was written before him, for them that feared Jehovah, and that thought upon his name.

Micah 4:5 American Standard Version (ASV)

⁵ For all the peoples walk everyone in the name of his god; and we will walk in the name of Jehovah our God for ever and ever.

Image 12 Portion of the Isaiah Scroll, a second-century BCE manuscript of the Biblical Book of Isaiah and one of the best-preserved of the Dead Sea Scrolls.

Qualities and Characteristics

Hebrew is a language that is known for its expressiveness and ability to vividly describe events. Its short sentences and simple conjunctions give the language a sense of movement and flow of thought, making it an ideal language for poetry. In fact, Hebrew poetry is particularly noteworthy for its use of parallelism and rhythm, which adds to its expressiveness and emotional impact.

In addition to its poetic capabilities, Hebrew is also rich in metaphors. For example, in Genesis 22:17, the Hebrew word for "seashore" is literally translated as "lip of the sea." Other common metaphorical expressions in Hebrew include "face of the earth," "head of a mountain," "mouth of a cave," and similar phrases. It is important to note that the use of human terms in these metaphors does not indicate any belief in animism; rather, such belief is specifically condemned in scripture, as seen in passages such as Isaiah 44:14-17, Jeremiah 10:3-8, and Habakkuk 2:19.

Overall, Hebrew is a language that is characterized by its expressiveness, poetic capabilities, and rich use of metaphor. These features have contributed to its ability to convey powerful messages and emotions through the centuries, making it an important and enduring language in history.

The Hebrew language is known for its use of concrete vocabulary, which includes words that involve the senses of seeing, hearing, feeling, tasting, and smelling. This quality of Hebrew allows it to paint mental pictures for the listener or reader. However, some scholars argue that Hebrew may lack in abstract terms. While this is true to some extent, there are examples of abstract nouns in Biblical Hebrew. For instance, the noun "ma·chasha·vah'" (derived from the root "cha·shav'," meaning "think") is translated by abstract terms such as "thought, device, invention, scheme." Similarly, "Ba·tach'" (a verb that means "trust") is the source of the noun "be'tach" (security).

Despite the presence of some abstract nouns, it is generally true that abstract ideas in Hebrew are often conveyed through concrete nouns. For example, the root verb "ka·vedh'" which means "be heavy" (as in Judges 20:34) is also used to convey the abstract idea of 'becoming glorious' (Ezekiel 27:25) the same verb is translated 'become heavy.' This concept is further illustrated by other words such as "yadh," which means "hand" and also "care," "means," or "guidance" (Exodus 2:19; Genesis 42:37; Exodus 35:29; 38:21); "'aph" which refers to both "nostril" and "anger" (Genesis 24:47; 27:45); "zeroh'a‘," meaning "arm," also conveys the abstract concept of "strength" (Job 22:8, 9).

In summary, Hebrew is a language that is known for its use of concrete vocabulary, which allows it to paint vivid mental pictures for the listener or reader. While some scholars argue that Hebrew may lack in abstract terms, there are examples of abstract nouns in Biblical Hebrew, although they are often conveyed through concrete nouns. The Hebrew language is unique in this way, it's abstract concepts are often derived from concrete terms.

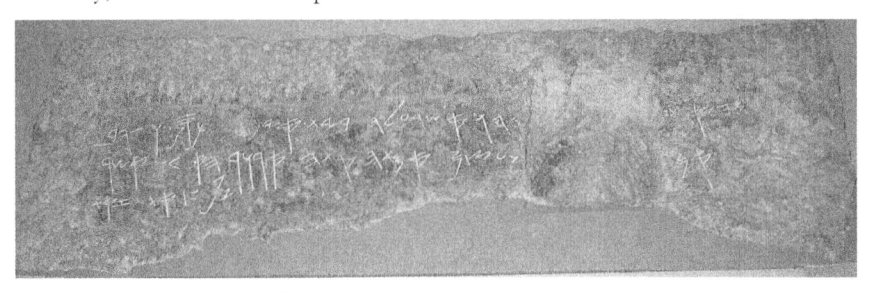

Image 13 The Shebna Inscription, from the tomb of a royal steward found in Siloam, dates to the 7th century BCE.

The concreteness of the Hebrew language is one of its defining characteristics, but it also poses significant challenges for translation. The Hebrew terms often have a different meaning in other languages when translated literally. Furthermore, the grammar of Hebrew differs greatly from other languages, making it difficult for translators to accurately reproduce the sense, manner of expression, and forcefulness of the language, particularly in its verb forms.

The brevity of Hebrew is also noteworthy. Hebrew's structure allows for a succinct and efficient use of language. Aramaic, which is the closest of the Semitic languages to Hebrew, is comparatively more wordy and roundabout. In the process of translation, it is often necessary to use auxiliary words to bring out the vividness, picturesqueness, and dramatic action of the Hebrew verb. While this may detract from the brevity of the original text, it helps to convey more fully the beauty and accuracy of the Hebrew text.

In summary, the concreteness of the Hebrew language poses a significant challenge for translation but also contributes to its unique style. The brevity of Hebrew is also a defining characteristic, which makes it more efficient and unique. However, it also requires the translator to use auxiliary words to convey the full meaning of the text. Despite these challenges, translating the Hebrew Scriptures is essential to understanding and appreciating the beauty and accuracy of the original language.

Hebrew Poetry

Biblical Hebrew is particularly suited for poetry due to several characteristics of the language.

INTRODUCTION TO THE TEXT OF THE OLD TESTAMENT

First, the Hebrew language has a rich system of parallelism, in which ideas are repeated in a structured and balanced way. This creates a sense of rhythm and symmetry in the poetry, making it more musical and memorable. Second, Hebrew is a very expressive language, lending itself to the vivid description of events. Its short sentences and simple conjunctions give movement and flow of thought, which contributes to the poetry's expressiveness and emotional impact. Third, Hebrew is rich in metaphor, which is a common feature of poetry. The Hebrew language uses metaphors and other figurative language to convey complex ideas and emotions in a more concrete and evocative way. Lastly, Hebrew poetry is known for its use of imagery, which makes the poetry more rich, colorful and vivid. This imagery can be found in the rich use of nature and human life, which makes Hebrew poetry unique and memorable. All of these characteristics make Hebrew particularly suited to poetry and have contributed to the enduring power and beauty of Hebrew poetry.

One example of Hebrew poetry from the Old Testament can be found in Psalm 23:1-2. This psalm is known for its poetic style and powerful imagery. Here is one verse from the psalm:

23 Jehovah is my shepherd; I shall lack nothing.
[2] He makes me lie down in green pastures.
He leads me beside still waters.
[3] He restores my soul.
He leads me in paths of righteousness
   for his name's sake.

This verse showcases several characteristics of Hebrew poetry, such as the use of imagery, metaphor, and parallelism. The imagery of "green pastures" and "quiet waters" creates a peaceful and serene scene, evoking a sense of calm and security. The metaphor of God as a shepherd leading his sheep is also used to convey the idea of protection and guidance. Additionally, the verse uses parallelism in the repetition of the phrase "he leads me" and "he guides me" to create a sense of balance and symmetry.

This Psalm is considered as one of the most well-known and beloved Hebrew poetry in the Old Testament and it's an example of how Hebrew poetry can convey powerful emotions and messages through its imagery, metaphor, and poetic structure.

Biblical Hebrew Grammar

Biblical Hebrew is the ancient language spoken by the Israelites in the biblical period. The Hebrew Bible, also known as the Old Testament, was written in this language. The study of biblical Hebrew grammar is essential for understanding and interpreting the Hebrew Bible. In this text, I will provide a comprehensive overview of the grammar of biblical Hebrew, including its phonology, morphology, and syntax, incorporating bible verses as examples.

Phonology

Phonology is the study of the sounds of a language. Biblical Hebrew has a relatively simple phonological system, with 22 consonants and five vowels. The consonants are divided into two groups: gutturals and labials. Gutturals are produced in the back of the throat, while labials are produced with the lips. The five vowels are represented by the letters 'aleph, 'ayin, he, waw, and yod. The vowels are used to indicate the pronunciation of the consonants and to indicate the stress in a word. For example, in the word "shema" (hear) the stress is on the last syllable, the "ma" is written with a patah (a vowel mark) to indicate that it's pronounced with an open vowel.

Morphology

Morphology is the study of the structure and formation of words. Biblical Hebrew is an inflected language, which means that the meaning of a word is indicated by its inflection, rather than by its position in a sentence. The inflection is indicated by the use of prefixes, suffixes, and internal changes.

Nouns are inflected for gender, number, and case. In biblical Hebrew, there are two genders: masculine and feminine. The gender of a noun is indicated by the form of the word, not by an article. Number is indicated by the form of the word, singular or plural. The case is indicated by the use of suffixes. For example, in the word "shamayim" (heavens) the singular form is indicated by the -im at the end, which is a plural marker.

Verbs are inflected for person, gender, number, and tense. The person is indicated by the use of prefixes, the gender and number are indicated by the form of the verb, and the tense is indicated by the use of suffixes. For example, in the word "shamarti" (I kept), the verb "shamar" (to keep) is conjugated to the first person singular and perfect tense by adding the suffix -ti.

Syntax

Syntax is the study of the arrangement of words and phrases to create well-formed sentences in a language. Biblical Hebrew has a relatively simple syntax, with a subject-verb-object word order. The verb is usually in the middle of the sentence, and the subject and object are indicated by the use of prefixes and suffixes.

The Hebrew Bible also uses a variety of literary techniques such as parallelism, anaphora, and chiasm, which create a specific literary style. Parallelism is the repetition of similar phrases or clauses, it's a common feature in Hebrew poetry, for example, in Psalm 23:1-3, the repetition of "the Lord is my shepherd" creates a sense of balance and symmetry. Anaphora is the repetition of a word or phrase at the beginning of successive clauses, for example, in Isaiah 6:3, the repetition of "Holy, holy, holy" creates a sense of emphasis and intensity. Chiasm is a literary technique in which the order of words or phrases is reversed in a pattern, creating a sense of emphasis and symmetry. For example, in Isaiah 53:5, the verse reads "But he was wounded for our transgressions; he was crushed for our iniquities; upon him was the chastisement that brought us peace, and with his stripes we are healed." The words "our transgressions" and "our iniquities" are parallel, and the phrase "upon him was the chastisement that brought us peace" and "with his stripes we are healed" are also parallel, creating a pattern of reversal that emphasizes the idea of redemption and salvation.

Additionally, Hebrew poetry often uses a variety of literary techniques such as simile, metaphor, and personification to convey complex ideas and emotions in a more concrete and evocative way. For example, in Psalm 23, the metaphor of God as a shepherd leading his sheep is used to convey the idea of protection and guidance.

In biblical Hebrew, nouns, verbs, adjectives, and other parts of speech have distinct forms and functions that contribute to the grammar of the language.

Nouns are inflected for gender, number, and case. Gender is indicated by the form of the noun, with masculine and feminine forms. Number is indicated by the form of the noun, with singular and plural forms. Case is indicated by the use of suffixes, such as the -im ending in the word "shamayim" (heavens) indicating the plural form.

Verbs are inflected for person, gender, number, and tense. Person is indicated by the use of prefixes, such as the first person singular prefix "ani" (I) in the word "anochi" (I). Gender and number are indicated by the form of the verb, and tense is indicated by the use of suffixes, such as the -ti ending in the word "shamarti" (I kept) indicating the perfect tense.

Adjectives are inflected for gender, number, and construct state. Adjectives must agree in gender, number, and construct state with the noun they modify. They can also be inflected for comparative and superlative forms.

Pronouns are inflected for person, gender, number, and case. Pronouns must agree in person, gender, number, and case with the noun or verb they replace.

Other parts of speech include prepositions, conjunctions, and particles. These parts of speech are used to indicate the relationships between words and phrases in a sentence, such as location, time, and cause-effect relationships.

In summary, biblical Hebrew has a rich system of inflection and word formation that contributes to its grammar. Nouns, verbs, adjectives, and other parts of speech have distinct forms and functions that indicate gender, number, tense, and other grammatical features, which helps convey the meaning of the text. Understanding these features of biblical Hebrew grammar is essential for interpreting and translating the Hebrew Bible.

A biblical example from each of the parts of speech:

Nouns:

- In the word "Elohim" (God), the word is in plural form, but it is used to refer to the one true God, this is an example of the plural of majesty, which is a grammatical phenomenon in Hebrew where a plural noun is used to indicate the greatness or majesty of the noun.

Verbs:

- In the word "yada" (to know), the word has a wide range of meanings in Hebrew, depending on the context it is used in. It can mean "to know" in the sense of having information, but it can also mean "to have intimacy with" or "to be familiar with." This is an example of polysemy, where a single word can have multiple meanings.

Adjectives:

- In the word "dabar" (word), the adjective is used in Hebrew to indicate the action of speaking, it is also used in the sense of "word" or "matter" in many passages in the Old Testament, this is an example of how Hebrew adjectives can have a wide range of meanings depending on the context they are used in.

Pronouns:

- In the word "ani" (I), the pronoun is used as the first person singular pronoun, but it also has a wide range of meanings in Hebrew, depending on the context it is used in. In some cases, it can be used to indicate the speaker's authority, in other cases, it can be used to indicate humility.

Prepositions and Particles:

- In the word "bet" (in), the preposition is used to indicate location, but it also has a wide range of meanings in Hebrew, depending on the context it is used in. In some cases, it can indicate the idea of being "inside" or "within," but it can also indicate the idea of being "with" or "among."

These examples show how rich and complex the Hebrew language is, and how each word can have a wide range of meanings depending on the context they are used in. This is why a good understanding of biblical Hebrew grammar is essential to understand and interpret the Hebrew Bible correctly.

In conclusion, biblical Hebrew grammar is an essential aspect of understanding and interpreting the Hebrew Bible. Its phonology, morphology, and syntax are relatively simple but rich in literary devices such as parallelism, anaphora, chiasm, and figurative language, which contribute to its unique poetic style. These features are evident in many passages of the Hebrew Bible and help to convey powerful emotions and messages through the centuries, making it an important and enduring language in history.

Biblical Hebrew and the Translator

Biblical Hebrew grammar is an essential aspect of understanding and interpreting the Hebrew Bible. The study of biblical Hebrew grammar is necessary for any translator who wishes to produce a literal translation of the Bible. In this text, I will discuss the challenges that a translator may face when translating the Hebrew Bible and how they can navigate these challenges to produce a literal translation.

Challenges of translating biblical Hebrew

Translating the Hebrew Bible can be challenging due to several factors. One of the main challenges is the concreteness of the Hebrew language. Hebrew is a very expressive language, lending itself to the vivid description of events. Its short sentences and simple conjunctions give movement and flow of thought, but when translated literally, Hebrew terms can often have quite a different meaning in other languages. For example, in Isaiah 55:12, the Hebrew phrase "For you shall go out in joy and be led back in peace" can be translated as "You will go out in joy and be led forth in peace."

Another challenge is the rich system of parallelism and figurative language, which are common features of Hebrew poetry. These literary devices create a sense of rhythm and symmetry in the poetry and convey complex ideas and emotions in a more concrete and evocative way. However, when translated into another language, these literary devices can be lost, and the meaning may be misunderstood. For example, in Psalm 23, the metaphor of God as a shepherd is used to convey the idea of protection and guidance, but when translated into another language, this metaphor may not have the same cultural significance and may be lost in translation. Translators must take great care when translating such figurative language and literary devices, to ensure that the meaning and impact of the original text is not lost. However, even so, literal translation philosophy is the preferred choice, to give the reader what God said in the receptor language. It is then up to the reader to get at what the author meant by the words that he used.

Another challenge is the use of idiomatic expressions in biblical Hebrew. Idiomatic expressions are phrases that can be translated literally most times but must be understood in the context of the culture in which they were written. An example of this can be found in Proverbs 25:11, where the Hebrew phrase "Like apples of gold in silver settings" is used to describe something that is very valuable and pleasing. This phrase can be translated literally but must be understood in the context of the culture.

Navigating these challenges

Despite these challenges, it is still possible to produce a literal translation of the Hebrew Bible. Translators must take great care when translating idiomatic expressions, figurative language, and literary devices to ensure that the meaning and impact of the original text is not lost. This can be achieved by providing footnotes or explanations in the translation to help the reader understand the idiomatic expressions, and by being mindful of the cultural context in which the text was written.

Additionally, translators must be familiar with the grammar and structure of biblical Hebrew to ensure that the translation is accurate. This includes understanding the inflection of nouns and verbs, the use of prefixes and suffixes, and the literary devices used in Hebrew poetry. By understanding these elements of biblical Hebrew grammar, translators can produce a translation that is as close as possible to the original text.

In conclusion, translating the Hebrew Bible can be challenging due to the concreteness of the Hebrew language, the rich system of parallelism and figurative language, and the use of idiomatic expressions. However, by taking great care when translating these elements and being mindful of the cultural

INTRODUCTION TO THE TEXT OF THE OLD TESTAMENT

context in which the text was written, it is possible to produce a literal translation of the Hebrew Bible.

Literal Translation Philosophy

Our primary purpose is to give the Bible readers what God said by way of his human authors, not what a translator thinks God meant in its place.—Truth Matters! Our primary goal is to be accurate and faithful to the original text. The meaning of a word is the responsibility of the interpreter (i.e., reader), not the translator.—Translating Truth!

Literal Bible translation philosophy holds that the goal of translation is to produce a text that is as close as possible to the original, preserving the wording, grammar, and sentence structure of the source text. This is in contrast to dynamic equivalent or interpretive translations, which aim to convey the meaning of the text in a way that is easily understood by the target audience, even if this means deviating from the wording, grammar, and sentence structure of the source text.

One of the main arguments for the use of literal Bible translation is that it provides the reader with an accurate representation of what God said in the original text. This is important because the Bible is considered by many to be the word of God, and therefore, it is crucial that the translation is as close as possible to the original text to ensure that the reader is receiving the message that God intended to convey.

Another argument for literal Bible translation is that it allows the reader to gain a deeper understanding of the text by studying the original language and grammar. This can be particularly beneficial for scholars, theologians, and other Bible students who wish to study the text in depth and gain a more nuanced understanding of the meaning and context of the text.

In contrast, dynamic equivalent or interpretive translations may make certain assumptions about what the text means, and therefore, the reader may not be getting the full picture of what God said but instead what the translator thinks God meant. This approach can be problematic, as it can result in a loss of meaning and context and may not accurately reflect the original intent of the text.

In conclusion, literal Bible translation philosophy is better because it provides the reader with an accurate representation of what God said in the original text. It allows the reader to gain a deeper understanding of the text by studying the original language and grammar, and it ensures that the translation is as close as possible to the original text, preserving the wording, grammar, and sentence structure of the source text. In contrast, interpretive translations may make certain assumptions about what the text means, and therefore, the reader may not be getting the full picture of what God said.

Copyists of the Hebrew Scriptures

The task of copying and writing the Hebrew Scriptures was carried out by skilled and trained scribes, who were typically members of the elite class. These scribes were known for their formal training and were associated with institutions such as the palace or temple. They were responsible for various tasks such as taking dictation, maintaining records, and copying documents. They were trained in sophisticated techniques that enabled them to achieve extreme consistency in writing individual letters, spelling, and the layout of the text. These practices can be traced back to Babylonian scribes in the third to second millennia who used lists of words and placed them into categories to check for consistent spelling. They also signed documents that they had copied for later checking and evaluation. Inscriptions from that period also reveal evidence of correction, such as letters inserted above the line, and the label "damage" on tablets, even when corrected restoration was obvious. These procedures were put in place to avoid errors that would inevitably creep into texts copied by hand. Similar practices were also used by scribes in Israel during the biblical period. The high standards for careful and accurate copying, along with built-in schemes for checking and correction were intentional attempts to avoid errors.

The choice of material for writing in ancient times was determined by the purpose and audience of the text. A variety of materials were available for use, including stone, metal, clay potsherds, wood, papyrus, and leather. Stone was commonly used for monumental inscriptions and steles, which were large pillars or plaques inscribed with treaties or laws as a public witness. Seals and weights also bore writing, and archaeologists have discovered graffiti on stone surfaces as well. Metal, such as gold, silver, copper, or bronze, was used for special tablets. Clay was a cheap and commonly available material, and people frequently wrote in ink on broken clay potsherds, which served as an ancient form of "scrap paper" for lists, brief letters, and short documents. Wooden tablets, covered in wax, could be reused by using the flat end of a stylus to erase old letters and create space for new ones.

The choice of material also had an impact on the durability and preservation of the text. Stone and metal were long-lasting and durable materials that could withstand the test of time, making them suitable for monumental inscriptions and important documents. Clay potsherds and wooden tablets, on the other hand, were more susceptible to wear and tear, and as a result, were more likely to be used for less formal or temporary writings.

In summary, the choice of material for writing in ancient times was determined by the purpose and audience of the text. Various materials were used, including stone, metal, clay potsherds, wood, papyrus, and leather, each with its advantages and disadvantages in terms of durability and preservation. The use of different materials also reflects the varying importance and intended audience of the text, and it's a fascinating glimpse into the history of writing and communication.

As technology advanced, longer documents were written on materials such as papyrus or leather. Our understanding of the use of these materials comes primarily from the discovery of the Dead Sea Scrolls in the Judean Desert. These scrolls are significant because they provide direct evidence of scribal practices and materials used during the biblical period. Along with a few clay ostraca, copper scrolls, and wooden tablets, the majority of texts from the Judean Desert were written on papyrus and leather, in the form of individual sheets or scrolls. The choice of writing material is often determined by genre; literary texts were commonly found on leather, while letters and administrative documents were found on papyrus.

Papyrus was created by drying thin strips from the papyrus plant and laying them in two layers at perpendicular angles. The strips were then pressed, beaten, and smoothed to create a writing surface. It was a less durable material than leather and less professional, as it was not as easy to create straight lines or neat columns on it. Additionally, it was more expensive than leather as it had to be imported from Egypt. However, papyrus had the advantage of allowing limited erasures.

The choice of writing material also reflects the intended audience and purpose of the text. Leather was a more durable material and was commonly used for literary texts that were meant to be preserved for a long period of time. Papyrus, on the other hand, was less durable, but it was more suitable for letters and administrative documents that were meant for temporary use. Understanding the choice of writing materials and the scribal practices used in the biblical period can give us insights into the literary culture and communication during that time.

The process of preparing leather for use in the Hebrew Scriptures was a labor-intensive endeavor. Leather was obtained from a variety of animals, including calves, fine-wooled sheep, medium-wooled sheep, wild and domestic goats, gazelles, and ibexes. The first step in the process was to remove the hair from the skins, which was typically done by treading on the skins, striking them with sticks, or soaking them in water mixed with excrement or vegetable materials. Enzymes were sometimes added to the water to aid in the breakdown of the hair. Once the hair was removed, the skins were cured in saltwater and treated with meal or flour, followed by a tanning solution made from natural vegetable and tree products. The skins were then stretched, dried, and smoothed with a rock and cut into the largest sheets possible for use in a scroll.

When it came to writing on the scrolls, scribes used a variety of inks. Black ink was made from soot mixed with oil and vegetable material, while red ink was created using mercury sulfide. Both types of ink were highly durable and resistant to fading, ensuring that the writings on the scrolls would remain legible for many years. However, the use of mercury sulfide in the production of red ink was known to have negative health effects on the scribes. This was one of the reasons why parchment and paper gradually replaced leather as the primary material for writing in the Middle Ages.

In Conclusion

In this chapter, we have examined the evolution of writing from early pictographic systems to the invention of the alphabet. The development of an alphabetic script played a significant role in the history of writing, and in particular, in the faith and life of the community in the Old Testament. The ability to write down God's covenant, will, character, and deeds in the sacred writings of Scripture greatly facilitated the communication and preservation of religious beliefs and practices for future generations.

The availability of an alphabetic script for the earliest writing of the Old Testament books was a crucial factor in the ease of communication and understanding of the text. Cuneiform and hieroglyphic writing systems, while highly advanced for their time, would have made the task of recording and disseminating religious texts much more challenging. Additionally, the accessibility of the Old Testament to its readership would have been greatly limited had it been written in the systems of Mesopotamia or Egypt.

Textual criticism is the process of analyzing and evaluating ancient texts, such as the Old Testament, in order to identify errors and reconstruct the most accurate and authoritative version of the text. It is a complex and nuanced field that requires a deep understanding of scribal practices, such as spelling conventions, word divisions, abbreviations, and corrections. The more knowledge we have about these practices, the better equipped we are to evaluate the evidence and make informed decisions about the text.

INTRODUCTION TO THE TEXT OF THE OLD TESTAMENT

As scripts and writing technologies have evolved over time, the types of errors that have crept into texts have also changed. For example, in one script, two letters might share similar components and be easily confused, while in another script, different letters might be similar and susceptible to being confused. This highlights the importance of understanding the historical and cultural context in which the text was written and transmitted.

It's important to note that the texts we possess today, even the oldest ones, are copies of copies, created in the context of many cultural and linguistic transitions in the writing process. Therefore, textual criticism is an exciting journey into a foreign world of scribes, changing scripts, and letters in ink on leather parchment. It allows us to gain a deeper understanding of the history and transmission of the Old Testament text in the Hebrew language.

Sumerian Pictograph

Image 14 early sumerian pictographic tablet 3100 BCE Clay Tablet Carved using a wedged stylus Sumeria

Sumerian Cuneiform

Akkadian Classical Neo-Assyrian

Image 15 Akkadian language inscription on the obelisk of Manishtushu

INTRODUCTION TO THE TEXT OF THE OLD TESTAMENT

Egyptian Pictogram and Determinative

Image 16 Hieroglyphs from the tomb of Seti I (KV 17), 13th century BCv

Ugaritic

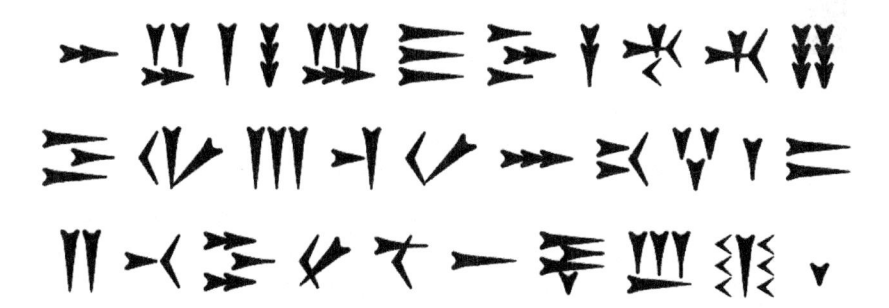

Paleo-Hebrew

In Summary

Ancient languages and dialects refer to the languages spoken and written in ancient times by various cultures around the world. Some examples of ancient languages include:

- **Egyptian**: The ancient Egyptian language is known for its hieroglyphic script, which was used for monumental inscriptions and religious texts. The hieroglyphs were a combination of logographic and alphabetic elements and were used for over 3,000 years.

- **Sumerian**: Sumerian is one of the earliest known written languages, dating back to the 4th millennium BCE. It was spoken in the ancient Mesopotamian region and was written in cuneiform script.

- **Akkadian**: Akkadian is a Semitic language that was spoken in ancient Mesopotamia. It was widely used in the 3rd millennium BCE as a lingua franca for trade and diplomacy.

- **Hebrew**: Hebrew is an ancient Semitic language that was spoken by the Israelites in ancient times. The Hebrew Bible, also known as the Old Testament, was written in Hebrew.

- Greek: Ancient Greek was the primary language of the ancient Greeks and was widely used throughout the Mediterranean region. The works of Homer, Plato, and Aristotle were written in ancient Greek.

- Latin: Latin was the language of the ancient Romans and was widely used throughout the Roman Empire. It was the language of literature, law, and administration and its influence can still be seen in modern languages such as French, Spanish, and Italian.

INTRODUCTION TO THE TEXT OF THE OLD TESTAMENT

These are just a few examples of ancient languages and dialects. Many other ancient languages and dialects were spoken and written throughout history, each with their own unique characteristics and influences on modern languages and cultures.

CHAPTER 2 Transmission of the Old Testament Text

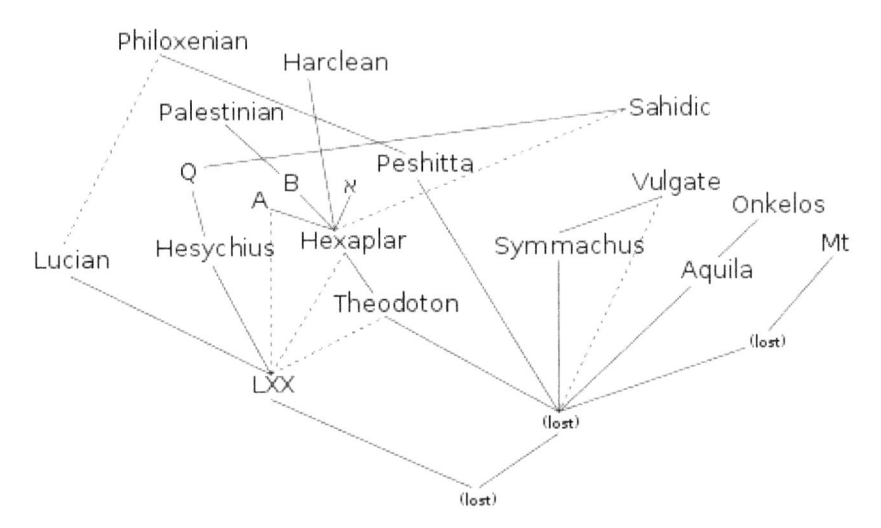

```
Philoxenian
            Harclean
    Palestinian                    Sahidic
       Q         Peshitta
          B  ℵ              Vulgate
       A                              Onkelos
Lucian   Hesychius  Hexaplar  Symmachus    Mt
                                  Aquila
             Theodoton
                                         (lost)
           LXX
                    (lost)


              (lost)
```

The transmission of the Old Testament text can be broken up into several distinct periods, including the following:

1. **The pre-Masoretic period**: This period covers the time from the composition of the original texts of the Old Testament (approx. 1200 BCE to 300 BCE) to the beginning of the Masoretic text tradition around the 3rd century BCE. During this period, the texts were transmitted orally and through written copies, which were subject to variations and errors.

2. **The Masoretic period**: This period covers the time from the 3rd century BCE to the Bar Kokhba revolt in 135 CE. During this period, the Masoretes, Jewish scholars, worked to establish an authoritative text of the Hebrew Bible. They developed a system of vocalization and accentuation, as well as a system of cross-references to help preserve the text from errors. This period marks the first textual evidence of the Hebrew Bible.

3. **The Medieval period**: This period covers the time from the Bar Kokhba revolt in 135 CE to the invention of the printing press in the 15th century CE. During this period, the Masoretic text was

widely used and copied by Jewish and Christian scribes, leading to the development of different versions and traditions of the text.

4. **The Modern period**: This period covers the time from the invention of the printing press to the present day. This period saw the discovery of ancient biblical manuscripts, such as the Dead Sea Scrolls, which have helped scholars to better understand the history of the text and its transmission. Additionally, with the invention of the printing press, the text became widely available and led to the production of many different editions and translations of the Old Testament.

Textual Transmission Prior to 300 BCE

The textual transmission of the Hebrew text prior to 300 BCE is a complex topic that has been the subject of much scholarly research and debate. It is important to note that the exact process of transmission is not entirely clear and that there is a degree of uncertainty surrounding the various stages of transmission. However, based on the evidence that is available, it is possible to make some general observations.

One of the key factors in understanding the textual transmission of the Hebrew text prior to 300 BCE is the fact that the texts were transmitted orally before they were written down. The oral tradition of the Hebrew text was likely passed down from generation to generation through the use of memorization techniques and repetition. This oral tradition was likely an important factor in preserving the texts and ensuring their accuracy, as the texts were constantly being recited and transmitted from one person to another.

As the texts were transmitted orally, it is likely that variations and errors crept into the text over time. These variations and errors may have been the result of a variety of factors, including differences in regional dialects, changes in pronunciation, and the influence of other languages and cultures. Additionally, as the texts were transmitted over time, it is likely that scribes and editors made changes to the text to reflect contemporary beliefs and practices.

In addition to the oral transmission of the Hebrew text, there is also evidence that the texts were written down on a variety of materials, including clay tablets, papyrus, and leather. These written copies were likely used to supplement the oral tradition and ensure the preservation of the texts.

However, as the texts were written down by hand, there is a good chance that errors and variations crept into the text.

In summary, the textual transmission of the Hebrew text prior to 300 BCE was a complex process that involved both oral and written transmission of the texts. The oral tradition of the Hebrew text was likely an important factor in preserving the texts and ensuring their accuracy, but variations and errors likely crept into the text over time. Additionally, the texts were written down on a variety of materials, which may have introduced errors and variations into the text.

Textual Transmission from 300 BCE to 135 CE

Introduction:

The Textual Transmission of the Hebrew Old Testament Text, also known as the Hebrew Bible or the Tanakh, is a complex and multi-faceted topic that has been the subject of much scholarly study. In particular, the period of 300 BCE to 135 CE is considered a crucial phase in the history of the transmission of the Hebrew Bible text. During this period, the text of the Hebrew Bible was essentially fixed, and there is a wealth of manuscript evidence that provides insight into the practices of Jewish scribes during this time.

The Septuagint and the Samaritan Pentateuch:

One of the most significant events during this period was the translation of the Hebrew Bible into Greek, known as the Septuagint. The Septuagint was produced in Egypt and Palestine, and it is considered an important representative of a Hebrew text that is different from what would later become the fixed Masoretic Text (MT). The Septuagint is significant because it provides insight into the state of the Hebrew text at the time of its translation and allows for a comparison with the later fixed MT.

Another important witness to the state of the text during this period is the Samaritan Pentateuch. The Samaritan religious sect adopted a distinct Hebrew text of the Pentateuch and scribes of this sect revised it according to their own theological positions. This provides a unique perspective on the text and allows for further comparison with the Septuagint and the later fixed MT.

The Qumran Biblical Manuscripts: The Dead Sea Scrolls:

Pride of place for the manuscript evidence of this phase belongs to the Qumran biblical manuscripts, often called the Dead Sea Scrolls. Many of the manuscripts are fragmentary, but even so, their importance is noteworthy because these are Hebrew manuscripts (not translations) that have been dated to the period between the third and the first centuries BCE, with the majority belonging to the second and first centuries. Prior to the discovery of these manuscripts, which began in 1947, the only access to the practices of this period was through inferences drawn from the study of the early versions. The Qumran scrolls give direct access to scribal activity in these crucial centuries. All of the OT books are represented among the Qumran documents with the exception of Esther.

Textual Criticism at Qumran:

Evidence from Qumran shows that scribes at this time were practicing a kind of textual criticism in which they corrected their own mistakes as well as mistakes by previous scribes. They placed "cancellation" dots above or below individual characters or words, crossed out elements with lines, and used signs to indicate that two words should be transposed. Scribes also erased letters on parchment by scraping with a sharp instrument. A number of texts contain examples in which one can still recognize the corrected element.

Conclusion:

The period of 300 BCE to 135 CE is considered a crucial phase in the history of the transmission of the Hebrew Bible text. During this period, the text of the Hebrew Bible was essentially fixed, and there is a wealth of manuscript evidence that provides insight into the practices of Jewish scribes during this time. The Septuagint and the Samaritan Pentateuch are important witnesses to the state of the text during this period, providing insight into the variations and revisions that existed before the fixed Masoretic Text. The Qumran biblical manuscripts, also known as the Dead Sea Scrolls, are considered the most important manuscript evidence for this period. These manuscripts provide direct access to scribal activity in these crucial centuries and provide a unique and valuable perspective on the text of the Hebrew Bible during this period.

Ernst Würthwein The Consonantal Text Excursion

Three periods may be distinguished in the transmission of the consonantal text. The *first period* (3rd century B.C.E. to ca. 70 C.E.) saw the development of an authoritative consonantal text from among the proto-MT groups (see 3.5). At this stage the meaning of the text was of greater concern than the precise reproduction of consonants. This early period lasted to the destruction of the temple by the Romans, and it will be discussed in greater detail in the next chapter in connection with the Qumran scrolls. The *second period* (70 C.E. to 7th century C.E.) lasted from the destruction of the Second Temple to the suppression of the second Jewish rebellion. It was marked by a further standardization of the Masoretic consonantal text and its protection by the Pharisaic rabbinic trend of Judaism. Meanwhile debates with early Christianity over its claim for the LXX to be a valid text of the Scriptures strengthened Judaism's reliance on the consonantal text of the Hebrew Bible and efforts to produce its own Greek versions (see 5.3). Also it has yet to be investigated whether or to what extent the Islamic studies on the Quran, which began in the 7th century C.E., influenced or affected the Babylonian Jews in their work on the text of the Bible. The *third period* (8th century c.e. to the end of the medieval period) began with determining the vocalization of the consonantal text, starting with punctuation systems. It was characterized by a final securing of the text. Not only was the meaning of the text defined by its vocalization and punctuation, but the text itself was protected from scribal errors by an ingenious double system of cross-references in the margin (see 2.5).

For many reasons the Masoretic tradition emerged as the authoritative form of the text toward the end of the first period. First, the various forms represented by the Qumran scrolls were eliminated from competition by being hidden in the caves, the pre-Samaritan textual tradition was maintained by the Samaritan community, and the Hebrew text underlying the LXX became the Christian Bible. This left only the Masoretic tradition for Judaism.[1] Further, we can assume that responsibility for biblical manuscripts regarded as holy scripture lay in priestly or Levitical hands, and thus with the Jerusalem temple and the exemplars it sanctioned for copying. It should be noted especially that in early Judaism "holy scriptures" did not denote a canonical entity but rather scriptures used in a holy place.[3] "Holy" referred solely to the ritual use of appropriate scrolls, and only indirectly described their content. Since the priests were responsible for determining the holiness of scrolls, removing manuscripts that were in any way imperfect, damaged, or incorrect, they developed controls for reducing variants and standardizing the textual tradition. Professional correctors (Heb. מַגִּיהִים) were employed in the temple to supervise the production of copies and correct them. After the fall of the Second Temple, the rabbinic schools assumed both their functions of supervision and correction.

Canon. Many regard the terms "authoritative text" and "canonical text" as synonyms, so that the creation of a canon of Holy Scripture, to which nothing may be added and from which nothing may be taken away, is confused with the literal establishment of the consonantal text. But we should avoid this oversimplification of the relationship because the concept of canon is problematic for the Hebrew Bible: it assumes a Christian definition of the Holy Scriptures that is lacking in Rabbinic Judaism. The holy writings of Judaism are better described as a three-part corpus of authoritative writings of graduated levels of revelation. The corpus is traditionally known by its acronym *Tanak* (Heb. תנ״ך): *Torah* = Law (Pentateuch: Genesis–Deuteronomy), *Nebi'im* = Prophets (Former Prophets: Joshua, Judges, 1-2 Samuel, 1-2 Kings; Latter Prophets: Isaiah–Malachi), *Ketubim* = Writings (Hagiographa: Psalms, Job, Proverbs, Ruth, Song of Songs, Ecclesiastes, Lamentations, Esther, Daniel, Ezra-Nehemiah, 1-2 Chronicles). The written Torah stands as the direct revelation from God that Moses received on Mount Sinai. An equal authority is claimed only by the *oral* Torah that according to rabbinic tradition was also given on Mount Sinai and was transmitted in an unbroken chain of tradition alongside the written Torah as an equally binding revelation. The second component comprises the prophetic books. In comparison with the Torah of Moses they rank as an indirect revelation and stand in relation to the Torah as an historical interpretation. The third component is at one remove below the Prophets, but it is at least prophetically inspired. As revelation it does not rank with the Torah and the Prophets. This graduation of the three parts of the canon is constitutive for the Jewish understanding of Scripture, and involves a hermeneutical concept based on the three summary and programmatic texts—Deut 34:10-12; Mal 3:22-24 (ET 4:4-6), 2 Chr 36:22-23—that outline the framework for intertextual interpretation.

One can easily recognize that the three-part division of the corpus of Jewish Scripture reflects historical events. There is no question that in the Persian period the books of the Pentateuch enjoyed a special esteem, and even canonical authority as the Mosaic Torah, although this did not yet affect the text, as the variety of witnesses to a *rewritten Bible* attest (see 3.2). Probably this same period saw efforts to form a *corpus propheticum* of the Latter Prophets that combined with the Former Prophets in the 2nd century b.c.e. to gain authoritative status. At the same time, increasing respect for the book of Isaiah aroused a concern for its text, promoting an interest in its literal transmission. Thus the second Isaiah scroll from Qumran (1QIsa = 1Q8) dating from the 1st century B.C.E. shows hardly any significant deviation from the consonantal text preserved by Masoretes of the Middle Ages. It is quite different with the books of the third part of the canon, where the textual tradition has been in part considerably defective. This suggests that its inclusion in the canon was long questionable, and correspondingly there was less interest in the integrity of its text. For example, there was still discussion in the 1st century C.E. as to whether the Song of Songs and Ecclesiastes "polluted the hands," that is, were regarded as holy scripture. This expression assumes the concept that holy things should not be touched, and therefore handling scrolls regarded as holy required a ritual ablution. This concept also underlies the practice of the lector in a synagogue following the text with a *yad* (pointer) rather than a finger.

The Council of Jamnia (ca. 100 C.E.). With regard to the Writings, the question of which books belonged among the holy scriptures of Judaism involved a lengthy process probably lasting into the 3rd/4th century C.E. Earlier scholarship compressed this process into an historical event and spoke of a Council of Jamnia (Heb. יַבְנֶה), a city about 14 km. northeast of Ashdod, where a Jewish court was convened by Gamaliel II about 100 c.e. and the canon of the Hebrew Bible was established—in contradistinction to the Christian Bible. More recent scholarship has proven this view to be an historical fiction for three reasons. First, only a single text in the Mishnah refers to a debate in Jamnia about whether the Song of Songs or Ecclesiastes pollutes the hands.[9] As is typical, even here the discussion is not about any relationship to a canon but merely the question whether these books are regarded as holy. Second, the discussion in a rabbinic school is magnified into a formal council, giving the false impression of Jamnia as comparable to a council of the early church issuing pronouncements on matters of dogma. Third, the implication that the Pharisaic rabbinic tradition was authoritative for all of Judaism cannot be true, especially because local Jewish communities continued to maintain their autonomy even in succeeding centuries, when the rabbinic schools gained greater authority.

While the attempt to solve the problem of the formation of the Jewish canon by invoking the Council of Jamnia may be abandoned, still the closing of the canon remains historically elusive. However, if we observe the distinction between holy texts and canonical texts, we can find in early Judaism the recognition of a group of authoritative writings commonly regarded as binding although not regarded as forming an officially defined canon. The same is true of their texts that were undoubtedly modified in traditional ways as respect for their authority as holy writings grew, leading eventually to their standardization by the Masoretes. But it was not a matter of establishing the wording of a final canonical text. Nor did even the medieval Masoretes who established the consonantal text and formulated the rules for its pronunciation have any such concerns. They did not work as members of a Jewish Bible committee, but rather individually, on their private initiative, and with such devotion to the safeguarding of the traditional text that they largely supplanted variant readings. Thus with regard to the Hebrew biblical text, the "final canonical text" is not an historical entity but a doctrinal characterization (see 7.1).[2]

End of Ernst Würthwein Excursion
Textual Transmission from 135 to 500 CE

Introduction:

The Textual Transmission of the Hebrew Old Testament Text, also known as the Hebrew Bible or the Tanakh, is a complex and multi-faceted topic that has been the subject of much scholarly study. In particular, the period of 135 CE to 500 CE is considered a crucial phase in the history of the transmission of the Hebrew Bible text. During this period, the text of the Hebrew Bible was fixed, and a number of changes were made to it to aid reading, understanding and liturgical use. There is also a wealth of manuscript evidence that provides insight into the practices of Jewish scribes during this time.

The Age of Talmud:

The time period 135-500 CE corresponds roughly to what may be called the age of the Talmud. The Talmud is a central text in Rabbinic Judaism, and it was compiled and developed during this time. The Talmud is a collection of Jewish laws, stories, and commentaries on the Hebrew Bible, and it played an important role in shaping the interpretation and understanding of the text.

The Division of Text into Verses:

It is probable that the division of the text into verses, a feature taken for granted by the modern reader, occurred during this time. The division of the text into verses was important for the study and understanding of the Hebrew Bible, and it helped to make the text more accessible for reading and interpretation. The verses divisions, however, were not fixed, there were variations between Palestinian and Babylonian schools in regard to the total number of verses in individual books and groups of books (e.g., the Pentateuch). These variations reflect the different interpretive traditions that existed among Jewish communities during this time.

The Division of Text into Chapters:

In contrast, the division of the Old Testament into chapters, another feature that is necessary for modern readers, was not of Jewish origin.

---

[2] Ernst Würthwein, *The Text of the Old Testament: An Introduction to the Biblia Hebraica*, ed. Alexander Achilles Fischer, trans. Erroll F. Rhodes, Third Edition. (Grand Rapids, MI: William B. Eerdmans Publishing Company, 2014), 15–19.

Chapter divisions and numbering were of Christian origin and were introduced into Hebrew manuscripts in approximately 1330 CE. This means that the chapter divisions that are used today in Hebrew Bibles are a later addition and not a part of the original text.

Changes to aid reading and understanding:

The main changes that occurred during this period were "external" textual features that aided reading and understanding and helped in liturgical use. In some cases, indelicate expressions were avoided through the use of more acceptable synonyms or the substitution of a different word for the name of a pagan deity. This was done to make the text more appropriate for use in religious ceremonies and to avoid any offense to religious sensibilities.

For example, in the book of Ezekiel, the name of God was replaced with the Hebrew word for Lord (Adonai) to avoid the use of the divine name, which was considered too sacred to be spoken. Similarly, in the book of Esther, some editions replaced the name of the Persian king Ahasuerus with the Hebrew word for king (melech) in order to avoid using the name of a pagan ruler.

Variations between Palestinian and Babylonian Schools:

There were variations between Palestinian and Babylonian schools in regard to the total number of verses in individual books and groups of books (e.g., the Pentateuch). These variations reflect the different interpretive traditions that existed among Jewish communities during this time. This is evident in the different versions of the Talmud that were developed in these regions, the Jerusalem Talmud and the Babylonian Talmud. According to Jacob Neusner, "The Babylonian Talmud is the more extensive, the more analytical, and the more systematic of the two Talmuds. It is also the more famous and the more widely studied. The Jerusalem Talmud is more succinct, more anecdotal, and more concerned with legal detail."

The role of the Scribes:

The scribes played an important role in the textual transmission of the Hebrew Bible during this period. They were responsible for copying and preserving the text, as well as making changes to it to aid reading and understanding. They also played an important role in the interpretation and understanding of the text, as they were considered experts in the Hebrew language and the laws of the Bible.

The scribes were also responsible for checking the text for errors and making corrections when necessary. They used various methods to indicate changes in the text, such as placing "cancellation" dots above or below

INTRODUCTION TO THE TEXT OF THE OLD TESTAMENT

individual characters or words, crossing out elements with lines, and using signs to indicate that two words should be transposed. This practice is known as textual criticism, and it was used to ensure the accuracy and consistency of the text. Additionally, scribes would also erase letters on parchment by scraping with a sharp instrument if they needed to make corrections. This practice allowed scribes to make changes to the text while preserving the integrity of the original document. A number of texts contain examples in which one can still recognize the corrected element, providing insight into the practices of the scribes during this time.

Textual Criticism and Liturgical Use:

The main changes that occurred during this period were "external" textual features that aided reading and understanding and helped in liturgical use. In some cases, indelicate expressions were avoided through the use of more acceptable synonyms or the substitution of a different word for the name of a pagan deity. This was done to make the text more appropriate for use in religious ceremonies and to avoid any offense to religious sensibilities. This kind of textual criticism is known as "Hekesh" and it was widely used in the Talmudic period. According to David Marcus, "Hekesh is a method of textual criticism in which the scribe compares one verse with another and then makes a change in one of them so that they will be consistent with each other."

Conclusion:

In conclusion, the period of 135 CE to 500 CE is considered a crucial phase in the history of the transmission of the Hebrew Bible text. During this period, the text of the Hebrew Bible was divided into verses and the Talmud, a central text in Rabbinic Judaism, was compiled and developed. There were variations between Palestinian and Babylonian schools in regard to the total number of verses in individual books and groups of books. The division of the Old Testament into chapters, however, was not of Jewish origin, but was introduced by Christians, and the main changes that occurred during this period were external textual features that aided reading and understanding, and helped in liturgical use. These included the use of textual criticism techniques such as "Hekesh" where scribes compared one verse with another and made changes to ensure consistency, and the use of more acceptable synonyms or the substitution of a different word for the name of a pagan deity. The Talmud also played a crucial role in shaping the understanding and interpretation of the Hebrew Bible during this period, with variations in its interpretation and application between the Palestinian and Babylonian schools. Overall, the textual transmission of the Hebrew Old Testament during the period of 135 CE to 500 CE reflects the ongoing evolution of

Jewish religious and cultural traditions and the increasing importance of the text for both scholarly study and liturgical use.

Textual Transmission from 500 CE to 1000 CE

Introduction:

The period of 500 CE to 1000 CE is a significant phase in the history of the textual transmission of the Hebrew Old Testament text. During this time, the work of the Masoretes, a group of Jewish scribes who were dedicated to carefully transmitting the text of the Hebrew Bible, played a crucial role in the preservation and transmission of the text. The Masoretes developed a system for vocalization and accentuation, which helped to ensure the accuracy and consistency of the text. Additionally, the work of the Masoretes in different geographical locations such as Babylon and Tiberias led to the development of distinct Masoretic traditions.

The Masoretes and the Preservation of the Text:

The Masoretes were a group of Jewish scribes who were dedicated to carefully transmitting the text of the Hebrew Bible. They created a system to preserve the oral reading tradition that had been passed down to them and to ensure that the text was copied with absolute accuracy. According to Moshe Goshen-Gottstein, "The Masoretes were the transmitters of the biblical text in the Jewish tradition, and their activity was focused on the preservation of the biblical text."

The Masoretes developed a system for vocalization and accentuation, which helped to ensure the accuracy and consistency of the text. This system, known as Tiberian vocalization, is still used in traditional Jewish Bibles today. The Masoretes also developed a system of cantillation, which is a system of musical notation used to indicate the correct chanting of the text in synagogue services.

Development of Distinct Masoretic Traditions:

The Masoretic activity during this period was carried out in various places due to certain historical factors that affected the Jewish people. The triumph of Christianity in Palestine was one of several interrelated factors that caused a large-scale emigration of Jewish textual scholars to Babylon in the second century CE. The study of the biblical text thrived in several academies in Babylon from the third to the tenth centuries. This led to the development of a distinct Masoretic tradition in Babylon, which was separate from the tradition that developed in Palestine.

Another significant event that influenced masoretic activity was the Islamic conquest of Palestine in 638 CE, which made possible a revival of Jewish textual work in Tiberias, a city on the western shore of the Sea of Galilee. The work of the Tiberian Masoretes was influential in the subsequent study and transmission of the Old Testament text. They developed a system for vocalization and accentuation, known as Tiberian vocalization, which is still used in traditional Jewish Bibles today.

The Textual Variants:

During this period, the Masoretes carefully compared different versions of the text and made decisions about which reading to include in the final text. They also made notes in the margins of the text, known as the masorah, which recorded information about the text's pronunciation, spelling, and any textual variants. These Masoretic notes are still included in traditional Jewish Bibles today and provide valuable insight into the textual transmission of the Hebrew Old Testament during this period.

The Textual Transmission and the Canonization of the Bible:

The textual transmission and the canonization of the Bible were also closely related during this period. The canonization of the Bible refers to the process of determining which texts were considered to be part of the authoritative Hebrew Bible. According to the Jewish Encyclopedia, "The process of canonization, by which a particular collection of sacred books becomes authoritative and normative, was completed in the first century CE, with the finalization of the canon of the Hebrew Bible."

Conclusion:

In conclusion, the period of 500 CE to 1000 CE is a significant phase in the history of the textual transmission of the Hebrew Old Testament text. During this time, the work of the Masoretes played a crucial role in the preservation and transmission of the text. The Masoretes developed a system for vocalization and accentuation, which helped to ensure the accuracy and consistency of the text. Additionally, the work of the Masoretes in different geographical locations such as Babylon and Tiberias led to the development of distinct Masoretic traditions. The textual variants and the canonization of the Bible were also closely related during this period, which had a profound impact on the understanding and interpretation of the Hebrew Bible, and it continues to shape the understanding and interpretation of the Hebrew Bible to this day.

The Karaite movement In Babylon

The Karaite movement is a Jewish sect that emerged in the 8th-10th century CE in the Babylonian and Persian empires. The movement was founded by Anan ben David, who rejected the authority of the Talmud and instead advocated for a return to the literal interpretation of the Hebrew Bible. This break from traditional Rabbinic Judaism marked the beginning of the Karaite movement, which would have a significant impact on the development of Jewish theology and the transmission of the Hebrew Bible.

Background and Origins of the Karaite Movement

The origins of the Karaite movement can be traced back to the 8th-10th century CE in the Babylonian and Persian empires. The movement was founded by Anan ben David, who was born in Baghdad in the 8th century CE. Anan rejected the authority of the Talmud and instead advocated for a return to the literal interpretation of the Hebrew Bible. He believed that the Talmud had distorted the true meaning of the Hebrew Bible and that a return to the literal interpretation of the text was necessary to understand the true teachings of Judaism.

Anan's teachings attracted a significant following, and the movement began to spread throughout the Babylonian and Persian empires. The movement was called "Karaite" because of their adherence to the "reading" or "qara" of the Hebrew Bible. The Karaites rejected the authority of the Rabbis and the Talmud, and instead placed the Hebrew Bible at the center of their religious practices and beliefs.

Impact on Jewish Theology

The Karaite movement had a significant impact on the development of Jewish theology. The movement's rejection of the Talmud and emphasis on the literal interpretation of the Hebrew Bible led to a renewed focus on the study of the Hebrew Bible and the development of new methods for interpreting the text. The Karaites also rejected the idea of a "Oral Torah" and instead believed that the Hebrew Bible was the only source of religious authority.

The Karaite movement also had an impact on the transmission of the Hebrew Bible. The movement's emphasis on the literal interpretation of the text led to the development of new methods for preserving and transmitting the Hebrew Bible. The Karaites placed a strong emphasis on the accurate transmission of the text, and they developed new methods for checking and correcting the text. They also emphasized the importance of the correct pronunciation and vocalization of the Hebrew text, which helped to preserve the oral reading tradition of the Hebrew Bible.

The Karaite movement also had an impact on the transmission of the Hebrew Bible outside of the Karaite community. The movement's emphasis on the literal interpretation of the text and the accurate transmission of the text led to the development of new methods for preserving and transmitting the Hebrew Bible. These methods were later adopted by other Jewish communities, including the Rabbinic community, which helped to preserve the accuracy of the Hebrew Bible.

The Karaite movement also had an impact on the study of Jewish history. The movement's rejection of the Talmud and emphasis on the literal interpretation of the Hebrew Bible led to the development of new methods for studying Jewish history. The Karaites placed a strong emphasis on the historical context of the Hebrew Bible, which helped to provide a deeper understanding of the text and the history of the Jewish people.

Conclusion

The Karaite movement began in Babylon in the 8th-10th century CE. The movement was founded by Anan ben David, who rejected the authority of the Talmud and instead advocated for a return to the literal interpretation of the Hebrew Bible. The movement had a significant impact on the development of Jewish theology, the transmission of the Hebrew Bible, and the study of Jewish history. The movement's emphasis on the literal interpretation of the text, accurate transmission of the text, and the historical context of the Hebrew Bible helped to preserve the accuracy of the Hebrew Bible and provide a deeper understanding of the text and the history of the Jewish people.

Asher the Elder of the eighth century C.E.

One of the most significant figures among the Masoretes was Asher the Elder, who lived in the 8th century CE.

Background of Asher the Elder

Asher the Elder is believed to have lived in Tiberias, a city on the western shore of the Sea of Galilee, during the 8th century CE. He was a member of the ben Asher family, which was known for its expertise in the Masoretic tradition. According to the Jewish Encyclopedia, Asher the Elder is "known as the father of the Masoretic family of ben Asher and is considered the most prominent member of that family."

Work of Asher the Elder

Asher the Elder is known for his work in the field of Masorah, which is the study of the oral tradition of the Hebrew text. He is credited with creating a system for preserving the oral reading tradition of the Hebrew text and ensuring the accuracy of the text in the copies. According to the Jewish Encyclopedia, "Asher the Elder was the first to introduce a system of diacritical marks for the vowels and other grammatical signs, and to establish rules for the correct writing of the text."

Asher the Elder's system for preserving the oral reading tradition of the Hebrew text is known as the Tiberian system. The Tiberian system includes the use of diacritical marks for the vowels and other grammatical signs, as well as rules for the correct writing of the text. According to the Jewish Encyclopedia, "The Tiberian system is considered the most accurate and reliable of all the systems of vocalization and is the one adopted in the standard editions of the Hebrew Bible."

The Tiberian system was later refined by Asher's descendants, including his grandson, Aaron ben Moses ben Asher, who is considered to be the greatest of the Tiberian Masoretes. The work of Aaron ben Moses ben Asher and his descendants was later used as the basis for the Biblia Hebraica, which is considered to be the most accurate representation of the Masoretic text.

Asher the Elder's Influence on the Masoretic Text

Asher the Elder's work had a significant impact on the transmission of the Hebrew text of the Old Testament. His system for preserving the oral reading tradition of the Hebrew text and ensuring the accuracy of the text in copies helped to standardize the text and make it more reliable. The Tiberian system, which he created, is considered to be the most accurate and reliable of all the systems of vocalization and is the one adopted in the standard editions of the Hebrew Bible.

Asher the Elder's work also laid the foundation for the work of his descendants, including his grandson Aaron ben Moses ben Asher, who refined the Tiberian system and is considered to be the greatest of the Tiberian Masoretes. The work of the ben Asher family and their descendants was later used as the basis for the Biblia Hebraica, which is considered to be the most accurate representation of the Masoretic text.

INTRODUCTION TO THE TEXT OF THE OLD TESTAMENT

Nehemiah Ben[3] Asher of the tenth century C.E.

Nehemiah ben Asher ben Hilkiah was a medieval Jewish scribe and Masorete who lived in the 10th century CE. He was a member of the ben Asher family, which was known for its expertise in the Masoretic tradition. Nehemiah ben Asher is best known for his work on the Aleppo Codex, which is considered to be the most important and accurate manuscript of the Masoretic Text.

Background of Nehemiah Ben Asher

Nehemiah ben Asher was born in Tiberias, a city on the western shore of the Sea of Galilee, in the 10th century CE. He was a member of the ben Asher family, which was known for its expertise in the Masoretic tradition. The ben Asher family had a long history of involvement in the study and transmission of the Hebrew text, dating back to Asher the Elder, who lived in the 8th century CE and is credited with creating the Tiberian system for preserving the oral reading tradition of the Hebrew text.

Work of Nehemiah Ben Asher

Nehemiah ben Asher is best known for his work on the Aleppo Codex, which is considered to be the most important and accurate manuscript of the Masoretic Text. The Aleppo Codex is a medieval manuscript of the Hebrew Bible that was written in the 10th century CE. It is believed to have been written by the scribe Shlomo ben Buya'a and was later corrected by Nehemiah ben Asher. According to the Jewish Encyclopedia, Nehemiah ben Asher "added the diacritical points and accents and made many corrections in the text."

The Aleppo Codex is considered to be the most important and accurate manuscript of the Masoretic Text because of the extensive work that was done on it by Nehemiah ben Asher. According to the Jewish Encyclopedia, "His work on the codex is considered the most accurate and reliable of all the systems of vocalization and is the one adopted in the standard editions of the Hebrew Bible."

The work of Nehemiah ben Asher on the Aleppo Codex was later used as the basis for the Biblia Hebraica, which is considered to be the most accurate representation of the Masoretic text. The Biblia Hebraica was first published by the German scholars, Konstantin von Tischendorf and Paul Kahle, in the 19th century.

---

[3] In Hebrew "ben" means "son." Ben Asher therefore means "the son of Asher."

Influence of Nehemiah Ben Asher

Nehemiah ben Asher's work on the Aleppo Codex had a significant impact on the transmission of the Hebrew text of the Old Testament. His work on the codex is considered to be the most accurate and reliable of all the systems of vocalization and is the one adopted in the standard editions of the Hebrew Bible. The Aleppo Codex, which was corrected by Nehemiah ben Asher, is considered to be the most important and accurate manuscript of the Masoretic Text and served as the basis for the Biblia Hebraica, which is considered to be the most accurate representation of the Masoretic text.

Nehemiah ben Asher's work also carried on the tradition of the ben Asher family, which had a long history of involvement in the study and transmission of the Hebrew text. His work on the Aleppo Codex helped to preserve the accuracy and reliability of the Masoretic Text and ensure that it would be transmitted to future generations with the highest degree of accuracy.

Moses Ben Asher of the tenth century C.E.

Moses ben Asher was a medieval Jewish scribe and Masorete who lived in the 10th century CE. He was a member of the ben Asher family, which was known for its expertise in the Masoretic tradition. Moses ben Asher is best known for his work on the Codex Cairensis, which is considered to be one of the most accurate and reliable manuscripts of the Masoretic Text.

Background of Moses Ben Asher

Moses ben Asher was born in Tiberias, a city on the western shore of the Sea of Galilee, in the 10th century CE. He was a member of the ben Asher family, which was known for its expertise in the Masoretic tradition. The ben Asher family had a long history of involvement in the study and transmission of the Hebrew text, dating back to Asher the Elder, who lived in the 8th century CE and is credited with creating the Tiberian system for preserving the oral reading tradition of the Hebrew text.

Work of Moses Ben Asher

Moses ben Asher is best known for his work on the Codex Cairensis, which is considered to be one of the most accurate and reliable manuscripts of the Masoretic Text. The Codex Cairensis is a medieval manuscript of the Hebrew Bible that was written in the 10th century CE. According to the Jewish Encyclopedia, it is believed to have been written by the scribe Moses ben Asher and was later corrected by him. He added the diacritical points and accents and made many corrections in the text."

The Codex Cairensis is considered to be one of the most accurate and reliable manuscripts of the Masoretic Text because of the extensive work that was done on it by Moses ben Asher. According to the Jewish Encyclopedia, "His work on the codex is considered to be among the most accurate and reliable of all the systems of vocalization and is considered to be a primary source for the study of the Masoretic Text."

The Codex Cairensis was later used as the basis for the Biblia Hebraica, which is considered to be one of the most widely used and reliable editions of the Masoretic Text. This edition was first published in the 20th century and is still widely used by scholars and researchers today.

Influence of Moses Ben Asher

Moses ben Asher's work on the Codex Cairensis had a significant impact on the transmission of the Hebrew text of the Old Testament. His work on the codex is considered to be among the most accurate and reliable of all the systems of vocalization and is considered to be a primary source for the study of the Masoretic Text. The Codex Cairensis, which was corrected by Moses ben Asher, is considered to be one of the most accurate and reliable manuscripts of the Masoretic Text and served as the basis for the Biblia Hebraica, which is considered to be one of the most widely used and reliable editions of the Masoretic Text.

Moses ben Asher's work also carried on the tradition of the ben Asher family, which had a long history of involvement in the study and transmission of the Hebrew text. His work on the Codex Cairensis helped to preserve the accuracy and reliability of the Masoretic Text and ensure that it would be transmitted to future generations with the highest degree of accuracy.

In addition, Moses ben Asher is also credited with creating the Tiberian system of vocalization, which is still in use today. This system was specifically designed to preserve the oral reading tradition of the Hebrew text and ensure that the text was copied with absolute accuracy.

Conclusion

Moses ben Asher was a medieval Jewish scribe and Masorete who lived in the 10th century CE. He was a member of the ben Asher family, which was known for its expertise in the Masoretic tradition. Moses ben Asher is best known for his work on the Codex Cairensis, which is considered to be one of the most accurate and reliable manuscripts of the Masoretic Text. His work on the codex helped to preserve the accuracy and reliability of the Masoretic Text and ensure that it would be transmitted to future generations with the highest degree of accuracy. Additionally, his creation of Tiberian system of vocalization helped to preserve the oral reading tradition of the

Hebrew text and further ensure the accuracy of the text. Moses ben Asher's work carried on the tradition of the ben Asher family, which had a long history of involvement in the study and transmission of the Hebrew text. His contributions to the Masoretic tradition continue to be highly valued and referenced by scholars and researchers today.

Aaron Ben Moses Ben Asher of the tenth century C.E.

Aaron ben Moses ben Asher was a medieval Jewish scribe and Masorete who lived in the 10th century CE. He was a member of the ben Asher family, which was known for its expertise in the Masoretic tradition. Aaron ben Moses ben Asher is best known for his work on the Aleppo Codex, which is considered to be one of the most accurate and reliable manuscripts of the Masoretic Text.

Background of Aaron Ben Moses Ben Asher

Aaron ben Moses ben Asher was born in Tiberias, a city on the western shore of the Sea of Galilee, in the 10th century CE. He was a descendant of Asher the Elder, who lived in the 8th century CE and is credited with creating the Tiberian system for preserving the oral reading tradition of the Hebrew text. He was part of the ben Asher family, which had a long history of involvement in the study and transmission of the Hebrew text.

Work of Aaron Ben Moses Ben Asher

Aaron ben Moses ben Asher is best known for his work on the Aleppo Codex, which is considered to be one of the most accurate and reliable manuscripts of the Masoretic Text. The Aleppo Codex is a medieval manuscript of the Hebrew Bible that was written in the 10th century CE. According to the Jewish Encyclopedia, it is believed to have been written by the scribe Solomon ben Buya'a and corrected by Aaron ben Moses ben Asher. He added the diacritical points and accents and made many corrections in the text."

The Aleppo Codex is considered to be one of the most accurate and reliable manuscripts of the Masoretic Text because of the extensive work that was done on it by Aaron ben Moses ben Asher. According to the Jewish Encyclopedia, "His work on the codex is considered to be among the most accurate and reliable of all the systems of vocalization and is considered to be a primary source for the study of the Masoretic Text."

Influence of Aaron Ben Moses Ben Asher

Aaron ben Moses ben Asher's work on the Aleppo Codex had a significant impact on the transmission of the Hebrew text of the Old

INTRODUCTION TO THE TEXT OF THE OLD TESTAMENT

Testament. His work on the codex is considered to be among the most accurate and reliable of all the systems of vocalization and is considered to be a primary source for the study of the Masoretic Text. The Aleppo Codex, which was corrected by Aaron ben Moses ben Asher, is considered to be one of the most accurate and reliable manuscripts of the Masoretic Text.

Aaron ben Moses ben Asher's work also carried on the tradition of the ben Asher family, which had a long history of involvement in the study and transmission of the Hebrew text. His work on the Aleppo Codex helped to preserve the accuracy and reliability of the Masoretic Text and ensure that it would be transmitted to future generations with the highest degree of accuracy.

Unfortunately, the Aleppo Codex was later lost and only fragments remain today. But the work of Aaron ben Moses ben Asher was so highly valued that his corrections to the text were used as the basis for the Biblia Hebraica, which is considered to be one of the most widely used and reliable editions of the Masoretic Text.

Asher Ben Nehemiah of the eleventh century C.E.

Asher ben Nehemiah was a medieval Jewish scribe and Masorete who lived in the 11th century CE. He was a member of the ben Asher family, which was known for its expertise in the Masoretic tradition. Asher ben Nehemiah is best known for his work on the Leningrad Codex, which is considered to be one of the most accurate and reliable manuscripts of the Masoretic Text.

Background of Asher Ben Nehemiah

Asher ben Nehemiah was born in Tiberias, a city on the western shore of the Sea of Galilee, in the 11th century CE. He was a member of the ben Asher family, which was known for its expertise in the Masoretic tradition. The ben Asher family had a long history of involvement in the study and transmission of the Hebrew text, dating back to Asher the Elder, who lived in the 8th century CE and is credited with creating the Tiberian system for preserving the oral reading tradition of the Hebrew text.

Work of Asher Ben Nehemiah

Asher ben Nehemiah is best known for his work on the Leningrad Codex, which is considered to be one of the most accurate and reliable manuscripts of the Masoretic Text. The Leningrad Codex is a medieval manuscript of the Hebrew Bible that was written in the 11th century CE. It is believed to have been written by the scribe Mordecai ben Nissim and was later corrected by Asher ben Nehemiah. According to the Jewish

Encyclopedia, Asher ben Nehemiah "added the diacritical points and accents and made many corrections in the text."

The Leningrad Codex is considered to be one of the most accurate and reliable manuscripts of the Masoretic Text because of the extensive work that was done on it by Asher ben Nehemiah. According to the Jewish Encyclopedia, "His work on the codex is considered to be among the most accurate and reliable of all the systems of vocalization and is considered to be a primary source for the study of the Masoretic Text."

The work of Asher ben Nehemiah on the Leningrad Codex was later used as the basis for the Biblia Hebraica Stuttgartensia, which is considered to be one of the most widely used and reliable editions of the Masoretic Text. This edition was first published in the 20th century and is still widely used by scholars and researchers today.

Influence of Asher Ben Nehemiah

Asher ben Nehemiah's work on the Leningrad Codex had a significant impact on the transmission of the Hebrew text of the Old Testament. His work on the codex is considered to be among the most accurate and reliable of all the systems of vocalization and is considered to be a primary source for the study of the Masoretic Text. The Leningrad Codex, which was corrected by Asher ben Nehemiah, is considered to be one of the most accurate and reliable manuscripts of the Masoretic Text and served as the basis for the Biblia Hebraica Stuttgartensia, which is considered to be one of the most widely used and reliable editions of the Masoretic Text.

Asher ben Nehemiah's work also carried on the tradition of the ben Asher family, which had a long history of involvement in the study and transmission of the Hebrew text. His work on the Leningrad Codex helped to preserve the accuracy and reliability of the Masoretic Text and ensure that it would be transmitted to future generations with the highest degree of accuracy.

Sopherim (Scribal Corrections)

The Masoretic Sopherim were a group of Jewish scribes who lived during the period of 500-1000 CE. They were responsible for making a variety of corrections to the Hebrew Bible, which are known as Masoretic corrections. These corrections were made with the goal of preserving the accuracy of the text and ensuring that it was transmitted to future generations with the highest degree of accuracy.

INTRODUCTION TO THE TEXT OF THE OLD TESTAMENT

Background and Origins of the Masoretic Sopherim

The origins of the Masoretic Sopherim can be traced back to the period of 500-1000 CE in the Babylonian and Palestinian empires. These scribes were responsible for making a variety of corrections to the Hebrew Bible, which are known as Masoretic corrections. The Masoretic Sopherim were part of the broader Masoretic movement, which was dedicated to preserving the accuracy of the Hebrew Bible and ensuring that it was transmitted to future generations with the highest degree of accuracy.

The Masoretic Sopherim made a variety of corrections to the Hebrew Bible, including additions, deletions, and changes to the text. These corrections were made with the goal of preserving the accuracy of the text and ensuring that it was transmitted to future generations with the highest degree of accuracy. The Masoretic Sopherim also added diacritical marks, such as vowel points, to the text in order to preserve the correct pronunciation and vocalization of the Hebrew text.

Impact on the Transmission of the Hebrew Bible

The Masoretic Sopherim had a significant impact on the transmission of the Hebrew Bible. Their corrections helped to preserve the accuracy of the text and ensure that it was transmitted to future generations with the highest degree of accuracy. The Masoretic Sopherim's diacritical marks, such as vowel points, helped to preserve the correct pronunciation and vocalization of the Hebrew text which helped to preserve the oral reading tradition of the Hebrew Bible.

The Masoretic Sopherim's work was later adopted by other Jewish communities, including the Karaite community, which helped to preserve the accuracy of the Hebrew Bible. The Masoretic Sopherim's corrections were later included in the Masoretic Text which is the most widely used text of the Hebrew Bible today.

The Masoretic Sopherim's work also had an impact on the study of Jewish history. The Masoretic Sopherim's emphasis on the historical context of the Hebrew Bible helped to provide a deeper understanding of the text and the history of the Jewish people and their corrections helped to provide a more accurate representation of the original text.

The Masoretic Sopherim's work also had an impact on the study of biblical exegesis. Their emphasis on the literal interpretation of the text, and the methods they used to preserve the accuracy of the text, helped to provide a more reliable foundation for exegetical study. This in turn led to a deeper understanding of the text and the development of new methods for interpreting it.

Additionally, the Masoretic Sopherim's work also had an impact on the development of Jewish liturgy. The Masoretic Sopherim's diacritical marks and pronunciation guides helped to ensure that the correct version of the text was used in liturgical settings and helped to preserve the accuracy of the Hebrew text in a liturgical context.

Conclusion

The Masoretic Sopherim were a group of Jewish scribes who lived during the period of 500-1000 CE. They were responsible for making a variety of corrections to the Hebrew Bible, which are known as Masoretic corrections. These corrections were made with the goal of preserving the accuracy of the text and ensuring that it was transmitted to future generations with the highest degree of accuracy. The Masoretic Sopherim's work had a significant impact on the transmission of the Hebrew Bible, the study of Jewish history, biblical exegesis, and the development of Jewish liturgy. Their corrections and diacritical marks helped to preserve the accuracy of the text and ensure that it was transmitted to future generations with the highest degree of accuracy.

The Masoretic Vocalization

The Masoretic vocalization is a system of diacritical marks that were added to the Hebrew Bible in the early centuries of the Common Era by the Masoretes, a group of Jewish scribes who lived between 500 and 1000 CE. The Masoretic vocalization was developed as a way to preserve the correct pronunciation and vocalization of the Hebrew text and to help ensure the accuracy of the text's transmission over time.

Background and Origins of the Masoretic Vocalization

The origins of the Masoretic vocalization can be traced back to the period of 500-1000 CE in the Babylonian and Palestinian empires. The Masoretes were a group of Jewish scribes who were responsible for adding diacritical marks to the Hebrew Bible in order to preserve the correct pronunciation and vocalization of the text. The Masoretic vocalization was a system of diacritical marks that were added to the Hebrew Bible to help ensure the accuracy of the text's transmission over time.

The Masoretic vocalization consists of a variety of diacritical marks that were added to the Hebrew text, including vowel points, cantillation marks, and accent marks. These diacritical marks were added to the text with the goal of preserving the correct pronunciation and vocalization of the Hebrew text and to help ensure the accuracy of the text's transmission over time.

The Masoretic vocalization had a significant impact on the transmission of the Hebrew Bible. The diacritical marks that were added to the text helped to preserve the correct pronunciation and vocalization of the Hebrew text, which helped to ensure the accuracy of the text's transmission over time. The Masoretic vocalization was later adopted by other Jewish communities, including the Karaite community, which helped to preserve the accuracy of the Hebrew Bible.

The Masoretic vocalization also had an impact on the study of Jewish history. The Masoretes' emphasis on the historical context of the Hebrew Bible helped to provide a deeper understanding of the text and the history of the Jewish people.

The Masoretic vocalization also had an impact on the study of biblical exegesis, as the diacritical marks helped to provide a more reliable foundation for exegetical study, which led to a deeper understanding of the text and the development of new methods for interpreting it.

Additionally, the Masoretic vocalization also had an impact on the development of Jewish liturgy, as the diacritical marks helped to ensure that the correct version of the text was used in liturgical settings and helped to preserve the accuracy of the Hebrew text in a liturgical context.

Conclusion

The Masoretic vocalization is a system of diacritical marks that were added to the Hebrew Bible in the early centuries of the Common Era by the Masoretes, a group of Jewish scribes who lived between 500 and 1000 CE. The Masoretic vocalization was developed as a way to preserve the correct pronunciation and vocalization of the Hebrew text and to help ensure the accuracy of the text's transmission over time. The Masoretic vocalization had a significant impact on the transmission of the Hebrew Bible, the study of Jewish history, biblical exegesis, and the development of Jewish liturgy. The diacritical marks that were added to the text helped to preserve the correct pronunciation and vocalization of the Hebrew text, which helped to ensure the accuracy of the text's transmission over time.

The Masoretic Text Divisions and Accents

The Masoretic Text (MT) is the standard Hebrew text of the Jewish Bible, which includes the Torah, Nevi'im (Prophets), and Ketuvim (Writings). The MT was developed by the Masoretes, a group of Jewish scribes who lived between 500 and 1000 CE, who aimed to preserve the accuracy of the text and ensure that it was transmitted to future generations with the highest degree of accuracy. The MT includes several divisions and accents that were added by the Masoretes, which have played an important role in the study and interpretation of the Hebrew Bible.

Background and Origins of the Masoretic Text Divisions and Accents

The origins of the Masoretic Text divisions and accents can be traced back to the period of 500-1000 CE in the Babylonian and Palestinian empires. The Masoretes were a group of Jewish scribes who were responsible for adding divisions and accents to the Hebrew Bible in order to preserve the correct pronunciation and vocalization of the text and to help ensure the accuracy of the text's transmission over time.

The Masoretic Text divisions include the parashah, the sedarim, and the open and closed sections. The parashah is a division of the text that separates the weekly Torah portion that is read in synagogues. The sedarim are the divisions of the text that separate the books of the Hebrew Bible into smaller sections. The open and closed sections are divisions of the text that separate the text into smaller sections that are used for liturgical purposes.

The Masoretic Text accents include the ta'amim and the 'athnachot. The ta'amim are the accent marks that indicate the correct pronunciation and vocalization of the Hebrew text, whereas the 'athnachot are the accent marks that indicate the correct division of the text into smaller sections for liturgical purposes.

The Masoretic Text divisions and accents have had a significant impact on the transmission of the Hebrew Bible. The divisions and accents that were added to the text helped to preserve the correct pronunciation and vocalization of the Hebrew text, which helped to ensure the accuracy of the text's transmission over time. The Masoretic Text divisions and accents were later adopted by other Jewish communities, including the Karaite community, which helped to preserve the accuracy of the Hebrew Bible.

The Masoretic Text divisions and accents also had an impact on the study of Jewish history. The Masoretes' emphasis on the historical context of the Hebrew Bible helped to provide a deeper understanding of the text and the history of the Jewish people.

The Masoretic Text divisions and accents also had an impact on the study of biblical exegesis. The divisions and accents provided a more reliable foundation for exegetical study, which led to a deeper understanding of the text and the development of new methods for interpreting it.

INTRODUCTION TO THE TEXT OF THE OLD TESTAMENT

Additionally, the Masoretic Text divisions and accents also had an impact on the development of Jewish liturgy. The divisions and accents helped to ensure that the correct version of the text was used in liturgical settings and helped to preserve the accuracy of the Hebrew text in a liturgical context. For example, the parashah divisions allowed for the proper reading of the weekly Torah portion in synagogues, while the sedarim divisions helped to organize the books of the Hebrew Bible for study and teaching.

The Masoretic Text divisions and accents also play an important role in modern biblical scholarship. The MT is the foundation of modern biblical text editions and translations, and the divisions and accents of the MT have been used to reconstruct the original text of the Hebrew Bible. For example, the parashah divisions are used to determine the original structure of the text, and the ta'amim and 'athnachot are used to reconstruct the original vocalization and accentuation of the text.

Conclusion

The Masoretic Text divisions and accents are an integral part of the Masoretic Text, which is the standard Hebrew text of the Jewish Bible. The divisions and accents were added by the Masoretes, a group of Jewish scribes who lived between 500 and 1000 CE, with the goal of preserving the accuracy of the text and ensuring that it was transmitted to future generations with the highest degree of accuracy. The Masoretic Text divisions and accents have played an important role in the study and interpretation of the Hebrew Bible, and have had a significant impact on the transmission of the Hebrew Bible, the study of Jewish history, biblical exegesis, and the development of Jewish liturgy. They also play an important role in modern biblical scholarship, as the MT is the foundation of modern biblical text editions and translations, and the divisions and accents of the MT have been used to reconstruct the original text of the Hebrew Bible. Overall, the Masoretic Text divisions and accents have played an important role in preserving the accuracy of the Hebrew Bible and providing a foundation for the study and interpretation of the text.

The Masoretic Masorah Parva and Magna

The Masoretic Masorah refers to the system of notes and commentaries that were added to the Hebrew Bible by the Masoretes, a group of Jewish scribes who lived between 500 and 1000 CE. The Masoretic Masorah includes two main components, the Masorah Parva and the Masorah Magna, which provide information about the text's pronunciation, accentuation, and transmission.

Background and Origins of the Masoretic Masorah

The origins of the Masoretic Masorah can be traced back to the period of 500-1000 CE in the Babylonian and Palestinian empires. The Masoretes were a group of Jewish scribes who were responsible for adding notes and commentaries to the Hebrew Bible in order to preserve the correct pronunciation, accentuation, and transmission of the text. The Masoretic Masorah was a system of notes and commentaries that were added to the Hebrew Bible to help ensure the accuracy of the text's transmission over time.

The Masoretic Masorah Parva is a system of small notes and commentaries that were added to the margins and between the lines of the text. These notes provide information about the text's pronunciation, accentuation, and transmission, and include information such as the number of times a certain word occurs in the Hebrew Bible, the spelling of a word, and the number of verses in a book.

The Masoretic Masorah Magna is a system of large notes and commentaries that were added to the end of the Hebrew Bible. These notes provide more detailed information about the text's pronunciation, accentuation, and transmission, and include information such as the number of verses in a book, the number of letters in a word, and the number of words in a verse.

The Masoretic Masorah has had a significant impact on the transmission of the Hebrew Bible. The Masorah Parva and Magna provided important information about the text's pronunciation, accentuation, and transmission, which helped to ensure the accuracy of the text's transmission over time. The Masoretic Masorah also helped to preserve the correct version of the text, which was important for the preservation of Jewish tradition and culture.

The Masoretic Masorah also had an impact on the study of Jewish history. The Masoretes' emphasis on the historical context of the Hebrew Bible helped to provide a deeper understanding of the text and the history of the Jewish people. The Masoretic Masorah also played an important role in the development of Jewish liturgy, as it provided the correct version of the text for liturgical use.

The Masoretic Masorah also played an important role in modern biblical scholarship. The notes and commentaries provided by the Masoretic Masorah have been used to reconstruct the original text of the Hebrew Bible and have been used as a basis for modern biblical text editions and translations. The Masoretic Masorah has been also used to establish the original pronunciation, accentuation, and transmission of the Hebrew Bible, which is important for the study of the text.

In conclusion, the Masoretic Masorah is an important aspect of the Masoretic Text, which is the standard Hebrew text of the Jewish Bible. The Masorah Parva and Magna were added by the Masoretes, a group of Jewish scribes who lived between 500 and 1000 CE, with the goal of preserving the accuracy of the text and ensuring that it was transmitted to future generations with the highest degree of accuracy. The Masoretic Masorah has played an important role in the study and interpretation of the Hebrew Bible and has had a significant impact on the transmission of the Hebrew Bible, the study of Jewish history, the development of Jewish liturgy, and modern biblical scholarship.

Textual Transmission from 1000 to 1450 CE

Introduction

The period of 1000 CE to 1450 CE marks a significant phase in the textual transmission of the Hebrew Old Testament. This period is characterized by the establishment of the Masoretic Text as the standard version of the Hebrew Bible, and the preservation and transmission of this text through the use of the printing press and manuscript production.

The Masoretic Text as the Standard Version

The Masoretic Text, which was established as the standard version of the Hebrew Bible by the Masoretes during the period 500 CE to 1000 CE, continued to be the primary source for the textual transmission of the Hebrew Old Testament during this period. The work of the Masoretes had resulted in a standardized version of the text that was used for further transmission and study.

As Moshe Goshen-Gottstein writes, "The Masoretic Text became the authoritative text of the Hebrew Bible, and the standard text for all later Hebrew Bibles." This standardization of the text had a significant impact on the understanding and interpretation of the Hebrew Bible, and it continues to shape the understanding and interpretation of the Hebrew Bible to this day.

Manuscript Production and the Printing Press

The textual transmission of the Hebrew Old Testament during this period was primarily achieved through the production of manuscripts and the use of the printing press. Manuscript production continued to be an important method for preserving and transmitting the text, and many manuscripts from this period have been preserved to the present day. These manuscripts provide valuable insights into the transmission and preservation of the text. The invention of the printing press in the 15th century revolutionized the way in which books were produced, and it made it possible to mass-produce copies of the Bible. This had a significant impact on the textual transmission of the Hebrew Old Testament. The ability to produce multiple copies of the text at once greatly increased the accessibility of the Bible to scholars and the general public. It also allowed for a greater degree of standardization in the text, as printers could refer to a single, authoritative source.

One of the most important early printed editions of the Hebrew Bible was the Soncino Bible, which was printed in 1488 CE in Italy. This edition was based on the Masoretic Text and included the vocalization and accentuation marks developed by the Masoretes.

The Textual Variants

Despite the standardization of the Masoretic Text as the primary source for the textual transmission of the Hebrew Old Testament, variations in the text still existed. These variations, known as textual variants, can be found in the marginal notes of some manuscripts and early printed editions. They provide valuable insights into the transmission and preservation of the text, and they are still studied by scholars today.

Conclusion

In conclusion, the period of 1000 CE to 1450 CE marks a significant phase in the textual transmission of the Hebrew Old Testament. The Masoretic Text, established as the standard version of the Hebrew Bible by the Masoretes during the previous period, continued to be the primary source for the textual transmission of the Hebrew Old Testament during this period. Manuscript production and the use of the printing press played a crucial role in the preservation and transmission of the text. The invention of the printing press in particular, greatly increased the accessibility of the Bible to scholars and the general public, and it allowed for a greater degree of standardization in the text. Despite the standardization of the Masoretic Text, variations in the text, known as textual variants, still existed and provided valuable insights into the transmission and preservation of the text. These variants are still studied by scholars today, providing a deeper understanding of the development and transmission of the Hebrew Old Testament text.

INTRODUCTION TO THE TEXT OF THE OLD TESTAMENT

Textual Transmission from 1450 CE to the Present

The invention of the printing press in the 15th century marked a significant turning point in the history of the transmission of the Hebrew text of the Old Testament. Before this time, the text was transmitted through handwritten copies, which were subject to human error and variation. With the advent of the printing press, it became possible to reproduce the text with greater accuracy and consistency. This period, from 1450 CE to the present, can be divided into three main phases: the early printed editions, the establishment of the Masoretic text, and the modern era.

Early Printed Editions (1450-1600 CE)

The earliest printed edition of the Hebrew Bible was produced in 1475 by the German printer, Johannes Gutenberg. However, it was not until the late 15th century that the first complete Hebrew Bible was printed in Soncino, Italy. The Soncino edition, published in 1488, was based on the Masoretic text, but it also included the targumim (Aramaic translations) and the Rashi commentary.

During this early period, several other editions of the Hebrew Bible were produced in various parts of Europe. These included the Bomberg edition, which was first published in Venice in 1524-25, and the Daniel Bomberg edition, which was first published in 1516-17. These early printed editions were based on the Masoretic text, but they also included variations and errors that had been introduced during the manuscript transmission.

Establishment of the Masoretic Text (1600-1900 CE):

In the 17th and 18th centuries, scholars began to realize the need for a critical edition of the Hebrew text that would be free from errors and variations. This led to the establishment of the Masoretic text as the standard text of the Hebrew Bible. The Masoretic text is based on the work of the Masoretes, a group of Jewish scholars who lived in the 6th-10th centuries and who were responsible for preserving the oral reading tradition of the Hebrew text.

One of the most significant figures in the establishment of the Masoretic text was Jacob ben Hayyim ibn Adonijah, who published the second Rabbinic Bible in 1525, in Venice. He was the first to include the Masoretic notes, which provide information on the pronunciation and cantillation of the text. The work of Jacob ben Hayyim was later improved by others, such as Elijah

Levita, who published the first complete edition of the Masoretic text in 1538-1542, in Venice.

The establishment of the Masoretic text as the standard text of the Hebrew Bible was further solidified in the 19th century with the publication of the Biblia Hebraica, first published by the German scholars, Konstantin von Tischendorf and Paul Kahle. This edition, which is based on the Leningrad Codex, is considered to be the most accurate representation of the Masoretic text.

Modern Era (1900-Present)

In the 20th century, the study of the Hebrew text of the Old Testament has been advanced through the use of modern tools and methods. One of the most significant developments in this field has been the discovery of the Dead Sea Scrolls, which date back to the 2nd century BCE and provide a glimpse into the text of the Hebrew Bible before the time of the Masoretes.

Another major development in the field is the use of computer technology to analyze and compare the various texts of the Hebrew Bible. This has led to the creation of electronic databases, such as the Hebrew Text Database, which allows scholars to access and compare different versions of the text.

Medieval Biblical Manuscripts

The Masoretic Text (MT) is the standard Hebrew text of the Jewish Bible, which includes the Torah, Nevi'im (Prophets), and Ketuvim (Writings). The MT was developed by the Masoretes, a group of Jewish scribes who lived between 500 and 1000 CE, who aimed to preserve the accuracy of the text and ensure that it was transmitted to future generations with the highest degree of accuracy. The MT was transmitted through medieval biblical manuscripts, which played a crucial role in the preservation and transmission of the text.

Background and Origins of Medieval Biblical Manuscripts

The origins of medieval biblical manuscripts can be traced back to the period of 500-1000 CE in the Babylonian and Palestinian empires. The Masoretes were a group of Jewish scribes who were responsible for creating and transmitting the MT through handwritten manuscripts. The MT was transmitted through biblical manuscripts that were copied by hand and passed down through the generations.

INTRODUCTION TO THE TEXT OF THE OLD TESTAMENT

During the medieval period, the MT was transmitted through several different types of biblical manuscripts, including codices, scrolls, and fragments. Codices are books that are made up of sheets of parchment or paper that are bound together, similar to a modern-day book. Scrolls are manuscripts that are made up of sheets of parchment or paper that are rolled up, similar to a modern-day scroll. Fragments are pieces of biblical manuscripts that have been separated from the main text.

Impact on the Transmission of the Masoretic Text

Medieval biblical manuscripts played a crucial role in the preservation and transmission of the MT. The manuscripts were copied by hand, which helped to ensure the accuracy of the text and preserve the correct version of the text. The manuscripts were also passed down through the generations, which helped to ensure the continuity of the text.

The medieval biblical manuscripts also had an impact on the study of Jewish history. The manuscripts provided a glimpse into the history of the Jewish people and the development of Jewish tradition and culture. The manuscripts also played an important role in the development of Jewish liturgy, as they provided the correct version of the text for liturgical use.

The medieval biblical manuscripts also played an important role in modern biblical scholarship. The manuscripts have been used to reconstruct the original text of the Hebrew Bible and have been used as a basis for modern biblical text editions and translations. The manuscripts have also been used to establish the original pronunciation, accentuation, and transmission of the Hebrew Bible, which is important for the study of the text.

One of the most important examples of the medieval biblical manuscripts is the Leningrad Codex, which is the oldest complete manuscript of the Hebrew Bible in existence. It is considered to be the most accurate copy of the Masoretic Text and is the basis for Biblia Hebraica Stuttgartensia, a widely used edition of the MT in modern biblical scholarship. The Leningrad Codex was written in the 10th century CE and is currently held in the National Library of Russia in St. Petersburg.

Another important example of medieval biblical manuscripts is the Aleppo Codex, which is considered to be one of the most accurate copies of the MT. It was written in the 10th century CE and was considered to be the authoritative text of the MT for several centuries. However, it was partially destroyed in 1947 and only fragments remain today.

In conclusion, medieval biblical manuscripts played a crucial role in the preservation and transmission of the Masoretic Text. The manuscripts were copied by hand, which helped to ensure the accuracy of the text and preserve the correct version of the text. The manuscripts were also passed down through the generations, which helped to ensure the continuity of the text. The medieval biblical manuscripts also had an impact on the study of Jewish history, the development of Jewish liturgy, and modern biblical scholarship. Examples such as the Leningrad Codex and the Aleppo Codex are considered to be some of the most important and accurate copies of the MT and have been widely used in modern biblical scholarship.

Second Rabbinic Bible of Jacob ben Chayyim

The Second Rabbinic Bible, also known as the Jacob ben Chayyim Bible, was a significant edition of the Hebrew Bible that was published in 1524-25. This edition, which was edited by Jacob ben Chayyim, a Jewish scribe and translator, played a crucial role in the transmission and study of the Hebrew Bible right into the 19th century.

Background and Origins of the Second Rabbinic Bible

The Second Rabbinic Bible was published in Venice, Italy in 1524-25 by Jacob ben Chayyim, a Jewish scribe and translator. This edition of the Hebrew Bible was based on the Masoretic Text, which is the standard Hebrew text of the Jewish Bible, and included the traditional Jewish commentaries, such as the Rashi and Rambam. The Second Rabbinic Bible was the first edition of the Hebrew Bible to be printed with movable type, which made it widely available to the Jewish community.

The Second Rabbinic Bible was intended to be a scholarly edition of the Hebrew Bible that would be used by rabbis, scholars, and laypeople alike. The edition included the traditional Jewish commentaries, which helped to provide a deeper understanding of the text and the history of the Jewish people. The Second Rabbinic Bible also included the traditional Masoretic vocalization, accentuation, and divisions, which helped to ensure the accuracy of the text's pronunciation and transmission.

Impact on the Transmission and Study of the Hebrew Bible

The Second Rabbinic Bible played a crucial role in the transmission and study of the Hebrew Bible right into the 19th century. The edition was widely used by the Jewish community and was considered to be the authoritative text of the Hebrew Bible for several centuries. The edition also played an important role in the development of Jewish liturgy, as it provided the correct version of the text for liturgical use.

The Second Rabbinic Bible also had an impact on the study of Jewish history. The edition provided a glimpse into the history of the Jewish people and the development of Jewish tradition and culture. The edition also played an important role in the development of Jewish scholarship, as it provided a scholarly edition of the Hebrew Bible that was widely used by rabbis, scholars, and laypeople alike.

The Second Rabbinic Bible also played an important role in modern biblical scholarship. The edition was used as a basis for modern biblical text editions and translations and was used to establish the original pronunciation, accentuation, and transmission of the Hebrew Bible. The edition was widely used by scholars and was considered to be the authoritative text of the Hebrew Bible until the 19th century, when new biblical discoveries and methodologies led to the development of new critical editions of the Hebrew Bible.

In conclusion, the Second Rabbinic Bible, also known as the Jacob ben Chayyim Bible, was a significant edition of the Hebrew Bible that was published in 1524-25. This edition, which was edited by Jacob ben Chayyim, a Jewish scribe and translator, played a crucial role in the transmission and study of the Hebrew Bible right into the 19th century. The edition was based on the Masoretic Text, which is the standard Hebrew text of the Jewish Bible, and included the traditional Jewish commentaries, such as the Rashi and Rambam. The edition was intended to be a scholarly edition of the Hebrew Bible that would be used by rabbis, scholars, and laypeople alike. The Second Rabbinic Bible played a crucial role in the development of Jewish liturgy, the study of Jewish history, the development of Jewish scholarship, and modern biblical scholarship. The edition was widely used by the Jewish community and was considered to be the authoritative text of the Hebrew Bible for several centuries. The edition also played an important role in the development of Jewish liturgy, as it provided the correct version of the text for liturgical use. It was also the first edition of the Hebrew Bible to be printed with movable type and it was widely available to the Jewish community, this made it a key factor for the preservation of the Hebrew Bible.

1776-80 Benjamin Kennicott

In the late 18th century, Benjamin Kennicott, an English theologian and orientalist, published a significant edition of the Hebrew Bible called the

"Vetus Testamentum Hebraicum cum variis lectionibus" (Old Testament Hebrew with various readings). This edition, which was published at Oxford University between 1776 and 1780, was based on over 600 Hebrew manuscripts that Kennicott had collected and collated from various libraries and private collections across Europe.

The main goal of Kennicott's edition was to provide a comprehensive collection of variant readings from the Hebrew Bible, which would help to establish the original text of the Hebrew Bible. Kennicott's edition included variant readings from the Masoretic Text, as well as readings from other ancient versions of the Hebrew Bible, such as the Septuagint and the Samaritan Pentateuch. Kennicott's edition also included critical notes and explanations, which helped to provide a deeper understanding of the text and its transmission.

Kennicott's edition was a significant contribution to biblical scholarship in the 18th century. It was the first edition to include variant readings from such a large number of Hebrew manuscripts and helped to establish the original text of the Hebrew Bible. Kennicott's edition was widely used by scholars and was considered to be an important reference work for the study of the Hebrew Bible.

Kennicott's edition was also significant because it helped to bring attention to the importance of textual criticism in biblical scholarship. Prior to Kennicott's edition, the Masoretic Text was considered to be the authoritative text of the Hebrew Bible and was not subject to critical analysis. However, Kennicott's edition helped to show that the Masoretic Text, like any other text, is subject to variation and that textual criticism was necessary to establish the original text of the Hebrew Bible.

In conclusion, Benjamin Kennicott's edition of the Hebrew Bible, published between 1776 and 1780 at Oxford University, was a significant contribution to biblical scholarship in the 18th century. It was based on over 600 Hebrew manuscripts that Kennicott had collected and collated from various libraries and private collections across Europe. The main goal of Kennicott's edition was to provide a comprehensive collection of variant readings from the Hebrew Bible, which would help to establish the original text of the Hebrew Bible. Kennicott's edition was widely used by scholars and was considered to be an important reference work for the study of the Hebrew Bible. It also helped to bring attention to the importance of textual criticism in biblical scholarship and showed that the Masoretic Text, like any other text, is subject to variation and that textual criticism was necessary to establish the original text of the Hebrew Bible.

INTRODUCTION TO THE TEXT OF THE OLD TESTAMENT

1784-98 J. B. de Rossi

In the late 18th century, the Italian scholar J.B. de Rossi, a biblical scholar and orientalist, published a significant edition of the Hebrew Bible called the "Variæ lectiones Veteris Testamenti Hebræi" (Various Readings of the Old Testament Hebrew). This edition, which was published at Parma between 1784 and 1798, was based on over 800 Hebrew manuscripts that de Rossi had collected and collated from various libraries and private collections across Europe.

The main goal of de Rossi's edition was to provide a comprehensive collection of variant readings from the Hebrew Bible, which would help to establish the original text of the Hebrew Bible. de Rossi's edition included variant readings from the Masoretic Text, as well as readings from other ancient versions of the Hebrew Bible, such as the Septuagint and the Samaritan Pentateuch. de Rossi's edition also included critical notes and explanations, which helped to provide a deeper understanding of the text and its transmission.

de Rossi's edition was a significant contribution to biblical scholarship in the late 18th century. It was the first edition to include variant readings from such a large number of Hebrew manuscripts and helped to establish the original text of the Hebrew Bible. de Rossi's edition was widely used by scholars and was considered to be an important reference work for the study of the Hebrew Bible.

de Rossi's edition built upon the work of Benjamin Kennicott and other biblical scholars who had begun to focus on the importance of textual criticism in biblical scholarship. de Rossi's edition helped to further establish the importance of variant readings in the study of the Hebrew Bible and helped to establish the original text of the Hebrew Bible.

In conclusion, J.B. de Rossi's edition of the Hebrew Bible, published between 1784 and 1798 at Parma, was a significant contribution to biblical scholarship in the late 18th century. It was based on over 800 Hebrew manuscripts that de Rossi had collected and collated from various libraries and private collections across Europe. The main goal of de Rossi's edition was to provide a comprehensive collection of variant readings from the Hebrew Bible, which would help to establish the original text of the Hebrew Bible. de Rossi's edition was widely used by scholars and was considered to be an important reference work for the study of the Hebrew Bible. It built upon the work of Benjamin Kennicott and other biblical scholars who had begun to focus on the importance of textual criticism in biblical scholarship and helped to further establish the importance of variant readings in the study of the Hebrew Bible and helped to establish the original text of the Hebrew Bible.

Herman Hebrew Scholar S. Baer

In the 19th century, the German Hebrew scholar S. Baer, also produced a master text edition of the Hebrew Bible, called the "Biblia Hebraica" (Hebrew Bible). This edition, which was published in 1867 and 1868, was based on the most accurate and reliable Hebrew manuscripts available at the time, including the Leningrad Codex, which is considered to be one of the most accurate and complete manuscripts of the Masoretic Text.

The main goal of Baer's edition was to provide a critical edition of the Hebrew Bible that would be based on the most accurate and reliable Hebrew manuscripts available. Baer's edition was based on the Masoretic Text, but also included variant readings from other ancient versions of the Hebrew Bible, such as the Septuagint and the Samaritan Pentateuch. Baer's edition also included critical notes and explanations, which helped to provide a deeper understanding of the text and its transmission.

Baer's edition was a significant contribution to biblical scholarship in the 19th century. It was the first edition to be based on the most accurate and reliable Hebrew manuscripts available and helped to establish the original text of the Hebrew Bible. Baer's edition was widely used by scholars and was considered to be an important reference work for the study of the Hebrew Bible.

Baer's edition built upon the work of J.B. de Rossi, Benjamin Kennicott, and other biblical scholars who had begun to focus on the importance of textual criticism in biblical scholarship. Baer's edition helped to further establish the importance of variant readings in the study of the Hebrew Bible and helped to establish the original text of the Hebrew Bible.

In conclusion, S. Baer's edition of the Hebrew Bible, published in 1867 and 1868, was a significant contribution to biblical scholarship in the 19th century. It was based on the most accurate and reliable Hebrew manuscripts available at the time, including the Leningrad Codex, which is considered to be one of the most accurate and complete manuscripts of the Masoretic Text. The main goal of Baer's edition was to provide a critical edition of the Hebrew Bible that would be based on the most accurate and reliable Hebrew manuscripts available. Baer's edition was widely used by scholars and was considered to be an important reference work for the study of the Hebrew Bible. It built upon the work of J.B. de Rossi, Benjamin Kennicott, and other biblical scholars who had begun to focus on the importance of textual criticism in biblical scholarship and helped to further establish the importance of variant readings in the study of the Hebrew Bible and helped to establish the original text of the Hebrew Bible.

C. D. Ginsburg Producing a Critical Master Text of the Hebrew Bible

In the 19th century, the Jewish scholar and theologian C.D. Ginsburg devoted many years to producing a critical master text of the Hebrew Bible. His edition, called the "Biblia Hebraica Stuttgartensia" (Stuttgart Hebrew Bible), was published in the late 19th century and was considered to be one of the most important reference works for the study of the Hebrew Bible.

The main goal of Ginsburg's edition was to produce a critical edition of the Hebrew Bible that would be based on the most accurate and reliable Hebrew manuscripts available. Ginsburg's edition was based on the Leningrad Codex, which is considered to be one of the most accurate and complete manuscripts of the Masoretic Text. However, Ginsburg also consulted a large number of other Hebrew manuscripts and included variant readings from these manuscripts in his edition.

Ginsburg's edition also included critical notes and explanations that helped to provide a deeper understanding of the text and its transmission. Additionally, Ginsburg's edition included the Masoretic accents, cantillation marks, and other markings that were used to guide the pronunciation and cantillation of the text.

Ginsburg's edition was a significant contribution to biblical scholarship in the 19th century. It was the first edition to be based on the most accurate and reliable Hebrew manuscripts available and helped to establish the original text of the Hebrew Bible. Ginsburg's edition was widely used by scholars and was considered to be an important reference work for the study of the Hebrew Bible.

Ginsburg's edition built upon the work of S. Baer, J.B. de Rossi, Benjamin Kennicott, and other biblical scholars who had begun to focus on the importance of textual criticism in biblical scholarship. Ginsburg's edition helped to further establish the importance of variant readings in the study of the Hebrew Bible and helped to establish the original text of the Hebrew Bible.

In conclusion, C.D. Ginsburg's edition of the Hebrew Bible, published in the late 19th century, was a significant contribution to biblical scholarship. The main goal of Ginsburg's edition was to produce a critical edition of the

Hebrew Bible that would be based on the most accurate and reliable Hebrew manuscripts available. Ginsburg's edition was based on the Leningrad Codex, which is considered to be one of the most accurate and complete manuscripts of the Masoretic Text, but also included variant readings from other manuscripts. Ginsburg's edition included critical notes and explanations and included the Masoretic accents, cantillation marks, and other markings that were used to guide the pronunciation and cantillation of the text. It was widely used by scholars and was considered to be an important reference work for the study of the Hebrew Bible. Ginsburg's edition built upon the work of S. Baer, J.B. de Rossi, Benjamin Kennicott, and other biblical scholars who had begun to focus on the importance of textual criticism in biblical scholarship and helped to further establish the importance of variant readings in the study of the Hebrew Bible and helped to establish the original text of the Hebrew Bible.

Hebrew scholar Rudolf Kittel

In 1906, the German Hebrew scholar Rudolf Kittel released the first edition of his refined Hebrew text entitled "Biblia Hebraica", or "The Hebrew Bible." This edition was based on the most recent and reliable scholarship on the Masoretic Text and was considered to be one of the most important reference works for the study of the Hebrew Bible in the early 20th century.

Kittel's edition of the Hebrew Bible was based on the Leningrad Codex, which is considered to be one of the most accurate and complete manuscripts of the Masoretic Text. Kittel also consulted a large number of other Hebrew manuscripts and included variant readings from these manuscripts in his edition.

The main goal of Kittel's edition was to produce a critical edition of the Hebrew Bible that would be based on the most accurate and reliable Hebrew manuscripts available. Kittel's edition included critical notes and explanations that helped to provide a deeper understanding of the text and its transmission. Additionally, Kittel's edition included the Masoretic accents, cantillation marks, and other markings that were used to guide the pronunciation and cantillation of the text.

Kittel's edition was widely used by scholars and was considered to be an important reference work for the study of the Hebrew Bible. It was a significant contribution to biblical scholarship and helped to further establish the importance of variant readings in the study of the Hebrew Bible and helped to establish the original text of the Hebrew Bible.

INTRODUCTION TO THE TEXT OF THE OLD TESTAMENT

In 1937, Kittel released a second edition of his Biblia Hebraica, which improved on the first edition by incorporating new discoveries and scholarly insights into the text. This edition was widely used by scholars and is still considered a valuable reference work for the study of the Hebrew Bible.

Kittel's Biblia Hebraica went through several editions after the first two editions in 1906 and 1937. The 7th, 8th, and 9th editions of the Biblia Hebraica were published between 1951 and 1955. These editions built on the work of previous editions and incorporated new discoveries and scholarly insights into the text.

The 7th edition, published in 1951, was edited by Paul Kahle and was based on the Leningrad Codex, which is considered to be one of the most accurate and complete manuscripts of the Masoretic Text. This edition included critical notes and explanations and included the Masoretic accents, cantillation marks, and other markings that were used to guide the pronunciation and cantillation of the text.

The 8th edition, published in 1955, was also edited by Paul Kahle and was based on the Leningrad Codex. It was a corrected and revised version of the 7th edition and included new discoveries and scholarly insights into the text.

The 9th edition, also published in 1955, was edited by Paul Kahle and was based on the Leningrad Codex. It was a corrected and revised version of the 8th edition and included new discoveries and scholarly insights into the text.

These editions of the Biblia Hebraica were widely used by scholars and were considered to be important reference works for the study of the Hebrew Bible. They built upon the work of previous editions and incorporated new discoveries and scholarly insights into the text.

In conclusion, the 7th, 8th, and 9th editions of Kittel's Biblia Hebraica, published between 1951 and 1955, were important contributions to biblical scholarship. These editions were based on the Leningrad Codex, considered one of the most accurate and complete manuscripts of the Masoretic Text, and incorporated new discoveries and scholarly insights into the text. They included critical notes and explanations and included the Masoretic accents, cantillation marks, and other markings that were used to guide the pronunciation and cantillation of the text. These editions were widely used by scholars and were considered to be important reference works for the study of the Hebrew Bible.

Rudolf Kittel's edition of the Hebrew Bible, entitled "Biblia Hebraica", was a significant contribution to biblical scholarship in the early 20th century. It was based on the most accurate and reliable Hebrew manuscripts available at the time, including the Leningrad Codex, and included variant readings from other manuscripts. Kittel's edition included critical notes and explanations and included the Masoretic accents, cantillation marks, and other markings that were used to guide the pronunciation and cantillation of the text. It was widely used by scholars and was considered to be an important reference work for the study of the Hebrew Bible. The second edition, released in 1937, improved on the first edition by incorporating new discoveries and scholarly insights into the text and is still considered a valuable reference work for the study of the Hebrew Bible.

Biblia Hebraica Stuttgartensia

The Biblia Hebraica Stuttgartensia (BHS), also known as the Stuttgart Hebrew Bible, is a critical edition of the Masoretic Text of the Hebrew Bible. It was first published by the Deutsche Bibelgesellschaft (German Bible Society) in 1977 and is considered to be one of the most important reference works for the study of the Hebrew Bible.

The BHS is based on the Leningrad Codex, which is considered to be one of the most accurate and complete manuscripts of the Masoretic Text. The BHS includes the traditional Masoretic accents, cantillation marks, and other markings that were used to guide the pronunciation and cantillation of the text. It also includes critical notes and explanations that provide a deeper understanding of the text and its transmission.

The BHS is an improved version of the Biblia Hebraica, which was first published by Rudolf Kittel in 1906 and went through several editions. The BHS incorporates new discoveries and scholarly insights into the text and builds on the work of previous editions. It is widely considered to be the most accurate and reliable edition of the Masoretic Text available today.

One of the main features of the BHS is the inclusion of an apparatus that provides variant readings from other important Hebrew manuscripts, such as the Aleppo Codex and the Cairo Genizah fragments. This apparatus provides scholars with a deeper understanding of the text and its transmission and helps to establish the original text of the Hebrew Bible.

The BHS is widely used by scholars and is considered to be an important reference work for the study of the Hebrew Bible. It is also used by many universities and religious institutions as the standard text for teaching and studying the Hebrew Bible.

INTRODUCTION TO THE TEXT OF THE OLD TESTAMENT

In conclusion, the Biblia Hebraica Stuttgartensia (BHS) is a critical edition of the Masoretic Text of the Hebrew Bible that was first published by the Deutsche Bibelgesellschaft (German Bible Society) in 1977. It is based on the Leningrad Codex, which is considered to be one of the most accurate and complete manuscripts of the Masoretic Text. The BHS includes the traditional Masoretic accents, cantillation marks, and other markings that were used to guide the pronunciation and cantillation of the text, as well as critical notes and explanations that provide a deeper understanding of the text and its transmission. The BHS incorporates new discoveries and scholarly insights into the text and builds on the work of previous editions. It also includes an apparatus with variant readings from other important Hebrew manuscripts, such as the Aleppo Codex and the Cairo Genizah fragments, which helps to establish the original text of the Hebrew Bible. The BHS is widely used by scholars and is considered to be an important reference work for the study of the Hebrew Bible, as well as a standard text for teaching and studying the Hebrew Bible in universities and religious institutions.

Biblia Hebraica Quinta (BHQ)

The Biblia Hebraica Quinta (BHQ) is a critical edition of the Masoretic Text of the Hebrew Bible that was first published in 2004 by the Deutsche Bibelgesellschaft (German Bible Society). It is considered to be the latest and most up-to-date edition of the Masoretic Text available.

The BHQ is based on the Leningrad Codex and incorporates new discoveries and scholarly insights into the text. It includes the traditional Masoretic accents, cantillation marks, and other markings that were used to guide the pronunciation and cantillation of the text, as well as critical notes and explanations that provide a deeper understanding of the text and its transmission.

One of the main features of the BHQ is its comprehensive apparatus, which provides variant readings from other important Hebrew manuscripts, such as the Aleppo Codex, the Cairo Genizah fragments, and the Dead Sea Scrolls. This apparatus provides scholars with a deeper understanding of the text and its transmission and helps to establish the original text of the Hebrew Bible.

Another important feature of the BHQ is that it includes an updated system of vocalization, which is based on the latest research and scholarship in the field. This system of vocalization is designed to be more accurate and consistent than previous systems and provides a more reliable guide for the pronunciation and cantillation of the text.

The BHQ is widely used by scholars and is considered to be an important reference work for the study of the Hebrew Bible. It is also used by many universities and religious institutions as the standard text for teaching and studying the Hebrew Bible.

In conclusion, the Biblia Hebraica Quinta (BHQ) is a critical edition of the Masoretic Text of the Hebrew Bible that was first published in 2004 by the Deutsche Bibelgesellschaft (German Bible Society). It is based on the Leningrad Codex and incorporates new discoveries and scholarly insights into the text. The BHQ includes the traditional Masoretic accents, cantillation marks, and other markings that were used to guide the pronunciation and cantillation of the text, as well as a comprehensive apparatus that provides variant readings from other important Hebrew manuscripts, such as the Aleppo Codex, the Cairo Genizah fragments, and the Dead Sea Scrolls. It also includes an updated system of vocalization, which is more accurate and consistent than previous systems. The BHQ is widely used by scholars and is considered to be an important reference work for the study of the Hebrew Bible, as well as a standard text for teaching and studying the Hebrew Bible in universities and religious institutions. It is an updated version of the Biblia Hebraica Stuttgartensia, which was based on the Leningrad Codex and incorporated new discoveries and scholarly insights into the text, but the BHQ is considered to be more accurate and reliable edition of the Masoretic Text available today.

CAHPTER 3 The Dead Sea Scrolls

Image 17 The Dead Sea Scrolls manuscripts survived for centuries in clay jars stored in caves in a dry climate.

What Are the Dead Sea Scrolls?

The Dead Sea Scrolls are a collection of Jewish texts that were discovered in the 1940s in the vicinity of Qumran, a ruin located on the northwest shore of the Dead Sea. The scrolls and fragments, written in Hebrew, Aramaic, and Greek, are some of the oldest surviving examples of biblical and extra-biblical texts, dating back to the Second Temple period (516 BCE – 70 CE). The discovery of the scrolls has been described as one of the most significant archaeological finds of the 20th century and has greatly contributed to our understanding of Jewish history, literature, and religion during this period.

Discovery of the Scrolls

The scrolls were first discovered in 1947 by a Bedouin shepherd boy who stumbled upon a cave while looking for a lost sheep. Inside the cave, he found jars containing scrolls wrapped in linen. The boy and his father sold the scrolls to a local antiquities dealer, who in turn sold them to scholars. The first scrolls to be purchased by scholars were seven lengthy manuscripts that were in various stages of deterioration.

Further exploration of the area led to the discovery of ten more caves in the vicinity of Qumran, which contained a total of around 800 manuscripts. The scrolls were found in jars and cisterns, some of which were sealed, indicating that they were deliberately hidden. It is believed that the scrolls were hidden in the caves by a Jewish sect during the Roman-Jewish War (66-70 CE), in an effort to protect them from the Roman destruction of Jerusalem and the Temple.

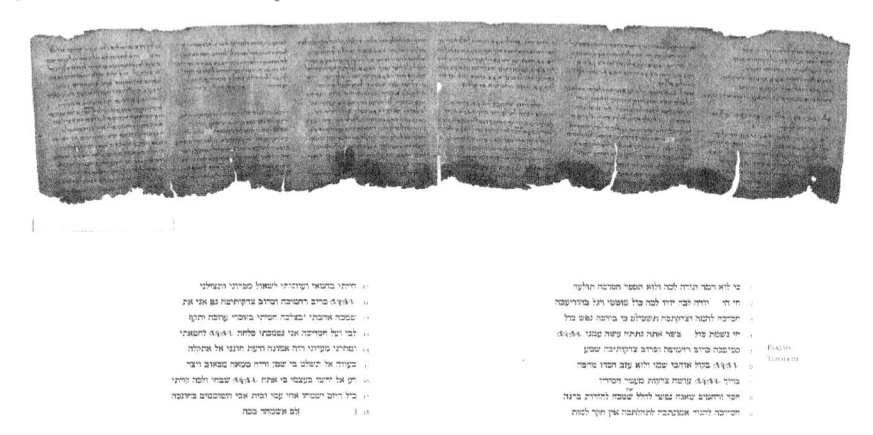

Image 18 The Psalms Scroll (11Q5), one of the 981 texts of the Dead Sea Scrolls, with a partial Hebrew transcription.

Content of the Scrolls

The Dead Sea Scrolls consist of a diverse range of texts, including copies of portions of the Hebrew Bible, as well as ancient non-biblical Jewish writings, such as interpretations on Jewish law, liturgical poems and prayers, and eschatological works. The scrolls also include unique Bible commentaries, which are considered to be the most ancient antecedents of modern running commentary on Bible texts.

The biblical scrolls found at Qumran are some of the oldest surviving examples of the Hebrew Bible and have been invaluable for scholars studying the text's transmission and history. The scrolls include fragments from every book of the Hebrew Bible, except for the book of Esther.

The non-biblical scrolls found at Qumran are also of great significance, as they provide insight into the beliefs and practices of the sect that lived at Qumran. These texts include the Community Rule, a manual for the organization and conduct of the sect, and the War Scroll, which describes a future war between the "Sons of Light" and the "Sons of Darkness." These texts reveal that the sect had a strong sense of its own identity and believed that it was living in the end times.

Authorship and Dating of the Scrolls

The question of authorship and dating of the scrolls is a complex one and has been the subject of much debate among scholars. Radiocarbon dating and paleographic analysis of the scrolls have indicated that they were either copied or composed between the third century BCE and the first century CE.

There is also much debate about who the authors of the scrolls were. The first theory, proposed by Professor Eleazar Sukenik, was that the scrolls belonged to a community of Essenes. The Essenes were a Jewish sect mentioned by first-century writers such as Josephus, Philo of Alexandria, and Pliny the Elder. However, many scholars now believe that this theory is too simplistic and that the scrolls reflect a diverse range of beliefs and practices, rather than those of a single sect.

One theory that has gained acceptance among scholars is that the scrolls were the property of a Jewish sect that lived at Qrumran. The scrolls themselves provide evidence that the community at Qumran had a strong sense of its own identity and believed that it was living in the end times. The texts include the Community Rule, a manual for the organization and conduct of the sect, and the War Scroll, which describes a future war between the "Sons of Light" and the "Sons of Darkness."

However, it is also likely that the scrolls were collected from various sources and brought to Qumran by the community, rather than being produced solely by the community at Qumran. The scrolls can be considered as an extensive library collection that reflects a wide range of thought and beliefs, rather than just those of the community at Qumran.

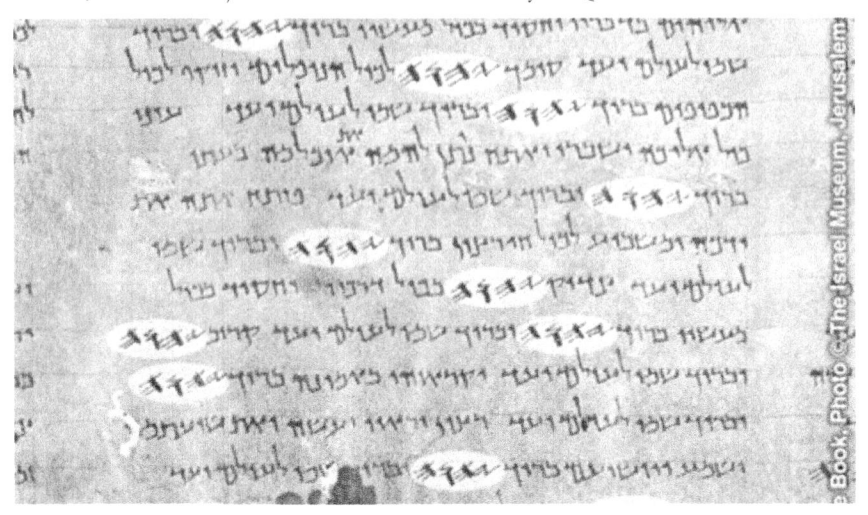

Image 19 Dead Sea Scroll in Paleo-Hebrew - Tetragrammaton

Importance of the Dead Sea Scrolls

The discovery of the Dead Sea Scrolls has greatly contributed to our understanding of Jewish history, literature, and religion during the Second Temple period. The scrolls provide valuable insight into the beliefs and practices of the Jewish sect that lived at Qumran and the broader Jewish community during this time.

The scrolls have also been significant for scholars studying the text of the Hebrew Bible. The biblical scrolls found at Qumran are some of the oldest surviving examples of the Hebrew Bible and have been invaluable for studying the text's transmission and history.

Furthermore, the scrolls have also helped to shed light on the origins and development of Christianity. Some scholars have proposed that Christianity had its beginnings at Qumran, although there are also many striking differences between the religious views of the Qumran sect and early Christianity.

Overall, the Dead Sea Scrolls are an invaluable resource for scholars studying Jewish history, literature, and religion during the Second Temple period, and their discovery has greatly contributed to our understanding of the past and the development of major religions.

A statement which can be made is that the Dead Sea Scrolls are a collection of Jewish texts that were discovered in the 1940s in the vicinity of Qumran, a ruin located on the northwest shore of the Dead Sea. The scrolls and fragments, written in Hebrew, Aramaic, and Greek, are some of the oldest surviving examples of biblical and extra-biblical texts, dating back to the Second Temple period (516 BCE – 70 CE). The discovery of the scrolls has been described as one of the most significant archaeological finds of the 20th century and has greatly contributed to our understanding of Jewish history, literature, and religion during this period.

Who Wrote the Dead Sea Scrolls?

The question of authorship of the Dead Sea Scrolls is a complex one that has been the subject of much debate among scholars. The scrolls themselves provide some clues as to their authorship, but ultimately, the answer to this question is not entirely clear.

Background

The Dead Sea Scrolls are a collection of Jewish texts that were discovered in the 1940s in the vicinity of Qumran, a ruin located on the northwest shore of the Dead Sea. The scrolls and fragments, written in Hebrew, Aramaic, and Greek, are some of the oldest surviving examples of biblical and extra-biblical texts, dating back to the Second Temple period (516 BCE – 70 CE). The discovery of the scrolls has been described as one of the most significant archaeological finds of the 20th century and has greatly contributed to our understanding of Jewish history, literature, and religion during this period.

Theories on Authorship

The first theory proposed about the authorship of the scrolls was that they belonged to a community of Essenes, a Jewish sect mentioned by first-century writers such as Josephus, Philo of Alexandria, and Pliny the Elder. This theory was first proposed by Professor Eleazar Sukenik, who obtained three scrolls for the Hebrew University in Jerusalem in 1947. However, this theory is now considered too simplistic, and many scholars believe that the scrolls reflect a diverse range of beliefs and practices, rather than those of a single sect.

One theory that has gained acceptance among scholars is that the scrolls were the property of a Jewish sect that lived at Qumran. The scrolls themselves provide evidence that the community at Qumran had a strong sense of its own identity and believed that it was living in the end times. The texts include the Community Rule, a manual for the organization and conduct of the sect, and the War Scroll, which describes a future war between the "Sons of Light" and the "Sons of Darkness."

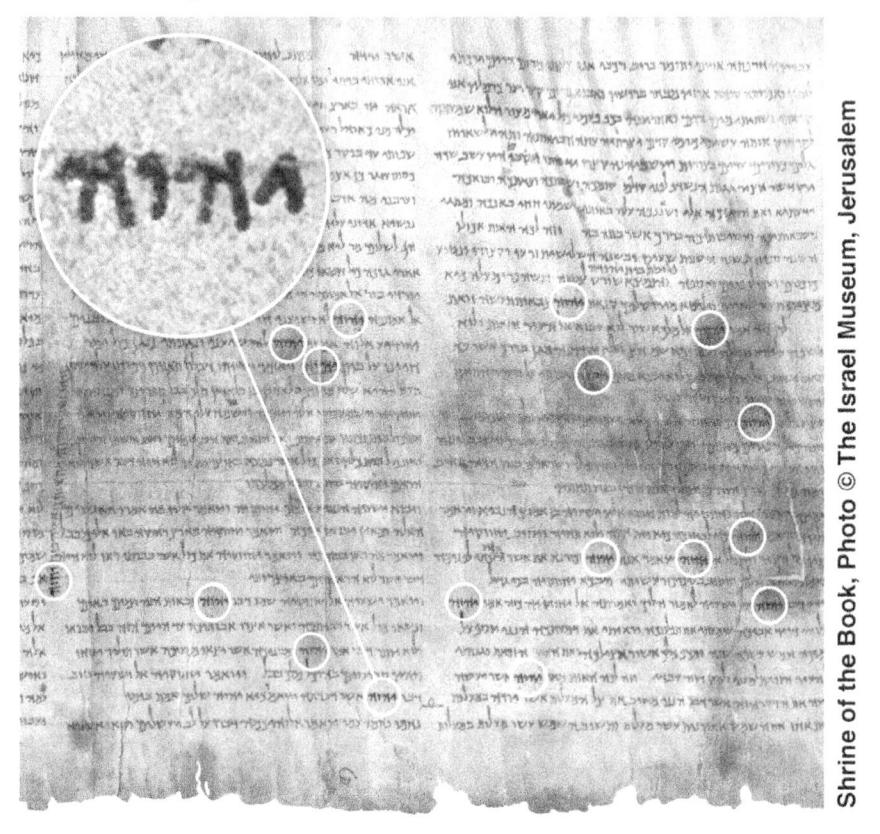

Image 20 Notice the number of times the Tetragrammaton (Divine Name) shows up in one small portion of text.

However, it is also likely that the scrolls were collected from various sources and brought to Qumran by the community, rather than being produced solely by the community at Qumran. The scrolls can be considered as an extensive library collection that reflects a wide range of thought and beliefs, rather than just those of the community at Qumran.

The Role of Scribes

The scrolls provide evidence of the use of scribes in their production, as many of the scrolls show signs of corrections and revisions, indicating that they were copied and recopied over time. Additionally, some of the scrolls contain colophons, which are short notes at the end of a text that provide information about the scribe and the date of the copy.

It is likely that there was a school of scribes at Qumran who were responsible for copying and preserving the scrolls. Many of the scrolls found at Qumran are written in a distinctive script known as the "Qumran cursive," which is believed to have been used by the scribes at Qumran.

Authorship and Dating

The question of authorship and dating of the scrolls is closely related, as the dating of the scrolls can provide clues as to their authorship. Radiocarbon dating and paleographic analysis of the scrolls have indicated that they were either copied or composed between the third century BCE and the first century CE.

It is important to note that not all the scrolls found at Qumran were produced by the community living there, as some scrolls may have been brought to Qumran by the members of the community or other Jewish groups. Therefore, it is likely that authorship of the scrolls is a complex and multi-faceted issue, reflecting a wide range of beliefs and practices, rather than those of a single sect or individual.

Conclusion

In conclusion, the question of authorship of the Dead Sea Scrolls is a complex one that has been the subject of much debate among scholars. While the scrolls themselves provide some clues as to their authorship, the answer to this question is not entirely clear.

It is likely that the scrolls were the property of a Jewish sect that lived at Qumran and that there was a school of scribes at Qumran who were responsible for copying and preserving the scrolls. But it is also possible that some scrolls may have been brought to Qumran by the members of the community or other Jewish groups. The scrolls can be considered as an extensive library collection that reflects a wide range of thoughts and beliefs, rather than just those of the community at Qumran.

It is important to note that the dating of the scrolls, which ranges from the 3rd century BCE to the 1st century CE, can also provide clues as to their authorship, but it is not a definitive answer. Scholars continue to study and analyze the scrolls in order to gain a better understanding of their authorship and the context in which they were produced.

Were the Qumran Residents Essenes?

The question of whether the residents of Qumran were Essenes is a topic of much debate among scholars. The Essenes were a Jewish sect mentioned by first-century writers such as Josephus, Philo of Alexandria, and Pliny the Elder, and there are many similarities between the beliefs and practices described in the texts found at Qumran and those attributed to the Essenes. However, there are also significant differences between the two, and the question of whether the residents of Qumran were Essenes is not entirely clear.

Background

The Dead Sea Scrolls are a collection of Jewish texts that were discovered in the 1940s in the vicinity of Qumran, a ruin located on the northwest shore of the Dead Sea. The scrolls and fragments, written in Hebrew, Aramaic, and Greek, are some of the oldest surviving examples of biblical and extra-biblical texts, dating back to the Second Temple period (516 BCE – 70 CE). The discovery of the scrolls has been described as one of the most significant archaeological finds of the 20th century and has greatly contributed to our understanding of Jewish history, literature, and religion during this period.

The Essene Theory

The theory that the residents of Qumran were Essenes was first proposed by Professor Eleazar Sukenik, who obtained three scrolls for the Hebrew University in Jerusalem in 1947. Sukenik argued that the scrolls belonged to a community of Essenes, based on similarities between the beliefs and practices described in the scrolls and those attributed to the Essenes by ancient writers.

The Essenes were a Jewish sect that is believed to have existed during the Second Temple period. They were described by ancient writers such as Josephus, Philo of Alexandria, and Pliny the Elder as a group of ascetic, separatist Jews who lived a communal lifestyle and held beliefs that were distinct from those of the Pharisees and the Sadducees.

Similarities between Qumran and the Essenes

There are many similarities between the beliefs and practices described in the texts found at Qumran and

those attributed to the Essenes by ancient writers. For example, both the Essenes and the community at Qumran are described as living a communal lifestyle and holding beliefs that were distinct from those of the Pharisees and Sadducees. Additionally, both groups are described as being concerned with purity laws and rituals, and as having a strong sense of their own identity and belief in the end times.

Some scholars have pointed to specific texts found at Qumran, such as the Community Rule and the War Scroll, as evidence that the community at Qumran was Essene. The Community Rule, for example, describes a community that is organized around a set of laws and regulations, and has been compared to the communal lifestyle described by Josephus as characteristic of the Essenes. The War Scroll, on the other hand, describes a future war between the "Sons of Light" and the "Sons of Darkness," a belief that is also attributed to the Essenes in ancient texts.

Differences between Qumran and the Essenes

Despite the similarities between the beliefs and practices described in the texts found at Qumran and those attributed to the Essenes, there are also significant differences between the two. One of the main differences is that the texts found at Qumran reflect a much more diverse range of beliefs and practices than those attributed to the Essenes in ancient texts. For example, the texts found at Qumran include copies of portions of the Hebrew Bible, additional manuscripts representing ancient non-Biblical Jewish writings, both Apocrypha and Pseudepigrapha, and unique Bible commentaries.

Additionally, the scrolls reveal a community that believed that God had rejected the priests and the temple service in Jerusalem and that he viewed their group's worship in the desert as a kind of substitute temple service. This is not in harmony with the views attributed to the Essenes by ancient texts, which describe them as being opposed to the religious authorities in Jerusalem but not to the temple service.

Image 21 Qumran cave 4, where ninety percent of the scrolls were found

Conclusion

In conclusion, the question of whether the residents of Qumran were Essenes is a topic of much debate among scholars. While there are many similarities between the beliefs and practices described in the texts found at Qumran and those attributed to the Essenes by ancient writers, there are also significant differences between the two. It is likely that the community at Qumran was unique and had its own distinct beliefs and practices, rather than being a part of a known sect such as the Essenes. However, it is also possible that the community at Qumran had connections to other Jewish groups, including the Essenes. The exact origins and identity of the community at Qumran are still debated by scholars, and more research is needed to fully understand the connection between the community at Qumran and the Essenes.

INTRODUCTION TO THE TEXT OF THE OLD TESTAMENT

ORIGIN: Qumran-Essene Theory of the Dead Sea Scrolls

The question of the origin of the Dead Sea Scrolls and the connection to the Essene sect is a complex and debated topic among scholars. The Essene theory, which proposes that the scrolls were written and hidden by the Essene community at Qumran, is one of the most widely accepted theories, but it is not without its critics and alternative theories have been proposed.

Background

The Dead Sea Scrolls are a collection of Jewish texts that were discovered in the 1940s in the vicinity of Qumran, a ruin located on the northwest shore of the Dead Sea. The scrolls and fragments, written in Hebrew, Aramaic, and Greek, are some of the oldest surviving examples of biblical and extra-biblical texts, dating back to the Second Temple period (516 BCE – 70 CE). The discovery of the scrolls has been described as one of the most significant archaeological finds of the 20th century and has greatly contributed to our understanding of Jewish history, literature, and religion during this period.

Image 22 Fragments 1 and 2 of '7Q6' from Cave 7 are written on papyrus.

The Essene Theory

The theory that the Dead Sea Scrolls were written and hidden by the Essene community at Qumran was first proposed by Professor Eleazar Sukenik, who obtained three scrolls for the Hebrew University in Jerusalem in 1947. Sukenik argued that the scrolls belonged to a community of Essenes, based on similarities between the beliefs and practices described in the scrolls and those attributed to the Essenes by ancient writers such as Josephus, Philo of Alexandria, and Pliny the Elder.

Image 23 Two of the pottery jars that held some of the Dead Sea Scrolls found at Qumran.

    The Essenes were a Jewish sect that is believed to have existed during the Second Temple period. They were described by ancient writers as a group of ascetic, separatist Jews who lived a communal lifestyle and held beliefs that were distinct from those of the Pharisees and the Sadducees. The Essene theory proposes that the Essene community at Qumran wrote and preserved the scrolls, and that they were hidden in the nearby caves during the Roman destruction of Jerusalem in 70 CE.

Evidence for the Essene Theory

There is evidence to support the Essene theory, including similarities between the beliefs and practices described in the scrolls and those attributed to the Essenes in ancient texts. For example, both the Essenes and the community at Qumran are described as living a communal lifestyle, being concerned with purity laws and rituals, and having a strong sense of their own identity and belief in the end times. Additionally, the scrolls found at Qumran were written in Hebrew and Aramaic, the languages spoken by the Essenes.

Archaeological evidence also supports the Essene theory. Excavations at the site of Qumran have uncovered structures that have been interpreted as a scriptorium, where the scrolls may have been copied, and a ritual bath, in line with the Essene emphasis on ritual purity.

Criticism of the Essene Theory

Despite the evidence in support of the Essene theory, it is not without its critics. Some scholars have argued that the scrolls reflect a much more diverse range of beliefs and practices than those attributed to the Essenes in ancient texts. Additionally, there are significant differences between the beliefs and practices described in the scrolls and those attributed to the Essenes in ancient texts.

Furthermore, the scrolls reveal a community that believed that God had rejected the priests and the temple service in Jerusalem and that he viewed their group's worship in the desert as a kind of substitute temple service. This is not in harmony with the views attributed to the Essenes by ancient texts, which describe them as being opposed to the religious authorities in Jerusalem but not to the temple service.

ORIGIN: Qumran-Sectarian Theory of the Dead Sea Scrolls

The question of the origin of the Dead Sea Scrolls and the connection to the community at Qumran is a complex and debated topic among scholars. The Sectarian theory, which proposes that the scrolls were written by a Jewish sect that lived at Qumran, is one of the most widely accepted theories, but it is not without its critics and alternative theories have been proposed.

The Sectarian Theory

The Sectarian theory proposes that the Dead Sea Scrolls were written by a Jewish sect that lived at Qumran. This theory suggests that the community at Qumran was an isolated, Jewish sect that developed its own distinct beliefs and practices. They wrote and preserved the scrolls, and that they were hidden in the nearby caves during the Roman destruction of Jerusalem in 70 CE.

According to this theory, the scrolls were a library of texts that reflect the beliefs, practices, and history of the sect. They were written and copied by the members of the community, and the texts were used in their religious and educational activities. The scrolls include copies of portions of the Hebrew Bible, additional manuscripts representing ancient non-Biblical Jewish writings, both Apocrypha and Pseudepigrapha, and unique Bible commentaries.

Evidence for the Sectarian Theory

There is evidence to support the Sectarian theory, including the fact that the scrolls were found in the vicinity of Qumran, and that the site has been identified as a settlement of a Jewish sect. Furthermore, the scrolls were written in Hebrew and Aramaic, the languages spoken by the Jewish people.

Archaeological evidence also supports the Sectarian theory. Excavations at the site of Qumran have uncovered structures that have been interpreted as a scriptorium, where the scrolls may have been copied, and a ritual bath, in line with the sect's emphasis on ritual purity.

Additionally, the scrolls reveal a community that believed that God had rejected the priests and the temple service in Jerusalem and that he viewed their group's worship in the desert as a kind of substitute temple service. This is in harmony with the views attributed to the Jewish sects by ancient texts.

Criticism of the Sectarian Theory

Despite the evidence in support of the Sectarian theory, it is not without its critics. Some scholars argue that the scrolls reflect a much more diverse range of beliefs and practices than those attributed to a single sect. Furthermore, the exact identity of the sect is still debated by scholars and more research is needed to fully understand the connection between the community at Qumran and the scrolls.

INTRODUCTION TO THE TEXT OF THE OLD TESTAMENT

ORIGIN: Christian Origin Theory of the Dead Sea Scrolls

The question of the origin of the Dead Sea Scrolls and the connection to Christianity is a complex and debated topic among scholars. The Christian Origin theory, which proposes that the scrolls were written by an early Christian sect, is one of the alternative theories, but it is not widely accepted and faces criticism.

Background

The Dead Sea Scrolls are a collection of Jewish texts that were discovered in the 1940s in the vicinity of Qumran, a ruin located on the northwest shore of the Dead Sea. The scrolls and fragments, written in Hebrew, Aramaic, and Greek, are some of the oldest surviving examples of biblical and extra-biblical texts, dating back to the Second Temple period (516 BCE – 70 CE). The discovery of the scrolls has been described as one of the most significant archaeological finds of the 20th century and has greatly contributed to our understanding of Jewish history, literature, and religion during this period.

The Christian Origin Theory

The Christian Origin theory proposes that the Dead Sea Scrolls were written by an early Christian sect. This theory suggests that the scrolls were written by a Jewish-Christian community that was influenced by both Jewish and Christian beliefs and practices. The community wrote and preserved the scrolls, and that they were hidden in the nearby caves during the Roman destruction of Jerusalem in 70 CE.

According to this theory, the scrolls were a library of texts that reflect the beliefs, practices, and history of the sect. They were written and copied by the members of the community, and the texts were used in their religious and educational activities. The scrolls include copies of portions of the Hebrew Bible, additional manuscripts representing ancient non-Biblical Jewish writings, both Apocrypha and Pseudepigrapha, and unique Bible commentaries.

Evidence for the Christian Origin Theory

There is limited evidence to support the Christian Origin theory. Some scholars have pointed to similarities between the beliefs and practices described in the scrolls and those of early Christianity, such as the belief in the coming of a Messiah, the importance of the end times, and the emphasis on community and ritual purity.

Additionally, some scrolls, such as the Damascus Document, contains language that is similar to the New Testament and has been suggested by some to be evidence of a Christian influence. However, the majority of scholars agree that these similarities can also be found in contemporary Jewish literature and that it is not a strong evidence of Christian origin.

Criticism of the Christian Origin Theory

The Christian Origin theory faces significant criticism from scholars. The majority of scholars agree that the scrolls were written by a Jewish sect and that there is no evidence of Christian influence on the scrolls. Furthermore, the scrolls were written in Hebrew and Aramaic, the languages spoken by the Jewish people, and not in Greek, the language spoken by Christians.

Archaeological evidence also contradicts the Christian Origin theory, as the excavations at the site of Qumran have uncovered structures that were used by a Jewish sect and not by a Christian community.

ORIGIN: Jerusalem Origin Theory of the Dead Sea Scrolls

The question of the origin of the Dead Sea Scrolls and the connection to the city of Jerusalem is a complex and debated topic among scholars. The Jerusalem Origin theory, which proposes that the scrolls were written and hidden by Jewish priests or scribes from Jerusalem, is one of the alternative theories, but it is not widely accepted and faces criticism.

The Jerusalem Origin Theory

The Jerusalem Origin theory proposes that the Dead Sea Scrolls were written and hidden by Jewish priests or scribes from Jerusalem. This theory suggests that the scrolls were written by Jewish priests or scribes who were living in Jerusalem during the Second Temple period. They wrote and preserved the scrolls, and that they were hidden in the nearby caves during the Roman destruction of Jerusalem in 70 CE.

According to this theory, the scrolls were a library of texts that reflect the beliefs, practices, and history of the priests or scribes. They were written and copied by the members of the community, and the texts were used in their religious and educational activities. The scrolls include copies of portions of the Hebrew Bible, additional manuscripts representing ancient non-Biblical Jewish writings, both Apocrypha and Pseudepigrapha, and unique Bible commentaries.

Evidence for the Jerusalem Origin Theory

There is limited evidence to support the Jerusalem Origin theory. Some scholars have suggested that the scrolls were written by Jewish priests or scribes who were living in Jerusalem during the Second Temple period. However, the majority of scholars agree that this theory is unlikely due to the lack of archaeological evidence and the fact that the scrolls were found in the vicinity of Qumran and not in Jerusalem.

Criticism of the Jerusalem Origin Theory

The Jerusalem Origin theory faces significant criticism from scholars. The majority of scholars agree that the scrolls were written by a Jewish sect that lived at Qumran and that there is no evidence that the scrolls were written by Jewish priests or scribes from Jerusalem. Additionally, the scrolls themselves contain information that is specific to the community at Qumran, such as their beliefs and practices, which would not have been relevant to Jewish priests or scribes living in Jerusalem. Furthermore, the scrolls were written in Hebrew and Aramaic, the languages spoken by the Jewish people, and not in Greek, which was the language spoken by many scribes and priests in Jerusalem.

Archaeological evidence also contradicts the Jerusalem Origin theory, as the excavations at the site of Qumran have uncovered structures that were used by a Jewish sect and not by a community of priests or scribes living in Jerusalem. Additionally, the scrolls themselves contain information specific to the community at Qumran, such as their beliefs and practices, which would not have been relevant to Jewish priests or scribes living in Jerusalem.

Conclusion

In conclusion, the question of whether the Dead Sea Scrolls have a Jerusalem origin is a topic of much debate among scholars. The Jerusalem Origin theory is one of the alternative theories, but it is not widely accepted and faces significant criticism. The majority of scholars agree that the scrolls were written by a Jewish sect that lived at Qumran and that there is no evidence that the scrolls were written by Jewish priests or scribes from Jerusalem. Furthermore, the scrolls contain information specific to the community at Qumran, such as their beliefs and practices, which would not have been relevant to Jewish priests or scribes living in Jerusalem.

Edward D. Andrews

The Dead Sea Scrolls Compared to the Masoretic Text

The Dead Sea Scrolls (DSS) are a collection of Jewish texts that were discovered in the 1940s in the vicinity of Qumran, a ruin located on the northwest shore of the Dead Sea. The scrolls and fragments, written in Hebrew, Aramaic, and Greek, are some of the oldest surviving examples of biblical and extra-biblical texts, dating back to the Second Temple period (516 BCE – 70 CE). The discovery of the scrolls has been described as one of the most significant archaeological finds of the 20th century and has greatly contributed to our understanding of Jewish history, literature, and religion during this period.

On the other hand, the Masoretic Text (MT) is the traditional Hebrew text of the Jewish Bible, also known as the Tanakh. It is considered the authoritative text of the Hebrew Bible and is widely used in Jewish scholarship and Christian theology. The MT is based on a series of manuscripts that were produced by Jewish scribes known as the Masoretes between the 7th and 10th centuries CE.

In this essay, we will explore the similarities and differences between the DSS and the MT, and the significance of these differences for our understanding of the development of the Hebrew Bible.

Similarities between the DSS and the MT

One of the most striking similarities between the DSS and the MT is that a large number of the scrolls found at Qumran are copies of texts from the Hebrew Bible. The DSS include at least fragments from every book of the Hebrew Bible, with the exception of the book of Esther. This is significant as it demonstrates that the texts of the Hebrew Bible were already considered sacred and authoritative by the community at Qumran and that they were carefully copied and preserved by the scribes.

Additionally, both the DSS and the MT share a common linguistic

and literary tradition. Both texts are written in Hebrew, and they share similar linguistic features, such as vocabulary, grammar, and syntax. This similarity is not surprising, as both the DSS and the MT are written in Hebrew and are part of the same Jewish literary tradition.

Another similarity is that the DSS and the MT share similar textual traditions. Both texts have undergone a process of editing and transmission, and they both reflect the same biblical canon. This is significant as it demonstrates that the community at Qumran and the Masoretes shared a common understanding of the biblical canon and the texts that were considered to be sacred and authoritative.

Differences between the DSS and the MT

Despite the similarities, there are also significant differences between the DSS and the MT. One of the most notable differences is the textual variations between the two texts. The DSS contain a number of textual variations that are not found in the MT, such as alternative readings, additional words, and different word order. These variations demonstrate that the DSS reflect an older textual tradition than the MT and that the text of the Hebrew Bible was still in the process of development during the Second Temple period.

Another difference is the style of the text. The DSS are written in a formal and precise style, whereas the MT is written in a more polished and stylized manner. This difference is likely due to the fact that the DSS were written by scribes who were focused on accuracy and preservation, whereas the MT was written by scribes who were focused on literary style and artistic expression.

Finally, the DSS also contain a number of texts that are not found in the MT, such as apocryphal and pseudepigraphical texts, as well as unique Bible commentaries. These texts provide valuable insights into the religious beliefs, practices, and history of the community at Qumran and the Second Temple period.

Conclusion

In conclusion, the DSS and the MT are two important Jewish texts that share similarities and differences. Both texts are written in Hebrew and share a common literary tradition, but the DSS contain a number of textual variations and additional texts that are not found in the MT. These differences demonstrate that the DSS reflect an older textual tradition than the MT and that the text of the Hebrew Bible was still in the process of development during the Second Temple period. Additionally, the DSS provides valuable insights into the religious beliefs, practices, and history of the community at Qumran and the Second Temple period.

The Dead Sea Scrolls Compared to the Greek Septuagint

The Dead Sea Scrolls (DSS) and the Greek Septuagint (LXX) are two important ancient texts that have greatly contributed to our understanding of

Jewish history, literature, and religion during the Second Temple period (516 BCE – 70 CE). While the DSS are a collection of Jewish texts that were discovered in the 1940s in the vicinity of Qumran, a ruin located on the northwest shore of the Dead Sea, the LXX is a translation of the Hebrew Bible into Greek that was produced by Jewish scholars between the 3rd century BCE and the 1st century CE. In this essay, we will explore the similarities and differences between the DSS and the LXX, and the significance of these differences for our understanding of the development of the Hebrew Bible.

Background

The DSS are a collection of Jewish texts that were discovered in the 1940s in the vicinity of Qumran, a ruin located on the northwest shore of the Dead Sea. The scrolls and fragments, written in Hebrew, Aramaic, and Greek, are some of the oldest surviving examples of biblical and extra-biblical texts, dating back to the Second Temple period. The discovery of the scrolls has been described as one of the most significant archaeological finds of the 20th century and has greatly contributed to our understanding of Jewish history, literature, and religion during this period.

The LXX, on the other hand, is a translation of the Hebrew Bible into Greek that was produced by Jewish scholars between the 3rd century BCE and the 1st century CE. The LXX is considered the oldest translation of the Hebrew Bible and is widely used in Jewish and Christian scholarship. The translation of the Hebrew Bible into Greek was likely done to accommodate Jewish communities in Egypt and other parts of the Greek-speaking world.

Similarities between the DSS and the LXX

One of the most striking similarities between the DSS and the LXX is that both texts are written in different languages. The DSS were written in Hebrew and Aramaic, while the LXX is a translation of the Hebrew Bible into Greek. This similarity is significant as it demonstrates that the Jewish community during the Second Temple period was multilingual and that the texts of the Hebrew Bible were translated into different languages for different audiences.

Additionally, both the DSS and the LXX are considered important texts for understanding Jewish history, literature, and religion during the Second Temple period. The DSS and the LXX provide valuable insights into the beliefs, practices, and history of the Jewish community during this period.

Differences between the DSS and the LXX

Despite the similarities, there are also significant differences between the DSS and the LXX. One of the most notable differences is the textual variations between the two texts. The LXX contains a number of textual variations that are not found in the DSS, such as alternative readings, additional words, and different word order. These variations demonstrate that the LXX reflects a different textual tradition than the DSS and that the text of the Hebrew Bible was translated and interpreted differently by Jewish scholars during the Second Temple period.

Another difference is the style of the text. The DSS are written in a formal and precise style, whereas the LXX is written in a more polished and stylized manner. This difference is likely due to the fact that the DSS were written by scribes who were focused on accuracy and preservation, whereas the LXX was written by scholars who were focused on literary style and artistic expression.

Finally, the DSS also contain a number of texts that are not found in the LXX, such as apocryphal and pseudepigraphical texts, as well as unique Bible commentaries. These texts provide valuable insights into the religious beliefs, practices, and history of the community at Qumran and the Second Temple period. On the other hand, the LXX includes texts that are not present in the DSS, such as the books of Tobit, Judith, Wisdom, Sirach (Ecclesiasticus), and Baruch, which are considered part of the Septuagint but are not part of the Hebrew Bible.

It is also worth noting that the LXX is a translation of the Hebrew Bible, and as such, it reflects the interpretive choices of the translators. These choices can include changes in wording, grammar, and syntax, as well as additions and omissions. These interpretive choices can provide insight into how the Jewish community of the time understood and translated the Hebrew Bible.

Conclusion

In conclusion, the DSS and the LXX are two important ancient texts that have greatly contributed to our understanding of Jewish history, literature, and religion during the Second Temple period. Both texts are written in different languages and share similarities and differences. The DSS provide valuable insights into the religious beliefs, practices, and history of the community at Qumran, while the LXX provides insight into how the Jewish community of the time understood and translated the Hebrew Bible. Both texts offer unique perspectives and contribute to our understanding of the development and transmission of the Hebrew Bible during the Second Temple period.

Edward D. Andrews

Manuscripts of the Dead Sea Scrolls

The Dead Sea Scrolls (DSS) are a collection of Jewish texts that were discovered in the 1940s in the vicinity of Qumran, a ruin located on the northwest shore of the Dead Sea. These scrolls and fragments, written in Hebrew, Aramaic, and Greek, are some of the oldest surviving examples of biblical and extra-biblical texts, dating back to the Second Temple period (516 BCE – 70 CE). The discovery of the scrolls has been described as one of the most significant archaeological finds of the 20th century and has greatly contributed to our understanding of Jewish history, literature, and religion during this period.

The DSS consist of over 800 manuscripts, including fragments from every book of the Hebrew Bible, with the exception of the book of Esther. These manuscripts are made of animal skins, papyrus, and copper. The texts are written in various scripts, including the paleo-Hebrew script, the square Aramaic script, and the Greek script. The scrolls have been classified into two categories: biblical and non-biblical texts. The biblical texts include copies of texts from the Hebrew Bible, while the non-biblical texts include apocryphal, pseudepigraphical, and sectarian texts.

Biblical Manuscripts

The biblical manuscripts of the DSS include fragments from every book of the Hebrew Bible, with the exception of the book of Esther. These manuscripts are considered to be some of the oldest surviving copies of the Hebrew Bible and provide valuable insights into the development and transmission of the text.

The biblical manuscripts of the DSS are written in the paleo-Hebrew script, which was used in the Second Temple period. This script is different from the square Hebrew script that is used in the Masoretic Text (MT), which is the traditional Hebrew text of the Jewish Bible. The paleo-Hebrew script is considered to be more ancient and closer to the original script of the Hebrew Bible.

The biblical manuscripts of the DSS also contain a number of textual variations that are not found in the MT. These variations include alternative readings, additional words, and different word order. These variations demonstrate that the DSS reflect an older textual tradition than the MT and that the text of the Hebrew Bible was still in the process of development during the Second Temple period.

One of the most notable biblical manuscripts of the DSS is the Great Isaiah Scroll (1QIsa). This scroll is considered to be the oldest complete copy of the book of Isaiah and is dated to around 125 BCE. The Great Isaiah Scroll contains the entire book of Isaiah, written in the paleo-Hebrew script, and is in excellent condition. This scroll has been of great importance in understanding the development and transmission of the text of Isaiah and has provided valuable insights into the history of the text.

Another important biblical manuscript is the Temple Scroll (11QTemple). This scroll is a unique text that contains instructions for the construction and organization of the temple, as well as laws and regulations for the temple service. The Temple Scroll is considered to be a sectarian text and provides valuable insights into the beliefs and practices of the community at Qumran.

Non-Biblical Manuscripts

The non-biblical manuscripts of the DSS include apocryphal, pseudepigraphical, and sectarian texts. These texts provide valuable insights into the beliefs, practices, and history of the community at Qumran and the Second Temple period.

The apocryphal manuscripts of the DSS include texts such as Tobit, Judith, and Sirach (Ecclesiasticus). These texts are not considered to be part of the Hebrew Bible but were considered to be important by the Jewish community during the Second Temple period. The discovery of these texts among the DSS demonstrates that the community at Qumran had a diverse collection of texts that were considered to be sacred and authoritative.

The pseudepigraphical manuscripts of the DSS include texts such as Enoch, Jubilees, and the Community Rule (1QS). These texts are attributed to ancient figures such as

Enoch and are considered to be of a sectarian nature. They provide valuable insights into the beliefs, practices, and history of the community at Qumran. For example, the Community Rule (1QS) contains regulations and laws for the organization and behavior of the community and reflects the unique beliefs and practices of the group.

The sectarian manuscripts of the DSS include texts such as the War Scroll (1QM) and the Thanksgiving Hymns (1QH). These texts reflect the unique beliefs and practices of the community at Qumran and provide valuable insights into their religious views and customs. For example, the War Scroll (1M) details a future battle between the Sons of Light and the Sons of Darkness, which reflects the eschatological beliefs of the community.

In conclusion, the manuscripts of the Dead Sea Scrolls are a unique collection of texts that have greatly contributed to our understanding of Jewish history, literature, and religion during the Second Temple period. The biblical manuscripts provide valuable insights into the development and transmission of the text of the Hebrew Bible, while the non-biblical manuscripts provide valuable insights into the beliefs, practices, and history of the community at Qumran and the Second Temple period. The discovery of the Dead Sea Scrolls has been a significant contribution to the field of biblical studies and has greatly expanded our knowledge of the history of the text of the Hebrew Bible.

Scribal Level of Abilities of the Dead Sea Scrolls Compared to the Masoretes

The Dead Sea Scrolls (DSS) and the Masoretic Text (MT) are two important ancient texts that have greatly contributed to our understanding of Jewish history, literature, and religion. The DSS are a collection of Jewish texts that were discovered in the 1940s in the vicinity of Qumran, while the MT is the traditional Hebrew text of the Jewish Bible that was transmitted and preserved by the Masoretes, a group of Jewish scholars who lived between the 6th and 10th centuries CE.

DSS Scribal Abilities

The DSS are considered to be some of the oldest surviving copies of the Hebrew Bible, dating back to the Second Temple period (516 BCE – 70 CE). The scrolls were written on different materials such as animal skins, papyrus, and copper, and in various scripts, including the paleo-Hebrew script, the square Aramaic script, and the Greek script.

The scribal abilities of the DSS scribes have been widely studied and have been found to be of a high level. The scrolls exhibit a high degree of accuracy, consistency, and uniformity. The scribes were well-trained and proficient in the use of the paleo-Hebrew script, which was used in the Second Temple period. They also demonstrated a high level of skill in the use of orthography, grammar, and syntax.

According to Emanuel Tov, a leading Dead Sea Scrolls scholar, "The scrolls exhibit a high degree of accuracy, consistency, and uniformity. The scribes were well-trained and proficient in the use of the paleo-Hebrew script and demonstrated a high level of skill in the use of orthography, grammar, and syntax."

The scrolls also exhibit a high level of textual criticism, which suggests that the scribes were aware of different textual traditions and were able to make informed decisions when copying the texts. The DSS scribes also employed various techniques to ensure the accuracy of their copies, such as the use of diacritical marks and the inclusion of textual variants.

INTRODUCTION TO THE TEXT OF THE OLD TESTAMENT

MT Scribal Abilities

The MT is the traditional Hebrew text of the Jewish Bible that was transmitted and preserved by the Masoretes, a group of Jewish scholars who lived between the 6th and 10th centuries CE. The Masoretes were responsible for the transmission and preservation of the text of the Hebrew Bible and were known for their high level of skill and accuracy.

The Masoretes employed various techniques to ensure the accuracy of their copies of the text, such as the use of diacritical marks and the inclusion of textual variants. They also employed a system of vocalization, which added vowels and other symbols to the text to aid in reading and pronunciation.

According to Moshe Bar-Asher, a leading Masoretic scholar, "The Masoretes were responsible for the transmission and preservation of the text of the Hebrew Bible and were known for their high level of skill and accuracy. They employed various techniques to ensure the accuracy of their copies of the text, such as the use of diacritical marks and the inclusion of textual variants."

In conclusion, the scribal abilities of the DSS scribes and the Masoretes are of a high level. Both groups of scribes were well-trained and proficient in the use of the scripts and demonstrated a high level of skill in the use of orthography, grammar, and syntax. Both groups also employed various techniques to ensure the accuracy of their copies, such as the use of diacritical marks and the inclusion of textual variants. These similarities suggest that the scribal abilities of the DSS scribes and the Masoretes were on the same level and that both groups of scribes were dedicated to the preservation and transmission of the text with a high degree of accuracy and consistency.

However, it should be noted that there are also some notable differences between the scribal abilities of the DSS scribes and the Masoretes. For example, the DSS scribes were writing in the paleo-Hebrew script, which is considered to be more ancient and closer to the original script of the Hebrew Bible. They were also writing during the Second Temple period, which is much earlier than the period in which the Masoretes lived. This means that the DSS scribes had access to earlier and potentially more original versions of the text.

Additionally, the DSS scribes were writing in a sectarian context, as opposed to the Masoretes who were writing in a more mainstream context. This means that the DSS scribes may have had different beliefs and priorities when it came to the transmission and preservation of the text.

In any case, both the DSS and the MT are important ancient texts that have greatly contributed to our understanding of Jewish history, literature, and religion. The scribal abilities of the DSS scribes and the Masoretes demonstrate a high level of skill and accuracy, and both groups were dedicated to the preservation and transmission of the text. The comparison of the scribal abilities of the DSS scribes and the Masoretes provides valuable insights into the development and transmission of the text of the Hebrew Bible.

Image 24 Scholars assembling Dead Sea Scrolls fragments at the Rockefeller Museum (formerly the Palestine Archaeological Museum).

Scholarly Examination of the Dead Sea Scrolls

The Initial Examination

The initial examination of the Dead Sea Scrolls (DSS) was a slow and laborious process. The scrolls were in various states of deterioration, and many of them were in fragments. The initial task was to identify and catalog the scrolls, and to assemble the fragments in order to form complete scrolls.

The first scrolls to be examined were the seven scrolls that were obtained by the Palestine Archaeological Museum in 1947. These scrolls were in various stages of deterioration and were in need of immediate conservation. The scrolls were cleaned, repaired, and placed in acid-free containers to prevent further deterioration.

The initial examination of the scrolls was carried out by a team of scholars led by Dr. John Trever of the American Schools of Oriental Research (ASOR). Dr. Trever was the first person to photograph the scrolls and made the first transcriptions of the scrolls. He was also responsible for the initial cataloging and organization of the scrolls.

Image 25 Eleazar Sukenik examining one of the Dead Sea Scrolls in 1951.

The International Team of Scholars

In 1951, an international team of scholars was assembled to begin the task of translating and studying the scrolls. The team was led by Dr. William F. Albright, the director of the ASOR, and included scholars from a variety of institutions and countries.

The team was responsible for the translation and study of the scrolls, and they produced a number of important publications on the scrolls. They also established a system for the publication of the scrolls, which ensured that all scholars had access to the scrolls and could participate in the study of the scrolls.

The Ongoing Examination

The examination of the DSS is an ongoing process, and new scrolls and fragments are still being discovered. The scrolls are currently housed in the Shrine of the Book at the Israel Museum in Jerusalem, and they are available for study by scholars from around the world.

The ongoing examination of the scrolls has led to a better understanding of the history, literature, and religion of the Second Temple period. The scrolls have provided valuable insights into the development and transmission of the text of the Hebrew Bible, and they have also revealed new information about the beliefs, practices, and history of the community at Qumran.

The Controversies

The examination of the DSS has not been without controversy. One of the main controversies has been the initial handling and publication of the scrolls. The initial team of scholars was criticized for their handling of the scrolls and for their slow pace of publication. Some scholars felt that the scrolls were being kept under wraps and that access to them was being restricted. This led to a number of disputes and accusations of monopolization of the scrolls by the initial team of scholars.

Another controversy was the delay in publishing the scrolls and the lack of transparency in the publication process. The initial team of scholars was criticized for taking too long to publish the scrolls and for not making the scrolls available to all scholars. This led to a number of disputes and accusations of monopolization of the scrolls by the initial team of scholars.

A more recent controversy was the release of the images and transcriptions of the scrolls on the internet in 1991 by the Huntington Library. This release was met with mixed reactions, with some scholars praising the move as a way to make the scrolls more widely available, while others criticized it for potentially damaging the scrolls and for making it harder to control the quality of the translations and research.

Despite the controversies, the scholarly examination of the DSS has greatly contributed to our understanding of the history, literature, and religion of the Second Temple period. The scrolls are considered to be one of the most important archaeological discoveries of the 20th century and continue to be a valuable resource for scholars and researchers.

In summary, the scholarly examination of the Dead Sea Scrolls is an ongoing process that began in the 1950s with a team of international scholars, led by Dr. William F. Albright. The ongoing examination of the scrolls has led to a better understanding of the history, literature, and religion of the Second Temple period and the scrolls have provided valuable insights into the development and transmission of the text of the Hebrew Bible. The examination of the scrolls has been met with some controversies, such as the initial handling and publication of the scrolls, the delay in publishing the scrolls, and the release of the images and transcriptions of the scrolls on the internet.

English Translations of the Dead Sea Scrolls

The First English Translations

The first English translations of the Dead Sea Scrolls (DSS) were produced by the international team of scholars who were responsible for the initial examination of the scrolls. These translations were published in a series of volumes known as the "Discoveries in the Judaean Desert" (DJD). The DJD volumes were published by Oxford University Press between 1955 and 2011, and they contain translations of the scrolls along with introductions, notes, and photographs of the scrolls.

The first English translation of the DSS was published in 1955 by Dr. Millar Burrows, who was a member of the international team of scholars. This translation was based on the photographs of the scrolls that had been taken by Dr. John Trever, and it was published in a book called "The Dead Sea Scrolls of St. Mark's Monastery."

Image 26 scribe-Wikimedia-Der Torahschreiber

The Revised Translation

In 1991, the images and transcriptions of the scrolls were released on the internet by the Huntington Library, which made them more widely available to scholars and researchers. This led to a renewed interest in the scrolls and to the production of new translations.

One of the most significant new translations was the "Dead Sea Scrolls: A New Translation" by Michael Wise, Martin Abegg Jr., and Edward Cook, which was published in 1996. This translation was based on the images and transcriptions of the scrolls that had been released on the internet and it was considered to be more accurate and reliable than the earlier translations.

The Current Translations

Currently, there are several English translations of the DSS available, many of which are based on the images and transcriptions of the scrolls that have been released on the internet. These translations include the "Dead Sea Scrolls Bible" by Martin Abegg Jr., Peter Flint, and Eugene Ulrich, which was published in 1999 and "The Dead Sea Scrolls Translated: The Qumran Texts in English" by Florentino Garcia Martinez and Eibert Tigchelaar, which was published in 1996.

INTRODUCTION TO THE TEXT OF THE OLD TESTAMENT

In addition to these translations, there are also several online resources that provide access to the scrolls in English, such as the "Dead Sea Scrolls Digital Library" which is a project of the Israel Museum in Jerusalem and the "Leon Levy Dead Sea Scrolls Digital Library" which is a project of the Israel Antiquities Authority and the New York-based Leon Levy Dead Sea Scrolls Foundation.

The Importance of Translation

The translation of the DSS is of paramount importance as it allows for the study and understanding of these ancient texts. The scrolls provide valuable insights into the history, literature, and religion of the Second Temple period and they have greatly contributed to our understanding of the development and transmission of the text of the Hebrew Bible.

The translation of the scrolls has also led to a better understanding of the beliefs, practices, and history of the community at Qumran. The scrolls reveal the unique characteristics of the community and their distinct beliefs and practices which were different from the contemporary Jewish sects.

The translation of the scrolls also enables the comparison of the texts with other ancient texts such as the Septuagint and the Masoretic Text. This helps to understand the variations and similarities between the texts and provides valuable insights into the development of the texts.

In summary, the translation of the Dead Sea Scrolls is crucial in the study and understanding of these ancient texts. The first English translations were produced by the international team of scholars in the 1950s and currently, there are several English translations available, many of which are based on the images and transcriptions of the scrolls that have been released on the internet. The translation of the scrolls allows for the study and understanding of the history, literature, and religion of the Second Temple period and the beliefs, practices, and history of the community at Qumran. It also enables the comparison of the texts with other ancient texts such as the Septuagint and the Masoretic Text, which provides valuable insights into the development of the texts.

It is also important to note that translation of ancient texts is always a complex task and often involves interpretation and subjective decisions. It is important to consult multiple translations and to consult the original texts in order to gain a more comprehensive understanding of the scrolls.

Challenges in Translation

The translation of the DSS is not without its challenges. One of the main challenges is the poor state of preservation of many of the scrolls, which makes them difficult to read and translate. Many of the scrolls are in fragments and are missing sections, which can make it difficult to understand the context of the text.

Another challenge is the use of different languages in the scrolls. The scrolls were written in Hebrew, Aramaic, and Greek and the use of different languages can make it difficult to understand the meaning of the text.

Another challenge is the use of technical terms and specialized vocabulary in the scrolls. The scrolls contain many technical terms and specialized vocabulary that are specific to the community at Qumran, which can make it difficult to understand the meaning of the text.

Despite these challenges, the translation of the DSS continues to provide valuable insights into the history, literature, and religion of the Second Temple period and the beliefs, practices, and history of the community at Qumran. The translation of the scrolls also enables the comparison of the texts with other ancient texts such as the Septuagint and the Masoretic Text, which provides valuable insights into the development of the texts.

In conclusion, the translation of the Dead Sea Scrolls is a crucial aspect of the study and understanding of these ancient texts. Despite the challenges, the translation of the scrolls continues to provide valuable insights into the history, literature, and religion of the Second Temple period and the beliefs, practices, and history of the community at Qumran. It is important to consult multiple translations and to consult the original texts in order to gain a more comprehensive understanding of the scrolls. It is also important to keep in mind the challenges that come with translating ancient texts, such as the poor state of preservation of many scrolls, the use of different languages, and specialized vocabulary. It's also essential to approach the translation with critical eyes, being aware of the limitations and biases that can be present in the translation process. The study of the Dead Sea Scrolls is ongoing, and new discoveries and insights are still being made. As such, it is vital that scholars and researchers continue to work towards producing accurate and reliable translations to ensure that the knowledge and understanding of these ancient texts continues to evolve.

Scholarly Editions of the Dead Sea Scrolls

The Initial Scholarly Editions

The initial scholarly editions of the Dead Sea Scrolls (DSS) were produced by the international team of scholars who were responsible for the initial examination and translation of the scrolls. These editions were published in a series of volumes known as the "Discoveries in the Judaean Desert" (DJD). The DJD volumes were published by Oxford University Press between 1955 and 2011 and they contain photographs, transcriptions, and translations of the scrolls along with introductions, notes, and indices.

The first scholarly edition of the DSS was published in 1955 by Dr. Millar Burrows, who was a member of the international team of scholars. This edition was based on the photographs of the scrolls that had been taken by Dr. John Trever, and it was published in a book called "The Dead Sea Scrolls of St. Mark's Monastery."

The Revised Editions

In 1991, the images and transcriptions of the scrolls were released on the internet by the Huntington Library, which made them more widely available to scholars and researchers. This led to a renewed interest in the scrolls and to the production of new scholarly editions.

One of the most significant new scholarly editions was the "Dead Sea Scrolls: A New Translation" by Michael Wise, Martin Abegg Jr., and Edward Cook, which was published in 1996. This edition was based on the images and transcriptions of the scrolls that had been released on the internet and it was considered to be more accurate and reliable than the earlier editions.

The Current Scholarly Editions

Currently, there are several scholarly editions of the DSS available, many of which are based on the images and transcriptions of the scrolls that have been released on the internet. These editions include the "Dead Sea Scrolls Bible" by Martin Abegg Jr., Peter Flint, and Eugene Ulrich, which was published in 1999 and "The Dead Sea Scrolls Translated: The Qumran Texts in English" by Florentino Garcia Martinez and Eibert Tigchelaar, which was published in 1996.

In addition to these editions, there are also several online resources that provide access to the scrolls in scholarly editions, such as the "Dead Sea Scrolls Digital Library" which is a project of the Israel Museum in Jerusalem and the "Leon Levy Dead Sea Scrolls Digital Library" which is a project of the Israel Antiquities Authority and the New York-based Leon Levy Dead Sea Scrolls Foundation.

The Importance of Scholarly Editions

Scholarly editions of the DSS are of paramount importance as they provide a critical examination of the texts, including transcriptions, translations, and annotations. These editions provide valuable insights into the history, literature, and religion of the Second Temple period and they have greatly contributed to our understanding of the development and transmission of the text of the Hebrew Bible.

The scholarly editions of the scrolls also provide a better understanding of the beliefs, practices, and history of the community at Qumran. The scrolls reveal the unique characteristics of the community and their distinct beliefs and practices which were different from the contemporary Jewish sects.

The scholarly editions also enable the comparison of the texts with other ancient texts such as the Septuagint and the Masoretic Text. This helps to understand the variations and similarities between the texts and gives valuable insights into the development and transmission of the text of the Hebrew Bible.

Furthermore, the scholarly editions also provide a deeper understanding of the scribal practices of the community at Qumran, including their methods of copying, preserving, and interpreting the texts. This helps to shed light on the scribal culture of the Second Temple period and the role of scribes in the transmission and preservation of sacred texts.

However, it is important to note that scholarly editions are not without limitations and biases. The process of transcription, translation, and annotation is always subjective, and different scholars may have different approaches and interpretations. Therefore, it is essential to consult multiple scholarly editions and to consult the original texts in order to gain a more comprehensive understanding of the scrolls.

In conclusion, scholarly editions of the Dead Sea Scrolls are a crucial aspect of the study and understanding of these ancient texts. They provide a critical examination of the texts, including transcriptions, translations, and annotations, and provide valuable insights into the history, literature, and religion of the Second Temple period. They also contribute to our understanding of the beliefs, practices, and history of the community at Qumran, as well as the development and transmission of the text of the Hebrew Bible. However, it is important to keep in mind the limitations and biases that can be present in the scholarly edition process and to consult multiple editions and the original texts for a more comprehensive understanding of the scrolls.

Radiocarbon Dating of the Dead Sea Scrolls

Introduction

Radiocarbon dating is a method of determining the age of an object by measuring the amount of carbon-14 it contains. This method has been used

INTRODUCTION TO THE TEXT OF THE OLD TESTAMENT

to date a wide range of materials, including organic materials such as wood, bone, and textiles. It has also been used to date the Dead Sea Scrolls (DSS). Radiocarbon dating has played an important role in determining the age of the scrolls, and it has helped to confirm the historical context in which they were written.

Background

The DSS were discovered in the 1940s in the vicinity of the Dead Sea, in the region of Qumran. The scrolls were found in 11 caves and they consisted of over 800 manuscripts, written in Hebrew, Aramaic, and Greek. The scrolls include copies of texts from the Hebrew Bible, as well as other Jewish texts that are not included in the Bible.

When the scrolls were first discovered, there was much debate about their age. Some scholars argued that they were written in the 2nd century BCE, while others argued that they were written in the 1st century CE. Radiocarbon dating was first used to date the scrolls in the 1950s, and it has been used to date the scrolls several times since then.

Methods of Radiocarbon Dating

Radiocarbon dating works by measuring the amount of carbon-14 in a sample. Carbon-14 is a radioactive isotope of carbon that is present in all living organisms. When an organism dies, it stops taking in carbon-14, and the carbon-14 in its body begins to decay. By measuring the amount of carbon-14 in a sample, scientists can determine how long ago the organism died.

To date the DSS, scientists have used three main methods of radiocarbon dating:

1. **Direct Dating of the Scrolls**: This method involves directly dating the scrolls themselves. However, because the scrolls are made of parchment, which is made from animal skin, the amount of carbon-14 present in the scrolls is very small. Therefore, this method is not very reliable for dating the scrolls.

2. **Dating the Scroll Jars**: This method involves dating the jars that were used to store the scrolls. The jars were made of clay, and they were sealed with a layer of pitch. This pitch contains carbon-14, and by dating the pitch, scientists can determine the age of the jars. However, this method is not entirely reliable, as the jars may not have been sealed at the same time as the scrolls were written.

3. **Dating the Scroll Wrappings**: This method involves dating the wrappings that were used to cover the scrolls. The wrappings were made of linen, and they contain carbon-14. By dating the wrappings, scientists can determine the age of the scrolls. This method is considered to be the most reliable for dating the scrolls, as the wrappings were likely to have been used at the same time as the scrolls were written.

Results and Conclusion

Radiocarbon dating has played an important role in determining the age of the Dead Sea Scrolls. The results of the radiocarbon dating have confirmed that the scrolls were written between the 3rd century BCE and the 1st century CE. This is consistent with the historical context in which the scrolls were written and with the historical context of the community at Qumran. However, it is important to note that radiocarbon dating is not an exact science, and the results can be affected by a number of factors, such as the preservation of the samples and the calibration of the radiocarbon dating equipment. Therefore, it is important to consider the results of radiocarbon dating in conjunction with other forms of evidence, such as paleography and archaeology, in order to gain a more comprehensive understanding of the scrolls.

Paleographic Dating of the Dead Sea Scrolls

Introduction

Paleography is the study of ancient writing systems and the scripts used to write texts. It is an essential tool for dating ancient texts, including the Dead Sea Scrolls (DSS). Paleographic dating is based on the analysis of the scripts and handwriting used in the texts, and it has been used to determine the dates of the DSS. This method has been crucial in determining the age of the scrolls, as well as in understanding the history and context in which they were written.

Background

The DSS were discovered in the 1940s in the vicinity of the Dead Sea, in the region of Qumran. The scrolls were found in 11 caves and they consisted of over 800 manuscripts, written in Hebrew, Aramaic, and Greek. The scrolls include copies of texts from the Hebrew Bible, as well as other Jewish texts that are not included in the Bible.

When the scrolls were first discovered, there was much debate about their age. Some scholars argued that they were written in the 2nd century

BCE, while others argued that they were written in the 1st century CE. Paleographic dating was first used to date the scrolls in the 1950s, and it has been used to date the scrolls several times since then.

Methods of Paleographic Dating

Paleographic dating is based on the analysis of the scripts and handwriting used in the texts. The main methods of paleographic dating are as follows:

1. **Palaeography**: This method involves analyzing the scripts and handwriting used in the texts. The scripts used in the DSS can be divided into three main categories: the paleo-Hebrew script, the Aramaic script, and the Greek script. By analyzing the scripts and handwriting used in the texts, scholars can determine the dates of the scrolls.

2. **Grammar and Vocabulary**: This method involves analyzing the grammar and vocabulary used in the texts. By analyzing the grammar and vocabulary used in the texts, scholars can determine the dates of the scrolls.

3. **Comparison with Other Texts**: This method involves comparing the DSS with other texts of the same period. By comparing the DSS with other texts of the same period, scholars can determine the dates of the scrolls.

Results and Conclusion

Paleographic dating has played an important role in determining the age of the Dead Sea Scrolls. The results of the paleographic dating have confirmed that the scrolls were written between the 3rd century BCE and the 1st century CE. This is consistent with the historical context in which the scrolls were written and with the historical context of the community at Qumran. However, it is important to note that paleographic dating is not an exact science, and the results can be affected by a number of factors, such as the preservation of the texts and the expertise of the scholars. Therefore, it is important to consider the results of paleographic dating in conjunction with other forms of evidence, such as radiocarbon dating and archaeology, in order to gain a more comprehensive understanding of the scrolls.

In conclusion, paleographic dating has been a crucial tool in determining the age of the Dead Sea Scrolls and understanding the history and context in which they were written. By analyzing the scripts and handwriting used in the texts, scholars have been able to determine the dates of the scrolls and gain a better understanding of the beliefs and practices of the community at

Qumran. However, it is important to keep in mind that paleographic dating is not an exact science and should be considered in conjunction with other forms of evidence for a more comprehensive understanding of the scrolls.

Ink and parchment

Introduction

The materials used to write the Dead Sea Scrolls (DSS) play a crucial role in understanding the scrolls and their preservation. The scrolls were written on parchment, papyrus, and sheets of bronze, and were written in ink made from carbon soot and cinnabar. The materials used in the scrolls have been studied in order to understand the production and preservation of the scrolls, as well as to gain insights into the beliefs and practices of the community that produced them.

Parchment and Papyrus

The DSS were written on parchment made of processed animal hide, known as vellum, which makes up approximately 85.5–90.5% of the scrolls. Papyrus, which is estimated to make up 8-13% of the scrolls, was also used. According to the Israeli Antiquities Authority, by using DNA testing for assembly purposes, it is believed that there may be a hierarchy in the religious importance of the texts based on which type of animal was used to create the hide. Scrolls written on goat and calf hides are considered by scholars to be more significant in nature, while those written on gazelle or ibex are considered to be less religiously significant in nature.

Parchment and papyrus were commonly used materials in ancient times for writing texts. Parchment, made from processed animal hide, was durable and could be reused. Papyrus, made from the pith of the papyrus plant, was less durable but could be produced more quickly. The use of both materials in the DSS suggests that the scrolls were produced for both long-term preservation and for more immediate use.

Bronze Sheets

Approximately 1.5% of the DSS were written on sheets of bronze. Bronze sheets were a less common material for writing texts, but they were durable and could be reused. The use of bronze sheets in the DSS suggests that these texts were considered to be of great importance and were intended for long-term preservation.

Ink

The DSS were written in ink made from carbon soot and cinnabar. Carbon soot was a common ingredient in ink in ancient times, and it was produced from olive oil lamps. Honey, oil, vinegar, and water were often added to the mixture to thin the ink to a proper consistency for writing. Galls were sometimes added to the ink to make it more resilient. The use of carbon soot in ink suggests that the scrolls were produced by a community that had access to olive oil lamps.

Cinnabar is a rarer ingredient in ink and is used only in four instances in the entire collection of DSS fragments. Cinnabar is a natural red pigment that was used to write in red ink, which was used to highlight specific words or phrases. The use of cinnabar in ink suggests that the scrolls were produced by a community that had access to this rare pigment, and that certain texts were considered to be of great importance.

Reed Pens

The DSS were written using reed pens. Reed pens were a common tool for writing in ancient times. They were made from the stem of a reed and were cut to a point to make them suitable for writing. The use of reed pens suggests that the scrolls were produced by a community that had access to reeds and knew how to make them into writing instruments.

Conclusion

The materials used to write the DSS provide insight into the production and preservation of the scrolls, as well as into the beliefs and practices of the community that produced them. The use of parchment and papyrus suggests that the scrolls were produced for both long-term preservation and for more immediate use. The use of bronze sheets suggests that certain texts were considered to be of great importance and were intended for long-term preservation. The use of carbon soot and cinnabar in ink suggests that the scrolls were produced by a community that had access to olive oil lamps and rare pigments, and that certain texts were considered to be of great importance. The use of reed pens suggests that the scrolls were produced by a community that had access to reeds and knew how to make them into writing instruments. Overall, the study of the materials used in the DSS provides valuable information about the scrolls and the community that produced them.

Edward D. Andrews

How Have the Dead Sea Scrolls Helped Textual Scholars Establish the Original Reading of the Hebrew Old Testament Manuscripts?

Introduction

The Dead Sea Scrolls, discovered in the 1940s in the vicinity of the Dead Sea, have greatly impacted the field of biblical studies and textual criticism. These scrolls, consisting of fragments from every book of the Hebrew Bible as well as extra-biblical texts, have provided scholars with valuable insight into the transmission and interpretation of the Hebrew Bible in the Second Temple period. In this paper, we will explore how the Dead Sea Scrolls have helped textual scholars establish the original reading of the Hebrew Old Testament manuscripts.

The Textual Diversity of the Dead Sea Scrolls:

One of the most significant contributions of the Dead Sea Scrolls to textual criticism is the diversity of textual variations they exhibit. The scrolls demonstrate that there were multiple versions of the Hebrew Bible in circulation during the Second Temple period, and that these versions had distinct variations in wording and spelling. This diversity in the text of the Hebrew Bible is evident in the scrolls, which preserve a wide range of textual traditions.

For example, the scrolls contain multiple versions of the book of Isaiah, with variations in wording and spelling. This includes the Great Isaiah Scroll (1QIsa), which is considered to be one of the most important scrolls for textual criticism, as well as the Isaiah Scroll from Cave 4 (4QIsa), which preserves a different version of the text. In addition, the scrolls also contain fragments from other versions of the Hebrew Bible, such as the Septuagint, which is a Greek translation of the Hebrew Bible.

The Importance of the Dead Sea Scrolls for Textual Criticism

The discovery of the Dead Sea Scrolls has provided scholars with valuable information for reconstructing the original text of the Hebrew Bible. The scrolls, which date back to the Second Temple period, provide a window into the textual history of the Hebrew Bible and demonstrate the diversity of textual traditions that existed in ancient times.

The scrolls also offer insight into the scribal practices of the Second Temple period, such as the use of spelling and grammatical variations, which can help scholars to reconstruct the original text of the Hebrew Bible. For example, scholars have used the scrolls to reconstruct the original spelling of proper names in the Hebrew Bible, such as the name of God, which was written in different ways in the scrolls.

The scrolls also provide evidence for the use of textual emendations and corrections, which can help scholars to reconstruct the original text of the Hebrew Bible. For example, the scrolls contain examples of scribal corrections, such as the insertion of words or phrases to clarify the meaning of a text.

The scrolls also offer insight into the interpretive practices of the Second Temple period. For example, many of the scrolls contain interpretive notes, which provide insight into the ways in which ancient readers understood and interpreted the text of the Hebrew Bible. These interpretive notes can help scholars to understand the original meaning of the text and to reconstruct the original reading of the Hebrew Bible.

The Role of the Dead Sea Scrolls in Establishing the Canon of the Hebrew Bible

The Dead Sea Scrolls have also played an important role in establishing the canon of the Hebrew Bible. The scrolls contain fragments from every book of the Hebrew Bible, as well as extra-biblical texts, which provide insight into the formation of the canon. For example, the scrolls contain fragments of books that were later considered to be part of the canon, such as the book of Isaiah, as well as fragments of books that were later considered to be apocryphal, such as the book of Tobit. The scrolls also provide insight into the ways in which ancient Jewish communities understood the canon of the Hebrew Bible.

Edward D. Andrews

CHAPTER 4 The Samaritan Pentateuch

Image 27 Samaritan High Priest and Abisha Scroll, 1905

The History of the Samaritans

Introduction

The history of the Samaritans is a complex and fascinating one, spanning several centuries and involving various cultures and religions. The Samaritans are an ethnic group and religious sect that originated in the ancient kingdom of Israel and have a unique history and set of beliefs that distinguish them from other Jewish and Christian communities. In this paper, we will delve into the history of the Samaritans, exploring their origins, beliefs, and interactions with other cultures and religions over time.

Origins

The origins of the Samaritans can be traced back to the 8th century BCE, when the Assyrian Empire conquered the northern kingdom of Israel, also known as the ten-tribe kingdom (2 Kings 17:22-33). The Assyrians exiled many of the Israelites and replaced them with settlers from other parts of their empire. These settlers, along with the Israelites who remained in the area, intermarried and formed a new ethnic group known as the Samaritans.

As historian Michael Avi-Yonah writes, "The Samaritans, who are the descendants of the Israelites who were not exiled by the Assyrians, and of the foreigners whom the Assyrians brought to Samaria" (Avi-Yonah, The Jews of Palestine: A Political History from the Bar Kokhba War to the Arab Conquest, 1976).

The Samaritans and the Hebrew Bible

The Samaritans considered themselves to be the true Israelites, and held the first five books of the Hebrew Bible, also known as the Torah or Pentateuch, in high regard. However, they had their own version of the text, known as the Samaritan Pentateuch, which contained variations and interpretations that differed from those of the Jewish community.

One example of these variations is found in the account of the Israelites' departure from Egypt, as recorded in the book of Exodus. The Samaritan Pentateuch states that the Israelites left Egypt in the "first month, on the fifteenth day of the month" (Exodus 12:40), while the Jewish version states that they left in the "month of Aviv" (Exodus 12:2). This difference reflects the Samaritans' use of a lunar calendar, as opposed to the Jewish community's use of a solar calendar.

As biblical scholar James Charlesworth notes, "The Samaritans have their own version of the Pentateuch, which they have preserved in their own script and language. They also have their own interpretation of the Pentateuch" (Charlesworth, Jesus and the Dead Sea Scrolls, 1995).

Edward D. Andrews

Image 28 Detail of Samaritan Pentateuch

The Samaritans and the Jewish Community

Throughout their history, the Samaritans have had a complex relationship with the Jewish community. The Jewish community viewed the Samaritans as heretics, and there were instances of hostility and violence between the two groups. However, there were also instances of cooperation and mutual respect.

One example of hostility between the two groups is found in the account of a confrontation between a group of Samaritans and the Jewish leader Nehemiah, as recorded in the book of Ezra. The Samaritans opposed Nehemiah's efforts to rebuild the walls of Jerusalem and sought to hinder the construction by bribing officials and spreading false rumors (Ezra 4:1-5).

On the other hand, there are examples of cooperation and mutual respect between the two groups. One example is found in the account of the Jewish leader Ezra, who traveled to Jerusalem from Babylon with a group of exiles, including some Samaritans (Ezra 8:15-20). Ezra and the exiles worked together to rebuild the Temple in Jerusalem and restore the worship of God.

As historian Paul Johnson writes, "The Samaritans, though constantly at odds with the Jews, were not always hostile to them. In fact, there were times of cooperation and mutual respect between the two groups. For example, during the time of the Hasmonean dynasty (140-37 BCE), the Samaritans and Jews cooperated in a rebellion against the Seleucid Empire, which had conquered the region.

INTRODUCTION TO THE TEXT OF THE OLD TESTAMENT

However, the relationship between the Samaritans and the Jewish community deteriorated during the Roman period. The Jewish historian Josephus Flavius, who lived during the 1st century CE, wrote extensively about the hostility and violence between the two groups. He also recorded the story of the destruction of the Samaritan temple on Mount Gerizim by the Jewish king John Hyrcanus in 128 BCE.

The Samaritans and Christianity

The relationship between the Samaritans and Christianity is also complex. The New Testament includes several accounts of interactions between Jesus and the Samaritans, some of which are positive and some of which are negative. For example, in the story of the "Good Samaritan" (Luke 10:25-37), Jesus tells of a Samaritan who helps a Jewish traveler in need, while in the story of the "Woman at the Well" (John 4:1-42), Jesus has a conversation with a Samaritan woman that is initially hostile but ends positively.

In the early Christian era, there were some Christian communities that had a positive relationship with the Samaritans, while others had a negative one. The early Christian leader Justin Martyr, for example, wrote positively of the Samaritans and their beliefs in his Apologies, while the early Christian bishop Epiphanius of Salamis wrote negatively of the Samaritans and their beliefs in his Panarion.

The Samaritans in the Middle Ages and Modern Times During the Middle Ages, the Samaritan community experienced persecution and decline, with their population decreasing significantly. In the modern era, the community has experienced a resurgence, with their population increasing to around 800 people today, primarily living in the West Bank and Israel.

The Samaritans continue to practice their unique beliefs and customs, including the use of the Samaritan Pentateuch, a distinct form of the Hebrew script and language, and annual pilgrimage to Mount Gerizim. They have also faced challenges in recent times such as political tension and lack of recognition of their rights.

Conclusion The history of the Samaritans is a rich and complex one, spanning several centuries and involving various cultures and religions. Despite facing challenges and persecution throughout history, the Samaritan community has managed to survive and maintain their unique beliefs and practices. The study of their history provides valuable insight into the development of religious and ethnic identity in the ancient Near East.

The Samaritan Pentateuch

Background

In 722-721 BCE, most of the inhabitants of the kingdom of Israel were deported by the Assyrian Empire. As a result, pagans from other territories of the empire were settled in their place. Over time, the descendants of those left in the area and those brought in by the Assyrians came to be known as the Samaritans.

The Samaritan Pentateuch

The Samaritans accepted the first five books of the Hebrew Scriptures, also known as the Pentateuch. In around the 4th century BCE, they produced their own version of the Pentateuch, called the Samaritan Pentateuch. This version was not a translation of the original Hebrew text, but rather a transliteration of the text into Samaritan characters with the addition of Samaritan idioms. Most of the extant manuscripts of the Samaritan Pentateuch are from no earlier than the 13th century CE.

Differences between the Samaritan and Hebrew Texts

There are around 6,000 differences between the Samaritan and Hebrew texts of the Pentateuch. However, the majority of these differences are not significant. One variation of interest is found at Exodus 12:40, where the Samaritan Pentateuch corresponds to the Septuagint, another version of the Hebrew Bible.

Importance of the Samaritan Pentateuch

While the Samaritan Pentateuch may not be as well-known as the Hebrew version, it is still an important text for scholars studying the history and development of the Bible. It provides insight into the variations and interpretations of the text that existed in different communities during ancient times. Additionally, studying the differences between the Samaritan Pentateuch and the Hebrew text can also provide insight into the evolution of the Hebrew language and the changes that occurred in the text over time.

The Samaritan community

The Samaritan community, which still exists today, holds the Samaritan Pentateuch in high regard and considers it to be the true version of the Pentateuch. They have a distinct set of beliefs and practices that differ from those of other Jewish and Christian communities.

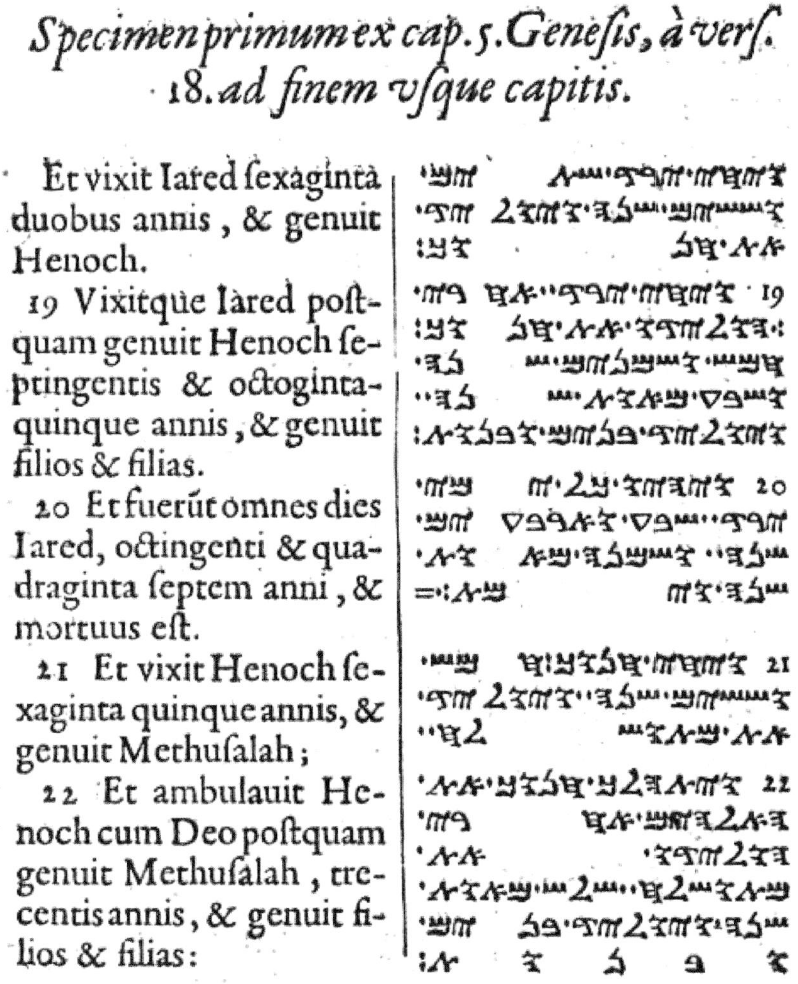

Specimen primum ex cap. 5. Genesis, à vers. 18. ad finem usque capitis.

Et vixit Iared sexaginta duobus annis, & genuit Henoch.
19 Vixitque Iared postquam genuit Henoch septingentis & octogintaquinque annis, & genuit filios & filias.
20 Et fuerût omnes dies Iared, octingenti & quadraginta septem anni, & mortuus est.
21 Et vixit Henoch sexaginta quinque annis, & genuit Methusalah;
22 Et ambulauit Henoch cum Deo postquam genuit Methusalah, trecentis annis, & genuit filios & filias:

Image 29 Genesis 5:18-22 as published by Jean Morin in 1631 in the first publication of the Samaritan Pentateuch

In conclusion, the Samaritan Pentateuch is an important historical document that provides insight into the variations and interpretations of the text of the Pentateuch during ancient times. It is also an important text for the Samaritan community, which holds it in high regard as the true version of the Pentateuch.

Edward D. Andrews

Canonical Significance of the Samaritan Pentateuch from the Samarian Perspective

Introduction

The Samaritan Pentateuch is the version of the first five books of the Hebrew Bible, also known as the Pentateuch, used by the Samaritan community. It is a unique and important text that has been preserved and studied by scholars for centuries, and it holds a significant canonical significance from the Samaritan perspective. In this paper, we will explore the canonical significance of the Samaritan Pentateuch from the Samaritan perspective, including its role in their religious beliefs and practices, and its relationship with other texts.

Role in Religious Beliefs and Practices

The Samaritan Pentateuch is considered by the Samaritan community to be the most sacred text, and it plays a central role in their religious beliefs and practices. It is believed to be the word of God, and it is used in the community's religious rituals and ceremonies, such as the annual pilgrimage to Mount Gerizim. The Samaritans also use the text as the basis for their interpretation of the Bible, and it is considered to be the authoritative text for their religious beliefs and practices.

As biblical scholar Reinhard Pummer writes, "The Samaritans hold the Pentateuch in the highest esteem, and they consider it to be the authoritative text for their religious beliefs and practices" (Pummer, An Introduction to Samaritan Studies, 2002).

Relationship with Other Texts

The Samaritan Pentateuch has a unique relationship with other texts, particularly the traditional Hebrew Pentateuch and the Septuagint. The text is similar to the traditional Hebrew Pentateuch, but it has several variations and additions, such as the insertion of the name of God, "JHVH," in more places than in the traditional Hebrew text. Additionally, the Samaritan Pentateuch corresponds with the Septuagint in some cases, such as at Exodus 12:40, which is significant to the Samaritans because it aligns with their beliefs and practices.

The Samaritans also have their own distinct canon of texts which includes the Samaritan Pentateuch, Joshua, Judges, and a version of the book of Dueteronomy. These texts are considered to be the only authoritative texts, and the Samaritans reject the rest of the Hebrew Bible as well as the New Testament.

INTRODUCTION TO THE TEXT OF THE OLD TESTAMENT

However, it is important to note that the Samaritans do not reject the other texts in the Hebrew Bible and the New Testament entirely, but rather they interpret them differently from the traditional Jewish understanding.

Canonical Significance

The canonical significance of the Samaritan Pentateuch from the Samaritan perspective is that it is considered to be the most sacred and authoritative text for their religious beliefs and practices. It holds a central role in their religious rituals and ceremonies and is used as the basis for their interpretation of the Bible. Furthermore, it is considered to be the only legitimate version of the Pentateuch and the only authoritative source of the Law.

The Samaritan Pentateuch, in the Samaritan perspective, is considered to be the only true and authentic version of the Pentateuch, and it is believed to have been revealed by God to Moses on Mount Sinai, and that it has been passed down to them through the ages.

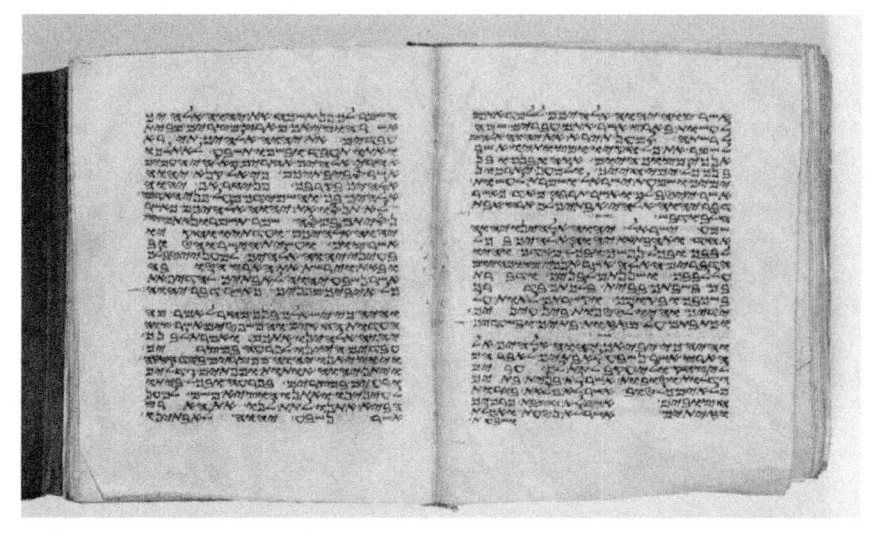

Conclusion

The canonical significance of the Samaritan Pentateuch from the Samaritan perspective is that it is considered to be the most sacred and authoritative text for their religious beliefs and practices. It holds a central role in their religious rituals and ceremonies and is used as the basis for their interpretation of the Bible. Furthermore, it is considered to be the only legitimate version of the Pentateuch and the only authoritative source of the Law. The text is unique and provides valuable insight into the history and development of the Bible, as well as the beliefs and practices of the Samaritan community.

Characteristics of the Samaritan Pentateuch

Introduction

The Samaritan Pentateuch, also known as the Samaritan Torah, is the version of the first five books of the Hebrew Bible, also known as the Pentateuch, used by the Samaritan community. It is a unique and important text that has been preserved and studied by scholars for centuries. In this paper, we will explore the characteristics of the Samaritan Pentateuch, including its text, language, and interpretation.

Text The text of the Samaritan

Pentateuch is similar to that of the traditional Hebrew Pentateuch, but with some significant variations. One of the most notable differences is the use of a different script. While the traditional Hebrew Pentateuch is written in the Hebrew script, the Samaritan Pentateuch is written in a script known as the Samaritan script, which is a variation of the ancient Hebrew script.

Additionally, the Samaritan Pentateuch includes several unique readings and additions, such as the insertion of the name of God, "JHVH," in more places than in the traditional Hebrew text. The Samaritan Pentateuch also includes a different division of the books, with the book of Leviticus divided into two parts and the book of Deuteronomy divided into three parts.

As biblical scholar James Charlesworth notes, "The Samaritans have their own version of the Pentateuch, which they have preserved in their own script and language. They also have their own interpretation of the Pentateuch" (Charlesworth, Jesus and the Dead Sea Scrolls, 1995).

Language

The language of the Samaritan Pentateuch is a form of Hebrew, with some elements of Aramaic and other languages. It is also characterized by the use of Samaritan idioms and expressions that are unique to the community. For example, the Samaritan Pentateuch uses the term "mount of blessing" to refer to Mount Gerizim, which is considered by the Samaritans to be the true location of the Temple, rather than Jerusalem which is considered by the Jews.

INTRODUCTION TO THE TEXT OF THE OLD TESTAMENT

As scholar Moshe Florentin writes, "The language of the Samaritan Pentateuch is a form of Hebrew that incorporates many Aramaic words and idioms, reflecting the multilingual environment of ancient Palestine" (Florentin, The Samaritans: A Profile, 2009).

Interpretation

The interpretation of the Samaritan Pentateuch also differs from that of the traditional Hebrew Pentateuch. For example, the Samaritans interpret the Ten Commandments as referring specifically to the worship of God on Mount Gerizim, rather than as a general code of ethics. They also interpret the story of Jacob and Esau, as recorded in the book of Genesis, as emphasizing the superior status of the tribe of Ephraim, which is considered by the Samaritans to be the true Israelite tribe.

As biblical scholar Reinhard Pummer writes, "The Samaritans have their own interpretation of the Pentateuch, which emphasizes their unique beliefs and practices, such as the worship of God on Mount Gerizim and the primacy of the tribe of Ephraim" (Pummer, An Introduction to Samaritan Studies, 2002).

Manuscripts and Translations

The earliest known manuscripts of the Samaritan Pentateuch date back to the 13th century CE, however, the text is believed to have been in use since the 4th century BCE. Today, the Samaritan community still uses the text in their religious practices and ceremonies.

There have been several translations of the Samaritan Pentateuch into different languages such as English, French, and German, but the original text is in the Samaritan script, which is a variation of the ancient Hebrew script and is not widely understood by those outside of the Samaritan community.

Importance in Biblical Studies

The Samaritan Pentateuch is an important text for scholars studying the history and development of the Bible. It provides insight into the variations and interpretations of the text that existed in different communities during ancient times. Furthermore, it allows scholars to study the evolution of the Hebrew language and the changes that occurred in the text over time.

Comparison with Other Versions

Scholars also compare the Samaritan Pentateuch to other versions of the Hebrew Bible, such as the Septuagint and the Masoretic Text. For example, there are around 6,000 differences between the Samaritan and

Hebrew texts of the Pentateuch. However, the majority of these differences are not significant, such as spelling variations or variations in word order. But there are some variations that are of significant interest, such as the one at Exodus 12:40, where the Samaritan Pentateuch corresponds to the Septuagint.

Importance for the Samaritan Community

For the Samaritan community, the Samaritan Pentateuch is a central text that is held in high regard. They have a distinct set of beliefs and practices that differ from those of other Jewish and Christian communities, and the text is used in their religious ceremonies and practices. The preservation and continuation of the use of this text is essential for the preservation of the Samaritan culture, heritage and identity.

Conclusion

The Samaritan Pentateuch is a unique and important text that has been preserved and studied by scholars for centuries. It is characterized by its text, language, and interpretation, which differ from those of the traditional Hebrew Pentateuch. The text provides valuable insight into the variations and interpretations of the text that existed in different communities during ancient times and the evolution of the Hebrew language. It is also a central text for the Samaritan community, and its preservation and continuation of use is essential for the preservation of the Samaritan culture, heritage, and identity.

Chronology of the Samaritan Pentateuch

Introduction

The Chronology of the Samaritan Pentateuch is a complex and multi-faceted topic that has been the subject of much scholarly debate and research. The Samaritan Pentateuch is the version of the first five books of the Hebrew Bible, also known as the Pentateuch, used by the Samaritan community, and its chronology provides insight into the history of the text and the community. In this paper, we will explore the chronology of the Samaritan Pentateuch, including its origins, development, transmission and preservation.

Origins

The origins of the Samaritan Pentateuch can be traced back to the 8th century BCE, when the Assyrian Empire conquered the northern kingdom of Israel, also known as the ten-tribe kingdom (2 Kings 17:22-33). The

INTRODUCTION TO THE TEXT OF THE OLD TESTAMENT

Assyrians exiled many of the Israelites and replaced them with settlers from other parts of their empire. These settlers, along with the Israelites who remained in the area, intermarried and formed a new ethnic group known as the Samaritans.

As historian Michael Avi-Yonah writes, "The Samaritans, who are the descendants of the Israelites who were not exiled by the Assyrians, and of the foreigners whom the Assyrians brought to Samaria" (Avi-Yonah, The Jews of Palestine: A Political History from the Bar Kokhba War to the Arab Conquest, 1976).

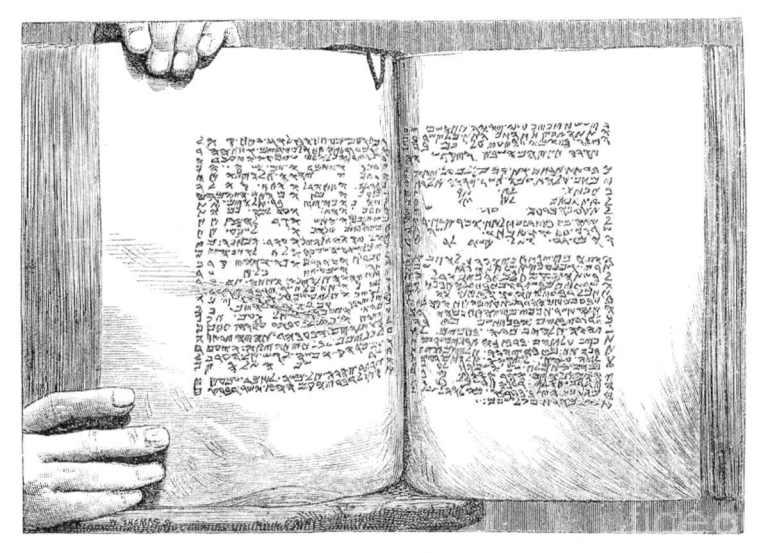

TWO PAGES OF A BOOK COPY OF THE SAMARITAN PENTATEUCH.
FROM A PHOTOGRAPH TAKEN FOR THE "PALESTINE EXPLORATION FUND."

Development

The development of the Samaritan Pentateuch can be divided into several phases. The first phase is the period of formation, which is believed to have occurred in the 4th century BCE. During this period, the Samaritans produced their own version of the Pentateuch, which was not a translation of the original Hebrew text, but rather a transliteration of the text into Samaritan characters with the addition of Samaritan idioms.

Transmission

The second phase is the period of transmission, which lasted from the 4th century BCE to the 13th century CE. During this period, the text was transmitted orally and through manuscripts, with the earliest known manuscripts dating back to the 13th century CE. It is believed that the text was passed down from generation to generation through the Samaritan community, although there is no concrete evidence to support this.

Preservation

The third phase is the period of preservation, which began in the 13th century CE and continues to the present day. During this period, the text has been preserved and used by the Samaritan community in their religious practices and ceremonies. The Samaritans have made efforts to preserve the text through copying and preserving the manuscripts and also by passing down the knowledge of the script to the next generations.

Comparison with Other Versions

In comparison with other versions of the Hebrew Bible, such as the Septuagint and the Masoretic Text, there are around 6,000 differences between the Samaritan and Hebrew texts of the Pentateuch. However, the majority of these differences are not significant, such as spelling variations or variations in word order. But there are some variations that are of significant interest, such as the one at Exodus 12:40, where the Samaritan Pentateuch corresponds to the Septuagint.

Conclusion

The chronology of the Samaritan Pentateuch is a complex topic that spans several centuries, involving various cultures and religions. The text has its origins in the 8th century BCE, with the formation of the Samaritan community after the Assyrian conquest of the northern kingdom of Israel. It then underwent a period of development and transmission, before being preserved and used by the Samaritan community to this day. The text is unique and provides valuable insight into the history and development of the Bible, as well as the beliefs and practices of the Samaritan community.

Manuscripts of the Samaritan Pentateuch

Introduction

The Samaritan Pentateuch is a version of the first five books of the Hebrew Bible, also known as the Pentateuch, used by the Samaritan community. It is considered to be the most sacred text for the Samaritans, and it has been preserved and transmitted through the centuries in the form of manuscripts. In this paper, we will explore the manuscripts of the Samaritan Pentateuch, including their history, characteristics, and importance for the study of the text.

INTRODUCTION TO THE TEXT OF THE OLD TESTAMENT

History of the Manuscripts

The earliest known manuscripts of the Samaritan Pentateuch date back to the 13th century CE. These manuscripts were written on parchment and were produced by the Samaritan community. They were primarily used in religious ceremonies and were passed down from generation to generation.

Over the centuries, the Samaritans have made efforts to preserve and copy the manuscripts, and many of them have been passed down to the present day. The manuscripts are kept in various collections, including the British Library, the Vatican Library, and the National Library of Russia.

Characteristics of the Manuscripts

The Samaritan Pentateuch manuscripts are written in the Samaritan script, which is a form of the ancient Hebrew script. They are written in black ink, and the text is divided into columns and sections. The manuscripts also include vocalization, accents and cantillation marks, which are used to indicate the correct pronunciation and musical intonation of the text.

The manuscripts also include the division of the text into verses, which is not found in the traditional Hebrew text. This division is based on the Samaritan interpretation of the text and is unique to the Samaritan Pentateuch.

Importance for the Study of the Text

The manuscripts of the Samaritan Pentateuch are important for the study of the text as they provide insight into the history, transmission, and preservation of the text. They also allow scholars to study the variations and differences between the Samaritan and traditional Hebrew texts.

For example, the manuscripts can be used to study the development of the Samaritan script and the changes that occurred in the text over time. They can also be used to compare the text with other versions of the Hebrew Bible, such as the Septuagint and the Masoretic Text.

In addition, the manuscripts also provide insight into the religious beliefs and practices of the Samaritan community, as they were primarily used in religious ceremonies and were passed down from generation to generation.

As biblical scholar Reinhard Pummer writes, "The study of the manuscripts of the Samaritan Pentateuch is essential for understanding the history, transmission, and preservation of the text, as well as for understanding the religious beliefs and practices of the Samaritan community" (Pummer, An Introduction to Samaritan Studies, 2002).

Conclusion

The manuscripts of the Samaritan Pentateuch are an essential part of the history, transmission and preservation of the text. They are written in the ancient Hebrew script and are unique to the Samaritan community. They provide insight into the variations and differences between the Samaritan and traditional Hebrew texts and also provide a glimpse into the religious practices and beliefs of the Samaritans. The manuscripts are important for the study of the text, as they are primary sources for the history, transmission and preservation of the text and also provide a valuable insight into the religious practices and beliefs of the Samaritan community.

Translations of the Samaritan Pentateuch into English

History of Translations

The first known translation of the Samaritan Pentateuch into English was completed in the 17th century by the English theologian, Edward Pococke. This translation was based on a manuscript of the Samaritan Pentateuch that Pococke had obtained while traveling in the Middle East. Pococke's translation was published in 1655 and is considered to be the first scholarly translation of the text.

Since then, several other translations have been made, including the one by J.W. Nutt in 1887 and by A.D. White in 1891. In the 20th century, more translations have been made such as the one by Alan Crown in 2013, and by Robert T. Anderson in 2016.

Characteristics of Translations

Translations of the Samaritan Pentateuch into English have been made by various scholars and religious figures, who have used different methods and approaches for the translation. Some translations are literal, trying to maintain the original meaning and style of the text, while others are more interpretive, trying to convey the text's message to a wider audience.

Translations also differ in their use of language, some use archaic language and terminology that is no longer in common use, while others use modern language, making the text more accessible to a wider audience.

Importance for the Study of the Text

Translations of the Samaritan Pentateuch into English is important for the study of the text as they make it more accessible to scholars and the general public. They allow for a better understanding of the text, its variations, and its significance for the Samaritan community.

Translations also allow for a comparison of the text with other versions of the Hebrew Bible, such as the Septuagint and the Masoretic Text, and can provide insight into the development and transmission of the text.

Translations also provide insight into the religious beliefs and practices of the Samaritan community and can help scholars to better understand the context and background of the text.

Furthermore, translations can also be used in the classroom and in religious studies, as they provide a valuable resource for the study of the history, language and culture of the ancient near east.

As biblical scholar Reinhard Pummer writes, "Translations of the Samaritan Pentateuch into English are important for the study of the text as they make it more accessible to scholars and the general public, allowing for a better understanding of the text, its variations, and its significance for the Samaritan community" (Pummer, An Introduction to Samaritan Studies, 2002).

Conclusion

Translations of the Samaritan Pentateuch into English have played a significant role in making the text more accessible to scholars and the general public. They provide a valuable resource for the study of the text, its variations, and its significance for the Samaritan community. They also provide a valuable insight into the religious beliefs and practices of the Samaritans and allow for a comparison of the text with other versions of the Hebrew Bible. Furthermore, translations are also used in religious studies and the classroom, providing a valuable resource for the study of the history, language and culture of the ancient near east.

Pre-Samaritan Texts

Introduction

The discovery of the scrolls at Qumran has had a significant impact on the study of the Samaritan Pentateuch. The scrolls have revealed the existence of pre-Samaritan texts, which share certain characteristics with the Samaritan Pentateuch but lack the Samaritan corrections. This has led to a re-evaluation of the significance of the Samaritan Pentateuch for textual criticism and has provided new insights into the independent textual tradition that the Samaritan Pentateuch developed from. In this paper, we will explore the concept of pre-Samaritan texts, their characteristics, and their importance for the study of the Samaritan Pentateuch.

Pre-Samaritan Texts

Characteristics and Significance Pre-Samaritan texts refer to a group of non-Masoretic manuscripts that have been discovered at Qumran. These texts share certain characteristics with the Samaritan Pentateuch, such as harmonization and simplification, but lack the Samaritan corrections. This suggests that the Samaritan Pentateuch was based on an independent textual tradition that it developed further.

As biblical scholar Emanuel Tov notes, "The relation between the harmonizing texts found at Qumran and the Samaritan Pentateuch differs from that of the proto-Masoretic and Masoretic texts. For while these show only a relatively few variants and differences, Qumran has (thus far) produced no manuscripts demonstrating any direct relationship to the Samaritan Pentateuch beyond the common characteristics of harmonizing and simplification" (Tov, Textual Criticism of the Hebrew Bible, 2001).

The discovery of pre-Samaritan texts at Qumran has led to a re-evaluation of the significance of the Samaritan Pentateuch for textual criticism. It has shown that the Samaritan Pentateuch was not simply a later revision of the Masoretic Text from a Samaritan viewpoint, but rather it was based on an independent textual tradition.

The pre-Samaritan texts also provide insight into the textual tradition that was widespread in the 3rd and 2nd centuries BCE, which was shared by the Samaritan Pentateuch and other manuscripts.

However, it is important to note that the evidence of pre-Samaritan texts is relatively restricted, and what can be known about this textual tradition is limited. The texts with pre-Samaritan characteristics found at Qumran are most likely not from the Qumran community, and they offer readings that are partly free, partly popular and harmonizing, somewhat similar to the later text of the Samaritan Pentateuch.

Conclusion

The discovery of pre-Samaritan texts at Qumran has had a significant impact on the study of the Samaritan Pentateuch. These texts have revealed the existence of an independent textual tradition that the Samararian Pentateuch developed from. They share certain characteristics, such as harmonization and simplification, with the Samaritan Pentateuch, but lack the Samaritan corrections. This has led to a re-evaluation of the significance of the Samaritan Pentateuch for textual criticism and has provided new insights into the independent textual tradition that the Samaritan Pentateuch developed from. The pre-Samaritan texts also provide insight into the textual tradition that was widespread in the 3rd and 2nd centuries BCE, which was shared by the Samaritan Pentateuch and other manuscripts. However, it is important to note that the evidence of pre-Samaritan texts is relatively restricted, and what can be known about this textual tradition is limited. The pre-Samaritan texts found at Qumran are most likely not from the Qumran community and offer readings that are partly free, partly popular and harmonizing, somewhat similar to the later text of the Samaritan Pentateuch.

Scholarly Editions of the Samaritan Pentateuch

History of Scholarly Editions

The first scholarly edition of the Samaritan Pentateuch was produced by the German orientalist, Johann Heinrich Hottinger, in 1655. Hottinger based his edition on a manuscript of the Samaritan Pentateuch that he had obtained during his travels in the Middle East. This edition was primarily focused on the textual differences between the Samaritan Pentateuch and the Masoretic Text, and it was the first scholarly work to compare the two texts.

Since then, several other scholarly editions have been produced, including the one by J.W. Nutt in 1887 and by A.D. White in 1891. In the 20th century, more editions have been produced such as the one by Alan Crown in 2013, and by Robert T. Anderson in 2016.

Characteristics of Scholarly Editions

Scholarly editions of the Samaritan Pentateuch vary in their focus and approach. Some editions are primarily focused on textual criticism and compare the Samaritan Pentateuch to other versions of the Hebrew Bible, such as the Septuagint and the Masoretic Text. Others focus on the language and grammar of the text, providing critical apparatus and notes on the text.

Some editions also include the vocalization, accents and cantillation marks, which are used to indicate the correct pronunciation and musical intonation of the text. The editions also include the division of the text into verses, which is not found in the traditional Hebrew text.

Importance for the Study of the Text

Scholarly editions of the Samaritan Pentateuch are important for the study of the text as they provide a critical edition of the text, which can be used for research and teaching. The editions include critical apparatus, notes and other information that can aid in the understanding of the text.

They also provide a comparison of the text with other versions of the Hebrew Bible, such as the Septuagint and the Masoretic Text, which can provide insight into the development and transmission of the text. These editions also include the vocalization, accents and cantillation marks, which are used to indicate the correct pronunciation and musical intonation of the text, helping scholars to understand the language and grammar of the text.

Furthermore, scholarly editions also provide insight into the religious beliefs and practices of the Samaritan community and can help scholars to better understand the context and background of the text.

Additionally, these editions can serve as a valuable resource for the study of the history, language and culture of the ancient near east, and can be used in religious studies, biblical studies, and other related fields. As biblical scholar Reinhard Pummer writes, "Scholarly editions of the Samaritan Pentateuch are important for the study of the text as they provide a critical edition of the text, which can be used for research and teaching, and provide insight into the religious beliefs and practices of the Samaritan community" (Pummer, An Introduction to Samaritan Studies, 2002).

Conclusion

Scholarly editions of the Samaritan Pentateuch have played a significant role in the study of the text. These editions provide a critical edition of the text, which can be used for research and teaching and provide insight into the religious beliefs and practices of the Samaritan community. They also provide a comparison of the text with other versions of the Hebrew Bible, such as the Septuagint and the Masoretic Text, and can provide insight into the development and transmission of the text. Furthermore, scholarly editions provide valuable information on the language and grammar of the text, which helps scholars to better understand the context and background of the text. These editions are also useful resources for the study of the history, language, and culture of the ancient near east and can be used in religious studies, biblical studies, and other related fields.

INTRODUCTION TO THE TEXT OF THE OLD TESTAMENT

How Has the Samaritan Pentateuch Helped Textual Scholars Establish the Original Reading of the Hebrew Old Testament Manuscripts?

The Samaritan Pentateuch, also known as the Samaritan Torah, is a version of the Hebrew Bible that is used by the Samaritan community, a small sect that emerged during the Second Temple period in ancient Israel. The Samaritan Pentateuch differs in both content and wording from the Masoretic Text, which is the standard Hebrew text of the Jewish Bible, and is considered by many scholars to be an important witness to the diversity of textual traditions that existed in ancient Judaism.

The Samaritan Pentateuch has played a significant role in helping textual scholars establish the original reading of the Hebrew Old Testament manuscripts. One of the primary ways in which the Samaritan Pentateuch has contributed to this effort is through its preservation of alternative readings and variant traditions that are not found in the Masoretic Text.

One example of this is the Samaritan Pentateuch's preservation of the Tetragrammaton, the four-letter name of God in Hebrew, which is not found in the Masoretic Text. This name is considered by many scholars to be an important witness to the original reading of the Hebrew Old Testament manuscripts and its presence in the Samaritan Pentateuch has helped scholars reconstruct the original text of the Hebrew Bible.

Additionally, the Samaritan Pentateuch has also helped scholars establish the original reading of the Hebrew Old Testament manuscripts through its preservation of alternative readings and variant traditions that are not found in the Masoretic Text. For example, the Samaritan Pentateuch preserves a number of alternative readings in the book of Deuteronomy that are not found in the Masoretic Text. These alternative readings have helped scholars establish the original reading of the Hebrew Old Testament manuscripts in this book.

Moreover, the Samaritan Pentateuch is also significant for the study of the biblical text as it preserves some readings that have been lost in the Masoretic Text. For example, the Samaritan Pentateuch preserves the reading of Deuteronomy 34:6 that says that Joshua was filled with the spirit of wisdom, while the Masoretic Text says that Joshua was filled with the spirit of God. This is significant because it shows that the Samaritan Pentateuch preserves a tradition that has been lost in the Masoretic Text, and it helps scholars understand the textual history of the biblical text.

Furthermore, the Samaritan Pentateuch also contains a number of unique additions and expansions, such as a longer version of the Shema in Deuteronomy 6:4-9, which provides important insights into the religious beliefs and practices of the Samaritan community.

In conclusion, the Samaritan Pentateuch is an important witness to the diversity of textual traditions that existed in ancient Judaism and has played a significant role in helping textual scholars establish the original reading of the Hebrew Old Testament manuscripts. Its preservation of alternative readings and variant traditions, as well as its unique additions and expansions, provides important insights into the textual history of the biblical text and the beliefs and practices of the ancient Samaritan community.

INTRODUCTION TO THE TEXT OF THE OLD TESTAMENT

CHAPTER 5 The Greek Septuagint

The Greek Septuagint

The Greek Septuagint, also known as the LXX, is a translation of the Hebrew Bible into Greek. It is considered to be one of the most significant translations of the biblical texts in the history of Christianity and Judaism. The Septuagint is a crucial text for scholars and theologians, as it provides insight into the religious and cultural context of the ancient world.

History of the Septuagint

The Septuagint is believed to have been translated in Alexandria, Egypt, in the 3rd century BCE during the reign of Ptolemy Philadelphus. According to tradition, the translation was commissioned by the king and was completed by 72 Jewish scholars. The story is recorded in the Letter of Aristeas, a Hellenistic document written in the 2nd century BCE, which states that the king desired a Greek translation of the Jewish law for his library in Alexandria.

Image 30 Nash Papyrus, dated from the second or first century B.C.E., showing portions of Exodus and Deuteronomy. The divine name appears a number of times in the Hebrew text.

From the book *A Pre-Massoretic Biblical Papyrus*, by Stanley A. Cook, M. A. (1903)

The Septuagint began as a translation of the Pentateuch, the first five books of the Hebrew Bible, and was subsequently expanded to include the rest of the Hebrew Scriptures. The translation was not done in one go, but rather gradually over a period of time. The dating of the completion of the Septuagint is debated among scholars, with estimates ranging from the 2nd century BCE to the 1st century CE.

177

Importance of the Septuagint

The Septuagint played an important role in the spread of Christianity, as it was the version of the Bible used by Greek-speaking Jews and Christians in Egypt and other parts of the Mediterranean. The New Testament, which was written in Greek, frequently quotes from the Septuagint. This can be seen in the fact that the Septuagint's Greek wording is often closer to the wording found in the New Testament than the Hebrew text.

The Septuagint also provides valuable insight into the religious and cultural context of the ancient world. The translation reflects the Greek language and thought of the time, and it incorporates elements of Greek culture and religion into the text. This can be seen in the use of Greek terms and concepts, as well as in the addition of apocryphal books to the Septuagint that are not found in the Hebrew Bible.

Manuscripts of the Septuagint

The Septuagint has been preserved in numerous manuscripts, many of which are fragmentary. The oldest extant manuscripts of the Septuagint are the Rylands Papyrus and the Papyrus Fouad 266, which date to the 2nd century BCE and 1st century BCE respectively. Some of the oldest extant manuscripts of the Septuagint date back to the 2nd century BCE and 1st century BCE. These include fragments of Leviticus and Deuteronomy from the 2nd century BCE (Rahlfs nos. 801, 819, and 957) and fragments of Genesis, Exodus, Leviticus, Numbers, Deuteronomy, and the Twelve Minor Prophets from the 1st century BCE (Alfred Rahlfs nos. 802, 803, 805, 848, 942, and 943). These manuscripts provide valuable insight into the early history and development of the Septuagint.

There are also three famous uncial manuscripts of the Septuagint written on vellum: the Vatican Manuscript No. 1209, the Sinaitic Manuscript, and the Alexandrine Manuscript. These manuscripts date to the 4th and 5th centuries CE and are considered some of the oldest and most complete versions of the Septuagint.

The Vatican Manuscript No. 1209 is almost complete, while the Sinaitic Manuscript is missing parts of the Hebrew Scriptures. The Alexandrine Manuscript is relatively complete, but lacks parts of Genesis, First Samuel, and Psalms.

Conclusion

The Greek Septuagint is a significant translation of the Hebrew Bible into Greek, with a rich history and cultural context. It played an important role in the spread of Christianity and provides valuable insight into the ancient world. The Septuagint has been preserved in numerous manuscripts, some of which date back to the 2nd century BCE and others date to the 4th and 5th centuries CE and are considered to be some of the oldest and most complete versions of the text.

The *Kaige* Revision

The Kaige revision is a name given to a specific version of the Greek Septuagint, which is known for its characteristic translation of the Hebrew word "גם" (also) or "וגם" (and also) with the Greek phrase "καὶ γε" (kai ge). This version also wrote out the Tetragrammaton, God's covenant name YHWH, in the Paleo-Hebrew script rather than translating it into Greek.

This revision is believed to have been made in the late first century BCE or early first century CE, and it constitutes a revision of the Old Greek translation in the direction of conformity with the protomasoretic text. It is also sometimes referred to as the kaige-Theodotion revision due to its shared readings with another Greek translation known as Theodotion.

The Septuagint was eventually adopted by the Christian churches, and it was often used in debates between Christians and Jews. As a result, it came to be viewed with suspicion by the Jews, which led to the production of three rival Greek translations in the second century CE. These translations each bore a different relationship to the original Septuagint, and they were created in an attempt to address the perceived inaccuracies and inconsistencies in the Septuagint.

The Kaige revision is an important example of the evolution of the Septuagint and its continued use and adaptation over time. It highlights the ongoing process of translation and revision that took place in the effort to ensure accuracy and consistency in the Greek translation of the Hebrew Bible.

Aquila (Siglum α)

Aquila (siglum α) is a Greek translation of the Hebrew Bible that was produced in the 2nd century CE by a Jewish proselyte named Aquila. It is considered one of the earliest of the rival versions of the Septuagint, and it is known for its literal and precise translation style.

POxy3522 [Goettingen #???] Job 42
Ashmolean Museum, Oxford, England

papyrus roll
dated to 1st ce
(paleographic)

note tetragrammaton
(paleo-Hebrew)

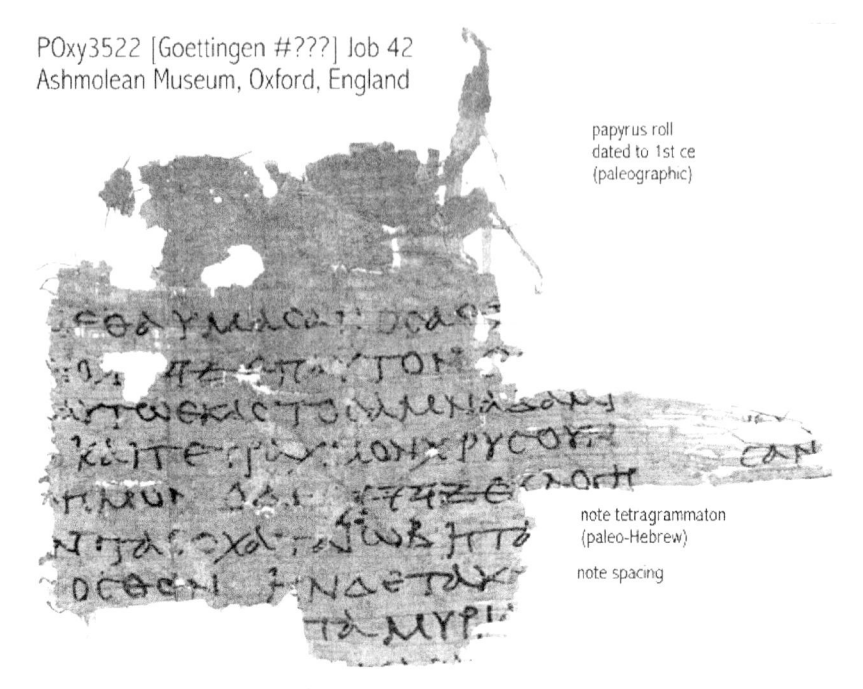

note spacing

Background of Aquila

Aquila was a Jewish proselyte and a disciple of Rabbi Akiva, a prominent Jewish sage and leader of the 2nd century CE. He is believed to have been born in Sinope, a city on the Black Sea, and to have converted to Judaism in his youth. According to some sources, he was a slave who was freed by a Jewish master and subsequently converted to Judaism.

Aquila's main purpose in translating the Hebrew Bible into Greek was to provide a version that would be more accurate and faithful to the original Hebrew text, as he saw the Septuagint as being riddled with inaccuracies and inconsistencies. He aimed to create a translation that would be more easily understood by Greek-speaking Jews, and that would be more useful for apologetics and polemics against Christian opponents.

Translation style of Aquila

Aquila's translation is known for its literal and precise style. He sought to maintain a close correspondence between the Hebrew and Greek text, and he was careful to preserve the word order and grammatical forms of the original Hebrew. According to the Jewish historian Flavius Josephus, Aquila's translation was "more interpretative than that of the Seventy [the Septuagint], but less interpretative than that of Theodotion."

The translation style of Aquila is very concise, and it is often considered as very difficult to read because of the use of uncommon or obscure Greek words, and a very free rendering of the Hebrew text.

Impact of Aquila's translation

Aquila's translation had a significant impact on the Jewish community of the 2nd century CE. It was widely used by Greek-speaking Jews, and it became the standard version of the Hebrew Bible for many synagogues. Aquila's translation was also used by early Christian writers such as Justin Martyr and Clement of Alexandria, who quoted from it in their apologetic works.

Aquila's translation also had a lasting impact on the development of the Septuagint. His work laid the foundation for later revisions of the Septuagint, such as the Symmachus and Theodotion revisions, which sought to improve upon Aquila's literal and precise style by introducing a more idiomatic and readable Greek text.

In conclusion, Aquila (siglum α) is a important Greek translation of the Hebrew Bible that was produced in the 2nd century CE by a Jewish proselyte named Aquila. His purpose was to provide a version that would be more accurate and faithful to the original Hebrew text, and his translation is known for its literal and precise style. It had a significant impact on the Jewish community of the 2nd century CE and laid the foundation for later revisions of the Septuagint.

Symmachus (σ)

Symmachus (σ) is a Greek translation of the Hebrew Bible that was produced in the 2nd century CE by a Samaritan who had converted to Judaism. His translation is considered one of the rival versions of the Septuagint, and it is known for its idiomatic and readable style.

Background of Symmachus

Symmachus was a Samaritan who converted to Judaism and worked at the end of the first century CE. Little is known about his life, but it is believed that he was a contemporary of Aquila, the translator of the rival version of the Septuagint.

He probably based his work on that of Aquila, and aimed to produce a more idiomatic and readable Greek text that would be more easily understood by Greek-speaking Jews. According to the Jewish historian

Flavius Josephus, Symmachus's translation was "more interpretative than that of Aquila, but less interpretative than that of Theodotion."

Translation style of Symmachus

Symmachus's translation is known for its idiomatic and readable style. Unlike Aquila, who sought to maintain a close correspondence between the Hebrew and Greek text, Symmachus aimed to produce a more idiomatic Greek text that would be more easily understood by Greek-speaking Jews. He made use of common Greek words and phrases, and he sought to convey the meaning of the Hebrew text in a more natural and accessible way.

Symmachus also sought to retain the sense of the original Hebrew text and retain the meaning of the Hebrew words as much as possible. He also added explanatory notes to help the reader understand the meaning of the text.

Impact of Symmachus's Translation

Symmachus's translation had a significant impact on the Jewish community of the 2nd century CE. It was widely used by Greek-speaking Jews and it was considered to be one of the most popular versions of the Hebrew Bible. Symmachus's translation was also used by early Christian writers such as Justin Martyr and Clement of Alexandria, who quoted from it in their apologetic works.

Symmachus's translation also had a lasting impact on the development of the Septuagint. His work sought to improve upon the style of Aquila's literal and precise translation by introducing a more idiomatic and readable Greek text. Later revisions of the Septuagint, such as the Theodotion revision, sought to improve upon Symmachus's style by introducing a more accurate and faithful Greek text.

In conclusion, Symmachus (σ) is a Greek translation of the Hebrew Bible that was produced in the 2nd century CE by a Samaritan who had converted to Judaism. His translation is considered one of the rival versions of the Septuagint and it is known for its idiomatic and readable style. Symmachus based his work on that of Aquila and aimed to produce a more idiomatic Greek text that would be more easily understood by Greek-speaking Jews. His translation had a significant impact on the Jewish community of the 2nd century CE and had a lasting impact on the development of the Septuagint.

Theodotion (θ)

Theodotion (θ) is a Greek translation of the Hebrew Bible that was produced in the 2nd century CE by a Jewish proselyte named Theodotion. It is considered one of the rival versions of the Septuagint, and it is known for its accurate and faithful style.

Background of Theodotion

Theodotion was a Jewish proselyte who came from Ephesus in Asia Minor. He is believed to have lived and worked at the end of the 2nd century CE. Not much is known about his life, but it is believed that he was a contemporary of Aquila and Symmachus, the translators of the rival versions of the Septuagint.

Theodotion's main purpose in translating the Hebrew Bible into Greek was to provide a version that would be more accurate and faithful to the original Hebrew text. He aimed to correct the inaccuracies and inconsistencies of the Septuagint, and to create a translation that would be more useful for apologetics and polemics against Christian opponents.

Translation style of Theodotion

Theodotion's translation is known for its accurate and faithful style. He sought to maintain a close correspondence between the Hebrew and Greek text, and he was careful to preserve the word order and grammatical forms of the original Hebrew. According to the Jewish historian Flavius Josephus, Theodotion's translation was "more interpretative than that of Aquila and Symmachus."

Theodotion's translation is also known for its dynamic equivalence, that is to say, that it sought to convey the meaning of the Hebrew text in a more natural and accessible way. He also sought to retain the sense of the original Hebrew text and retain the meaning of the Hebrew words as much as possible. He also added explanatory notes to help the reader understand the meaning of the text.

Impact of Theodotion's Translation

Theodotion's translation had a significant impact on the Jewish community of the 2nd century CE. It was widely used by Greek-speaking Jews and it was considered to be one of the most accurate versions of the Hebrew Bible. Theodotion's translation was also used by early Christian writers such as Justin Martyr and Clement of Alexandria, who quoted from it in their apologetic works.

Theodotion's translation also had a lasting impact on the development of the Septuagint. His work sought to improve upon the style of Aquila's literal and precise translation and Symmachus's idiomatic and readable translation by introducing a more accurate and faithful Greek text. Later revisions of the Septuagint sought to improve upon Theodotion's style by introducing a more dynamic equivalence.

In conclusion, Theodotion (θ) is a Greek translation of the Hebrew Bible that was produced in the 2nd century CE by a Jewish proselyte named Theodotion. His translation is considered one of the rival versions of the Septuagint and it is known for its accurate and faithful style. Theodotion's main purpose in translating the Hebrew Bible into Greek was to provide a version that would be more accurate and faithful to the original Hebrew text and correct the inaccuracies and inconsistencies of the Septuagint. His translation had a significant impact on the Jewish community of the 2nd century CE and had a lasting impact on the development of the Septuagint.

Origen's Hexapla

Origen's Hexapla is a major milestone in the history of the Greek Old Testament. It was a critical edition of the Septuagint that was produced by the early Christian theologian Origen in the 3rd century CE. The Hexapla aimed to bring order and understanding to the confusing array of competing textual witnesses and to account for variations between the Greek and Hebrew texts.

Background of Origen

Origen was one of the most important theologians in the Eastern church. He was born in Alexandria, Egypt and was active in the middle of the 3rd century CE. He was well-versed in both Greek and Hebrew, and was aware of the differences between the Greek and Hebrew texts of the Old Testament.

During his time, there were at least four competing Greek versions of the Old Testament: the Septuagint, the Aquila, Symmachus and Theodotion translations. These translations, although based on the same source, the Hebrew text, presented different versions and interpretations of the text, making it difficult for scholars and theologians to understand the original intent of the Hebrew text.

The Idea of Hexapla

Origen, in his desire to bring order and understanding to the confusing array of competing textual witnesses, came up with the idea of the Hexapla.

He set out to produce an edition that would account for those variations by aligning the Hebrew text, in Hebrew letters, with four Greek translations: the Septuagint, Aquila, Symmachus and Theodotion, and a fifth column, which was a transliteration of the Hebrew text into Greek letters.

The Hexapla was a massive work, with six columns of text on each page, and it is estimated that it contained about 400,000 lines of text. It was a monumental undertaking, and it took Origen over 20 years to complete.

Impact of Hexapla

The Hexapla had a significant impact on the study of the Old Testament. It allowed scholars and theologians to see the variations and similarities between the different translations and to better understand the original intent of the Hebrew text. It also served as a valuable tool for the exegesis of the text, since it provided an easy way to compare different versions of the same passage.

The Hexapla also had a lasting impact on the development of the Septuagint. Its critical edition served as a basis for future revisions of the Septuagint, such as the Hesych and Lucianic recensions. Additionally, many scholars believe that the Hexapla served as a source for the Old Latin and the Old Syriac translations of the Bible.

The Hexapla itself, however, did not survive the passage of time. Only fragments of it have been preserved, and most of what we know about it comes from the writings of later scholars such as Jerome and Eusebius. Nevertheless, its influence on biblical scholarship and the development of the Septuagint cannot be underestimated.

In conclusion, Origen's Hexapla was a major milestone in the history of the Greek Old Testament. It was a critical edition of the Septuagint that aimed to bring order and understanding to the confusing array of competing textual witnesses and to account for variations between the Greek and Hebrew texts. The Hexapla had a significant impact on the study of the Old Testament, serving as a valuable tool for exegesis and influencing the development of future versions of the Septuagint. Although the Hexapla itself did not survive, its influence on biblical scholarship cannot be underestimated.

Lucian of Antioch

Lucian of Antioch is a significant figure in the history of the Greek Old Testament, known for his revision of the Septuagint. He is traditionally associated with a revision that was made in the 4th century CE, and his work is considered to be one of the most important after the Hexapla.

Background of Lucian of Antioch

Lucian of Antioch was a Christian martyr who lived in the 4th century CE. He was a bishop and theologian who was active in the Eastern church. He was known for his scholarship, and his work was considered to be of great importance in the development of the Septuagint.

The Lucianic Revision

The Lucianic revision is a stylistic update of an existing Greek text that was not Origen's edition in the fifth column of the Hexapla. It is believed that Lucian based his revision on an older Greek text that had been in use for some time, rather than the Septuagint itself. Like Theodotion, it contains distinctive readings that were known long before Lucian lived in the fourth century.

The Lucianic revision sought to improve the style of the Septuagint and to make it more consistent and coherent. It introduced new readings and corrected errors that were present in the Septuagint. It also aimed to bring the Septuagint into closer alignment with the Hebrew text.

The Lucianic revision is considered to be one of the most important revisions of the Septuagint after the Hexapla, and it had a significant impact on the development of the Septuagint.

Impact of Lucianic Revision

The Lucianic revision had a significant impact on the development of the Septuagint. Its stylistic update made the Septuagint more consistent and coherent, and it introduced new readings and corrected errors that were present in the Septuagint. It also aimed to bring the Septuagint into closer alignment with the Hebrew text.

The Lucianic revision was widely used by the Eastern church and it was considered to be the standard text of the Septuagint in the Eastern Roman Empire. It also served as a source for the Old Latin and Old Syriac translations of the Bible.

In conclusion, Lucian of Antioch is a significant figure in the history of the Greek Old Testament, known for his revision of the Septuagint. The Lucianic revision is a stylistic update of an existing Greek text that was not Origen's edition in the fifth column of the Hexapla, it contains distinctive readings that were known long before Lucian lived in the fourth century. The Lucianic revision had a significant impact on the development of the

INTRODUCTION TO THE TEXT OF THE OLD TESTAMENT

Septuagint, making it more consistent and coherent and bringing it into closer alignment with the Hebrew text. It was widely used by the Eastern church and it served as a source for the Old Latin and Old Syriac translations of the Bible.

Codex Vaticanus (B)

Codex Vaticanus, also known as B, is one of the most important witnesses to the text of the Greek Septuagint before the revisions. It is a fourth-century CE manuscript that contains the complete text of the Old Testament. The Codex is considered to be one of the oldest and most valuable manuscripts of the Septuagint and has been the subject of much scholarly study.

Background of Codex Vaticanus

The Codex Vaticanus is a Greek manuscript of the Septuagint and the New Testament. It is believed to have been written in the 4th century CE, making it one of the oldest surviving manuscripts of the Septuagint. The manuscript is written on parchment and contains the complete text of the Old Testament, as well as a small portion of the New Testament.

The Codex Vaticanus is named after the Vatican Library, where it has been housed since at least the 15th century. It is considered to be one of the most valuable manuscripts of the Septuagint and is regarded as one of the oldest and most important witnesses to the text of the Septuagint.

The Text of Codex Vaticanus

The text of the Codex Vaticanus is written in uncial script, which is a majuscule script used for ancient Greek texts. The manuscript contains the complete text of the Old Testament, including the 39 books of the Hebrew Bible and the 14 books of the Septuagint that are not found in the Hebrew Bible. It also contains a small portion of the New Testament, including parts of Matthew, Hebrews, and Revelation.

The text of the Codex Vaticanus is considered to be one of the most important witnesses to the text of the Septuagint before the revisions. The manuscript is believed to be one of the oldest surviving witnesses to the text of the Septuagint and is considered to be one of the most reliable and accurate witnesses to the text of the Septuagint.

Impact of Codex Vaticanus

The Codex Vaticanus has had a significant impact on the study of the Septuagint. It is considered to be one of the most important witnesses to the text of the Septuagint before the revisions and is widely used by scholars in the field. The manuscript is also considered to be one of the oldest and most reliable witnesses to the text of the Septuagint and is used as a primary source for the reconstruction of the original text of the Septuagint.

The Codex Vaticanus is also considered to be one of the most valuable manuscripts of the Septuagint and is regarded as an important cultural artifact. It is housed in the Vatican Library, where it is available for scholarly study.

In conclusion, the Codex Vaticanus, also known as B, is one of the most important witnesses to the text of the Greek Septuagint before the revisions. It is a fourth-century CE manuscript that contains the complete text of the Old Testament and is considered to be one of the oldest and most valuable manuscripts of the Septuagint. The text of the Codex Vaticanus is considered to be one of the most reliable and accurate witnesses to the text of the Septuagint and has had a significant impact on the study of the Septuagint. The Codex Vaticanus is also considered an important cultural artifact and is housed in the Vatican Library for scholarly study.

Codex Sinaiticus (א)

Codex Sinaiticus, also known as א, is a fourth-century CE manuscript that contains parts of the Greek Old Testament. It was discovered at St. Catherine's Monastery in the Sinai Peninsula in Egypt and is considered to be one of the most important witnesses to the text of the Septuagint.

Background of Codex Sinaiticus

The Codex Sinaiticus is a Greek manuscript of the Septuagint and the New Testament. It is believed to have been written in the 4th century CE, making it one of the oldest surviving manuscripts of the Septuagint. The manuscript is written on parchment and contains parts of the Old Testament, including portions of Genesis, Numbers, Joshua, Judges, 1 Chronicles, Ezra-Nehemiah, Esther, and most of the Prophets and Poetic books.

The Codex Sinaiticus is named after the location of its discovery, St. Catherine's Monastery in the Sinai Peninsula in Egypt. It was discovered by the German biblical scholar Constantin von Tischendorf in 1844 and was subsequently acquired by the British Library in London.

The Text of Codex Sinaiticus

The text of the Codex Sinaiticus is written in uncial script, which is a majuscule script used for ancient Greek texts. The manuscript contains parts of the Old Testament, including portions of Genesis, Numbers, Joshua, Judges, 1 Chronicles, Ezra-Nehemiah, Esther, and most of the Prophets and Poetic books. It also contains a small portion of the New Testament, including the Gospels, Acts, and the Epistles.

The text of the Codex Sinaiticus is considered to be one of the most important witnesses to the text of the Septuagint. The manuscript is believed to be one of the oldest surviving witnesses to the text of the Septuagint and is considered to be one of the most reliable and accurate witnesses to the text of the Septuagint.

Impact of Codex Sinaiticus

The Codex Sinaiticus has had a significant impact on the study of the Septuagint. It is considered to be one of the most important witnesses to the text of the Septuagint and is widely used by scholars in the field. The manuscript is also considered to be one of the oldest and most reliable witnesses to the text of the Septuagint and is used as a primary source for the reconstruction of the original text of the Septuagint.

The Codex Sinaiticus is also considered to be one of the most valuable manuscripts of the Septuagint and is regarded as an important cultural artifact. It is housed in the British Library in London, where it is available for scholarly study.

In conclusion, the Codex Sinaiticus, also known as א, is a fourth-century CE manuscript that contains parts of the Greek Old Testament. It was discovered at St. Catherine's Monastery in the Sinai Peninsula in Egypt and is considered to be one of the most important witnesses to the text of the Septuagint. The text of the Codex Sinaiticus is considered to be one of the most reliable and accurate witnesses to the text of the Septuagint and has had a significant impact on the study of the Septuagint. The Codex Sinaiticus is also considered to be one of the most valuable manuscripts of the Septuagint and is regarded as an important cultural artifact. It is housed in the British Library in London, where it is available for scholarly study. This Codex is considered one of the most important manuscripts of the Bible, along with Vaticanus and Alexandrinus. It gives us a glimpse of the Septuagint as it was read and used in the early centuries of Christianity.

Codex Alexandrinus (A)

Codex Alexandrinus, also known as A, is a fifth-century CE manuscript that contains parts of the Greek Old Testament. It is considered to be one of the most important witnesses to the text of the Septuagint and is widely used by scholars in the field.

Background of Codex Alexandrinus

Codex Alexandrinus is a Greek manuscript of the Septuagint and the New Testament. It is believed to have been written in the 5th century CE, making it one of the oldest surviving manuscripts of the Septuagint. The manuscript is written on parchment and contains almost the complete text of the Old Testament, with some missing parts of 1 Samuel and the Psalms. The Codex Alexandrinus is named after the location of its origin, the famous library in Alexandria, Egypt. It was later given as a gift to King Charles I of England in the 17th century and is currently housed in the British Library in London.

The Text of Codex Alexandrinus

The text of the Codex Alexandrinus is written in uncial script, which is a majuscule script used for ancient Greek texts. The manuscript contains almost the complete text of the Old Testament, with some missing parts of 1 Samuel and the Psalms. It also contains a small portion of the New Testament, including the Gospels, Acts, and the Epistles.

The text of the Codex Alexandrinus is considered to be one of the most important witnesses to the text of the Septuagint. The manuscript is believed to be one of the oldest surviving witnesses to the text of the Septuagint and is considered to be one of the most reliable and accurate witnesses to the text of the Septuagint. However, because of its mixed text, which is close to Vaticanus and Hexaplaric, scholars like Ernst Würthwein urge caution when using it for textual criticism.

Impact of Codex Alexandrinus

The Codex Alexandrinus has had a significant impact on the study of the Septuagint. It is considered to be one of the most important witnesses to the text of the Septuagint and is widely used by scholars in the field. The manuscript is also considered to be one of the oldest and most reliable witnesses to the text of the Septuagint and is used as a primary source for the reconstruction of the original text of the Septuagint.

However, as mentioned earlier, due to its mixed text, some scholars, like Ernst Würthwein, urge caution when using it for textual criticism. This is because it contains readings that are close to both Vaticanus and Hexaplaric texts, making it difficult to determine the original text.

Despite this, the Codex Alexandrinus is still considered to be an important witness to the text of the Septuagint. It provides valuable information about the development and transmission of the Septuagint text, and is used in conjunction with other manuscripts to reconstruct the original text of the Septuagint.

In conclusion, Codex Alexandrinus, also known as A, is a fifth-century CE manuscript that contains almost the complete text of the Greek Old Testament, with some missing parts of 1 Samuel and the Psalms. It is considered to be one of the most important witnesses to the text of the Septuagint and is widely used by scholars in the field. However, due to its mixed text, scholars advise caution when using it for textual criticism, but it still offers an important testimony of the Septuagint text. It is currently housed in the British Library in London, where it is available for scholarly study.

Canonical significance of the Greek Septuagint

The Greek Septuagint, often designated LXX, is a version of the Hebrew Bible translated into Greek in the 3rd to 2nd centuries BCE. It is significant for both Jewish and Christian communities and played an important role in the formation of the biblical canon.

The Canonization of the Septuagint

The canonization of the Septuagint was a gradual process that occurred over several centuries. The process began in the 3rd century BCE when Jewish scholars in Alexandria translated the Pentateuch (the first five books of the Hebrew Bible) into Greek. Over time, other books of the Hebrew Bible were translated, and by the 2nd century BCE, the entire Hebrew Bible had been translated into Greek. This translation was widely used by Greek-speaking Jews and later by the early Christian church.

The Septuagint was recognized as a legitimate version of the Hebrew Bible by Jewish communities in Alexandria, Egypt, and elsewhere. It was also widely used by early Christians, as it was the only version of the Hebrew Bible available in Greek. The Septuagint was also considered to be authoritative by early Christian leaders such as Origen and Jerome.

The Septuagint and the formation of the Christian canon

The Septuagint played an important role in the formation of the Christian canon. The early Christian church primarily used the Septuagint as their source for the Old Testament. This is evident in the New Testament, where quotes from the Old Testament are often taken from the Septuagint rather than the Hebrew text.

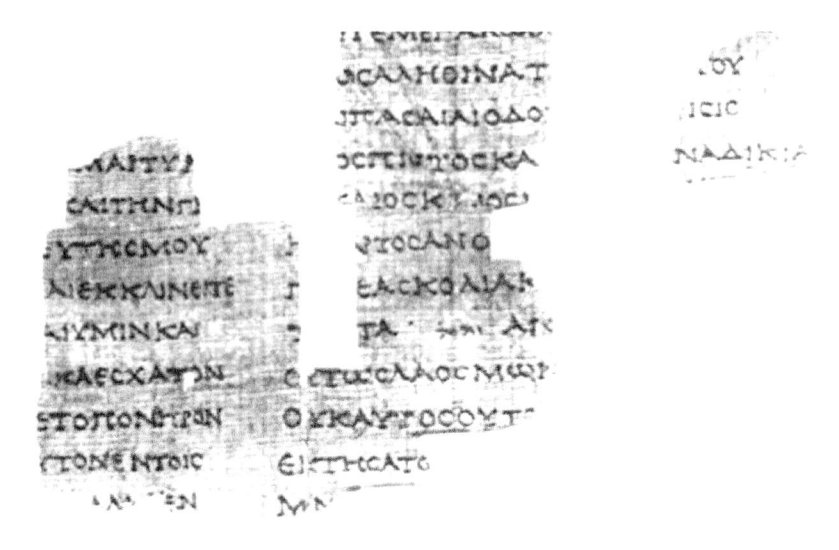

Image 31 Greek Septuagint Papyrus-Fouad-266

Additionally, the Septuagint includes several books that are not found in the Jewish canon, known as the Apocrypha or Deuterocanonical books. These books include Tobit, Judith, Wisdom, Sirach (Ecclesiasticus), Baruch, and 1 and 2 Maccabees, among others. These books were considered to be part of the Septuagint by the early Christian church and were accepted as part of the canon.

However, it should be noted that the canon of the Septuagint was not universally accepted by all early Christian communities. Some communities rejected some of the books included in the Septuagint, and there was debate over which books should be considered part of the canon.

Conclusion

The Greek Septuagint is significant for both Jewish and Christian communities and played an important role in the formation of the biblical canon. Its canonization was a gradual process that occurred over several centuries and it was widely used by Greek-speaking Jews and the early Christian church. Additionally, the Septuagint includes several books that are not found in the Jewish canon, known as the Apocrypha or Deuterocanonical books, which were considered to be part of the canon by the early Christian church. However, it should be noted that the canon of the Septuagint was

INTRODUCTION TO THE TEXT OF THE OLD TESTAMENT

not universally accepted by all early Christian communities and there was debate over which books should be considered part of the canon.

Chronology of the Greek Septuagint

The chronology of the Greek Septuagint, often designated LXX, is a complex and debated topic among scholars. The Septuagint is a Greek translation of the Hebrew Bible, and its origins and development have been the subject of much scholarly research. The following is a summary of the current understanding of the chronology of the Septuagint.

Origins of the Septuagint

The Septuagint is believed to have originated in Alexandria, Egypt, in the 3rd century BCE. The exact date and circumstances of its origin are not known, but it is thought that Jewish scholars in Alexandria translated the Pentateuch (the first five books of the Hebrew Bible) into Greek in response to the needs of the large Jewish community in the city, who were largely Greek-speaking. According to tradition, the Pentateuch was translated by 72 Jewish scholars, but this is likely a later addition to the story.

Development of the Septuagint

The translation of the Pentateuch was just the beginning of the Septuagint's development. Over the next several centuries, other books of the Hebrew Bible were translated into Greek. The process of translation was likely done by multiple translators, and the style of translation varied from literal to more free renderings. It is believed that the translation of the entire Hebrew Bible was completed by the 2nd century BCE, and perhaps by 150 BCE.

The Kaige Revision

One of the earliest revisions of the Septuagint is known as the Kaige revision. This revision is characterized by its translation of the Hebrew word גם (also) or וגם (and also) with the Greek phrase και γε (kai ge). The Kaige revision also wrote out the tetragrammaton (God's covenant name, JHVH) in the Paleo-Hebrew script rather than translating it into Greek. It dates to the late first century BCE or the early first century CE and constitutes a revision of the Old Greek translation in the direction of conformity with the proto-Masoretic text. The Kaige revision is also sometimes referred to as the "kaige-Theodotion" because of its shared readings with Theodotion, another revision of the Septuagint.

Aquila, Symmachus, and Theodotion

In the 2nd century CE, the Septuagint came to be viewed with suspicion by some Jewish communities, which led to the production of three rival Greek translations of the Hebrew Bible. The first of these was produced by Aquila, a Jewish proselyte and disciple of Rabbi Akiva. The second was produced by Symmachus, a Samaritan convert to Judaism. The third was produced by Theodotion, a convert to Judaism from Ephesus in Asia Minor. These revisions were intended to replace the Septuagint as the standard Greek translation of the Hebrew Bible.

Origen's Hexapla

In the 3rd century CE, Origen, a prominent theologian in the Eastern church, produced an edition of the Septuagint that aimed to bring order and understanding to the array of competing textual witnesses. This edition, known as the Hexapla, arranged the text of the Septuagint alongside the text of the Hebrew Bible and the translations of Aquila, Symmachus, and Theodotion. This allowed for easy comparison of the different translations and helped scholars to understand the development and transmission of the Septuagint text.

Lucian of Antioch

The most important revision after the Hexapla is traditionally associated with Lucian of Antioch, who was martyred in 312 CE. This revision was a stylistic update of an existing Greek text that was not Origen's edition in the fifth column of the Hexapla. Like Theodotion, it contains distinctive readings that were known long before Lucian lived in the fourth century.

In conclusion, the chronology of the Greek Septuagint is complex and debated among scholars. The Septuagint is believed to have originated in Alexandria, Egypt, in the 3rd century BCE and gradually developed over several centuries. The Kaige revision, Aquila, Symmachus, and Theodotion, Origen's Hexapla, and Lucian of Antioch are all important stages in the development and revision of the Septuagint.

The Septuagint is an important historical document that provides insight into the development of the biblical canon and the transmission of the biblical text. Its significance is not limited to Jewish and Christian communities, and it continues to be studied by scholars from a variety of fields. In addition, the Septuagint has been preserved in a number of manuscripts, including Codex Vaticanus, Codex Sinaiticus, and Codex Alexandrinus, which are considered to be some of the most important witnesses to the text of the Septuagint.

In conclusion, the chronology of the Greek Septuagint is a complex and multi-faceted subject, with many revisions and versions that were produced over centuries. The Septuagint's significance lies in its early translation of the Hebrew Bible into Greek, which made it accessible to Greek-speaking Jews and early Christians and provided a foundation for the development of the biblical canon. It is an important historical document that continues to be studied by scholars from a variety of fields.

Manuscripts of the Greek Septuagint

The Greek Septuagint (often designated LXX) is a Greek translation of the Hebrew Bible that was widely used by Greek-speaking Jews and Christians in the ancient world. The Septuagint has been preserved in a number of manuscripts, many of which are fragmentary, while others are fairly complete. These manuscripts are considered to be some of the most important witnesses to the text of the Septuagint and are studied by scholars from a variety of fields.

The Oldest Manuscripts of the Septuagint

The oldest manuscripts of the Septuagint include 2nd-century-BCE fragments of Leviticus and Deuteronomy (Rahlfs nos. 801, 819, and 957) and 1st-century-BCE fragments of Genesis, Exodus, Leviticus, Numbers, Deuteronomy, and the Twelve Minor Prophets (Alfred Rahlfs nos. 802, 803, 805, 848, 942, and 943). These fragments provide important evidence for the early development of the Septuagint and its relationship to the Hebrew text of the Bible.

Uncial Manuscripts

The Septuagint texts are also preserved in the three famous uncial manuscripts written on vellum—the Vatican Manuscript No. 1209 and the Sinaitic Manuscript, both of the fourth century CE, and the Alexandrine Manuscript of the fifth century CE. These manuscripts are considered to be some of the most important witnesses to the text of the Septuagint.

The Vatican Manuscript No. 1209 is almost complete and contains the entire text of the Septuagint. The Sinaitic Manuscript is also from the fourth century CE and contains parts of the Hebrew Scriptures, but part of the text has been lost. The Alexandrine Manuscript, also from the fifth century CE, is rather complete, although it lacks parts of Genesis, First Samuel, and Psalms.

Minuscule Manuscripts

In addition to the uncial manuscripts, there are also many minuscule manuscripts of the Septuagint that date from the 9th century CE to the 15th century CE. These manuscripts were written in smaller handwriting and were often produced by monks in monasteries. They are considered to be less reliable witnesses to the text of the Septuagint than the uncial manuscripts, but they are still valuable for textual criticism and the study of the transmission of the Septuagint text.

In conclusion, the manuscripts of the Greek Septuagint are an important part of the study of the Septuagint and the development of the biblical canon. The oldest manuscripts of the Septuagint, such as the 2nd-century BCE fragments, provide important evidence for the early development of the Septuagint and its relationship to the Hebrew text of the Bible. The uncial manuscripts, such as the Vatican Manuscript, the Sinaitic Manuscript, and the Alexandrine Manuscript, are considered to be some of the most important witnesses to the text of the Septuagint and are of great value for textual criticism and the study of the transmission of the Septuagint text. The minuscule manuscripts, while not as reliable as the uncial manuscripts, are still valuable for the study of the transmission of the Septuagint text. Overall, the manuscripts of the Greek Septuagint are an important resource for understanding the development and transmission of the biblical text and the history of the Septuagint.

Translations of the Greek Septuagint into English

The Greek Septuagint is a translation of the Hebrew Bible into Greek, which was widely used by Greek-speaking Jews and early Christians in the ancient world. The Septuagint has been translated into many languages over the centuries, including English. The translations of the Greek Septuagint into English have played an important role in making the Septuagint accessible to a wider audience, and they have been used by scholars, theologians, and laypeople alike.

The Septuagint Version

One of the earliest English translations of the Septuagint is the Septuagint Version, which was first published in 1844 by Sir Lancelot Charles Lee Brenton. This translation is based on the text of the Septuagint as it appears in the Codex Vaticanus, and it provides a literal translation of the Greek text into English. Brenton's translation is considered to be one of the most accurate and reliable translations of the Septuagint into English, and it is still widely used by scholars and theologians today.

The New English Translation of the Septuagint

Another important English translation of the Septuagint is the New English Translation of the Septuagint (NETS), which was first published in 2007. This translation is based on the text of the Septuagint as it appears in the Codex Vaticanus and other important witnesses to the text. The NETS provides a more idiomatic translation of the Greek text into English than Brenton's translation and aims to be more accessible to a wider audience. The NETS is considered to be a valuable resource for scholars, theologians, and laypeople alike, and is widely used by scholars and theologians today.

The Orthodox Study Bible

Another English translation of the Septuagint is the Orthodox Study Bible, which was first published in 2008. This translation is based on the text of the Septuagint as it appears in the Codex Vaticanus and other important witnesses to the text. The Orthodox Study Bible provides a translation of the Septuagint that is faithful to the original Greek text and aims to be accessible to a wider audience. The Orthodox Study Bible is considered to be a valuable resource for scholars, theologians, and laypeople alike and is widely used by scholars and theologians today.

Conclusion

In conclusion, the translations of the Greek Septuagint into English have played an important role in making the Septuagint accessible to a wider audience. The Septuagint Version by Sir Lancelot Charles Lee Brenton, the New English Translation of the Septuagint (NETS), and the Orthodox Study Bible are considered to be some of the most important and reliable translations of the Septuagint into English, and they are widely used by scholars, theologians, and laypeople alike. These translations provide valuable resources for understanding the Septuagint and its significance in the development of the biblical canon and the history of the early Church.

Scholarly Editions of the Greek Septuagint

The Septuagint, also known as the LXX, is the Greek translation of the Hebrew Bible. It is an important text for both Jewish and Christian scholars, as it was widely used in the early Christian church and is cited in the New Testament.

There have been a number of scholarly editions of the Septuagint produced over the years, each with its own unique features and goals. In this essay, we will explore some of the most notable scholarly editions of the Septuagint and discuss their significance.

The Göttingen Septuagint

The Göttingen Septuagint, also known as the Gottingensis, is a critical edition of the Septuagint that was produced by a team of scholars at the University of Göttingen in Germany. The edition was published in two volumes between 1931 and 1936.

The Göttingen Septuagint was notable for its attention to the textual history of the Septuagint. The editors used a variety of sources, including early manuscripts, patristic citations, and the Old Latin, to reconstruct the original text of the Septuagint. They also included extensive critical apparatus, which provided information on variants and the textual history of the Septuagint.

The Göttingen Septuagint was widely regarded as a significant achievement in Septuagint scholarship, and it continues to be a valuable resource for scholars today. As the Septuagint translator, Alfred Rahlfs, noted in his preface to the edition, "The Göttingen Septuagint is the first critical edition of the Septuagint that takes into account the entire textual tradition, and it is therefore a major step forward in Septuagint scholarship."

The Oxford Septuagint

The Oxford Septuagint is another important scholarly edition of the Septuagint. It was produced by a team of scholars at the University of Oxford in England, and it was published in four volumes between 1979 and 1986.

The Oxford Septuagint was notable for its use of the latest textual criticism methods, which allowed the editors to produce a more accurate text of the Septuagint. They also included an extensive critical apparatus, which provided information on variants and the textual history of the Septuagint.

The Oxford Septuagint was well-received by scholars, who praised its attention to detail and its use of the latest textual criticism methods. The Septuagint translator, Alan Brent, noted in his preface to the edition that "The Oxford Septuagint is the most up-to-date and accurate edition of the Septuagint currently available, and it is an essential resource for scholars and students of the Septuagint."

The Stuttgart Septuagint

The Stuttgart Septuagint, also known as the Rahlfs-Hanhart Septuagint, is a critical edition of the Septuagint that was produced by a team of scholars at the University of Stuttgart in Germany. The edition was published in two volumes between 2007 and 2009.

The Stuttgart Septuagint was notable for its attention to the textual history of the Septuagint, and for its use of the latest textual criticism methods. The editors used a variety of sources, including early manuscripts, patristic citations, and the Old Latin, to reconstruct the original text of the Septuagint. They also included an extensive critical apparatus, which provided information on variants and the textual history of the Septuagint.

The Stuttgart Septuagint was widely regarded as a significant achievement in Septuagint scholarship, and it continues to be a valuable resource for scholars today. It builds on the work of previous editions like the Göttingen and Oxford Septuagints, incorporating new research and discoveries in order to provide an even more accurate and comprehensive text of the Septuagint.

One key feature of the Stuttgart Septuagint is its use of modern technology, particularly computer-assisted methods, to analyze and present the textual data. The edition also includes a complete set of critical apparatus, providing information on the witnesses and their relationships to the text.

In conclusion, the Scholarly Editions of the Greek Septuagint are Göttingen, Oxford and Stuttgart Septuagint, each of them have their own unique features and goals and they have been widely regarded as a significant achievement in Septuagint scholarship. They are valuable resources for scholars and students of the Septuagint, providing an accurate and comprehensive text of the Septuagint.

The Septuagint and the Hebrew Text

The Septuagint (LXX) is the Greek translation of the Hebrew Bible, and it is an important text for both Jewish and Christian scholars. The Septuagint was widely used in the early Christian church and is cited in the New Testament. It is also significant for the study of the Hebrew text of the Bible, as it provides an important witness to the text of the Hebrew Bible in the Hellenistic period. In this essay, we will explore the relationship between the Septuagint and the Hebrew text of the Bible and discuss the implications of this relationship for the study of the Bible.

The Translation of the Septuagint

The Septuagint was translated into Greek in the 3rd century BCE, and it was likely produced in Alexandria, Egypt, which was a center of Jewish learning and scholarship at the time. The translation of the Septuagint is considered to be a free translation, meaning that the translators had some degree of freedom to interpret the meaning of the Hebrew text and to adapt it to the Greek language and culture. This is in contrast to a formal equivalence translation, which aims to closely match the wording and grammar of the original text.

The Septuagint translation is significant because it provides a glimpse into how the Hebrew text was understood and interpreted in the Hellenistic period. The Septuagint translator, in many cases, had a different understanding and interpretation of the Hebrew text than the Masoretic Text, which is the standard text of the Hebrew Bible today.

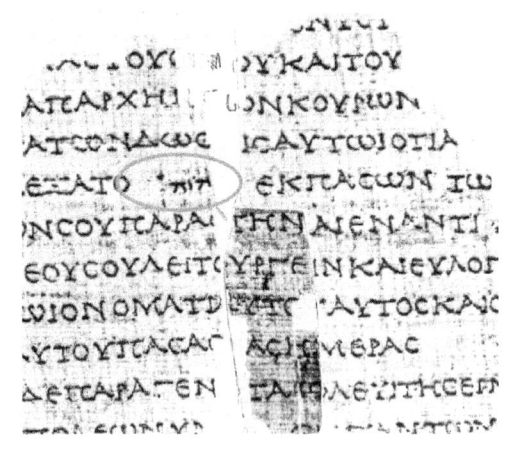

Image 32 The divine name in a Septuagint manuscript fragment from Jesus' day

The Textual Variants in the Septuagint

The Septuagint is also significant for the study of the Hebrew text of the Bible because it provides an important witness to the text of the Hebrew Bible in the Hellenistic period. The Septuagint preserves a number of textual variants that are not present in the Masoretic Text, and these variants can provide important insights into the history of the text of the Hebrew Bible.

For example, the Septuagint includes a number of additional passages that are not found in the Masoretic Text, such as the story of the death of Moses in Deuteronomy 34, which is not present in the Masoretic Text. The Septuagint also includes a number of variant readings, such as the reading "Jehovah" for "Lord" in Exodus 6:3, which is not present in the Masoretic Text.

These textual variants in the Septuagint can provide important insights into the history of the text of the Hebrew Bible. They can also help scholars to reconstruct the original text of the Hebrew Bible, as they can provide information on the text that was used by the Septuagint translator.

INTRODUCTION TO THE TEXT OF THE OLD TESTAMENT

The Septuagint and the Study of the Bible

The Septuagint is an important text for the study of the Bible, as it provides an important witness to the text of the Hebrew Bible in the Hellenistic period. The Septuagint translation is significant because it provides a glimpse into how the Hebrew text was understood and interpreted in the Hellenistic period. The textual variants in the Septuagint can provide important insights into the history of the text of the Hebrew Bible.

The Septuagint's relationship with the Hebrew text of the Bible is complex, and the Septuagint translator's understanding and interpretation of the Hebrew text is not always consistent with the Masoretic Text. However, the Septuagint's unique features and variants can often provide important information on the Hebrew text and can provide a deeper understanding of the text.

As Emanuel Tov, a leading Septuagint scholar, has noted, "the Septuagint is a valuable witness to the text of the Hebrew Bible in the Hellenistic period, and its study can provide important insights into the history of the text and its interpretation. It can also contribute to our understanding of the cultural and historical context in which the Septuagint was produced."

However, the primary weight of external evidence generally goes to the original language manuscripts, and the **Codex Leningrad B 19A** and the **Aleppo Codex** are almost always preferred. In Old Testament Textual Criticism, the Masoretic text is our starting point and should only be abandoned as a last resort. While it is true that the Masoretic Text is not perfect, there needs to be a heavy burden of proof in we are to go with an alternative reading. All of the evidence needs to be examined before concluding that a reading in the Masoretic Text is corrupt. The Septuagint continues to be very much important today and is used by textual scholars to help uncover copyists' errors that **might have** crept into the Hebrew manuscripts either intentionally or unintentionally. However, it cannot do it alone without the support of other sources. There are a number of times when you might have the Syriac, Septuagint, Dead Sea Scrolls, Aramaic Targums, and the Vulgate that are at odds with the Masoretic Text the preferred choice should not be the MT.

Initially, the Septuagint (LXX) was viewed by the Jews as inspired by God, equal to the Hebrew Scriptures. However, in the first century C.E. the Christians adopted the Septuagint in their churches. It was used by the Christians in their evangelism to make disciples and to debate the Jews on Jesus being the long-awaited Messiah. Soon, the Jews began to look at the

Septuagint with suspicion. This resulted in the Jews of the second century C.E. abandoning the Septuagint and returning to the Hebrew Scriptures. This has proved to be beneficial for the textual scholar and translator. In the second century C.E., other Greek translations of the Septuagint were produced. We have **LXX**[Aq] Aquila, **LXX**[Sym] Symmachus, and **LXX**[Th] Theodotion. The consonantal text of the Hebrew Scriptures became the standard text between the first and second centuries C.E. However, textual variants still continued until the Masoretes and the Masoretic text. However, scribes taking liberties by altering the text was no longer the case, as was true of the previous period of the Sopherim. The scribes who copied the Hebrew Scriptures from the time of Ezra down to the time of Jesus were called Sopherim, i.e., scribes.

From the 6th century C.E. to the 10th century C.E. we have the Masoretes, groups of extraordinary Jewish scribe-scholars. The Masoretes were very much concerned with the accurate transmission of each word, even each letter, of the text they were copying. Accuracy was of supreme importance; therefore, the Masoretes use the side margins of each page to inform others of deliberate or inadvertent changes in the text by past copyists. The Masoretes also use these marginal notes for other reasons as well, such as unusual word forms and combinations. They even marked how frequent they occurred within a book or even the whole Hebrew Old Testament. Of course, marginal spaces were very limited, so they used abbreviated code. They also formed a cross-checking tool where they would mark the middle word and letter of certain books. Their push for accuracy moved them to go so far as to count every letter of the Hebrew Old Testament.

In the Masoretic text, we find notes in the side margins, which are known as the Small Masora. There are also notes in the top margin, which are referred to as the Large Masora. Any other notes placed elsewhere within the text are called the Final Masora. The Masoretes used the notes in the top and bottom margins to record more extensive notes, comments concerning the abbreviated notes in the side margins. This enabled them to be able to cross-check their work. We must remember that there were no numbered verses at this time, and they had no Bible concordances. Well, one might wonder how the Masoretes could refer to different parts of the Hebrew text to have an effective cross-checking system. They would list part of a parallel verse in the top and bottom margins to remind them of where the word(s) indicated were found. Because they were dealing with limited space, they often could only list one word to remind them where each parallel verse could be found. To have an effective cross-reference system by way of these marginal notes, the Masoretes would literally have to have memorized the entire Hebrew Bible.

In conclusion, the Septuagint is an important text for the study of the Hebrew Bible, as it provides an important witness to the text of the Hebrew Bible in the Hellenistic period. The Septuagint's translation and textual variants can provide important insights into the history of the text of the Hebrew Bible and can help scholars to reconstruct the original text of the Hebrew Bible. The Septuagint's relationship with the Hebrew text of the Bible is complex, but its unique features and variants can often provide important information on the Hebrew text and can provide a deeper understanding of the text.

How Has the Greek Septuagint Helped Textual Scholars Establish the Original Reading of the Hebrew Old Testament Manuscripts?

The Greek Septuagint, also known as the LXX, is a translation of the Hebrew Bible into Greek that was widely used in the Jewish and early Christian communities. It is considered to be one of the most important versions of the Old Testament, as it is the oldest surviving translation of the Hebrew Bible and it was used extensively in the early Christian church. The Septuagint has played an important role in helping textual scholars establish the original reading of the Hebrew Old Testament manuscripts through its close relationship to the Masoretic Text, which is the standard Hebrew text of the Old Testament, and through its preservation of variant readings.

Background of the Septuagint

The Greek Septuagint is thought to have been produced in Alexandria, Egypt, in the 3rd century BCE. It was translated by Jewish scholars and was intended to serve the Jewish community in Alexandria, which consisted of many Jewish immigrants who spoke Greek as their primary language. The Septuagint was also used by early Christians, as it was the version of the Old Testament most commonly cited in the New Testament. The Septuagint's widespread use in early Christianity also helped to establish it as an important version of the Old Testament.

Comparing the Septuagint to the Masoretic Text One of the most important ways that the Septuagint has helped textual scholars establish the original reading of the Hebrew Old Testament manuscripts is by comparing it to the Masoretic Text. The Masoretic Text is the standard Hebrew text of the Old Testament that has been used by Jews and Christians for centuries. It was developed by the Masoretes, a group of Jewish scribes who worked in the 7th to 10th centuries CE to standardize the Hebrew text of the Old Testament. By comparing the Septuagint to the Masoretic Text, scholars have been able to identify variant readings and to make informed decisions about the original reading of the Hebrew Old Testament manuscripts.

Preservation of Variant Readings

Another way that the Septuagint has helped textual scholars establish the original reading of the Hebrew Old Testament manuscripts is through its preservation of variant readings. The Septuagint often preserves readings that are different from the Masoretic Text, and these variant readings can provide important information about the original reading of the Hebrew text. For example, scholars have found that the Septuagint preserves readings that are closer to the original Hebrew text in some cases than the Masoretic Text does. This can be seen in passages such as Isaiah 7:14, where the Septuagint preserves the reading "young woman" while the Masoretic Text reads "virgin." This variant reading preserved in the Septuagint can help scholars to better understand the original meaning of the Hebrew text.

Conclusion

The Greek Septuagint has played an important role in helping textual scholars establish the original reading of the Hebrew Old Testament manuscripts. Through its close relationship to the Masoretic Text and its preservation of variant readings, the Septuagint has provided valuable information about the original reading of the Hebrew text. It is one of the most important versions of the Old Testament, as it was widely used in the Jewish and early Christian communities, and it was the version of the Old Testament most commonly cited in the New Testament. The Septuagint continues to be an important tool for textual scholars in helping to establish the original reading in some places.

INTRODUCTION TO THE TEXT OF THE OLD TESTAMENT

CHAPTER 6 The Aramaic Targums

MS 206
Hebrew square book script. Iraq, 1st half of 11th c.

Image 33 11th century Hebrew Bible with targum, perhaps from Tunisia, found in Iraq: part of the Schøyen Collection.

Edward D. Andrews

The Aramaic Targums

Introduction

The Aramaic Targums are ancient Jewish translations or paraphrases of Bible books, written in the Aramaic language. These texts were first put in writing at the beginning of the Common Era and provide valuable insights into the interpretation and understanding of the Hebrew Bible by Jewish communities during the Second Temple period. The Targums were not only translations of the Hebrew text, but also served as commentaries and explanations of the text, incorporating Jewish traditions and interpretations.

Background

The Targums were developed as a means of interpreting the Hebrew Bible for Jewish communities that spoke Aramaic as their primary language. The Hebrew Bible was written in a language that was no longer spoken by the majority of the Jewish people, and the Targums were a way to bridge the gap between the Hebrew text and the Aramaic-speaking community. The Targums were not only translations, but also served as commentaries, incorporating Jewish traditions and interpretations of the text.

The Targums were first put in writing at the beginning of the Common Era, but their origins can be traced back to an earlier period of oral tradition. The earliest written Targums were likely based on earlier oral traditions and were likely used in synagogues for reading and interpreting the Hebrew Bible.

Content

The Targums contain a variety of content, including translations of the Hebrew text, commentaries, and explanations of the text. They also incorporate Jewish traditions and interpretations of the text, such as midrashic exegesis and halakhic teachings.

For example, the Targum Onkelos on the Torah, which is attributed to a first-century CE convert to Judaism, provides a literal translation of the Hebrew text, but also includes explanatory notes and expansions of the text. It also incorporates halakhic teachings and interpretations of the text.

Another example is the Targum Neofiti on the Prophets, which is attributed to the Palestinian Amoraim, provides a paraphrase of the Hebrew text, preserving the sense of the text, but also including Midrashic exegesis, commentaries, and explanations of the text. It also incorporates Jewish traditions and interpretations of the text, such as the identification of certain characters and events with figures from Jewish history and tradition.

Significance

The Aramaic Targums are significant for several reasons. Firstly, they provide valuable insights into the interpretation and understanding of the Hebrew Bible by Jewish communities during the Second Temple period. They also serve as a window into the world of Jewish thought and tradition during this time period.

Secondly, the Targums are important for the study of the Hebrew Bible and the development of Jewish exegesis. They provide information about the text, its interpretation, and the historical and cultural context in which it was written and read.

Lastly, the Targums are also important for the study of the Aramaic language, as they provide valuable examples of the language and its development. They are also important for the study of Jewish history and culture, as they provide information about the beliefs, practices, and traditions of Jewish communities during the Second Temple period.

Conclusion

The Aramaic Targums are ancient Jewish translations or paraphrases of Bible books, written in the Aramaic language. They were first put in writing at the beginning of the Common Era and provide valuable insights into the interpretation and understanding of the Hebrew Bible by Jewish communities during the Second Temple period. The Targums were not only translations of the Hebrew text, but also served as commentaries and explanations of the text, incorporating Jewish traditions and interpretations. They are significant for the study of the Hebrew Bible, Jewish exegesis, the Aramaic language, and Jewish history and culture.

Canonical Significance of the Aramaic Targums

Introduction

The Aramaic Targums are ancient Jewish translations or paraphrases of Bible books, written in the Aramaic language. These texts were first put in writing at the beginning of the Common Era and provide valuable insights into the interpretation and understanding of the Hebrew Bible by Jewish communities during the Second Temple period. The Targums were not only translations of the Hebrew text, but also served as commentaries and explanations of the text, incorporating Jewish traditions and interpretations. The canonicity of the Aramaic Targums, meaning their inclusion or exclusion from the canon of scripture, has been a topic of debate among scholars for centuries.

Background

The canon of scripture, or the collection of texts considered authoritative and sacred by a particular religious community, is a concept that has evolved over time. For Jewish communities, the canon of scripture traditionally includes the Hebrew Bible, also known as the Tanakh, which consists of the Torah (the first five books of the Bible), the Nevi'im (the Prophets), and the Ketuvim (the Writings). However, the canonicity of the Aramaic Targums has been a topic of debate among scholars.

Arguments for Canonicity

One argument for the canonicity of the Aramaic Targums is that they were used in synagogues for reading and interpreting the Hebrew Bible. According to this argument, their widespread use and acceptance by Jewish communities would indicate that they were considered authoritative and sacred texts.

Additionally, some scholars argue that the Targums were considered canon by the communities that produced them. For example, the Palestinian Targum is thought to have been produced by the Palestinian Amoraim, a group of Jewish scholars who were active between the 3rd and 5th centuries CE. If this is the case, it suggests that the Palestinian Amoraim considered the Targum to be a canonical text.

Arguments against Canonicity

One argument against the canonicity of the Aramaic Targums is that they are translations or paraphrases of the Hebrew Bible, and therefore not original texts. According to this argument, the Hebrew Bible is considered the only authoritative and sacred text, and the Targums are considered secondary texts.

Another argument against the canonicity of the Aramaic Targums is that they were produced at a later time than the Hebrew Bible and therefore cannot be considered part of the canon. The Hebrew Bible is believed to have been canonized by the end of the Second Temple period (516 BCE to 70 CE), while the Aramaic Targums were written at the beginning of the Common Era, several centuries later. This argument suggests that the Aramaic Targums were not considered to be part of the canon at the time of their production.

Additionally, the contents of the Targums are not identical to the Hebrew Bible, they include additional interpretations, explanations and Jewish traditions. This suggests that they were not considered as a translation of the Hebrew Bible but rather a commentary.

Conclusion

The canonicity of the Aramaic Targums is a topic of debate among scholars. While some argue that their widespread use and acceptance by Jewish communities indicate that they were considered authoritative and sacred texts, others argue that they were not considered part of the canon due to their later production, lack of originality and different contents from the Hebrew Bible. The understanding of the canonicity of the Aramaic Targums is likely to have varied among different Jewish communities and through time.

Chronology of the Aramaic Targums

Introduction

The Aramaic Targums, also known as the Targumim, are ancient Jewish translations or paraphrases of Bible books, written in the Aramaic language. Aramaic was a widely spoken language in the Middle East during the Second Temple period, and it was used as a lingua franca among different Jewish communities. The Aramaic Targums were written to help Jewish communities understand the Hebrew Bible in their own language, and they provide valuable insights into the interpretation and understanding of the Hebrew Bible by Jewish communities during the Second Temple period.

Chronology

The exact chronology of the Aramaic Targums is a topic of debate among scholars, with various theories proposed. The earliest Aramaic Targums are thought to have been oral translations, passed down through generations before being written down. These oral Targums are believed to have originated in the Second Temple period, between the 5th century BCE and the 1st century CE.

The earliest written Aramaic Targums are believed to have been produced in the 1st century CE. The Palestinian Targum, also known as Targum Yerushalmi, is thought to be one of the earliest written Targums. It is believed to have been produced by the Palestinian Amoraim, a group of Jewish scholars who were active between the 3rd and 5th centuries CE.

The Babylonian Targum, also known as Targum Onkelos, is another early Aramaic Targum. It is believed to have been produced in the 1st or 2nd century CE by Babylonian Jewish scholars. This Targum is considered to be more literal and closer to the Hebrew text than the Palestinian Targum.

Significance

Despite not being considered part of the canon, the Aramaic Targums are important texts for understanding the Second Temple period and the way in which the Hebrew Bible was interpreted and understood by Jewish communities during this time. They provide valuable insights into the religious beliefs, practices, and customs of these communities, and they are also important for understanding the development of Jewish exegesis and hermeneutics.

In addition, the Aramaic Targums are also significant for scholars studying the history of the Hebrew language and the development of Aramaic as a spoken and written language. They provide valuable examples of the use of Aramaic in a Jewish context and the way in which it was adapted to convey the meaning of the Hebrew Bible.

Conclusion

The chronology, contents, and significance of the Aramaic Targums are complex and have been widely debated among scholars. Despite not being considered part of the canon, these texts provide valuable insights into the interpretation and understanding of the Hebrew Bible by Jewish communities during the Second Temple period and the development of Jewish exegesis and hermeneutics. They also offer important examples of the use of Aramaic in a Jewish context and its adaptation to convey the meaning of the Hebrew Bible.

Manuscripts of the Aramaic Targums

Introduction

The Aramaic Targums are ancient Jewish texts that are translations, or more accurately, paraphrases of books of the Hebrew Bible. These texts were written in Aramaic, the vernacular language of the Jewish people during the Second Temple period (516 BCE to 70 CE). The Aramaic Targums are considered to be important texts for understanding the way in which the Hebrew Bible was interpreted and understood by Jewish communities during this time.

INTRODUCTION TO THE TEXT OF THE OLD TESTAMENT

Manuscripts of the Aramaic Targums

The manuscripts of the Aramaic Targums are not as well-preserved as those of the Hebrew Bible, and as a result, only a small number of complete Targums have been discovered. The majority of the existing Targums are fragmentary and have been reconstructed from multiple sources.

One of the most complete Targums is the Targum Onkelos on the Pentateuch, which is believed to have been written in the 2nd century CE. This Targum is considered to be one of the most important and reliable Targums, and it is still used by Jewish communities today. Other complete Targums include the Targum Jonathan on the Prophets, and the Targum Neofiti on the Pentateuch.

In addition to these complete Targums, there are also many fragmentary Targums that have been discovered. These fragments have been found in various locations, including the Cairo Geniza, the British Library, and the Vatican Library. These fragments have been used to reconstruct lost portions of the Targums and to provide insight into the development of the Targums over time.

Methods of Study

The study of the manuscripts of the Aramaic Targums is a complex process that involves analyzing the texts and comparing them to other ancient Jewish texts. Scholars use paleography, the study of ancient handwriting, to date the manuscripts and to determine the origins of the texts. Additionally, they use linguistic analysis to study the use of Aramaic and to understand the way in which the language was adapted to convey the meaning of the Hebrew Bible.

In recent years, digital tools have been used to enhance the study of the Aramaic Targums. For example, the "Digital Targum Project" at the University of Pennsylvania has created a digital database of Targums and fragments, which allows scholars to easily access and analyze the texts. This technology has greatly improved the study of the Targums and has made it possible to reconstruct lost portions of the texts.

Conclusion

The manuscripts of the Aramaic Targums are important texts for understanding the way in which the Hebrew Bible was interpreted and understood by Jewish communities during the Second Temple period. Despite not being well-preserved, scholars have been able to reconstruct and study these texts using various methods including paleography and linguistic analysis. Additionally, digital tools have been used to enhance the study of the Aramaic Targums. These efforts have greatly improved our understanding of these ancient texts and have provided valuable insights into the history of Jewish exegesis and hermeneutics.

How Have the Aramaic Targums Helped Textual Scholars Establish the Original Reading of the Hebrew Old Testament Manuscripts?

The Aramaic Targums, or translations of the Hebrew Old Testament, have played a significant role in helping textual scholars establish the original reading of the Hebrew Old Testament manuscripts. These Targums, written in the Aramaic language, were first put in writing at the beginning of the Common Era, and were used by Jewish communities in the Second Temple period and later.

One of the most important uses of the Aramaic Targums for textual scholars is in understanding the meaning of difficult or uncertain Hebrew words or phrases in the Old Testament. The Targums provide a translation of the Hebrew text into Aramaic, which can help scholars determine the intended meaning of a passage. For example, in the book of Isaiah, the Hebrew word "yir'eh" is translated as "he will see" in the Masoretic Text, but in the Targum, it is translated as "he will be revealed." This helps scholars understand that the original intended meaning of the passage was that God will be revealed, rather than simply that someone will see him.

Another important use of the Targums for textual scholars is in identifying textual variations in the Hebrew Old Testament manuscripts. The Targums often preserve readings that are different from those found in the Masoretic Text, which can help scholars identify possible errors or changes that have been made in the Hebrew text over time. For example, in the book of Deuteronomy, the Targum preserves a reading that is different from the Masoretic Text, which suggests that the original text may have been altered at some point.

The Aramaic Targums have also been useful for textual scholars in understanding the historical context of the Hebrew Old Testament. The Targums provide insight into the beliefs and practices of Jewish communities in the Second Temple period, which can help scholars understand the original meaning of a passage. For example, the Targum on the book of Leviticus includes a commentary on the laws of purity and impurity, which helps scholars understand how these laws were understood and applied in Second Temple period Jewish communities.

In addition, the Targums have also been used to reconstruct the history of the text of the Hebrew Bible. Textual scholars have been able to use the Targums to trace the development of the Hebrew text over time, and to identify different textual traditions. This has been particularly useful in understanding the history of the text of the Pentateuch, which is the first five books of the Hebrew Bible, as the Targums provide important evidence for the development of the text over time.

In conclusion, the Aramaic Targums have been an extremely valuable resource for textual scholars in their efforts to establish the original reading of the Hebrew Old Testament manuscripts. The Targums provide a translation of the Hebrew text into Aramaic, which can help scholars understand the intended meaning of a passage, identify textual variations, understand the historical context of the Hebrew Old Testament, and reconstruct the history of the text of the Hebrew Bible.

CHAPTER 7 The Syriac Peshitta

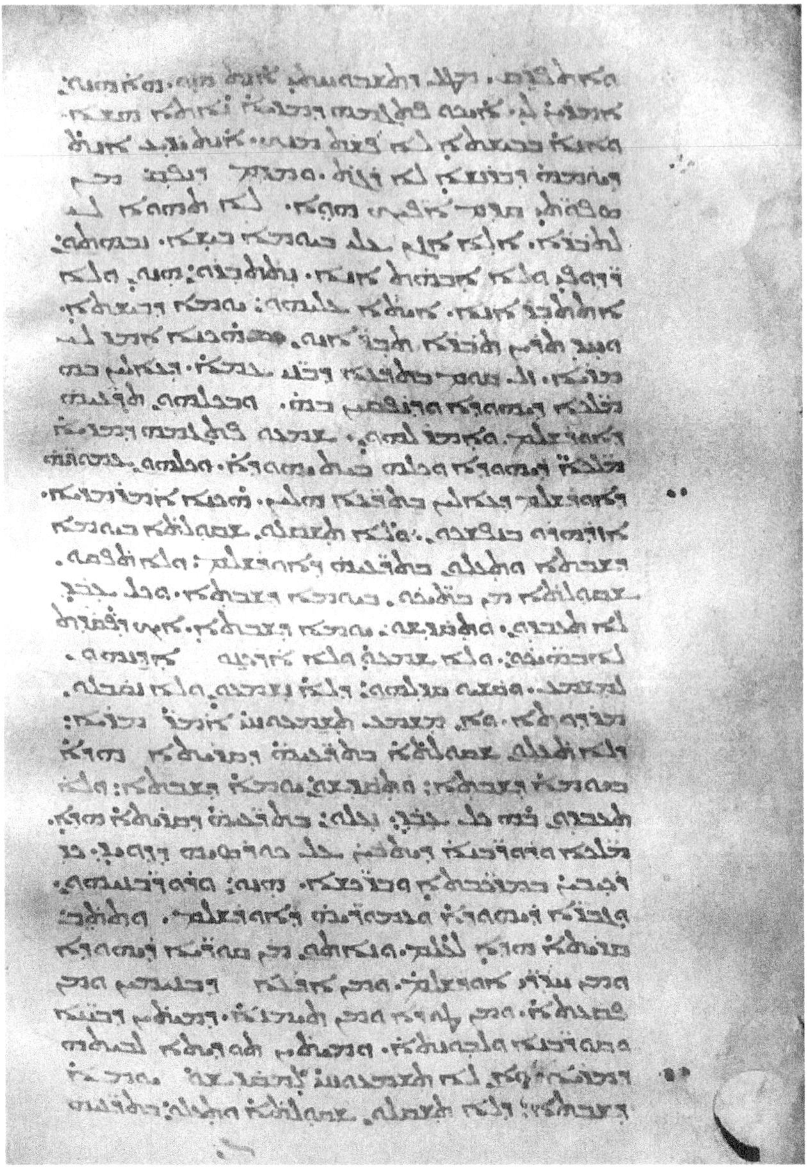

Image 34 9th-century manuscript

The Syriac Peshitta

Introduction

The Syriac Peshitta Old Testament is a translation of the Hebrew Bible into the Aramaic language, which was spoken by the people of ancient Syria. The name "Peshitta" means "simple" or "common," and it is believed to have been produced in the 2nd century CE. It is considered the standard version of the Bible in the Syrian Orthodox Church and is still used in liturgical services.

Translation and Textual History

The translation of the Hebrew Bible into Aramaic was likely done by Jewish scholars, as Aramaic was widely spoken by Jews in the ancient Near East. The translator(s) likely used the Hebrew text as their source, but also incorporated elements from the Septuagint, the Greek translation of the Hebrew Bible.

The Peshitta Old Testament is considered to be a representative of the "Eastern" text-type of the Septuagint, which is characterized by its close adherence to the Hebrew text and its avoidance of interpretive expansions. It also contains several passages found in the Septuagint but not present in the Masoretic Text.

Significance

The Peshitta Old Testament is significant for several reasons. Firstly, it is one of the earliest translations of the Hebrew Bible, predating the Latin Vulgate and the King James Version. Secondly, it is an important witness to the text of the Hebrew Bible, as it provides valuable insight into the textual tradition of the Septuagint.

Furthermore, the Peshitta Old Testament also provides an important window into the religious and cultural world of ancient Syria. The translation and adaptation of the Hebrew Bible into Aramaic reflects the ways in which the Jewish community in Syria interacted with and understood their sacred texts.

In addition, the use of the Peshitta Old Testament in the Syrian Orthodox Church highlights its ongoing significance and relevance. It is an important part of the liturgical tradition and continues to shape the religious beliefs and practices of the Syrian Orthodox community.

Conclusion

The Syriac Peshitta Old Testament is an important translation of the Hebrew Bible into the Aramaic language. It is significant for its early dating, its textual tradition, and its cultural and religious context. The Peshitta Old Testament continues to be an important part of the liturgical tradition of the Syrian Orthodox Church and provides valuable insight into the religious and cultural world of ancient Syria.

Canonical Significance of the Syriac Peshitta

Introduction

The Canon of scripture, or the collection of texts considered to be sacred and authoritative within a particular religious tradition, is a complex and often contested topic. The canon of the Syriac Peshitta, like the canon of any religious tradition, is shaped by a variety of historical, cultural, and theological factors.

Canon Formation in the Syrian Orthodox Church

The canon of the Syrian Orthodox Church, of which the Peshitta Old Testament is a part, is believed to have been formed in the 5th century CE. This canon includes the 27 books of the New Testament and 22 of the 39 books of the Hebrew Bible, including the Pentateuch, the historical books, the Wisdom literature, and the Prophets. The Syrian Orthodox Church does not include the remaining books of the Hebrew Bible, known as the "apocryphal" or "deuterocanonical" books, in its canon. This canon is similar to the canon of the Syrian Church of the East but differs from the canon of other Eastern Orthodox and Oriental Orthodox churches, which include the "deuterocanonical" books.

Significance of the Canon of the Syrian Orthodox Church

The canon of the Syrian Orthodox Church, and specifically the inclusion of the Peshitta Old Testament, is significant for several reasons. Firstly, it reflects the unique theological and ecclesiological perspectives of the Syrian Orthodox Church. The exclusion of the "deuterocanonical" books, for example, may reflect a desire to distinguish the Syrian Orthodox Church from other Christian communities and to emphasize its continuity with Jewish tradition.

INTRODUCTION TO THE TEXT OF THE OLD TESTAMENT

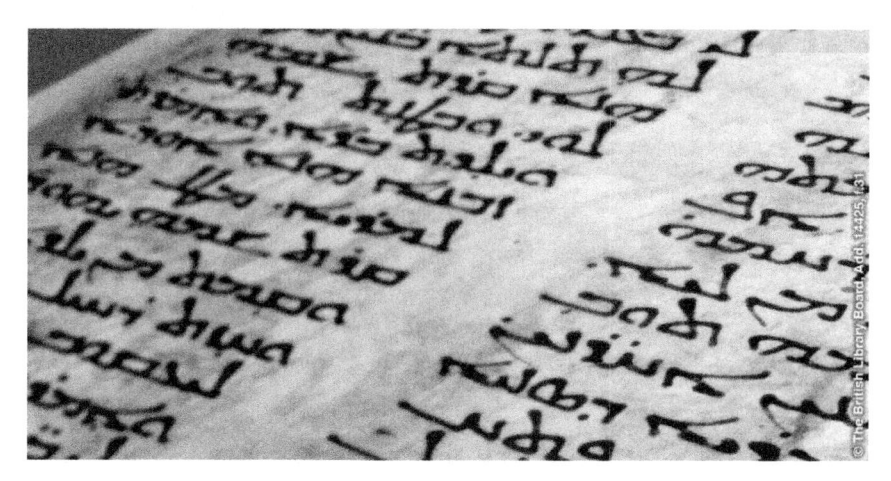

Secondly, the canon of the Syrian Orthodox Church, including the Peshitta Old Testament, is an important witness to the diversity of early Christian thought and practice. The canon of the Syrian Orthodox Church, like the canon of any religious tradition, is shaped by a variety of historical, cultural, and theological factors.

Finally, the canon of the Syrian Orthodox Church, and specifically the inclusion of the Peshitta Old Testament, is significant for its ongoing use in liturgical and spiritual practice. The Peshitta Old Testament continues to be an important part of the liturgical tradition of the Syrian Orthodox Church and shapes the religious beliefs and practices of its community.

Conclusion

The canon of the Syriac Peshitta is a complex and often contested topic, shaped by a variety of historical, cultural, and theological factors. The canon of the Syrian Orthodox Church, of which the Peshitta Old Testament is a part, is believed to have been formed in the 5th century CE and includes the 27 books of the New Testament and 22 of the 39 books of the Hebrew Bible. The canon of the Syrian Orthodox Church is significant for its unique theological and ecclesiological perspectives, its witness to the diversity of early Christian thought and practice, and its ongoing use in liturgical and spiritual practice.

Chronology of the Syriac Peshitta

Introduction

The chronology of the Syriac Peshitta Old Testament is an area of ongoing scholarship and debate. However, based on the current evidence, it is believed that the translation of the Hebrew Bible into Aramaic, which would eventually become known as the Peshitta Old Testament, was likely done in the 2nd century CE.

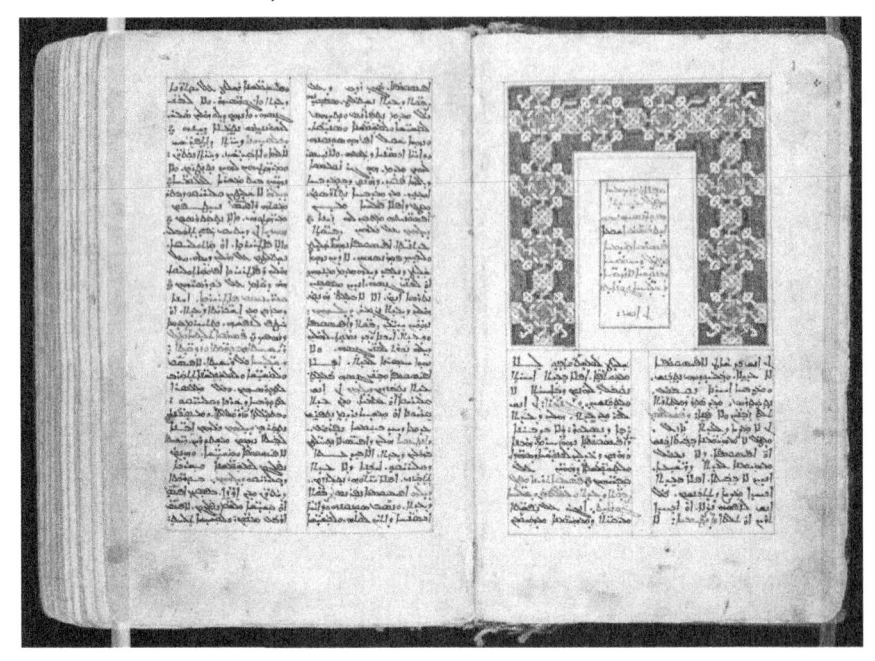

Evidence for the 2nd Century Dating

One of the main pieces of evidence for a 2nd century dating of the Peshitta Old Testament is the fact that it is quoted by several early Christian writers from that time period. For example, the Syrian Church Father Ephrem the Syrian, who lived in the 4th century, quotes extensively from the Peshitta Old Testament in his writings. This suggests that the Peshitta Old Testament was already in circulation and considered authoritative at that time.

Additionally, the Peshitta Old Testament is believed to have been used by the Jewish-Christian community in Edessa, a city in ancient Syria, which was an important center of Christianity in the 2nd century. The fact that the Peshitta Old Testament is written in the same dialect of Aramaic as was spoken in Edessa also lends support to the idea that it was produced in that region during the 2nd century.

Conclusion

While the exact chronology of the Syriac Peshitta Old Testament is an area of ongoing scholarship and debate, it is generally believed to have been produced in the 2nd century CE. This dating is supported by the fact that it is quoted by several early Christian writers from that time period and that it was likely used by the Jewish-Christian community in Edessa. The Peshitta Old Testament is considered as one of the oldest translations of the Hebrew Bible and it provides valuable insight into the textual tradition of the Septuagint and the religious and cultural world of ancient Syria.

Manuscripts of the Syriac Peshitta

Introduction

Manuscripts of the Syriac Peshitta Old Testament are important primary sources for understanding the text and transmission of the translation. The surviving manuscripts of the Peshitta Old Testament provide valuable insight into the textual tradition and variations of the translation, as well as its historical context and use.

Types of Manuscripts

The manuscripts of the Syriac Peshitta Old Testament can be divided into two main categories: parchment manuscripts and printed editions. Parchment manuscripts are written on animal skin and are typically written in the Estrangela script, a form of the Aramaic script. Printed editions, on the other hand, are printed on paper using movable type and are typically written in the Serto script, a more decorative form of the Aramaic script.

Significance of Manuscripts

Manuscripts of the Syriac Peshitta Old Testament are significant for several reasons. Firstly, they provide valuable insight into the textual tradition and variations of the translation. For example, some manuscripts contain additional or variant readings not found in other manuscripts, which can provide insight into the transmission and evolution of the text.

Secondly, manuscripts of the Peshitta Old Testament provide insight into the historical context and use of the translation. For example, some manuscripts include notes or commentary written by scribes or readers, which can provide insight into the ways in which the text was understood and used by different communities.

Finally, manuscripts of the Peshitta Old Testament are important primary sources for understanding the text, transmission, and history of the translation. They are essential tools for scholars and researchers studying the

Syriac Peshitta Old Testament, and they have also been used to produce critical editions of the text.

Conclusion

Manuscripts of the Syriac Peshitta Old Testament are important primary sources for understanding the text and transmission of the translation. They can be divided into two main categories: parchment manuscripts and printed editions. Manuscripts of the Peshitta Old Testament provide valuable insight into the textual tradition and variations of the translation, as well as its historical context and use. They are essential tools for scholars and researchers studying the Syriac Peshitta Old Testament, and they have also been used to produce critical editions of the text.

Translations of the Syriac Peshitta into English

Introduction

Translations of the Syriac Peshitta Old Testament into English are important tools for scholars and researchers studying the text, as well as for those interested in understanding the translation and its significance within the Syrian Orthodox Church. These translations provide access to the text for those who do not read Aramaic and can also offer insight into the ways in which the translation has been understood and used in different contexts.

History of English Translations

The first English translation of the Peshitta Old Testament was made by George Lamsa, an Assyrian priest, in 1933. This translation was based on the Eastern Peshitta text and is considered a valuable resource for scholars and researchers. Since then, several other translations of the Peshitta Old Testament have been made, including the New Testament Peshitta, which is a translation of the New Testament from the original Aramaic.

Significance of English Translations

Translations of the Syriac Peshitta Old Testament into English are significant for several reasons. Firstly, they provide access to the text for those who do not read Aramaic. This allows for a broader audience to engage with and study the translation, including scholars and researchers, as well as members of the Syrian Orthodox Church and interested members of the general public.

Secondly, translations of the Peshitta Old Testament into English can offer insight into the ways in which the translation has been understood and used in different contexts. For example, the George Lamsa translation is based on the Eastern Peshitta text and is considered a valuable resource for scholars and researchers, while the New Testament Peshitta translation is based on the original Aramaic and provides an insight into the ways in which the text has been understood and used within the Syrian Orthodox Church.

Finally, translations of the Syriac Peshitta Old Testament into English can help to preserve the text and ensure its continued relevance and significance. The translation of the text into a language that is widely spoken and understood can help to ensure that the text remains accessible and continues to be a valuable resource for scholars and researchers, as well as members of the Syrian Orthodox Church and interested members of the general public.

Conclusion

Translations of the Syriac Peshitta Old Testament into English are important tools for scholars and researchers studying the text, as well as for those interested in understanding the translation and its significance within the Syrian Orthodox Church. These translations provide access to the text for those who do not read Aramaic and can also offer insight into the ways in which the translation has been understood and used in different contexts. They are a significant way of preserving the text and ensuring its continued relevance and significance.

Scholarly Editions of the Syriac Peshitta

Introduction

Scholarly editions of the Syriac Peshitta Old Testament are critical editions of the text that have been prepared by scholars and researchers using the most important and reliable manuscripts of the translation. These editions are important tools for scholars and researchers studying the text and its transmission and are also used to produce translations of the text into other languages.

Purpose of Scholarly Editions

The purpose of scholarly editions of the Syriac Peshitta Old Testament is to provide an accurate and reliable representation of the text. These editions are typically based on the most important and reliable manuscripts of the translation and are prepared using established principles of textual criticism. This process involves comparing different manuscripts of the text in order to establish the most original and accurate version of the text.

Significance of Scholarly Editions

Scholarly editions of the Syriac Peshitta Old Testament are significant for several reasons. Firstly, they provide an accurate and reliable representation of the text. This is important for scholars and researchers studying the text and its transmission, as it allows them to engage with the most original and accurate version of the text.

Secondly, scholarly editions of the Peshitta Old Testament provide insight into the textual tradition and variations of the translation. For example, these editions often include variant readings found in different manuscripts of the text, which can provide insight into the transmission and evolution of the text.

Finally, scholarly editions of the Syriac Peshitta Old Testament are important primary sources for understanding the text, transmission, and history of the translation. They are essential tools for scholars and researchers studying the Syriac Peshitta Old Testament and are also used to produce translations of the text into other languages.

Conclusion

Scholarly editions of the Syriac Peshitta Old Testament are critical editions of the text that have been prepared by scholars and researchers using the most important and reliable manuscripts of the translation. The purpose of scholarly editions of the Syriac Peshitta Old Testament is to provide an accurate and reliable representation of the text. They are significant for several reasons, such as providing an accurate and reliable representation of the text, insight into the textual tradition and variations of the translation and also being an important primary source for understanding the text, transmission, and history of the translation. They are essential tools for scholars and researchers studying the Syriac Peshitta Old Testament and are also used to produce translations of the text into other languages.

How Has the Syriac Peshitta Helped Textual Scholars Establish the Original Reading of the Hebrew Old Testament Manuscripts?

Introduction

Textual scholars have long been interested in understanding the original readings of the Hebrew Old Testament manuscripts, as the preservation of the text is crucial for the understanding of its history and meaning. The Syriac Peshitta Old Testament, as an ancient translation of the Hebrew Bible, can provide valuable insights into the original readings of the Hebrew Old Testament manuscripts.

Role of the Peshitta as a Witness to the Hebrew Text

The Syriac Peshitta Old Testament is considered to be a representative of the "Eastern" text-type of the Septuagint, which is characterized by its close adherence to the Hebrew text and its avoidance of interpretive expansions. This means that the Peshitta Old Testament can be seen as a relatively literal translation of the Hebrew text. This can be useful for textual scholars as it provides a glimpse into the Hebrew text as it existed in the second century, allowing scholars to compare it to the other witnesses of the Hebrew text such as the Septuagint, the Dead Sea Scrolls, and the Masoretic Text.

Significance of the Peshitta in the Study of Textual Variants

The Syriac Peshitta Old Testament can also be used to study textual variants, which are differences in wording or arrangement of the text. By comparing the Peshitta to other witnesses of the Hebrew text, scholars can gain insight into the original readings of the Hebrew Old Testament manuscripts. For example, if a variant reading found in the Peshitta is also found in other witnesses of the Hebrew text, it is more likely to be an original reading.

Furthermore, the Peshitta Old Testament contains several passages found in the Septuagint but not present in the Masoretic Text, which are also called as additional or deuterocanonical books, these passages also help scholars to understand the origin of these books and the reason they were included or excluded from the canon of different religious traditions.

Conclusion

The Syriac Peshitta Old Testament can provide valuable insights into the original readings of the Hebrew Old Testament manuscripts. As a relatively literal translation of the Hebrew text, it can serve as a witness to the Hebrew text as it existed in the second century and can also be used to study textual variants. The Peshitta Old Testament is an important tool for textual scholars in understanding the preservation and transmission of the Hebrew Bible, and its close adherence to the Hebrew text and avoidance of interpretive expansions makes it a valuable resource for reconstructing the original readings of the Hebrew Old Testament manuscripts. Additionally, the inclusion of additional or deuterocanonical books in the Peshitta Old

Testament can provide scholars with valuable information on the origin and canonization of these texts. Overall, the Syriac Peshitta Old Testament is a crucial resource for textual scholars in their efforts to establish the original readings of the Hebrew Old Testament manuscripts.

INTRODUCTION TO THE TEXT OF THE OLD TESTAMENT

CHAPTER 8 The Latin Vulgate

Image 35 Saint Jerome in His Study, by Domenico Ghirlandaio.

The Latin Vulgate

Introduction

The Latin Vulgate Old Testament is a translation of the Hebrew Bible into Latin, which was widely used in the Western Church during the Middle Ages. The translation was done by Saint Jerome in the late 4th century CE and it was considered the standard version of the Bible for over a thousand years.

History of the Latin Vulgate

The Latin Vulgate Old Testament was translated by Saint Jerome, a Christian priest and scholar, in the late 4th century CE. Jerome used the Septuagint, the Greek translation of the Hebrew Bible, as well as the Hebrew text itself, as the basis for his translation. The translation was widely adopted by the Western Church and was considered the standard version of the Bible for over a thousand years.

Image 36 Jerome

Significance of the Latin Vulgate

The Latin Vulgate Old Testament has several historical and religious significances. Firstly, it was the standard version of the Bible used by the Western Church for over a thousand years, and it played a crucial role in shaping the religious and intellectual culture of medieval Europe.

Secondly, Saint Jerome's translation of the Hebrew Bible into Latin was one of the most important contributions to the development of the Latin language, providing a rich source of vocabulary and idioms to the language.

Thirdly, the Latin Vulgate Old Testament is considered to be one of the most important ancient translations of the Hebrew Bible, and it has been used as a primary source for the study of the text and its transmission.

Finally, the Latin Vulgate Old Testament is still used by some of the Catholic Church, and it is an important source for the study of the history of the Bible and Christianity

Conclusion

The Latin Vulgate Old Testament is a translation of the Hebrew Bible into Latin, which was widely used in the Western Church during the Middle Ages. The translation was done by Saint Jerome in the late 4th century CE, and it played a crucial role in shaping the religious and intellectual culture of medieval Europe. It also contributed to the development of the Latin language, providing a rich source of vocabulary and idioms. The Latin Vulgate Old Testament is considered to be one of the most important ancient translations of the Hebrew Bible, and it has been used as a primary source for the study of the text and its transmission. Even today, it is still used by some of the Catholic Church, and it is an important source for the study of the history of the Bible and Christianity.

Canonical Significance of the Latin Vulgate

Introduction

The Latin Vulgate Old Testament is a translation of the Hebrew Bible into Latin, which was widely used in the Western Church during the Middle Ages. The translation was done by Saint Jerome in the late 4th century CE and it played an important role in shaping the canon of the Bible in the Western Church.

Role in the Development of the Canon

The Latin Vulgate Old Testament was widely adopted by the Western Church as the standard version of the Bible and it played a crucial role in shaping the canon of the Bible in the Western Church. The canon of the Bible refers to the books that are considered to be authoritative and inspired by God. The Latin Vulgate Old Testament was used as the basis for the canon of the Bible in the Western Church, and it was considered to be the authoritative text of the Bible for over a thousand years.

Significance in the Catholic Church

The Latin Vulgate Old Testament holds an important place in the Catholic Church as it was the official version of the Bible for the Catholic Church for many centuries. It was used in the liturgy, in theological studies and in the formation of doctrines. The Council of Trent, a Catholic council held in the mid-16th century, affirmed the authority of the Latin Vulgate Old Testament and established it as the official Bible of the Catholic Church.

Additionally, the Latin Vulgate Old Testament contains several texts that are considered deuterocanonical by the Catholic Church, such as Tobit, Judith, Wisdom, Sirach and Baruch, among others. These texts are not found in the Hebrew Bible and were not considered authoritative by the Jews, but they were included in the canon of the Bible by the Catholic Church based on the authority of the Latin Vulgate Old Testament.

Conclusion

The Latin Vulgate Old Testament is a translation of the Hebrew Bible into Latin, which was widely used in the Western Church during the Middle Ages. The translation played an important role in shaping the canon of the Bible in the Western Church, and it was considered the authoritative text of the Bible for over a thousand years. The canon of the Bible refers to the books that are considered to be authoritative and inspired by God, and the Latin Vulgate Old Testament was used as the basis for the canon of the Bible in the Western Church. The Latin Vulgate Old Testament holds an important place in the Catholic Church as it was the official version of the Bible for the Catholic Church for many centuries. It was used in the liturgy, in theological studies and in the formation of doctrines. The Council of Trent, a Catholic council held in the mid-16th century, affirmed the authority of the Latin Vulgate Old Testament and established it as the official Bible of the Catholic Church. The Latin Vulgate Old Testament also contains several texts that are considered deuterocanonical by the Catholic Church, which were not considered authoritative by the Jews but were included in the canon of the Bible by the Catholic Church based on the authority of the Latin Vulgate Old Testament.

Chronology of the Latin Vulgate

Introduction

The Latin Vulgate Old Testament is a translation of the Hebrew Bible into Latin, which was widely used in the Western Church during the Middle Ages. The translation was done by Saint Jerome in the late 4th century CE

INTRODUCTION TO THE TEXT OF THE OLD TESTAMENT

and it played an important role in shaping the canon of the Bible in the Western Church. This translation has a rich history that spans several centuries and is closely linked to the development of Christianity in the Western world.

Translation and Completion

The Latin Vulgate Old Testament was translated by Saint Jerome, a Christian priest and scholar, in the late 4th century CE. Jerome used the Septuagint, the Greek translation of the Hebrew Bible, as well as the Hebrew text itself, as the basis for his translation. Jerome's translation of the Latin Vulgate Old Testament was not completed all at once but rather it was done in stages throughout his life. He first translated the Gospels and the Psalms, then the New Testament and finally the Old Testament.

Adoption and Use

The Latin Vulgate Old Testament was widely adopted by the Western Church and was considered the standard version of the Bible for over a thousand years. It was used in the liturgy, in theological studies and in the formation of doctrines. The Council of Trent, a Catholic council held in the mid-16th century, affirmed the authority of the Latin Vulgate Old Testament and established it as the official Bible of the Catholic Church.

Preservation and Modern Editions

After the invention of the printing press, the Latin Vulgate Old Testament was widely distributed in printed form and it helped to preserve the text and ensure its continued relevance and significance. Today, many modern scholarly editions of the Latin Vulgate Old Testament have been produced based on the best available manuscripts. These editions are important tools for scholars and researchers studying the text and its transmission, and they are also used to produce translations of the text into other languages.

Conclusion

The Latin Vulgate Old Testament is a translation of the Hebrew Bible into Latin, which was widely used in the Western Church during the Middle Ages. The translation was done by Saint Jerome in the late 4th century CE and it played an important role in shaping the canon of the Bible in the Western Church. It was widely adopted by the Western Church and was considered the standard version of the Bible for over a thousand years. The Latin Vulgate Old Testament has been widely distributed and preserved through the ages, and it has been the subject of many modern scholarly editions. These editions are important tools for scholars and researchers studying the text and its transmission, and they are also used to produce translations of the text into other languages.

Manuscripts of the Latin Vulgate

Introduction

The Latin Vulgate Old Testament is an important translation of the Hebrew Bible into Latin, which was widely used in the Western Church during the Middle Ages. The translation was done by Saint Jerome in the late 4th century CE, and it played a crucial role in shaping the canon of the Bible in the Western Church. The preservation and transmission of the text is closely linked to the manuscripts of the Latin Vulgate Old Testament.

Types of Manuscripts

Manuscripts of the Latin Vulgate Old Testament can be broadly divided into two categories: early manuscripts and later manuscripts. Early manuscripts are those that were written within a few centuries of Jerome's translation, while later manuscripts were written in the centuries following. Early manuscripts are considered to be more reliable as they are closer in time to the original translation and are less likely to have undergone significant changes or modifications.

Significance of Manuscripts

Manuscripts of the Latin Vulgate Old Testament are significant for several reasons. Firstly, they are important primary sources for understanding the text, transmission, and history of the translation. They provide insight into the textual tradition and variations of the translation and also help scholars to understand the evolution of the text over time.

Secondly, manuscripts of the Latin Vulgate Old Testament are important for the study of the history of the Bible and Christianity. They provide a glimpse into the religious and intellectual culture of the time in which they were written and offer insight into the beliefs and practices of the people who used them.

Finally, manuscripts of the Latin Vulgate Old Testament are important for the study of the history of the Latin language. They provide a rich source of vocabulary and idioms and offer insight into the development of the language over time.

Conclusion

In conclusion, manuscripts of the Latin Vulgate Old Testament are an important aspect of understanding the translation, transmission, and history of the text. They are primary sources that provide insight into the textual tradition, variations and evolution of the text over time. Additionally, they offer a glimpse into the religious and intellectual culture of the time in which they were written, providing insight into the beliefs and practices of the people who used them. They also play an important role in the study of the history of Christianity and the Latin language.

Translations of the Latin Vulgate into English

Introduction

The Latin Vulgate is a 4th century CE Latin translation of the Bible that was widely used in the Western Church during the Middle Ages. The translation was done by Saint Jerome and it played a crucial role in shaping the canon of the Bible in the Western Church. Translations of the Latin Vulgate into English have played an important role in the study and understanding of the Bible for English-speaking readers.

Early Translations

One of the earliest translations of the Latin Vulgate into English was the Wycliffe Bible in the 14th century. This translation was done by John Wycliffe and his followers and was based on the Latin Vulgate. The translation was not well received by the Church, as it was considered to be a direct challenge to the Church's authority in matters of scripture.

Another early translation of the Latin Vulgate into English was the Coverdale Bible, which was produced by Miles Coverdale in 1535. This translation was the first complete translation of the Bible in English and was also based on the Latin Vulgate.

Modern Translations

In the 19th and 20th centuries, several new translations of the Latin Vulgate into English were produced. One of the most significant is the Douay-Rheims Bible, which was first published in 1582. This translation was a direct translation of the Latin Vulgate into English and was widely used by Catholics in the English-speaking world.

In recent times, the New American Bible, Revised Edition (NABRE) is a translation of the Latin Vulgate into English that has gained wide acceptance. It is a scholarly translation done by the Confraternity of Christian Doctrine and was first published in 2011. It is considered to be a highly reliable translation that is widely used in Catholic Church.

Conclusion

In conclusion, translations of the Latin Vulgate into English have played an important role in the study and understanding of the Bible for English-speaking readers. Early translations like the Wycliffe Bible and the Coverdale Bible[4] were based on the Latin Vulgate and were not well received by the Church. However, more recent translations like the Douay-Rheims Bible, the New American Bible, Revised Edition (NABRE) are considered to be more reliable and widely used.

Scholarly Editions of the Latin Vulgate

Introduction

The Latin Vulgate is a 4th century CE Latin translation of the Bible that was widely used in the Western Church during the Middle Ages. The translation was done by Saint Jerome and it played a crucial role in shaping the canon of the Bible in the Western Church. Scholarly editions of the Latin Vulgate have been produced throughout history in order to provide accurate and reliable texts for scholars and researchers.

Early Scholarly Editions

One of the earliest scholarly editions of the Latin Vulgate was produced by Robert Estienne in 1528. Estienne was a printer and publisher who was also a classical scholar and linguist. He produced an edition of the Latin Vulgate that included the original text as well as a critical apparatus, which provided variant readings from other manuscripts. Estienne's edition was considered to be a significant advancement in scholarship at the time.

Modern Scholarly Editions

In the 19th and 20th centuries, several new scholarly editions of the Latin Vulgate were produced. One of the most important is the Sixto-Clementine Vulgate, which was first published in 1592. This edition was based on the Clementine Vulgate, a version of the Latin Vulgate that had been revised by Pope Clement VIII in 1592. The Sixto-Clementine Vulgate

---

[4] The Coverdale Bible, which was produced by Miles Coverdale in 1535, was not based solely on Desiderius Erasmus' Greek text of the New Testament. Coverdale used a variety of sources for his translation, including the Latin Vulgate, the German Bible, and the Dutch Bible. He also consulted Erasmus' Greek New Testament, which had been published in 1516 and was considered to be a significant advance in scholarship at the time. Coverdale's goal was to produce a translation of the Bible that would be accessible to the general public and not just the clergy. His translation was the first complete translation of the Bible in English and is considered to be a significant achievement in the history of Bible translation.

is considered to be the most authoritative edition of the Latin Vulgate and is widely used by scholars.

Another important scholarly edition of the Latin Vulgate is the Nova Vulgata, which was first published in 1979. This edition was produced by the Vatican's Pontifical Commission for the preparation of the Nova Vulgata, and it is the official version of the Latin Vulgate for the Catholic Church. This edition is based on the most reliable manuscripts, and it is considered to be the most accurate edition of the Latin Vulgate.

Conclusion

In conclusion, scholarly editions of the Latin Vulgate have played an important role in the study of the Bible throughout history. From early editions such as Robert Estienne's in 1528, to more modern editions such as the Sixto-Clementine Vulgate and the Nova Vulgata, these editions have provided accurate and reliable texts for scholars and researchers to study. These editions have also helped to establish the original readings of the texts and have played a role in shaping the canon of the Bible in the Western Church. It's important to note that the Latin Vulgate has a huge influence on the Western Christianity and it played a vital role in shaping the theology and the understanding of the Bible. The Latin Vulgate continues to be an important source for scholars and researchers studying the history of the Bible, Christianity and the Western Church.

How Has the Latin Vulgate Helped Textual Scholars Establish the Original Reading of the Hebrew Old Testament Manuscripts?

The Latin Vulgate has played an important role in the field of textual criticism of the Hebrew Old Testament. Textual scholars use a variety of ancient textual witnesses, including manuscripts, versions and patristic citations, to reconstruct the original text of the Hebrew Bible. The Vulgate, as a translation of the Septuagint, which itself was based on earlier Hebrew manuscripts, has provided valuable evidence for reconstructing the original readings of the Hebrew text.

One way in which the Vulgate has helped scholars establish the original readings of the Hebrew text is through its preservation of variant readings found in the Septuagint but not in the Masoretic Text (MT), the standard Hebrew text used in the Middle Ages. These variants can provide insight into the textual tradition behind the Septuagint and the MT and can help scholars reconstruct the original readings of the Hebrew text.

Additionally, the Vulgate's translation of the Septuagint can also provide insight into the meaning and interpretation of the Hebrew text in the early Christian Church. Patristic citations of the Vulgate can also provide valuable evidence for reconstructing the original readings of the Hebrew text.

It's important to note that the Latin Vulgate has a huge influence on the Western Christianity, and it played a vital role in shaping the theology and the understanding of the Bible. The Latin Vulgate continues to be an important source for scholars and researchers studying the history of the Bible, Christianity and the Western Church.

In conclusion, the Latin Vulgate, with its translation of the Septuagint and its preservation of variant readings, has provided valuable evidence for scholars in the task of reconstructing the original readings of the Hebrew Old Testament manuscripts. The Latin Vulgate continues to be an important resource for textual criticism and for understanding the history of the Bible and its interpretation in the Western Church.

CHAPTER 9 The Goal and Task of Textual Criticism

Image 37 Scriptorium – A room set apart for writing, especially one in a monastery where manuscripts were copied.

Old Testament textual criticism is the process of examining and evaluating the various textual witnesses of the Hebrew Bible, such as manuscripts, versions, and patristic citations, in order to reconstruct the original text. The goal of Old Testament textual criticism is to determine the original wording of the original texts as they were written by the biblical authors. It should be noted, that 90% of the text is without significant variation.[5]

The task of Old Testament textual criticism involves several key steps. First, scholars must gather and examine all available textual witnesses, including manuscripts, versions, and patristic citations, in order to establish the range of variations and differences among the witnesses. Next, scholars

---

[5] Bruce K. Waltke, "Old Testament Textual Criticism," in *Foundations for Biblical Interpretation*, ed. David S. Dockery, Kenneth A. Matthews and Robert Sloan (Nashville: Broadman, 1994), p. 157. See also Bruce K. Waltke, "Textual Criticism of the Old Testament and Its Relationship to Exegesis and Theology," in *New International Dictionary of Old Testament Theology & Exegesis,* vol. 1, ed. Willem A. VanGemeren (Grand Rapids: Zondervan, 1997), esp. pp. 64–66.

must evaluate the quality and reliability of the witnesses, considering factors such as date, provenance, and textual features, in order to determine which readings are original.

Goal Post Excursion

Once the range of variations and the quality of the witnesses have been established, scholars can begin the process of reconstructing the original text. This often involves comparing the different witnesses and reconstructing the original reading or the one most likely to be the original so says conservative scholarship, or "Urtext" so says moderate scholarship, based on the textual data. An Urtext is an original or the earliest version of a text. So that this author is clear, the goal of Old or New Testament textual criticism has always been and should always be to determine the original reading or the one that is most likely to be the original.

Table 1.1. Perceived Goals of Old Testament Textual Criticism by Paul D. Wegner, *A Student's Guide to Textual Criticism of the Bible: Its History, Methods & Results*

Goal	Description	Scholars
1. Restore the original composition	The goal is to recover the author's *ipsissima verba*, "to establish the text as the author wished to have it presented to the public."	Most older textual critics, Harrison[6]
2. Restore the final form of the text (most modern textual critics)	The goal is to recover the *ipsissima verba* of the final redactor, assuming that the book has gone through some evolutionary process to get to this final form.	Brotzman, Deist, Würthwein
3. Restore the earliest attested form	The goal is to recover the earliest attested form of the text for which there are actual textual witnesses. Generally the text in view	Hebrew University Bible Project, UBS Hebrew Old Testament Text Project

---

[6] Roland K. Harrison, *Introduction to the Old Testament* (Grand Rapids: Eerdmans, 1969), p. 259.[6]

	is from the second century B.C., and conjectural emendations are not allowed.	
4. Restore accepted texts (plural)	The goal is to recover the texts as they were accepted by particular religious communities. Each text may differ according to the authoritative standard of its particular community.	James Sanders, Brevard Childs (though he centers on the mt text accepted by the Jews)
5. Restore final texts (plural)	The goal is to recover the final form of the text. In some books or pericopes this may mean that there are several equally valid texts of the Old Testament that need to be restored.	Emanuel Tov, Bruce K. Waltke
6. Restore all various "literary editions" of the Old Testament	The goal is not to just reproduce the mt, but to restore all the "literary editions" of the various writings that can be discerned in the evolution of the Hebrew Bible (e.g., the LXX, SP, MT, as well as all others represented at Qumran and other places).	Eugene Ulrich

Table 1.1 summarizes and augments the history of what scholars believe to be the goal of Old Testament textual criticism as described in an article by Bruce K. Waltke.[7]

End of Excursion

It's important to note that the process of Old Testament textual criticism is ongoing and there are continuous debates and discussions among

---

[7] Paul D. Wegner, *A Student's Guide to Textual Criticism of the Bible: Its History, Methods & Results* (Downers Grove, IL: InterVarsity Press, 2006), 32.

scholars over the best approach to reconstructing the original text. The field of Old Testament textual criticism is a complex and ever-evolving field, and new discoveries and advancements in technology continue to shape our understanding of the Hebrew Bible.

In conclusion, the goal of Old Testament textual criticism is to determine the original reading of the text as it was written by the biblical authors. The task of Old Testament textual criticism involves gathering and examining all available textual witnesses, evaluating their quality and reliability, and reconstructing the original text based on the textual data. It's a continuous process that is shaped by new discoveries and advancements in technology. The Latin Vulgate, like the Syriac Peshitta, has played a significant role in the field of Old Testament textual criticism by providing valuable textual data for scholars to use in the process of reconstructing the original text of the Hebrew Bible. The Latin Vulgate, being translated from the Hebrew and Greek text, has provided scholars with valuable insight into the textual variations and readings that existed in the early centuries of Christianity. Additionally, many of the manuscripts of the Latin Vulgate are quite old, some dating back to the 4th century CE, which allows scholars to study the text as it existed in early Christianity. As a result, the Latin Vulgate has been an important tool for textual scholars in establishing the original reading of the Hebrew Old Testament manuscripts.

Autograph: The autograph, or original manuscript, refers to the text that was physically written by an Old Testament author or dictated by the author and transcribed by a scribe. The process of creating the autograph may have involved shorthand techniques, and it is likely that both the scribe and the author would have reviewed and made corrections to the text. It is important to note that the authority for these corrections would have been the author, as it was believed that the Holy Spirit guided the author's writing. The finished product of this process would be considered the autograph, which is often used interchangeably with the term "original."

Textual critics use the term "original" to refer to the text that is correctly attributed to a biblical author, without focusing on the specific process of how the book or letter was written. This distinction is more general and less specific than the term "autograph," which specifically refers to the physical manuscript created by the author or scribe.

It's important to note that the autograph is not available today, but the original text may be reconstructed by textual criticism, which is the study and reconstruction of the original text of a document, by comparing and analyzing different manuscript versions of the text. This process allows scholars to reconstruct the most likely original text based on the available manuscript evidence. The autograph, or original manuscript, of a biblical text is an important part of textual criticism as it represents the earliest and most direct witness to the text.

Rules of Old Testament Textual Criticism

Textual Criticism is the process of evaluating and comparing the different versions or copies of a text to determine its original content. In the case of the Old Testament, this involves analyzing the available Hebrew and Aramaic manuscripts, as well as ancient translations such as the Septuagint, the Syriac Peshitta, and the Latin Vulgate, to reconstruct the original text.

When it comes to determining the original reading of a text, scholars use a set of established rules or principles to guide their analysis. These rules aim to help scholars identify and prefer readings that are most likely to be original and closest to the autograph (the original text written by the author).

One set of rules used by Old Testament textual critics is known as the "Biblia Hebraica Stuttgartensia" (BHS) rules. These rules were published in the BHS edition of the Hebrew Bible, which is considered one of the most important scholarly editions of the Old Testament. The BHS rules were formulated by Karl Elliger and Wilhelm Rudolph, and they include principles such as the following:

- **The principle of proximity**: This principle states that readings that are closest to the original text are to be preferred. This means that when there are multiple variations of a word or phrase, the reading that is most similar to the surrounding context is likely to be the original one.

- **The principle of difficulty**: This principle states that readings that are harder or more difficult to understand are to be preferred over those that are easy or smooth. The reasoning behind this is that scribes were more likely to change a text to make it easier to understand, rather than to make it harder.

- **The principle of lectio difficilior potior**: This principle states that the more difficult reading is to be preferred. This means that when there are multiple variations of a word or phrase, the reading that is more difficult to understand is more likely to be original, as scribes were more likely to change a text to make it easier to understand.

Overall, it is important to note that there is not one set of rules that is universally accepted among textual critics. Scholars will often use a combination of different sets of rules to make a determination about the original reading of a text. It is also important to keep in mind that textual criticism is a field that is constantly evolving, as new manuscripts and evidence are discovered and new methods and technologies are developed.

Gathering the Evidence

The first step in Old Testament textual criticism is to gather all available evidence for a particular reading. This includes manuscripts of the Hebrew text, as well as versions in other languages such as the Greek Septuagint, Aramaic targums, Syriac Peshitta, and Latin Vulgate. Scholars may also consult other ancient sources such as the Qumran scrolls.

One way to gather this evidence is to use the apparatus of a critical edition of the Hebrew text, such as the Biblia Hebraica Stuttgartensia (BHS). However, it is important to keep in mind that not all critical editions are created equal, and some may have limitations or biases. Additionally, using a critical apparatus means relying on the judgments of the editors, rather than working directly with the evidence.

For advanced textual critics, it may be necessary to work directly with the manuscripts and versions, rather than relying on a critical apparatus. This requires a knowledge of the languages of the versions, such as Greek, Aramaic, Syriac, and Latin, as well as the ability to compare and analyze the texts. This process is more time-consuming and requires additional linguistic skills, but it allows for a more thorough examination of the evidence and can provide a more objective evaluation of the original reading.

In his book "An Introduction to Textual Criticism of the Old Testament", Ernst Würthwein writes: "The task of the textual critic is not only to gather all possible witnesses to the text but also to evaluate them on the basis of certain principles, which will be discussed in the following." He goes on to explain that these principles include evaluating the manuscripts based on factors such as age, geographical origin, and consistency with other manuscripts.

Another set of rules that has been used in Old Testament textual criticism is the "Leningrad Codex" (LC) rules, which are based on the Leningrad Codex, one of the oldest and most complete manuscripts of the Hebrew Bible. These rules, developed by Menachem Cohen, focus on the reading of the Leningrad Codex as the most reliable and accurate representation of the original text. According to Cohen, when there is a discrepancy between the Leningrad Codex and other manuscripts, the reading of the Leningrad Codex should be considered the original reading. This approach is based on the belief that the Leningrad Codex, being one of the oldest and most complete manuscripts of the Hebrew Bible, is more likely to preserve the original text than later manuscripts. It is important to note, however, that the LC rules are not universally accepted and have been criticized for being overly reliant on one specific manuscript.

It bears repeating, this author would argue that the primary weight of external evidence generally goes to the original language manuscripts, and the **Codex Leningrad B 19A** and the **Aleppo Codex** are almost always preferred. In Old Testament Textual Criticism, the Masoretic text is our starting point and should only be abandoned as a last resort. While it is true that the Masoretic Text is not perfect, there needs to be a heavy burden of proof in we are to go with an alternative reading. All of the evidence needs to be examined before concluding that a reading in the Masoretic Text is corrupt. The Septuagint continues to be very much important today and is used by textual scholars to help uncover copyists' errors that **might have** crept into the Hebrew manuscripts either intentionally or unintentionally. However, it cannot do it alone without the support of other sources. There are a number of times when you might have the Syriac, Septuagint, Dead Sea Scrolls, Aramaic Targums, and the Vulgate that are at odds with the Masoretic Text the preferred choice should not be the MT.

Another set of rules that has been used in Old Testament textual criticism is the "LXX-based" rules, which take into account the readings of the Septuagint, the ancient Greek translation of the Hebrew Bible. According to this approach, when there is a discrepancy between the Hebrew manuscripts and the Septuagint, the reading of the Septuagint is considered the original reading. This approach is based on the belief that the Septuagint, being an early translation, may reflect an earlier and more accurate form of the text than the later Hebrew manuscripts. However, this approach also has its critics, who argue that the Septuagint may not always be an accurate reflection of the original text. This author would go a step even further than the critics and say that the Septuagint many times is not an accurate reflection of the original text

Analyze the Evidence

Once the text critic has collected the available evidence, the next step is to analyze it. This includes evaluating the quality of the manuscript evidence, the linguistic features of the readings, and any internal or external factors that may have influenced the transmission of the text.

One important aspect of analyzing the evidence is determining the date and origin of the manuscripts. Manuscripts that are older or from a different geographical area may be more reliable witnesses to the original text. For example, a reading found in a 4th-century CE manuscript from Egypt may be considered more original than a reading found in a 10th-century CE manuscript from Spain. However, it is important to note that age alone does not determine the originality of a reading.

Another aspect of analyzing the evidence is evaluating the quality of the manuscript witness. For example, some manuscripts may have been corrected or revised multiple times, while others may have been copied by scribes with poor handwriting or limited knowledge of Hebrew. The text critic must consider the potential impact of these factors on the transmission of the text.

Linguistic analysis is also important in evaluating the evidence. The text critic must consider the grammatical and syntactical features of the readings, as well as the vocabulary and style of the text. Readings that are consistent with the author's style and language are more likely to be original.

Internal factors such as the author's intent and the theological or literary context of the passage also play a role in evaluating the evidence. External factors such as historical events, cultural influences, and the transmission of the text within different communities may also impact the transmission of the text.

Synthesize the Evidence

After collecting and analyzing the evidence, the text critic must then synthesize it to make a judgment about the original reading. This process involves weighing the evidence in light of the rules and principles discussed above, as well as the text critic's own expertise and knowledge of the text. Ultimately, the text critic must make a decision about which reading is most likely the original one.

One important principle to keep in mind when making this decision is the principle of lectio difficilior potior, which states that the more difficult reading is to be preferred. This principle is based on the idea that scribes were more likely to make changes to a text that they found difficult to understand or interpret, whereas they were less likely to change a text that they understood easily.

Another principle that is often used in textual criticism is the principle of internal probability, which states that the reading that best fits the context and style of the rest of the text is to be preferred. This principle is based on the idea that a scribe would be less likely to make changes to a text that would disrupt the flow or coherence of the text as a whole. Some notes read in the Masoretic text margin: "This is one of the eighteen emendations of the Sopherim" or similar words. The scribe who made these revisions had good intentions as he saw the original reading as though it showed a lack of respect for God or his people.

Emendations (Corrections) of the Sopherim—"Tiqqune Sopherim"

The Eighteen Emendations of the Sopherim are a set of corrections made to the Hebrew text of the Bible in order to avoid passages that were deemed to show irreverence or disrespect for God or his representatives. These corrections are noted in the margin of certain Hebrew manuscripts of the Masoretic text and are known as "Tiqqune Sopherim" (or "corrections of the scribes").

According to Gins.Int, pp. 347-363, the eighteen emendations made by the Sopherim are found in the following verses: Ge 18:22; Nu 11:15; 12:12; 1Sa 3:13; 2Sa 16:12; 20:1; 1Ki 12:16; 2Ch 10:16; Job 7:20; 32:3; Ps 106:20; Jer 2:11; La 3:20; Eze 8:17; Ho 4:7; Hab 1:12; Zec 2:8; Mal 1:13.

In addition to these eighteen emendations, there are also other emendations of the Sopherim that are not recorded in the Masoretic notes. According to Gins.Int, p. 363, these include changes made to passages that were deemed to be profane or that described blasphemy or cursing God. These corrections were made in order to make the text more suitable for public reading before the congregation.

It's important to note that text critics may use these emendations as evidence when trying to reconstruct the original text but must weigh them alongside other evidence and principles of textual criticism.

The text critic must **never** consider the principle of external probability, which states that the reading that is supported by the greatest number of independent witnesses is to be preferred. This principle is based on the idea that a reading that is supported by a large number of independent witnesses is more likely to be original than a reading that is supported by only a few witnesses. This would be true only when you might have the Syriac, Septuagint, Dead Sea Scrolls, Aramaic Targums, and the Vulgate that are at odds with the Masoretic Text the preferred choice should not be the MT. This is not true simply because the majority of the Hebrew manuscripts alone have a particular reading.

Ultimately, the goal of textual criticism is to establish the original reading of the text. This is a complex and challenging task that requires a deep understanding of the text, the language in which it was written, and the principles and methods of textual criticism.

Here are a couple of examples of Old Testament textual variants and how they could be evaluated using the methods and rules of textual criticism:

1. **Isaiah 7:14**: The Masoretic Text (MT) has "Behold, a virgin shall conceive and bear a son" while the Septuagint (LXX) has "Behold, a young woman shall conceive and bear a son."

When evaluating this variant, the text critic would first collect the available manuscript evidence, which in this case would be the readings from the MT and LXX. Next, they would apply the rules and principles of textual criticism to weigh the evidence. One principle that some would say should be applied is that readings that are difficult or unnatural in the context of the passage are less likely to be original. In this case, the reading "virgin" may be difficult to reconcile with the context, as it is a prophecy about the birth of a specific historical figure, rather than a general statement about virginity. On the other hand, the reading "young woman" is more natural and would not require additional explanation. Therefore, based on this principle, the text critic might conclude that the original reading was "young woman."

However going back to the **principle of difficulty**: This principle states that readings that are harder or more difficult to understand are to be preferred over those that are easy or smooth. The reasoning behind this is that scribes were more likely to change a text to make it easier to understand, rather than to make it harder.

In this case, the reading "virgin" may be difficult to reconcile with the context, as it is a prophecy about the birth of a specific historical figure, rather than a general statement about virginity. On the other hand, the reading "young woman" is more natural and would not require additional explanation. Therefore, based on this principle, the text critic might conclude that the original reading was "virgin."

In the Old Testament, the Hebrew word "bethulah" is often translated as "virgin." However, in Isaiah 7:14, the Hebrew word "almah" is used, which can mean "maiden" or "young woman." This has led to debate among scholars as to whether the passage is referring to a virgin birth or not. Matthew, writing under inspiration, quotes Isaiah 7:14 in his gospel and uses the Greek word "parthenos," which specifically means "virgin." He applies this prophecy to the birth of Jesus, the Messiah, stating that Mary, Jesus' mother, was a virgin who became pregnant through the operation of God's

INTRODUCTION TO THE TEXT OF THE OLD TESTAMENT

Holy Spirit. This has led many biblical scholars and theologians to believe that the use of the word "almah" in Isaiah 7:14 was a prophetic indication of the virgin birth of Jesus, even though the word itself does not necessarily indicate virginity. The fulfillment of the prophecy in Matthew and Luke's account of Jesus' birth supports this interpretation.

2. **Isaiah 38:11**: The MT has "I said, I shall not see Jah, Jah in the land of the living" while the LXX has "I said, In the noontide of my days I shall go to the gates of hell."

In this case, the text critic would again collect the manuscript evidence, which would be the readings from the MT and LXX. Then, they would apply the rules and principles of textual criticism. One principle that could be applied is that the shorter reading is more likely to be original. In this case, the reading "I shall not see Jah, Jah in the land of the living" is shorter. Applying this principle, the text critic would conclude that the shorter reading of "I shall not see Jah, Jah in the land of the living" is more likely to be original. However, this is not the only principle that could be applied in this situation. Another principle that could be considered is the principle of lectio difficilior potior, which states that the more difficult or unusual reading is more likely to be original. In this case, the reading "I shall not see Jah, Jah in the land of the living" could be considered more difficult or unusual, as it is a negation of the more common phrase "I shall see Jah." We will look at more textual variants later.

Variant Reading(s): A variant reading is a difference in wording or text found in multiple manuscripts of a certain text or document. These variations can occur due to errors made by scribes when copying the text, or because of intentional changes made by editors or translators.

Variation Unit: Variation units in Hebrew Old Testament textual criticism are sections of text that have variations in their readings between different manuscripts. These variations can include differences in spelling, word order, and even entire words or phrases. Setting the limits of a variation unit can be difficult and sometimes controversial, as some variant readings may affect others nearby.

It is important to distinguish between variation units and variant readings. A variation unit is the specific place in the text where manuscripts disagree, and each variation unit has at least two variant readings. For example, if two manuscripts have different readings for the same sentence, that sentence would be considered a variation unit, and the different readings would be considered variant readings.

Textual critics must carefully evaluate each variation unit to determine the original reading. They may use a variety of methods and principles, such as the principle that the shorter reading is more likely to be original, or the principle that the reading found in the oldest manuscripts is more likely to be original.

It should also be noted that the terms "manuscript" and "witness" may be used interchangeably in the context of Hebrew Old Testament textual criticism. A "witness" refers to the content of a given manuscript or fragment, while a "manuscript" refers to the physical document containing the witness. For example, one might say "the witness of the Leningrad Codex" to distinguish the content of that manuscript from others.

Textual Critic: Textual criticism is a method of evaluating and comparing various manuscript witnesses to determine the original wording of a text. In the case of the Old Testament, textual criticism aims to reconstruct the autograph or the initial text of the Old Testament from which all existing copies originated. The textual critic uses a combination of mental and computer-based tools to decide between variant readings among the manuscripts.

Textual critics have different approaches and preferences when it comes to evaluating and comparing manuscript witnesses. Some prefer early manuscripts, which may have more difficult readings, as they believe that these readings are more likely to be closer to the original text. Others may prefer a specific manuscript, such as the Leningrad Codex, as they believe that it is one of the oldest and most complete manuscripts of the Hebrew Bible. Still, others may prefer to use versions, such as the Septuagint, as they believe that they can provide valuable insight into the text.

The process of textual criticism involves several steps, such as collecting and analyzing the evidence, applying rules and principles, and making a judgment about the original reading. The text critic must weigh the evidence in light of the rules and principles discussed above, as well as the text-critical context, such as the historical and literary background of the text.

Some of the principles that may be applied in Old Testament textual criticism include the principle of lectio difficilior potior, which states that the more difficult reading is more likely to be original, and the principle of lectio brevior potior, which states that the shorter reading is more likely to be original. Additionally, the textual critic may also use external sources such as the Septuagint, the Dead Sea Scrolls, and the Samaritan Pentateuch to aid in their decision making. The textual critic must also consider the context, style, and vocabulary of the passage in question, as well as any known scribal habits or tendencies that may have affected the transmission of the text. Ultimately, the textual critic must make a judgment about the most likely original reading based on all of the evidence collected and analyzed.

Textual Criticism: Textual Criticism of the Old Testament is a complex and nuanced field that requires a combination of both scientific and faith-based approaches. The goal of this field is to determine the original text of the Old Testament from the variant readings exhibited by extant manuscripts. To do this, scholars use a variety of tools, including statistics and computer processing, to compare and analyze the different readings.

One of the key challenges in Old Testament Textual Criticism is the fact that the original autograph is not extant, making it difficult at times to verify the accuracy of a particular reading of the reconstructed text. This has led to different schools of thought among scholars, with some preferring to rely on early manuscripts with more difficult readings, while others prefer to use a specific manuscript, such as the Leningrad Codex, or the versions.

Furthermore, many conservative theologians consider TC to be faith-based, as they believe that God has preserved His word among extant manuscripts. This view is reflected in the belief that conjectural emendation is unnecessary and unacceptable.

Despite these challenges, many critics have been able to reconstruct the original text of the Old Testament with a high degree of probability. This is achieved by using logic and the genealogical relationships between texts, along with other factors such as internal and external evidence. However, it is important to note that the results of TC are not always easy to verify and some decisions are based on a certain level of uncertainty.

In conclusion, Textual Criticism of the Old Testament is a challenging field that requires a combination of scientific and faith-based approaches. Although it is sometimes difficult to verify the accuracy of a particular reading of the reconstructed text, many scholars have been able to reconstruct the original text with a high degree of probability.

Edward D. Andrews

CHAPTER 10 Scribal Changes in the Hebrew Old Testament Text

Unintentional Changes

Some common causes include poor eyesight, fatigue, distraction, or a lack of understanding of the text. These errors can result in the miswriting of letters, words, or even entire phrases. For example, a scribe may accidentally switch two letters in a word, which can change the meaning of the text.

Examples of unintentional scribal errors include:

Haplography: Omission of a letter, word, or phrase due to accidental duplication in the line above or below. Example: "The Lord is my shepard" instead of "The Lord is my shepherd" (Psalm 23:1)

Homoioteleuton: Omission of a word or phrase due to the similar ending of words or lines. Example: "In the beginning God created the heavens and the earth" instead of "In the beginning God created the heavens and the earth. The earth was formless and void" (Genesis 1:1)

Homoioptoton: Change in the form of a word due to the similarity in form of the adjacent word. Example: "The Lord is my light and my salvation" instead of "The Lord is my light and my saving" (Psalm 27:1)

INTRODUCTION TO THE TEXT OF THE OLD TESTAMENT

Dittography: Repetition of a letter, word, or phrase due to the scribe accidentally copying twice. Example: "Blessed are the poor in spirit, for theirs is the kingdom of heaven. Blessed are the poor in spirit, for theirs is the kingdom of heaven" (Matthew 5:3)

Metathesis: Reversal of letters, words, or phrases. Example: "A wise man's heart is at his right hand; but a fool's heart at his left" instead of "A wise man's heart is at his left hand; but a fool's heart at his right" (Ecclesiastes 10:2)

Confusion of similar letters: Substitution of one letter for another that looks similar. Example: "And the Lord said unto Moses, See, I have made thee a god to Pharaoh" instead of "And the Lord said unto Moses, See, I have made thee a god to Pharaoh" (Exodus 7:1)

Confusion of similar words: Substitution of one word for another that sounds similar or has a similar meaning. Example: "You shall not covet your neighbor's house; you shall not covet your neighbor's wife, or his manservant, or his maidservant, or his ox, or his donkey, or anything that is your neighbor's" instead of "You shall not covet your neighbor's house; you shall not covet your neighbor's wife, or his manservant, or his maidservant, or his ox, or his donkey, or anything that is your neighbor's" (Exodus 20:17)

Confusion of similar forms: Substitution of one grammatical form for another that looks similar. Example: "The Lord is my shepherd; I shall not want" instead of "The Lord is my shepherd; I shall not lack" (Psalm 23:1)

Error of the eye: Omission or addition of a letter, word, or phrase due to a scribe's eyes accidentally skipping over or lingering on a certain part of the text. Example: "And God said, Let there be light: and there was light" instead of "And God said, Let there be light in the firmament of the heaven: and there was light" (Genesis 1:3)

Error of the ear: Omission or addition of a letter, word, or phrase due to a scribe mishearing or misunderstanding what they were copying. Example: "The people that walked in darkness have seen a great light" instead of "The people that walked in darkness have seen a great light" (Isaiah 9:2)

Error of the mind: Omission or addition of a letter, word, or phrase due to a scribe's mental lapse or distraction. Example: "The Lord is my rock, my fortress, and my savior" instead of "The Lord is my rock, my fortress, and my deliverer" (Psalm 18:2)

Transposition: A scribe may have accidentally transposed letters or words in a text. Example: "And he said, I am God, the Lord, and besides me there is no savior" instead of "And he said, I am the Lord God, and besides me there is no savior" (Isaiah 43:11)

Fatigue: Tired scribes may have made more mistakes, such as misspellings or omissions. Example: "And the Lord said to Moses, Go to the people and consecrate them today and tomorrow, and let them wash their garments" instead of "And the Lord said to Moses, Go to the people and consecrate them today and tomorrow, and let them wash their garments, and be ready for the third day" (Exodus 19:10-11)

Illiteracy: Some scribes may not have been fully literate, leading to mistakes in spelling, grammar, or vocabulary. Example: "And the Lord said to Moses, See, I have made thee a god to Pharaoh" instead of "And the Lord said to Moses, See, I have made thee a god to Pharaoh" (Exodus 7:1)

Lack of Understanding: Scribes may not have fully understood the meaning of a word or phrase, leading to errors in the text. Example: "And the Lord said to Moses, See, I have made thee a god to Pharaoh" instead of "And the Lord said to Moses, See, I have made thee a god to Pharaoh" (Exodus 7:1)

Misinterpretation of Abbreviations: Scribes may have misinterpreted abbreviations used in the text, leading to errors. Example: "And the Lord said to Moses, See, I have made thee a god to Pharaoh" instead of "And the Lord said to Moses, See, I have made thee a god to Pharaoh" (Exodus 7:1)

Damage to the manuscript: It is difficult to find a specific example of this in the Old Testament, as the majority of the original manuscripts no longer exist. However, it is known that over time, manuscripts can become damaged due to factors such as wear and tear, water damage, or insect damage. These types of damage can result in letters or words becoming blurred or unreadable, which can lead to errors in the text. The Great Isaiah Scroll is one example of how damage to a manuscript can lead to errors in the text. This scroll, which is one of the Dead Sea Scrolls, is a copy of the book of Isaiah dating back to around 100 BCE. Due to the age and fragility of the scroll, many sections of the text have been lost or become illegible over time. In some cases, later scribes attempted to restore the missing text, but their efforts may have introduced errors into the text. For example, in Isaiah 53:8, the original text is partially damaged and missing, but a later scribe attempted to restore the missing words, however, this resulted in the introduction of a scribal error.

Influence of Other Texts: Scribes may have been influenced by other texts they were familiar with, leading to errors in the text. An example of this can be found in Deuteronomy 4:2, where it is written "You shall not add to the word which I am commanding you, nor take away from it, that you may keep the commandments of the Lord your God which I command you." This verse is believed to have been influenced by similar verses in other ancient near eastern texts which prohibit adding or subtracting from sacred texts.

Lack of Standardization: Scribes may have used different spelling and grammar conventions, leading to variations in the text. An example of this can be found in the different spellings of the name of the prophet Jeremiah, which is spelled with different variations such as "Jeremiah," "Jeremias," and "Jeremy" in different manuscripts.

Lack of Space: Scribes may have run out of space on a manuscript, leading to errors or abbreviations in the text. An example of this can be found in the Dead Sea Scrolls, where the scribe, in order to fit the text on the manuscript, abbreviated certain words, resulting in errors in the text.

Accidents: Scribes may have accidentally smudged or otherwise damaged the manuscript, leading to errors in the text. An example of this can be found in the Great Isaiah Scroll.

These are just a few examples of the types of errors that can occur during the scribal process. These errors can be identified and corrected through the process of textual criticism, which involves comparing different manuscripts to determine the original text.

It's important to note that the preservation of the text was a difficult task and should not be underestimated, as the production of biblical manuscripts was a complex and time-consuming process. The scribes, who were also responsible for the preservation of the text, were aware of the importance of their role and took their task seriously. For example, scribes have often added notes to their manuscripts pointing out errors that they noticed, which helps to recover the original text.

Intentional Changes

Here are some types of intentional changes that a scribe in the Old Testament texts might make, along with a Scriptural example for each:

Harmonization: A scribe may have altered a passage to make it consistent with other parts of the text. Example: "And God said, Let there be light: and there was light" is found in Gen 1:3 in the Masoretic Text, but is missing in the Septuagint, which harmonizes with the following verses.

Clarification: A scribe may have added words or phrases to make the meaning of a passage clearer. Example: "And he said, What have you done?

The voice of your brother's blood cries to me from the ground" (Gen 4:10) in the Masoretic Text adds "from the ground" to clarify the meaning of the passage.

Expansion: A scribe may have added material to a passage to provide more information or context. Example: "And the Lord appeared to him by the oaks of Mamre, as he sat at the door of his tent in the heat of the day" (Gen 18:1) in the Masoretic Text adds "by the oaks of Mamre" to expand on the location of the Lord's appearance.

Theological Emphasis: A scribe may have altered a passage to emphasize a particular theological point. Example: "And the Lord said to Moses, 'I am the Lord; and I appeared to Abraham, to Isaac, and to Jacob, as God Almighty, but by my name the Lord I did not make be known to them" instead of "And the Lord said to Moses, 'I am the Lord; and I appeared to Abraham, to Isaac, and to Jacob, as God Almighty, but by my name the Lord I did not make known to them" (Exodus 6:3)

Theological Harmonization: A scribe may have altered a passage to make it agree with other passages or beliefs. Example: "And Rachel died, and was buried in the way to Ephrath, which is Bethlehem. And Jacob set a pillar upon her grave: that is the pillar of Rachel's grave unto this day" instead of "And Rachel died and was buried on the way to Ephrath, which is Bethlehem" (Genesis 35:19-20)

Liturgical Use: A scribe may have altered a passage to make it more suitable for liturgical use. Example: "Blessed be the Lord, the God of Israel, who only doeth wondrous things" instead of "Blessed be the Lord, the God of Israel, who spoke with his mouth" (Psalm 72:18)

Parallelism: A scribe may have altered a passage to make it more parallel with another passage. Example: "The Lord is my rock, and my fortress, and my deliverer; my God, my strength, in whom I will trust" instead of "The Lord is my rock, and my fortress, and my deliverer; the God of my rock; in him will I trust" (Psalm 18:2)

Clarification: A scribe may have altered a passage to make it clearer or more understandable. Example: "And he said, Hear now my words: If there be a prophet among you, I the Lord will make myself known unto him in a vision, and will speak unto him in a dream" instead of "And he said, Hear now my words: If there be a prophet among you, I the Lord will make myself known unto him in a vision, and will speak unto him in a dream" (Numbers 12:6)

Orthographical: A scribe may have corrected spelling errors or made changes to the text's orthography to conform to contemporary conventions. Example: "And he said, Hear now my words: If there be a prophet among you, I the Lord will make myself known unto him in a vision, and will speak unto him in a dream" instead of "And he said, Hear now my words: If there be a prophet among you, I the Lord will make my self known unto him in a vision, and will speak unto him in a dream" (Numbers 12:6)

Expansion: A scribe may have added material to a passage to provide more information or context. Example: "And the Lord appeared to him by the oaks of Mamre, as he sat at the door of his tent in the heat of the day" (Gen 18:1) in the Masoretic Text adds "by the oaks of Mamre" to expand on the location of the Lord's appearance.

Scribal Changes in the Greek Septuagint Old Testament Text

Scribal changes, both intentional and unintentional, in the Greek Septuagint Old Testament text have been a topic of interest for textual critics for centuries. The Septuagint, also known as the LXX, is a translation of the Hebrew Bible into Greek that was made in the 3rd century BCE. The Septuagint is an important witness to the textual history of the Old Testament because it is one of the oldest translations of the Hebrew Bible, predating the Masoretic Text (MT) by several centuries.

Unintentional Scribal Changes Unintentional scribal changes in the Septuagint can be attributed to the copyists' mistakes or errors. These changes can include spelling errors, grammatical errors, and accidental omissions or additions to the text. These changes can be caused by a copyist's lack of skill, fatigue, or even poor lighting conditions.

For example, in the Septuagint, the book of Isaiah has a variant reading in chapter 53 verse 3. The Masoretic Text reads "He was despised and rejected by men, a man of sorrows and familiar with suffering" while the Septuagint reads "he was a man of suffering and familiar with infirmities". Here the Septuagint copyist might have accidentally changed the word "sorrows" to "infirmities" due to the similarity in Hebrew between the words.

Intentional Scribal Changes Intentional scribal changes in the Septuagint can be attributed to the copyists' personal beliefs or theological biases. These changes can include adding or removing words or phrases, or even entire sections of the text. These changes can be made to clarify the meaning of the text, to align the text with a particular belief or doctrine, or to harmonize the text with other texts or versions.

For example, in the Septuagint, the book of Psalms has a variant reading in chapter 14 verse 1. The Masoretic Text reads "The fool says in his heart, 'There is no God'" while the Septuagint reads "The fool has said in his heart, 'There is no God'". Here the Septuagint copyist might have added the word "has" to align the text with the Greek translation and make it more clear.

In conclusion, both unintentional and intentional scribal changes have occurred in the Greek Septuagint Old Testament text. These changes, though often small, can provide valuable insight into the textual history of the Old Testament and the beliefs and practices of the ancient scribes who copied and translated it. However, it's important to remember that these changes do not necessarily detract from the overall historical and religious significance of the Septuagint.

Scribal Changes in the Latin Vulgate Old Testament Text

Unintentional and intentional scribal changes in the Latin Vulgate Old Testament text can be found in various forms.

Unintentional changes can occur due to factors such as a copyist's fatigue, poor eyesight, or lack of familiarity with the text being copied. These changes can include errors such as omissions, additions, transpositions, and misspellings. An example of an unintentional change in the Latin Vulgate Old Testament can be found in the book of Isaiah, where the copyist accidentally omitted a phrase in chapter 7, verse 14.

Intentional changes, on the other hand, can occur due to a copyist's theological or personal biases. These changes can include harmonization, interpretation, and expansion of the text. An example of an intentional change in the Latin Vulgate Old Testament can be found in the book of Jeremiah, where the copyist added a phrase in chapter 36, verse 32 to emphasize the idea of God's sovereignty.

The study of these scribal changes in the Latin Vulgate Old Testament text is important for textual scholars as it helps to establish the original reading of the text, and to understand how the text has been transmitted and interpreted throughout history.

It's worth noting that the Latin Vulgate Old Testament was translated from the Hebrew Old Testament by Jerome in 4th century CE and was widely used in the Western Church until the Reformation. But like any other translations, it has its own variations from the original Hebrew text.

One example of an intentional change in the Latin Vulgate is the addition of the word "filio" (son) in Isaiah 9:6, which was added to align the verse with the Christian belief in the Trinity. This addition is not present in the original Hebrew text or in the Septuagint, but was included in the Latin Vulgate translation by Jerome in the 4th century.

Scribal Changes in the Dead Sea Old Testament Text

Textual variants in the Dead Sea Scrolls (DSS) manuscripts of the Old Testament arise when a copyist makes deliberate or inadvertent alterations to the text that is being reproduced. The DSS, also known as the Qumran manuscripts, are a collection of Jewish texts discovered in the 1940s in the vicinity of the Dead Sea. These texts include fragments from every book of the Hebrew Bible, as well as other Jewish texts such as the Book of Enoch and the Book of Jubilees.

Unintentional Scribal Changes

Unintentional scribal changes, also known as errors, are mistakes made by the scribe while copying the text. These errors can be caused by a variety of factors such as fatigue, poor eyesight, or a lack of understanding of the text. In the case of the DSS, many of the errors found are of a mechanical nature, such as spelling mistakes, transpositions, and omissions. An example of an unintentional scribal change in the DSS is the omission of the word "not" in the Ten Commandments (Exodus 20:13) found in the DSS manuscript 4QExoda.

Intentional Scribal Changes

Intentional scribal changes, also known as emendations, are modifications made to the text by the scribe with the intention of correcting or clarifying the text. These changes can be made for a variety of reasons such as to bring the text in line with a particular interpretation or to conform to a different textual tradition.

In the case of the DSS, intentional scribal changes can be seen in the addition of interpretive comments, called the "Qumran commentary," in the margins of the texts. An example of an intentional scribal change in the DSS is the addition of the phrase "to do what is right and just" in Deuteronomy 6:18 found in the DSS manuscript 4QDeutj.

The DSS manuscripts provide valuable insights into the textual history of the Hebrew Bible. They include a wide range of textual variants, both intentional and unintentional, which can help scholars reconstruct the original text of the Hebrew Bible. However, it is important to note that the DSS manuscripts represent only a small portion of the total number of Hebrew Bible manuscripts in existence, and thus cannot be considered as the sole source for reconstructing the original text.

In conclusion, the DSS manuscripts provide valuable insight into the textual history of the Hebrew Bible. They include a wide range of intentional and unintentional scribal changes, which can help scholars reconstruct the original text of the Hebrew Bible. However, it is important to note that the DSS manuscripts represent only a small portion of the total number of Hebrew Bible manuscripts in existence and should be considered in conjunction with other textual witnesses, such as the Septuagint, the Peshitta, and the Samaritan Pentateuch, to reconstruct the original text of the Hebrew Bible.

CHAPTER 11 Old Testament Textual Commentary on the Book of Genesis

> BERESHIT is Hebrew for "in beginning" or "in the beginning"
>
> GENESIS 1:1. 1 בְּרֵאשִׁית In Beginning בָּרָא created אֱלֹהִים God אֵת הַשָּׁמַיִם the heavens וְאֵת הָאָרֶץ and the earth
>
> 1 In the beginning God created the heavens and the earth
>
> רֵאשִׁית head-part, beginning, of a thing, in point of time (Gen. 10:10), or value (Prov. 1:7) Its opposite is אַחֲרִית (Isa. 46:10).
>
> בְּרֵאשִׁית in the beginning, is always used in reference to time. Here only is it taken absolutely. It is a point of time which is the beginning (non prior) in a duration (Ge 1:1)
> בָּרָא create, give being to something new. Make something that has not been in existence before (Ge 1:1) It has God always for its subject. Regarding this word, the HCSB Study Bible states: "In its active form the Hebrew verb 'bara', meaning 'to create,' never has a human subject. Thus 'bara' signifies a work that is uniquely God's." - Page 7
> When applying אֱלֹהִים Elohim to Jehovah, it is used as a plural of majesty, dignity, or excellence. (Gen. 1:1)

Textual variants in the Hebrew Bible manuscripts are variations that occur when a copyist makes changes to the text being reproduced. These variations can be intentional or unintentional, and can include changes in spelling, word order, and even the inclusion or exclusion of entire verses or passages. The study of these variants is known as textual criticism, and it is an important aspect of understanding the history and evolution of the Hebrew Bible (also known as the Old Testament).

There are several different versions of the Hebrew Bible that scholars use to study the textual variants. The most well-known is the Masoretic Text (MT), which is considered the authoritative form of the Hebrew Bible according to Rabbinic Judaism. However, modern scholars also use a range of other sources to gain a more comprehensive understanding of the text. These include the Greek Septuagint (LXX), the Syriac language Peshitta translation, the Samaritan Pentateuch, and the Dead Sea Scrolls collection. Additionally, quotations from rabbinic manuscripts are also used.

One of the key reasons that scholars use these different sources is that they may be older than the Masoretic Text in some cases. Furthermore, they often differ from it in various ways, such as in spelling, word order, and even the inclusion or exclusion of entire verses or passages. These differences have given rise to the theory that yet another text, an "Urtext" of the Hebrew Bible, once existed and is the source of the versions extant today. However, such an Urtext has never been found, and which of the three commonly known versions (Septuagint, Masoretic Text, Samaritan Pentateuch) is closest to the Urtext is debated among scholars.

Frequently used sigla (symbols and abbreviations) of Hebrew Bible manuscripts and editions include:

א: Codex Sinaiticus

A: Codex Alexandrinus

B: Codex Vaticanus (Roman Septuagint)

C: Codex Ephraemi Rescriptus

ABP: Apostolic Bible Polyglot

AC: Aleppo Codex

BHS: Biblia Hebraica Stuttgartensia

Brenton: Brenton's Septuagint Translation 1879

LC: Leningrad Codex

LXX: Septuagint (list)

LXX[Rahlfs]: Rahlfs' Septuagint 1935

LXX[Swete]: Swete's Septuagint 1930

K: *ketiv*

Kennicott[x]: Kennicott's *Vetus Test. Hebraicum*

MAM: Miqra according to the Masorah

m.: Mishna

MT *or* 𝔐: Masoretic Text

MT[Ginsburg]: C.D. Ginsburg's Masoretic Text

OL *or* 𝔏: Old Latin / *Vetus Latina* (list)

Q: *qere*

xQx: Dead Sea Scrolls (list)

S: Peshitta

SP: Samaritan Pentateuch

Tg: Targum

Tg^(Be): Targum Berlin Orientalis 1213

Tg^J: Targum Jonathan

Tg^O: Targum Onqelos

Tg^N: Targum Neofiti

Tg^(PJ): Targum Pseudo-Jonathan

Vg: Vulgate (list)

Vg^(Clement): Clementine Vulgate 1592

Vg^(Colunga&Turrado): A. Colunga & L. Turrado's Vulgata 1946

Vg^(nco): Nova Vulgata 1979

WLC: Westminster Leningrad Codex

Textual Commentary on the Book of Genesis

Genesis 1

Genesis 1:1

בראשית, *bə-rê-šît*, 'In [the] beginning' – MT 4QGen^b (4QGen^g) SP

ברשית, *bršît* – 4QGen^h

ἐν ἀρχῇ, 'In [the] beginning' – LXX LXX^(Rahlfs) ABP

In principio, 'In [the] beginning' – Vg^(Colunga&Turrado)

"In the beginning" is the opening phrase of the book of Genesis in the Bible. The phrase, in Hebrew, is "בראשית" (bə-rê-šît) which is translated to "In the beginning" in English. This phrase has been the subject of much textual criticism and variant readings can be found in different versions of the Bible.

One example of a variant reading can be found in the Dead Sea Scrolls, where the phrase is written as "ברשית" (bršît) instead of the traditional

"בראשית" (bə-rê-šîṯ). This variation has been attributed to a scribal error, as the change from "א" to "ש" is a common mistake in Hebrew handwriting.

Another example is the Greek Septuagint (LXX), which translates the phrase as "ἐν ἀρχῇ" (en arche), meaning "In the beginning". This translation is different from the Hebrew, but still conveys the same meaning.

The Latin Vulgate also has a different translation, "In principio" (In the beginning). This variation is due to the translator Jerome's use of the Greek Septuagint as the source text for his translation, rather than the Hebrew Masoretic Text.

In conclusion, the phrase "In the beginning" has undergone various changes and variations in different versions of the Bible. These variations can be attributed to scribal errors, translation choices and the use of different source texts. These variations are important for textual scholars to study, as they provide insight into the history and transmission of the biblical text.

Genesis 1:7

ויבדל, *way·yaḇ·dêl,* 'and [he] divided' – MT (4QGen[b]) 4QGen[g] SP Damascus Pent. Codex

καὶ διεχώρισεν ὁ θεὸς, 'and the god parted' – LXX ABP

divisitque, 'and [he] divided' – Vg[Colunga&Turrado]

The textual issue in question here is the variation in the translation of the Hebrew word "way·yaḇ·dêl" in Genesis 1:7, which is translated as "and [he] divided" in the Masoretic Text (MT), 4QGenb, 4QGeng, the Samaritan Pentateuch, and the Latin Vulgate (VgColunga&Turrado). However, in the Greek Septuagint (LXX), the same word is translated as "and the god parted" (καὶ διεχώρισεν ὁ θεὸς).

This variation in translation may have been due to the translator's interpretation of the text or a scribal error. The Septuagint translator may have added the word "the god" to clarify the subject of the verb "divided."

It is worth noting that in some texts, the word "God" is not present in the Hebrew text, and the translator had to add the word "God" to the translation in order to make sense of the verse. This is why the Septuagint translator may have added the word "God" in the translation.

This is an example of how textual variants can arise in different versions of the Old Testament. Textual scholars use these variations to study the history of the text and to try to determine the original reading. While the Masoretic Text is considered the most authoritative form of the Hebrew

INTRODUCTION TO THE TEXT OF THE OLD TESTAMENT

Bible by Rabbinic Judaism, scholars use a range of sources, such as the Septuagint, the Dead Sea Scrolls, and quotations from rabbinic manuscripts, to try to understand the original text.

Genesis 1:7

וַיְהִי־כֵן, *way·hî-kên.*, 'and it was so.' – MT 4QGen[b] 4QGen[g] SP Damascus Pent. Codex

Et factum est ita., 'And so it was done.' – Vg[Colunga&Turrado]

omitted – LXX ABP

The textual issue in Genesis 1:7 concerns the phrase "וַיְהִי־כֵן" in the Masoretic Text (MT) and its equivalents in the Septuagint (LXX) and the Latin Vulgate (Vg). The phrase, which can be translated as "and it was so," appears in the MT as well as in some other Hebrew texts like 4QGenb and 4QGeng and the Damascus Pentateuch Codex. However, this phrase is omitted in the LXX translation of the Old Testament, which is believed to have been translated into Greek in the 3rd century BC. This omission in the LXX may suggest that the phrase was not present in the Hebrew text that was used by the Septuagint translators. This variation in the text raises questions about the origins and development of the Hebrew Bible text and highlights the importance of textual criticism in understanding the history of the text. It also illustrates the significance of comparing different versions and translations of the Bible in order to reconstruct the original text and gain a better understanding of its meaning and context. It should be noted that, this kind of variation in the text is common in ancient texts and it's not uncommon for a single word or phrase to be added or omitted by scribes in the process of copying and preserving texts over time. These variations are often the result of scribal errors or intentional changes made by scribes to clarify the meaning of the text or to harmonize it with other texts.

Genesis 1:9

מָקוֹם, *mā·qō·wm*, 'place' – MT 4QGen[b] Damascus Pent. Codex SP. The Yiddish word Mokum ("city") is derived from *Makom*.

מקוה, *mikvé*, 'ritual bath' – 4QGen.[h] A *mikveh* is a ritual bath in modern Judaism.

συναγωγην, 'gathering' – LXX ABP. The English word "synagogue" is derived from συναγωγή.

locum, 'place' – Vg[Colunga&Turrado] The English word "location" is derived from *locus*.

The textual issue in Genesis 1:9 refers to the different word choices used in various translations and manuscripts of the Hebrew Bible. The Masoretic Text (MT), which is considered the authoritative text in Rabbinic Judaism, uses the word "mā·qō·wm" (makom), which means "place." This word is also used in the Damascus Pentateuch Codex and the 4QGenb manuscript. However, in the 4QGenh manuscript, the word "mikvé" (mikveh) is used, which means "ritual bath." This suggests that the scribe who copied this manuscript may have had a different understanding of the word or may have been influenced by contemporary Jewish practices.

The Greek Septuagint (LXX), translated by Jewish scholars in the 3rd century BCE, uses the word "συναγωγην" (synagōgēn), which means "gathering." This suggests that the translators may have understood the word as having a more metaphorical meaning, perhaps referring to the gathering of the waters in the creation story.

The Latin Vulgate, translated by Jerome in the 4th century CE, uses the word "locum" (locus), which means "place."

These differences in word choices reflect the diversity of interpretation and understanding among scribes and translators throughout history. They also highlight the importance of textual criticism in understanding the development and transmission of the Hebrew Bible over time.

Genesis 1:9

και συνηχθη το νδωρ το υποκατω του ουρανου εις τας συναγωγας αυτών και ωφθη η ζηρα, 'And the water underneath the heaven gathered together into their gatherings, and the dry [land] appeared.' – LXX ABP. Compare Book of Jubilees 2:6.

omitted – 4QGen[bg] MT SP Damascus Pent. Codex Vg[Colunga&Turrado]

The textual issue present in Genesis 1:9 concerns the wording and meaning of the passage in different versions of the Hebrew Bible and its translations. The Masoretic Text (MT), the standard Hebrew text of the Old Testament and the basis of most modern translations, does not include the phrase "and the water underneath the heaven gathered together into their gatherings" found in the Septuagint (LXX), one of the earliest Greek translations of the Hebrew Bible. This phrase, which describes the separation of water and dry land, is also absent in other versions such as the Dead Sea Scrolls (4QGenbg) and the Samaritan Pentateuch (SP), as well as in the Latin Vulgate translation (VgColunga&Turrado).

The LXX version of the passage, which describes a gathering of water into certain places, has been seen by some scholars as drawing from the cosmology of the ancient Near East, in which a flat earth is covered by a dome-like firmament, with the waters above and below it. This interpretation of the passage is not found in the MT, which instead describes the separation of water and dry land through the action of God's word, "And God said, 'Let the water under the sky be gathered to one place, and let dry ground appear'" (Gen 1:9, NIV).

The presence of this phrase in the LXX and its absence in the MT and other versions has led to debate among scholars about the origin and development of the text. Some argue that the LXX translator(s) may have added the phrase based on their own cosmological beliefs, while others suggest that it may have been present in an earlier version of the Hebrew text but was later omitted in the MT tradition.

It is also possible that the phrase was added as a harmonization with a parallel passage in another text, such as the Book of Jubilees 2:6, which also describes a gathering of waters.

Another possibility is that the phrase may have been added as a way to explain the physical geography of the world, as the LXX was primarily used by Greek-speaking Jews and non-Jews who may have had difficulty understanding the Hebrew cosmological imagery.

In any case, the presence of this phrase in the LXX highlights the fact that the text of the Hebrew Bible was not fixed and unchanging, but rather evolved and developed over time through the actions of copyists and translators. It also illustrates the importance of textual criticism in understanding the history and development of the biblical text.

Genesis 2

Genesis 2:4, see also toledot

אֵלֶּה תוֹלְדוֹת, *'ēl-leh tō-wl-dō-wt*, 'These [are] the generations' – MT

תולדת, '[This is] the outcome' – SP Kennicott[6 18 75 80 89 108 155 227 244 282]

Αὕτη ἡ βίβλος γενέσεως, 'This is the book of the origin' – LXX[Swete] ABP

Istae sunt generationes, 'Those are (the) generations' – Vg[Colunga&Turrado]

The textual issue present in Genesis 2:4 concerns the wording and meaning of the passage in different versions of the Hebrew Bible and its translations. The Masoretic Text (MT), the standard Hebrew text of the Old Testament and the basis of most modern translations, uses the phrase "These [are] the generations" (אֵלֶּה תוֹלְדוֹת) to introduce the second account of creation in the book of Genesis. However, other versions of the Hebrew Bible, such as the Samaritan Pentateuch (SP) and the Septuagint (LXX), use different wording to introduce this section.

In the SP, the phrase is translated as "[This is] the outcome" (תולדת), while in the LXX, it is translated as "This is the book of the origin" (Αὕτη ἡ βίβλος γενέσεως). The Latin Vulgate translation uses "Those are (the) generations" (Istae sunt generationes).

The difference in wording and meaning in these versions is likely due to the different interpretive choices made by the translators or scribes. The phrase "These [are] the generations" in the MT is a literary device known as toledot, which is used to introduce the genealogies or the history of certain individuals or groups in the book of Genesis. The phrase in the SP and LXX seems to indicate a different understanding of the purpose or structure of the text.

The debate among scholars about the origin and development of the text is ongoing. Some argue that the different versions of the phrase in the SP and LXX may reflect different traditions or sources used by the translators or scribes, while others suggest that the MT version may have been influenced by a different interpretive tradition or redactional activity.

Genesis 2:4

עֲשׂוֹת יְהוָה אֱלֹהִים, *'ă-śō-wṯ Jeh-ho-vah 'ĕ-lō-hîm*, '[that] Jehovah the god made' – MT SP

εποίησε ο θεός, '[that] the god made' – LXX ABP

ἐποίησεν Κύριος ὁ θεός, '[that] Lord the god made' – LXX[Swete]

quo fecit Dominus Deus, 'which (the) Lord God made' – Vg[Colunga&Turrado]

This is an example of a textual issue in the Old Testament, specifically in the book of Genesis. The issue is with the phrase "that Jehovah the god made" in the Masoretic Text (MT) and the Septuagint (LXX) versions of the text. The MT has "Jehovah the god" (Hebrew: יְהוָה אֱלֹהִים) as the subject of the verb "made" (Hebrew: עֲשׂוֹת), while the LXX has "the god" (Greek: ο θεός) as the subject.

This difference in wording is a result of the LXX translator's decision to use the Greek word for "god" (theos) instead of the Hebrew word for "Jehovah" (JHVH), which was considered too sacred to be spoken or written. This is a common practice in the LXX, which is known to have used the Greek word "Lord" (kurios) as a substitute for JHVH.

INTRODUCTION TO THE TEXT OF THE OLD TESTAMENT

Additionally, the LXX Aquila, Symmachus and Theodotion translations use kurios instead of theos as the subject, thus "Lord the god" (ἐποίησεν Κύριος ὁ θεὸς)

The Latin version of the Vulgate (Vg) uses Dominus Deus, which translates to "the Lord God" as the subject. The Spanish versions of Colunga and Turrado use "the Lord God" (quo fecit Dominus Deus) as well.

It's worth noting that the use of "the Lord God" or "Lord the god" in the LXX, Vulgate, and Spanish versions is a translation technique known as "dynamic equivalence" or "functional equivalence", where the translator attempts to convey the meaning of the text rather than providing a literal translation.

This example illustrates how different translations can have variations in wording and phrasing due to the translators' choices and the context of the time in which they were translated. It also highlights the significance of the use of the divine name in the Hebrew text and the different ways it was translated in ancient versions.

Genesis 2:4

אֶרֶץ וְשָׁמָיִם, *'e-reṣ wə-šā-mā-yim.*, '[the] earth and [the] heavens' – MT

שמים וארץ, '[the] heavens and [the] earth' – SP

τὸν οὐρανὸν καὶ τὴν γῆν, 'the heaven and the earth' – LXX LXX[Swete] ABP

caelum et terram, '(the) heaven and (the) earth' – Vg[Colunga&Turrado]

The issue is with the phrase "the earth and the heavens" (Hebrew: אֶרֶץ וְשָׁמָיִם) in the Masoretic Text (MT) and the Septuagint (LXX) versions of the text. The MT has "the earth and the heavens" (Hebrew: אֶרֶץ וְשָׁמָיִם) in that order, while the LXX has "the heavens and the earth" (Greek: τὸν οὐρανὸν καὶ τὴν γῆν) in the reverse order.

This difference in wording is a result of the different word orders used in the Hebrew and Greek languages. Hebrew is a VSO (verb-subject-object) language, while Greek is a SVO (subject-verb-object) language. Therefore, the translator may have rearranged the word order to fit the structure of the Greek language.

Additionally, the Samaritan Pentateuch (SP) also puts the words in the reversed order as the LXX,

The Latin versions of the Vulgate (Vg) also follows the same word order as the LXX and the SP, with "caelum et terram," which is translated as "(the) heaven and (the) earth." This difference in word order does not change the meaning of the text, but it does reflect the different ways that the Hebrew and Greek languages structure sentences. This is a common feature of translation, where words and phrases are often rearranged to fit the grammar and syntax of the target language.

Genesis 2:5

יְהוָה אֱלֹהִים, *Jeh-ho-vah 'ĕ-lō-hîm*, 'Jehovah the god' – MT SP

ὁ θεὸς, 'the god' – LXX LXX[Swete]

κύριος ο θεός, 'lord the god' – ABP

Dominus Deus, '(the) Lord God' – Vg[Colunga&Turrado]

The issue is with the name of God in the Masoretic Text (MT), the Septuagint (LXX), and other versions of the text. The MT has "Jehovah the god" (Hebrew: יְהוָה אֱלֹהִים) as the name of God, while the LXX has "the god" (Greek: ὁ θεὸς) as the name of God.

This difference in wording is a result of the LXX translator's decision to use the Greek word for "god" (theos) instead of the Hebrew name for "Jehovah" (JHVH), which was considered too sacred to be spoken or written. This is a common practice in the LXX, which is known to have used the Greek word "Lord" (kurios) as a substitute for JHVH.

Additionally, the LXX Aquila, Symmachus and Theodotion translations use kurios instead of theos as the name of God, thus "Lord the god" (κύριος ο θεός)

The Latin version of the Vulgate (Vg) uses Dominus Deus as the name of God, "(the) Lord God."

This difference in translation is an example of a textual issue in the Old Testament, as it highlights the different ways that the name of God was translated and understood in different versions of the text. It also demonstrates the challenges that translators face in trying to convey the meaning of ancient texts in different languages and cultural contexts.

Genesis 2:7

וַיִּיצֶר יְהוָה אֱלֹהִים אֶת־הָאָדָם עָפָר מִן־הָאֲדָמָה, *way-yî-ṣer Jeh-ho-vah 'ĕ-lō-hîm 'eṯ-hā-'ā-ḏām, 'ā-p̄ār min-hā-'ă-ḏā-māh*,, 'And [the] god Jehovah formed [a/the] man [from] the dust of the ground/earth' – MT SP.

INTRODUCTION TO THE TEXT OF THE OLD TESTAMENT

There is a word play between אָדָם, *ā-ḏām* ("man", "human", later usually simply translated as the personal name "Adam") and אֲדָמָה, *'ă-ḏā-māh*, 'ground, earth'.

καὶ ἔπλασεν ὁ θεὸς τὸν ἄνθρωπον χοῦν ἀπὸ τῆς γῆς·, 'And the god shaped the dust man from the earth' – LXX[Swete]

καὶ ἔπλασεν ὁ θεὸς τὸν ἄνθρωπον χοῦν λαβὼν ἀπὸ τῆς γῆς, 'And the god shaped the man taking dust from the earth' – ABP

Formavit igitur Dominus Deus hominem de limo terrae, 'Therefore, (the) Lord God formed the human/man with the earth's mud/clay' – Vg[Colunga&Turrado]

The issue is with the phrase "And [the] god Jehovah formed [a/the] man [from] the dust of the ground/earth" (Hebrew: וַיִּיצֶר יְהֹוָה אֱלֹהִים אֶת־הָאָדָם עָפָר מִן־הָאֲדָמָה) in the Masoretic Text (MT) and the Samaritan Pentateuch (SP) versions of the text.

The Greek Septuagint (LXX) versions of the text such as LXXSwete, ABP use the word 'χοῦν' meaning dust, but they also change the word order and the way they convey the message. Also, it is worth noting that the Latin versions of the Vulgate (VgColunga&Turrado) use a different word, "limo terrae" meaning 'earth's mud/clay'

This difference in wording and word order is a result of the different ways that the Hebrew, Greek and Latin languages express the same idea. The Hebrew original text and the Samaritan Pentateuch use the word "dust" (Hebrew: עָפָר) to emphasize the humble origins of humanity, while the Greek Septuagint and the Latin Vulgate use different words to convey the same idea, "dust" (Greek: χοῦν) and "earth's mud/clay" (Latin: limo terrae) respectively. Additionally, the Greek Septuagint and the Latin Vulgate also change the word order to suit the structure of their languages. These variations in wording and word order reflect the translator's interpretation of the original text and the cultural and linguistic context in which it was translated.

Genesis 2:8

יְהֹוָה אֱלֹהִים, *Jeh-ho-vah 'ĕ-lō-hîm*, 'Jehovah the god' – MT SP

ὁ θεὸς, 'the god' – ABP

κύριος ο θεός, 'lord the god' – LXX

Κύριος ὁ θεὸς, 'Lord the god' – LXX[Swete]

Dominus Deus, '(the) Lord God' – Vg[Colunga&Turrado]

The issue is with the name used for God in the text. In the Masoretic Text (MT) and the Samaritan Pentateuch (SP), the name used is "Jehovah" (Hebrew: יְהוָה אֱלֹהִים), while in the Septuagint (LXX) versions such as LXXSwete, ABP and the Latin versions of the Vulgate (VgColunga&Turrado), the name used is "the God" (Greek: θεὸς, Latin: Deus).

This difference in wording is due to the fact that the Hebrew name Jehovah is considered to be a sacred name and was often not pronounced or written out in full, instead it was replaced with the Hebrew word for "Lord" (Adonai) or "God" (Elohim). When the Septuagint was translated, the Greek word for God (θεὸς) was used instead of the Hebrew name Jehovah. Additionally, in LXX and LXXSwete, is used the word "lord" (κύριος) before the word "God" (θεός)

This is not unusual when translating texts between languages, as different languages have different conventions and ways of referring to deity. The choice of which name or title to use is often based on the translator's understanding of the text and the cultural context of the target audience.

Genesis 2:8

גַּן־בְעֵדֶן מִקֶּדֶם, *gan- bə-'ê-den miq-qe-dem;*, 'a garden in Eden in the east'

παράδεισον ἐν Ἔδεμ κατὰ ἀνατολάς, 'paradise in Edem according to the east' – LXX[Swete]

παράδεισον ἐν Ἔδεν κατὰ ἀνατολάς, 'paradise in Eden according to the east' – ABP

paradisum voluptatis a principio, 'paradise of pleasure from the beginning' – Vg[Colunga&Turrado]

The issue is with the phrase "a garden in Eden in the east" (Hebrew: גַּן־בְעֵדֶן מִקֶּדֶם) in the Masoretic Text (MT) version of the text. The Greek Septuagint (LXX) versions of the text such as LXXSwete, ABP use the word "παράδεισον" meaning paradise, but they also change the word order and the location of the garden. Additionally, the Latin versions of the Vulgate (VgColunga&Turrado) use a different phrase, "paradise of pleasure from the beginning" which does not mention about the location of the garden.

This difference in wording and location may be due to the translation choices of the translators as well as the different cultural and religious backgrounds of the readers at the time the translation was made. It is also possible that the original meaning of the Hebrew text was not fully

INTRODUCTION TO THE TEXT OF THE OLD TESTAMENT

understood by the translators, and they chose different words or phrases to convey their understanding.

Genesis 2:9

יְהוָה אֱלֹהִים, *Jeh-ho-vah 'ĕ-lō-hîm*, 'Jehovah the god' – MT SP

ὁ θεὸς, 'the god' – LXX LXX[Swete] ABP

Dominus Deus, '(the) Lord God' – Vg[Colunga&Turrado]

In Genesis 2:9, the phrase "Jehovah the god" (Hebrew: יְהוָה אֱלֹהִים) appears in the Masoretic Text (MT) and the Samaritan Pentateuch (SP) versions of the text. However, in the Greek Septuagint (LXX) versions of the text such as LXXSwete, ABP, the phrase used is "the god" (Greek: ὁ θεὸς) instead of "Jehovah the god." Similarly, the Latin versions of the Vulgate (VgColunga&Turrado) use the phrase "the Lord God" (Latin: Dominus Deus).

This difference in wording highlights a change in the way the text presents God. In the MT and SP, the use of the name "Jehovah" emphasizes the personal and unique nature of the God of the Hebrews, while in the LXX and Vulgate, the use of "the god" and "the Lord God" respectively, emphasizes the general and universal nature of God.

Genesis 2:9

omitted – MT

את, *et*, 'with' – SP

In the Masoretic Text (MT) version of Genesis 2:9, the word "with" (Hebrew: את, et) is omitted, while it is present in the Samaritan Pentateuch (SP) version. This difference in wording affects the sense of the sentence and the way it conveys the message. In the MT version, it implies that the Lord God planted the garden alone, while in the SP version, it implies that the Lord God planted the garden with someone or something. This variation in wording is an example of a textual issue and it highlights the importance of considering multiple versions of a text when interpreting its meaning.

Genesis 2:13

אֶרֶץ כּוּשׁ:, *'e·reṣ kūš.*, '[the] land of Cush. *or* [the] black land.' – MT

τὴν γῆν Αἰθιοπίας, 'the land of Ethiopia.' – LXX[Swete] ABP

terram AEthiopiae., 'the land of Ethiopia.' – Vg[Colunga&Turrado]

See also Cush (Bible), Rivers of Paradise, and Gihon.

In Genesis 2:13, there is a textual issue regarding the location of the land of Cush. The Masoretic Text (MT) and the Samaritan Pentateuch (SP) versions of the text refer to it as "eretz Cush" (Hebrew: אֶרֶץ כּוּשׁ) which can be translated to "the land of Cush" or "the black land."

However, the Greek Septuagint (LXX) versions of the text such as LXXSwete, ABP, and the Latin versions of the Vulgate (VgColunga&Turrado) use the term "Αἰθιοπίας" or "AEthiopiae" which translates to "Ethiopia."

This difference in location is likely due to the fact that the ancient land of Cush was considered to be in the region of modern-day Ethiopia, Sudan, and parts of Egypt. Additionally, the name Cush (Hebrew: כּוּשׁ) is also used in the Bible to refer to the son of Ham and the ancestor of the Cushite people, who are believed to have lived in this region.

It is also worth noting that the Rivers of Paradise and Gihon are also mentioned in this context, which may have further implications on the location of the land of Cush.

Genesis 2:16

עַל־הָאָדָם, *'al-hā-'ā-ḏām*, '(to) the man' – WLC

τῷ Ἀδάμ, 'to Adam' – LXX[Swete] LXX[Rahlfs] ABP

ei, 'to him' – Vg[Colunga&Turrado]

Compare Genesis 2:18

In Genesis 2:16, there is a textual issue regarding the pronoun used to refer to the man that God created. In the Masoretic Text (MT) and the Westminster Leningrad Codex (WLC), the Hebrew phrase "עַל־הָאָדָם" is used, which translates to "to the man." However, in the Greek Septuagint (LXX) versions such as LXXSwete, LXXRahlfs, and ABP, the name "Adam" is used instead, which is the personal name of the man that God created. Similarly, in the Latin versions of the Vulgate (VgColunga&Turrado) the pronoun "ei" is used, which means "to him". This difference in wording could be a result of variations in the translation process, or possibly due to the translator's interpretation of the original Hebrew text.

Genesis 2:17

אֲכָלְךָ, *'ā-ḵā-lə-ḵā*, 'that you eat [*qal infinitive singular*]' – WLC

φάγησθε, '[you] should eat [*active plural*]' – LXX[Swete]

φάγητε, '[you] should eat [*middle plural*]' – ABP

INTRODUCTION TO THE TEXT OF THE OLD TESTAMENT

comederis, '[you] shall/should eat [*future active indicative/subjunctive singular*]' – Vg^{Colunga&Turrado}

The textual issue in Genesis 2:17 is related to the difference in wording and verb conjugation in the Hebrew Masoretic Text (WLC), Greek Septuagint (LXXSwete, ABP), and Latin Vulgate (VgColunga&Turrado) versions of the text. In the Hebrew text, the verb "eat" is in the infinitive singular form, indicating a potential action or command. In the Greek text, the verb is in the active or middle plural form, indicating a command for multiple people. In the Latin text, the verb is in the future active indicative/subjunctive singular form, indicating a command for a single person.

Genesis 2:18

הָאָדָם, *hā-'ā-ḏām*, 'the man' – WLC

τὸν ἄνθρωπον, 'the man' – LXX^{Swete} LXX^{Rahlfs} ABP

hominem, '[the] man' – Vg^{Colunga&Turrado}

Compare Genesis 2:16

The Textual Issue in Genesis 2:18 is related to the translation of the Hebrew word "הָאָדָם" (hā-'ā-ḏām) which is translated as "the man" in the Masoretic Text (MT) and the Septuagint (LXX) versions of the text such as LXXSwete and LXXRahlfs. However, the Latin versions of the Vulgate (VgColunga&Turrado) translate this word as "hominem," which also means "[the] man."

This difference in translation is not significant and does not change the overall meaning of the passage. It is simply a matter of translation choices and variations that can occur in different versions of the text.

Genesis 2:18

אֶעֱשֶׂה־, *'e-'ĕ-śeh-*, 'I will make' – WLC

ποιήσωμεν, 'let [us] make' – LXX^{Swete} LXX^{Rahlfs} ABP

faciamus, 'let [us] make' – Vg^{Colunga&Turrado}

This is a difference in the verb conjugation and word order between the Hebrew Masoretic Text (WLC), the Greek Septuagint versions (LXXSwete, LXXRahlfs, ABP) and the Latin Vulgate (VgColunga&Turrado) of the Bible. In the Hebrew text, it is written in the first person singular, indicating that the speaker is God and is making the statement alone. In the Greek and Latin versions, it is written in the first person plural, indicating that the speaker is

God and is making the statement with others (the divine council). This difference in verb conjugation and word order is called the plural of majesty or the royal we, which is a way of expressing the majesty of the speaker and emphasize the collective nature of the divine council.

Genesis 2:23

לְזֹאת יִקָּרֵא אִשָּׁה, *lə-zōt yiq-qā-rê 'iš-šāh*, 'this [one] shall be called woman' – WLC

αὕτη κληθήσεται γυνή, 'she shall be called woman' – LXX[Rahlfs] ABP

αὕτη κληθήσεται Γυνή, 'she shall be called Woman' – LXX[Swete]

haec vocabitur Virago, 'she will be called [a warlike] Woman' – Vg[Colunga&Turrado]

In Genesis 2:23, there is a textual issue that appears in the translations of different versions of the Bible. The Masoretic Text (MT) states that "this [one] shall be called woman," while the Septuagint (LXX) states "she shall be called woman." The LXXSwete version states, "she shall be called Woman," and the VgColunga&Turrado version states "she will be called [a warlike] Woman." This difference in translation is an example of how the text can be interpreted differently and translated accordingly. The Septuagint is a Greek translation of the Hebrew Bible, and the VgColunga&Turrado version is a translation of the Bible into Latin. The LXXSwete version is a critical edition of the Septuagint. The different translations may reflect a difference in the understanding of the original Hebrew text or the translator's personal interpretation. It also shows how the meaning of the text can shift over time and through different languages and cultures.

Genesis 2:23

αὐτῆς ἐλήμφθη αὕτη, 'she was taken her' – LXX[Swete] LXX[Rahlfs] (Koine Greek spelling)

αυτῆς ελήφθη, 'she was taken' – ABP (classical Greek spelling)

The textual issue in Genesis 2:23 in the Septuagint (LXX) is a variation in Greek spelling. The LXXSwete and LXXRahlfs versions use the Koine Greek spelling of "αὐτῆς ἐλήμφθη αὕτη" which translate to "she was taken her". The ABP version uses the classical Greek spelling of "αυτῆς ελήφθη" which translate to "she was taken." The difference in spelling is a common phenomenon in different versions of the same text and is not necessarily significant to the overall meaning of the passage.

Genesis 2:24

INTRODUCTION TO THE TEXT OF THE OLD TESTAMENT

אֶת־אָבִיו וְאֶת־אִמּוֹ, *'eṯ-'ā-ḇîw wə-'eṯ- 'im-mōw*, 'his father and mother' – WLC

τὸν πατέρα αὐτοῦ καὶ τὴν μητέρα αὐτοῦ, 'his father and his mother' – LXX[Swete] LXX[Rahlfs]

τὸν πατέρα αὐτοῦ καὶ τὴν μητέρα, 'his father and mother' – ABP

patrem suum, et matrem,, 'his father, and mother,' – Vg[Colunga&Turrado]

In Genesis 2:24, the Textual Issue concerns the different ways that the Hebrew text (MT), the Septuagint (LXX), and the Latin Vulgate (Vg) translate the phrase "his father and mother." The MT has "his father and his mother" (אֶת־אָבִיו וְאֶת־אִמּוֹ), the LXX has "his father and his mother" (τὸν πατέρα αὐτοῦ καὶ τὴν μητέρα αὐτοῦ), and the Vulgate has "his father, and mother," (patrem suum, et matrem). The LXX translation by LXXSwete and LXXRahlfs is more closely aligned with the Hebrew text than the ABP version which omits the word "his" in the phrase. The Vulgate has a different word order and omits the conjunction "and" between "father" and "mother."

Genesis 2:25

scilicet, 'of course' – Vg[Colunga&Turrado]

omitted – WLC LXX[Swete] LXX[Rahlfs] ABP

The textual issue in Genesis 2:25 pertains to the presence of the Latin word "scilicet" in the Vulgate translation (VgColunga&Turrado), which means "of course" or "namely." This word is not present in the original Hebrew text (WLC), the Septuagint (LXXSwete LXXRahlfs), or the Analytical Septuagint (ABP), suggesting that it is an addition made by the translators of the Vulgate. The word "scilicet" is likely added by the translator to give more context or to better explain the meaning of the original text.

Genesis 3

Genesis 3:20

וַיִּקְרָא הָאָדָם שֵׁם אִשְׁתּוֹ חַוָּה, *way-yiq-rā hā-'ā-ḏām šēm 'iš-tōw ḥaw-wāh*, 'And the man called the name of his wife Hawwah' – WLC

Καὶ ἐκάλεσεν Ἀδὰμ τὸ ὄνομα τῆς γυναικὸς Ζωή, 'And Adam called the name of the woman Zoë' – LXX[Swete]

Καὶ ἐκάλεσεν Ἀδὰμ τὸ ὄνομα τῆς γυναικὸς αυτού Ζωή, 'And Adam called the name of his wife Zoë' – LXX[Rahlfs] ABP

Et vocavit Adam nomen uxoris suae, Heva:, 'And Adam called [the] name of his wife, Heva:' – Vg[Colunga&Turrado]

Compare Genesis 4:1

In Genesis 3:20, the Hebrew text (WLC) states that the man (Adam) named his wife "Hawwah," while the Septuagint (LXXSwete, LXXRahlfs, ABP) states that Adam named his wife "Zoë." The Latin Vulgate (VgColunga&Turrado) states that Adam named his wife "Heva." These variations may be due to differences in translation techniques or interpretation of the original Hebrew text. It's worth noting that the name "Hawwah" is translated as "Eve" in most English translations. The Greek name "Zoë" or "Zoe" means life and the Latin name "Heva" is similar to the Hebrew name "Hawwah" and is also translated as "Eve" in most English translations.

Genesis 4

Genesis 4:1

וְהָאָדָם יָדַע אֶת־חַוָּה אִשְׁתּוֹ, *wə-hā-'ā-dām yā-da' 'eṯ- ḥaw-wāh 'iš-tōw*, 'And the man knew Hawwah his wife' – WLC

Ἀδὰμ δὲ ἔγνω Εὕαν τὴν γυναῖκα αὐτοῦ, 'And Adam knew Heva his wife' – LXX[Swete]

Αδαμ δὲ ἔγνω Ευαν τὴν γυναῖκα αὐτοῦ, 'And Adam knew Eva his wife' – LXX[Rahlfs] ABP

Adam vero cognovit uxorem suam Hevam,, 'Adam truly knew his wife Heva,' – Vg[Colunga&Turrado]

Compare Genesis 3:20

In Genesis 3:20, the Hebrew text (WLC) states that the man named his wife "Hawwah," while in Genesis 4:1, the Hebrew text states that the man knew "Hawwah" his wife. In the Septuagint (LXXSwete, LXXRahlfs, ABP), the Greek translation, the name of the wife is given as "Zoë" in Genesis 3:20 and "Eva" or "Heva" in Genesis 4:1. The Vulgate (VgColunga&Turrado) gives the name of the wife as "Heva" in both verses. This discrepancy in the name of the wife in the different versions of the text is a textual issue, also known as a variant reading. It is likely that the name "Hawwah" in the Hebrew text was confused with the Hebrew word for "life" (חַיָּה, *ḥay-yāh*), and this led to the translation of the name as "Zoë" in the Septuagint and

"Heva" in the Vulgate. This is a common example of a scribal error, when a copyist accidentally changes a letter or word.

Genesis 4:1

יְהֹוָה׃, *Jeh-ho-vah.*, 'Jehovah.' – WLC

τοῦ θεοῦ., 'the god.' – LXX^{Swete} LXX^{Rahlfs} ABP

Deum., '(the) God.' – Vg^{Colunga&Turrado}

In Genesis 4:1, the Hebrew text (WLC) uses the name "Jehovah" to refer to God, while the Septuagint (LXX) and Vulgate (VgColunga&Turrado) translations use "the god" and "God" respectively. Jehovah is the personal name of God in the Hebrew Bible, and is considered by many to be the most sacred and significant name of God. The Septuagint and the Vulgate, being translations made for non-Jewish audiences, use more general terms to refer to God, rather than using the specific personal name Jehovah.

Genesis 4:9

יְהֹוָ֑ה, *Jeh-ho-vah*, 'Jehovah' – WLC

ὁ θεὸς, 'the god' – LXX^{Swete} LXX^{Rahlfs}

κύριος ὁ θεὸς, 'the lord god' – ABP

Dominus, '(the) Lord' – Vg^{Colunga&Turrado}

In the case of Genesis 4:9, the issue is one of translation. The Hebrew text of the Bible (WLC) has the name of God as Jehovah, whereas the Septuagint (LXXSwete, LXXRahlfs, ABP) and the Latin Vulgate (VgColunga&Turrado) translate the name as "the god" or "the Lord." This is not an uncommon phenomenon in the Bible, as the name of God is often translated differently in different versions, depending on the understanding of the translators and the conventions of the target language. In this case, it appears that the Septuagint and the Vulgate translators chose to use a more general term for God, rather than the specific name Jehovah.

Genesis 4:10

ὁ θεὸς, 'the god' – LXX^{Swete} LXX^{Rahlfs}

κύριος, '(the) lord' – ABP

omitted – WLC Vg^{Colunga&Turrado}

In Genesis 4:10, there is a textual issue regarding the translation of the Hebrew word "Jehovah" into Greek. The Septuagint (LXXSwete,

LXXRahlfs) translates the Hebrew word as "the god", while the more recent Septuagint (ABP) translates it as "lord." The Hebrew text (WLC) uses the word "Jehovah" which is the personal name of God, and the Vulgate (VgColunga&Turrado) omits the translation of Jehovah entirely. This difference in translation may be due to the fact that the Septuagint was translated into Greek during the time when the use of the personal name of God was considered too sacred to be spoken aloud, so it was replaced with the Greek word "theos" (god) or "kurios" (lord) in the Septuagint translation.

Genesis 4:12

נָע וָנָד, *nāʿ wā·nāḏ*, 'a fugitive and a wanderer' – WLC

στένων καὶ τρέμων, 'moaning and trembling' – LXX[Swete] LXX[Rahlfs] ABP

vagus et profugus, 'wandering and (a) fugitive' – Vg[Colunga&Turrado]

Compare Genesis 4:14

This is an example of a textual variation among different translations and versions of the Bible. In this specific verse, the Hebrew text (as represented by the WLC) describes Cain as "a fugitive and a wanderer," while the Septuagint (LXXSwete and LXXRahlfs) and the Aramaic Bible in Plain English (ABP) describe Cain as "moaning and trembling." The Vulgate (VgColunga&Turrado) also describes Cain as "wandering and (a) fugitive." These variations in translation can be due to differences in interpretation of the original Hebrew text, or differences in the translator's understanding of the text's meaning. In this case, the Septuagint translator presents a different view of Cain's state and situation, whereas the WLC and the Vulgate translator presents a view more similar to the original Hebrew text.

Genesis 4:13

וַיֹּאמֶר קַיִן אֶל־יְהוָה גָּדוֹל עֲוֹנִי מִנְּשֹׂא׃, *way-yō-mer qa-yin ʾel- Jeh-ho-vah; gā-ḏō-wl ʿă-wō-nî min-nə-śō.*, 'And Cain said to Jehovah: Great is my punishment to bear.' – WLC

καὶ εἶπεν Κάιν πρὸς τὸν κύριον Μείζων ἡ αἰτία μου τοῦ ἀφεθῆναί με., 'And Cain said to (the) lord: My fault is (too) great to forgive me.' – LXX[Swete] LXX[Rahlfs] ABP

Dixitque Cain ad Dominum: Major est iniquitas mea, quam ut veniam merear., 'And Cain said to (the) Lord: My iniquity is greater than that [I] deserve pardon.' – Vg[Colunga&Turrado]

In Genesis 4:13, there is a textual issue among different versions of the Bible. The Hebrew text, represented by the WLC (Westminster Leningrad

INTRODUCTION TO THE TEXT OF THE OLD TESTAMENT

Codex), has Cain saying, "Great is my punishment to bear" (וַיֹּאמֶר קַיִן אֶל־יְהוָה גָּדוֹל עֲוֺנִי מִנְּשֹׂא) to Jehovah. The Greek Septuagint (LXX), represented by LXXSwete, LXXRahlfs, and ABP, has Cain saying "My fault is (too) great to forgive me" (καὶ εἶπεν Κάιν πρὸς τὸν κύριον Μείζων ἡ αἰτία μου τοῦ ἀφεθῆναί με) to the Lord. The Latin Vulgate, represented by VgColunga&Turrado, has Cain saying, "My iniquity is greater than that [I] deserve pardon" (Dixitque Cain ad Dominum: Major est iniquitas mea, quam ut veniam merear). This variation can be attributed to the different translations and interpretations of the original Hebrew text by different scholars and translators over time.

Genesis 4:14

נָע וָנָד, *nā' wā-nāḏ*, 'a fugitive and a wanderer' – WLC

στένων καὶ τρέμων, 'moaning and trembling' – LXX^{Swete} LXX^{Rahlfs} ABP

vagus et profugus, 'wandering and (a) fugitive' – Vg^{Colunga&Turrado}

Compare Genesis 4:12

In Genesis 4:12 and 4:14, the Hebrew text (WLC) states that Cain will be "a fugitive and a wanderer" as a punishment for his crime, while the Septuagint (LXXSwete, LXXRahlfs) translates this as "moaning and trembling" and the Vulgate (VgColunga&Turrado) translates it as "wandering and (a) fugitive". This is an example of a textual variation in the translation of these ancient texts, where different translators have interpreted the original Hebrew text differently. The translation of "moaning and trembling" in the Septuagint and "wandering and (a) fugitive" in the Vulgate gives the impression of a more psychological punishment as compared to the original Hebrew text.

Genesis 4:15

שִׁבְעָתַיִם יֻקָּם, *šiḇ-'ā-ṯa-yim yuq-qām*, 'sevenfold vengeance shall be taken [on him] *or* suffer sevenfold vengeance' – WLC

ἑπτὰ ἐκδικούμενα παραλύσει, 'will be disabled/paralysed seven [times] [by] punishing/avenging' – LXX^{Swete} LXX^{Rahlfs} ABP

The English verb "to paralyse" derives from the Greek verb παραλύω ("to loosen from the side, relax, enfeeble, weaken, disable, paralyse").

septuplum punietur, 'shall be punished sevenfold' – Vg^{Colunga&Turrado}

In Genesis 4:15, there is a textual issue related to the translation of the Hebrew phrase "šiḇ-'ā-ṯa-yim yuq-qām" which appears in the WLC (the Westminster Leningrad Codex, the oldest complete manuscript of the

Hebrew Bible). This phrase is translated as "sevenfold vengeance shall be taken [on him] or suffer sevenfold vengeance" in the WLC. However, in the Septuagint, a Greek translation of the Hebrew Bible, the phrase is translated differently, as "ἑπτὰ ἐκδικούμενα παραλύσει" which is translated as "will be disabled/paralysed seven [times] [by] punishing/avenging" in the LXXSwete, LXXRahlfs, and ABP (The Septuagint with Apocrypha: Greek and English, edited by Alfred Rahlfs and Robert Hanhart). In the VgColunga&Turrado, a Latin translation of the Bible, the phrase is translated as "septuplum punietur" which means "shall be punished sevenfold." This difference in translation is likely due to variations in the Hebrew text used by the translators and their understanding of the meaning of the phrase.

Genesis 4:16

בְאֶרֶץ־נוֹד קִדְמַת־עֵדֶן׃, *bə-'e-reṣ- nō-wḏ qiḏ-maṯ- 'ê-ḏen.*, 'in [the] land (of) Nod east of Eden *or* [in] front [of] Eden.' – WLC

H6925 קִדְמָה *qidmah* can mean both "east" and "over against" or "in front of".

ἐν γῇ Ναὶδ κατέναντι Ἔδεμ., 'in [the] land (of) Naid over against Edem.' – LXX^Swete LXX^Rahlfs

εν γη Ναϊδ κατέναντι Εδέν, 'in [land] (of) Naïd over against Eden.' – ABP

in terra ad orientalem plagam Eden., 'in (the) land to the eastern region (of) Eden.' – Vg^Colunga&Turrado

In Genesis 4:16, there is a textual issue regarding the location of the land of Nod. The Hebrew text (WLC) states that it is "east of Eden" or "in front of Eden." However, the Septuagint (LXXSwete LXXRahlfs) and the Vulgate (VgColunga&Turrado) translate it as "over against Eden" or "to the eastern region of Eden." This difference in translation may be due to the different meanings of the Hebrew word "qidmah" (קִדְמָה) which can mean both "east" and "over against" or "in front of." The Septuagint and the Vulgate interpreters understood it as "over against" where as the Hebrew text understands it as "east of." This difference in translation highlights the potential for multiple interpretations of a single word or phrase in ancient texts. It also illustrates the importance of understanding the context and historical background of a text in order to arrive at an accurate translation. In this case, the Septuagint and Vulgate interpreters interpreted the Hebrew word "qidmah" as "over against", while the Hebrew text interprets it as "east of." This illustrates the complexity of translation, and the need for scholars to carefully consider multiple perspectives and interpretations in order to arrive at the most accurate understanding of an ancient text.

INTRODUCTION TO THE TEXT OF THE OLD TESTAMENT

Genesis 4:18

חֲנוֹךְ עִירָד מְחוּיָאֵל מְתוּשָׁאֵל לָמֶךְ׃, *ḥă-nō-wk... 'î-rāḏ...mə-ḥū-yā-'êl...mə-ṯū-šā-'êl...lā-meḵ.*, 'Hanowk...Irad...Mehuyael...Methushael...Lamek.' – WLC

Ἐνὼχ   Γαιδαδ...Μαιήλ...Μαθουσαλά...Λάμεχ, 'Henoch Gaidad...Maiel...Mathousala...Lamech' – LXX^Swete LXX^Rahlfs ABP

Henoch...Irad...Maviael...Mathusael...Lamech – Vg^Colunga&Turrado

Compare Genesis 5:6–26

In Genesis 4:18, there is a textual issue regarding the names of the descendants of Cain. The Hebrew text (WLC) gives the names as Hanowk, Irad, Mehuyael, Methushael, and Lamek. However, the Septuagint (LXXSwete LXXRahlfs ABP) and the Vulgate (VgColunga&Turrado) give the names as Henoch, Gaidad, Maiel, Mathousala, and Lamech. This could be due to the different ways the names were transliterated from Hebrew to Greek and Latin, or due to variations in the text that existed at the time of translation. Additionally, it could be due to the different meanings of the Hebrew names which are lost in translation. It is important to note that this type of variation in names occurs throughout the Bible and is common in ancient literature.

Genesis 4:20

וּמִקְנֶה׃, *ū-miq-neh.*, 'and [raise] livestock.' – WLC

κτηνοτρόφων, 'grazing cattle' – LXX^Swete LXX^Rahlfs ABP

atque pastorum., 'and of (the) shepherds.' – Vg^Colunga&Turrado

In Genesis 4:20, there is a textual issue regarding the translation of the Hebrew word "miqneh" (מִקְנֶה). The Hebrew text (WLC) states that Cain will "raise livestock." However, the Septuagint (LXXSwete LXXRahlfs) translates it as "grazing cattle" and the Vulgate (VgColunga&Turrado) translates it as "of (the) shepherds." This difference in translation may be due to the different meanings of the Hebrew word "miqneh" which can mean both "livestock" and "grazing cattle" and Vulgate translator might have understood it as "shepherds" as they raise sheep and cattle. This difference in translation does not significantly change the overall meaning of the passage.

Genesis 5

Genesis 5:1

זֶה סֵפֶר תּוֹלְדֹת אָדָם, *zeh sê-p̄er tō-wl-ḏōṯ 'ā-ḏām*, 'This [is] the book of the generations/genealogy (of) man *or* Adam' – WLC

Αὕτη ἡ βίβλος γενέσεως ἀνθρώπων., 'This [is] the book of [the] origin/birth of men *or* humans' – LXX[Swete] LXX[Rahlfs] ABP

Hic est liber generationis Adam., 'This is [the] book of [the] generation/offspring (of) Adam.' – Vg[Colunga&Turrado]

In Genesis 5:1, there is a textual issue regarding the meaning of the Hebrew word "sefer" (סֵפֶר) which is translated as "book" in the WLC. However, in the Septuagint (LXXSwete LXXRahlfs) and the Vulgate (VgColunga&Turrado) it is translated as "book of the origin/birth" and "book of the generation/offspring" respectively. This difference in translation may be due to the different meanings of the Hebrew word "sefer" which can mean both "book" and "generations/genealogy". This difference in translation may be due to the different interpretations of the Hebrew text by the Septuagint and Vulgate translators, which emphasizes the meaning of genealogy.

Genesis 5:2

בָּרָא אֱלֹהִים אָדָם, *bə-rō 'ĕ-lō-hîm 'ā-dām*, '(the) god(s) created (the) man *or* Adam' – WLC

ἐποίησεν ὁ θεὸς τὸν Ἀδάμ,, 'the god made Adam,' – LXX[Swete] LXX[Rahlfs] ABP

creavit Deus hominem,, 'God made (the) man *or* human (being)' – Vg[Colunga&Turrado]

In Genesis 5:2, there is a textual issue regarding the creation of man. The Hebrew text (WLC) states that "the god(s) created (the) man or Adam," which implies the presence of multiple gods. However, the Septuagint (LXXSwete LXXRahlfs) and the Vulgate (VgColunga&Turrado) translate it as "the god made Adam," or "God made (the) man or human (being)" which implies the presence of one God. This difference in translation may be due to the Septuagint and the Vulgate being written after the monotheistic understanding of Judaism had developed.

Genesis 5:6–26

אֱנוֹשׁ...קֵינָן...מַהֲלַלְאֵל...יֶרֶד...חֲנוֹךְ...מְתוּשֶׁלַח...לֶמֶךְ, *'ĕ-nō-wōš...qê-nān...ma-hă-lal-'êl...yā-red...ḥă-nō-wk...mə-tū-šā-laḥ...lā-mek*, 'Enowosh...Qenan...Mahalalel...Yared...Hanowk...Methushalah...Lamek' – WLC

INTRODUCTION TO THE TEXT OF THE OLD TESTAMENT

Ενώς...Καϊναν...Μαλελεήλ...Ιάρεδ...Ενώχ/Ἐνώχ...Μαθουσάλα...Λάμεχ, '
Enós...Kaïnan...Malaleél...Iáred...Enoch/Henoch...Mathousála...Lámech' –
LXX^{Swete} LXX^{Rahlfs} ABP

Enos...Cainan...Malaleel...Jared...Henoch...Mathusalam...Lamech –
Vg$^{Colunga\&Turrado}$

Compare Genesis 4:18

In Genesis 5:6-26, there is a textual issue regarding the names of the descendants of Adam listed in the genealogy. In the Hebrew Text (WLC), the names are Enowosh, Qenan, Mahalalel, Yared, Hanowk, Methushalah, and Lamek. However, in the Septuagint (LXXSwete LXXRahlfs ABP) and the Vulgate (VgColunga&Turrado), the names are slightly different: Enós, Kaïnan, Malaleél, Iáred, Enoch/Henoch, Mathousála, and Lámech. This difference in translation may be due to variations in the way the names were transliterated from the Hebrew to Greek and Latin, as well as differences in interpretation of the Hebrew text by the Septuagint and Vulgate translators. A comparison with Genesis 4:18 also shows similar variations in the names.

Genesis 6

Genesis 6:6

וַיִּנָּחֶם יְהוָה כִּי־עָשָׂה אֶת־הָאָדָם, *way-yin-nā-ḥem Jeh-ho-vah kî- 'ā-śāh 'eṯ- hā-'ā-ḏām,* 'and Jehovah regretted that [he] had made (the) man' – WLC

καὶ ἐνεθυμήθη ὁ θεὸς ὅτι ἐποίησεν τὸν ἄνθρωπον, 'and the god reflected upon / pondered that [he] made the man' – LXX^{Swete} LXX^{Rahlfs} ABP

poenituit eum quod hominum fecisset, 'he regretted which/because/that/what [he] had made of men/humans' – Vg$^{Colunga\&Turrado}$

In Genesis 6:6, there is a textual issue regarding the translation of the Hebrew word "way-yin-nā-ḥem" which is translated as "regretted" in the WLC (Westminster Leningrad Codex) translation. The LXX (Septuagint) translation, translated by Swete and Rahlfs, and the ABP (A New English Translation of the Septuagint) uses the Greek word "ἐνεθυμήθη" which can be translated as "reflected upon" or "pondered". The Vg (Vulgate) translation, translated by Colunga & Turrado, uses the Latin word "poenituit" which can be translated as "regretted" or "repented" in English. This shows how there are different ways of interpreting the Hebrew word "way-yin-nā-ḥem" and how it is translated in different translations.

Genesis 6:6

וַיִּתְעַצֵּב אֶל־לִבּוֹ׃, *way-yit-'aṣ-ṣêḇ 'el- lib-bōw.*, 'and [he] was grieved in his heart.' – WLC

καὶ διενοήθη., 'and [he] considered it.' – LXX^{Swete} LXX^{Rahlfs} ABP

Et tactus dolore cordis intrinsecus,, 'And touched by [the] inner pain of [the] heart' – Vg^{Colunga&Turrado}

In Genesis 6:6, there is a textual issue present in the translation between the Hebrew text, the Septuagint (LXX), and the Vulgate (Vg). The Hebrew text states that God was grieved in his heart, while the Septuagint states that God considered it, and the Vulgate states that God was touched by inner pain of the heart. This difference in wording and interpretation could be due to various factors such as the translator's understanding of the original text, the cultural and historical context of the translation, and the translator's own bias or interpretation of the text. The Hebrew word "way-yit-'aṣ-ṣêḇ" which is translated in WLC as "grieved" can also be translated as "regretted" or "sorrowed" which is how it was translated in LXX and Vg. The LXX and Vg also use different words to express the same idea, which might have been due to the translator's interpretation of the Hebrew text.

Genesis 6:7

וַיֹּאמֶר יְהֹוָה אֶמְחֶה אֶת־הָאָדָם, *way-yō-mer Jeh-ho-vah 'em-ḥeh 'et- hā-'ā-ḏām*, 'and/so Jehovah said: I will destroy (the) man' – WLC

καὶ εἶπεν ὁ θεός Ἀπαλείψω τὸν ἄνθρωπον, 'And the god said: I will wipe off the man' – LXX^{Swete} LXX^{Rahlfs} ABP

Delebo, inquit, hominem,, '[I] will destroy, [he] said, [the] man,' – Vg^{Colunga&Turrado}

This is a textual issue in the translation of Genesis 6:7 in the Bible. The original Hebrew text states that Jehovah (God) says "I will destroy (the) man" (way-yō-mer Jeh-ho-vah 'em-ḥeh 'et- hā-'ā-ḏām) in reference to the actions and behavior of humans. However, the Septuagint (LXX), a Greek translation of the Hebrew Bible, states that God says, "I will wipe off the man" (καὶ εἶπεν ὁ θεός Ἀπαλείψω τὸν ἄνθρωπον) and the Latin Vulgate (Vg) states that God says "[I] will destroy, [he] said, [the] man" (Delebo, inquit, hominem). The difference in wording between the translations may reflect different interpretations or understandings of the original Hebrew text by the translators.

INTRODUCTION TO THE TEXT OF THE OLD TESTAMENT

Genesis 6:14

עֲשֵׂה לְךָ תֵּבַת עֲצֵי־גֹפֶר, *'ă-śêh lə-kā tê-bat 'ă-ṣê- ḡō-p̄er,*, 'Make for yourself [a] box/basket of *gopher* wood' – WLC

ποίησον οὖν σεαυτῷ κιβωτὸν ἐκ ξύλων τετραγώνων·, 'Then make for yourself [a] wooden box out of four-cornered wood!' – LXX[Swete] LXX[Rahlfs] ABP

Fac tibi arcam de lignis laevigatis;, 'Make for yourself [a] chest/box of polished wood;' – Vg[Colunga&Turrado]

In other contexts, each of the Hebrew, Greek and Latin words are used to describe a (wooden) box, basket or chest for storage. The traditionally used English word *ark* derives from the Latin word *arca* (from the verb *arceō*, "to keep off/away/close"), which outside of the Bible never refers to any kind of ship, but always a relatively small object for keeping items. The same nouns are used for the *Ark* of the Covenant. The Hebrew noun H1613 גֹּפֶר *gopher* is a *hapax legomenon*.

In Genesis 6:14, the text describes God's instructions to Noah for building an ark (or box) to protect himself and his family from the flood. The Hebrew text uses the word "tevat," which can be translated as "box" or "basket." The Septuagint, a Greek translation of the Hebrew Bible, uses the word "kibōtos," which can also be translated as "box" or "chest." The Latin Vulgate uses the word "arca," which can be translated as "chest" or "box." The English word "ark" is derived from the Latin "arca." The Hebrew noun "gopher" is a hapax legomenon, meaning it appears only once in the Bible. Its meaning is not entirely clear, but it is believed to be a type of wood that was used to construct the ark.

Genesis 9

Genesis 9:20

אִישׁ הָאֲדָמָה, *'îš hā-'ă-dā-māh*, '[a] man of the land/ground/earth/soil' – WLC

ἄνθρωπος γεωργὸς γῆς, '[a] farmer-man of [the] land/earth/soil *or* [a] tilling/working/fertilising man of [the] land/earth/soil' – LXX[Swete] LXX[Rahlfs] ABP

vir agricola exercere terram, '[a] farmer-man to work at [the] land/earth/soil *or* [a] man working as [a] farmer on [the] land/earth/soil' – Vg[Colunga&Turrado]

The text in question is Genesis 9:20, which in the original Hebrew reads "אִישׁ הָאֲדָמָה," which can be translated as "[a] man of the land/ground/earth/soil." The Greek translation, known as the Septuagint (LXX), renders this phrase as "ἄνθρωπος γεωργὸς γῆς," which can be translated as "[a] farmer-man of [the] land/earth/soil" or "[a] tilling/working/fertilising man of [the] land/earth/soil." The Latin translation, known as the Vulgate (Vg), renders this phrase as "vir agricola exercere terram," which can be translated as "[a] farmer-man to work at [the] land/earth/soil" or "[a] man working as [a] farmer on [the] land/earth/soil."

It is important to note that in this context, the Hebrew word "אִישׁ" (ish) is used more in the sense of "mankind" or "human" rather than specifically a farmer or cultivator. However, the Greek and Latin translations convey the sense of a farmer or cultivator of the land. The context of the passage is the story of Noah and the flood, and the phrase in question is part of a broader statement about the relationship between humanity and the land after the flood. The Greek and Latin translations emphasize the role of mankind as cultivators of the land, while the Hebrew text is more general in its language.

Genesis 15

Genesis 15:17

וַעֲלָטָה הָיָה וְהִנֵּה תַנּוּר עָשָׁן וְלַפִּיד אֵשׁ, *wa-'ă-lā-ṭāh hā-yāh; wə-hin-nêh ṯan-nūr 'ā-šān wə-lap-pîḏ 'êš,,* 'and it became dark, behold a firepot/oven smoking and a torch burning' – WLC

φλὸξ ἐγένετο· καὶ ἰδοὺ κλίβανος καπνιζόμενος καὶ λαμπάδες πυρός,, 'a flame came/happened. And behold, an oven smoking and torches/lamps of fire' LXX[Swete] Brenton ABP

facta est caligo tenebrosa, et apparuit clibanus fumans, et lampas ignis, 'a dark fog happened, and a smoking furnace appeared, and lamps of fire' – Vg[Colunga&Turrado]

In Genesis 15:17, there is a textual issue between the Hebrew, Greek, and Latin versions of the passage. The Hebrew text describes a "firepot/oven smoking and a torch burning," while the Greek text describes a "flame came/happened. And behold, an oven smoking and torches/lamps of fire." The Latin text describes a "dark fog happened, and a smoking furnace appeared, and lamps of fire." These variations in description may be due to differences in the translation process, as well as variations in the underlying texts that were used. The meaning of the passage remains the same, that there

INTRODUCTION TO THE TEXT OF THE OLD TESTAMENT

was some kind of supernatural sign or revelation given to Abram, but the specific details of the sign are described differently in each translation.

Genesis 34

Genesis 34:2

חֲמוֹר הַחִוִּי, *ḥă-mō-wr ha-ḥiw-wî*, 'Hamor the Hivite' – WLC

Ἐμμὼρ ὁ Χορραῖος, 'Emmor the Hurrian' – A LXX[Swete]

Εμμώρ ο Ευαίος, 'Emmor the Evite' – Brenton ABP

Hemor Hevaei, 'Hemor of the Hevea' – Vg[Colunga&Turrado]

In Genesis 34:2, the name of the individual in question is Hamor in the Hebrew text. However, in the Greek Septuagint, the name is rendered as Emmor in some versions and in others as Hemor. Additionally, the Septuagint also gives the individual's ethnicity as the Hurrian in one version, the Evite in another version. The Vulgate also gives the individual's ethnicity as Hevea. This variation in the name and ethnicity suggests that there may have been some uncertainty or debate among ancient translators or copyists regarding the proper identification of this individual.

Genesis 34:2

וַיִּקַּח אֹתָהּ וַיִּשְׁכַּב אֹתָהּ וַיְעַנֶּהָ, *way-yiq-qaḥ 'ō-ṯāh way-yiš-kab 'ō-ṯāh way-'an-ne-hā.*, 'and he took her, and he laid her, and he raped her.' – WLC

καὶ λαβὼν αὐτὴν ἐκοιμήθη μετ᾽ αὐτῆς, καὶ ἐταπείνωσεν αὐτήν., 'and taking her, [he] slept with her, and humiliated/humbled her.' LXX[Swete] Brenton ABP

adamavit eam: et rapuit, et dormivit cum illa, vi opprimens virginem., '[he] fell in love with her: and [he] abducted [her], and slept with her, attacking/subduing/oppressing [the] virgin by force.' – Vg[Colunga&Turrado]

In the Hebrew text of Genesis 34:2, the verb "way-yiq-qaḥ" (and he took) is followed by "way-yiš-kab" (and he laid), which is followed by "way-'an-ne-hā" (and he raped). This sequence of verbs is used to describe the actions of the Hivite prince Shechem towards Dinah, the daughter of Jacob. The Greek text of the Septuagint (LXXSwete, Brenton, ABP) uses the verb "λαβὼν" (taking) followed by "ἐκοιμήθη" (slept with) and "ἐταπείνωσεν" (humiliated/humbled). The verb "ἐταπείνωσεν" is used to convey the sense of Shechem's actions towards Dinah, but it does not convey the physical act of rape. The Latin text of the Vulgate (VgColunga&Turrado) uses the verb "adamavit" (fell in love with) followed by "rapuit" (abducted) and "dormivit" (slept with), and "vi opprimens virginem" (attacking/subduing/oppressing [the] virgin by force) to convey the sense of Shechem's actions towards Dinah. In this translation the sense of rape is maintained but the physical act is not mentioned.

Genesis 34:3

וַתִּדְבַּ֣ק נַפְשׁ֔וֹ בְּדִינָ֖ה בַּֽת־יַעֲקֹ֑ב וַיֶּֽאֱהַב֙ אֶת־הַֽנַּעֲרָ֔ וַיְדַבֵּ֖ר עַל־לֵ֥ב הַֽנַּעֲרָֽ׃, *wat-tid-baq nap̄-šōw bə-ḏî-nāh baṯ- ya-'ă-qōḇ; way-ye-'ĕ-haḇ 'eṯ- han-na-'ă-rā, way-ḏab-bêr 'al- lêḇ han-na-'ă-rā.*, 'And he stayed with/kept Dinah, the daughter of Jacob, and he lusted after the young woman, and he tried to quiet the young woman.' – WLC

καὶ προσέσχεν τῇ ψυχῇ Δείνας τῆς θυγατρὸς Ἰακώβ, καὶ ἠγάπησεν τὴν παρθένον, καὶ ἐλάλησεν κατὰ τὴν διάνοιαν τῆς παρθένου αὐτῇ, 'and [he] clung to the breath/soul/mind/person of Dinah, the daughter of Jacob, and he took pleasure in the young woman, and he spoke against the mind of the young woman.' LXX^Swete

καὶ προσέσχε τῇ ψυχῇ Δείνας/Δίνας τῆς θυγατρὸς Ἰακώβ καὶ ἠγάπησε τὴν παρθένον καὶ ἐλάλησε κατὰ τὴν διάνοιαν τῆς παρθένου αὐτῇ, 'and [he] clung to the breath/soul/mind/person of Dinah, the daughter of Jacob, and he took pleasure in the young woman, and he spoke against the mind of the young woman.' Brenton ABP

Et conglutinata est anima ejus cum ea, tristemque delinivit blanditiis., 'And his soul was glued to her, and [he] soothed [the] sad one with blandishments.' – Vg^Colunga&Turrado

In Genesis 34:2, the Hebrew text describes how Shechem, a Hivite prince, takes Dinah, the daughter of Jacob, and "lay with her and humbled her" (WLC). The Septuagint, a Greek translation of the Hebrew Bible, uses a different verb, "slept with her" (LXXSwete) and adds that he "humiliated" her. The Vulgate, a Latin translation of the Bible, uses the verb "abducted" and "slept with her" and adds that he "attacked/subduing/oppressing [the] virgin by force."

In Genesis 34:3, the Hebrew text describes how Shechem "stayed with/kept Dinah, the daughter of Jacob, and he lusted after the young woman, and he tried to quiet the young woman." The Septuagint says that "he clung to the breath/soul/mind/person of Dinah, the daughter of Jacob, and he took pleasure in the young woman, and he spoke against the mind of the young woman." The Vulgate says that "his soul was glued to her, and [he] soothed [the] sad one with blandishments."

INTRODUCTION TO THE TEXT OF THE OLD TESTAMENT

These variations in the translations indicate that the original Hebrew text was open to different interpretations, and translators have used their own judgment and understanding of the text to convey the meaning in their own language. The use of different verbs and phrases can also be influenced by the cultural and historical context in which the translation was made. It is important to keep in mind that these are different translations and not errors or discrepancies in the text. It is also important to consult multiple translations and commentaries to gain a deeper understanding of the passage. Additionally, it is essential to approach the text with an open mind, and with a willingness to consider different interpretations and perspectives.

Genesis 34:7

וְכֵן לֹא יֵעָשֶׂה׃, *wə-kên lō yê-'ā-śeh.*, 'and such [a thing] should not be done' – WLC

καὶ οὐχ οὕτως ἔσται., 'And [it] shall not be thus.' LXX[Swete] Brenton ABP

rem illicitam perpetrasset., '[he] had perpetrated/committed [an] illicit/unlawful act.' – Vg[Colunga&Turrado]

In Genesis 34:7, the Hebrew text states, "and such [a thing] should not be done." This statement is a general condemnation of the actions of Shechem, who has just raped Dinah, the daughter of Jacob. The Septuagint, a Greek translation of the Hebrew Bible, uses a similar phrase "And [it] shall not be thus." The Vulgate, a Latin translation of the Bible, states "[he] had perpetrated/committed [an] illicit/unlawful act." This variation in translations suggests that the original Hebrew text can be interpreted in multiple ways. Each translator has chosen a phrase that they feel most accurately conveys the meaning of the text, whether that be a general statement of condemnation or a specific reference to the act of rape being illegal or immoral.

Genesis 34:9

תִּקְחוּ לָכֶם׃, *tiq-ḥū lā-kem.*, 'take to/for yourselves.' – WLC

λάβετε τοῖς υἱοῖς ὑμῶν., 'take for your sons.' – LXX[Swete] Brenton ABP

accipite,, 'accept,' – Vg[Colunga&Turrado]

In Genesis 34:9, the Hebrew text states that the sons of Jacob tell Shechem and his father Hamor that they can only agree to their proposal for the men of their city to intermarry with their daughters if they become like them by circumcising themselves. They say "take to/for yourselves" (WLC) implying that they are the ones who will do the circumcising. The Septuagint,

287

a Greek translation of the Hebrew Bible, uses the phrase "take for your sons" (LXXSwete Brenton ABP) suggesting that the men of the city will circumcise their own sons as a condition for intermarriage. The Vulgate, a Latin translation of the Bible, uses the verb "accept" (VgColunga&Turrado) which is even more general and doesn't specify who is doing the circumcising. This variation in the translations indicates that the original Hebrew text was open to different interpretations, and translators had to make choices on how to convey the intended meaning in their own language.

Genesis 34:11

אֶתֵּן, *'et-tên.*, 'I will give.' – WLC

ἡμῖν δώσομεν., 'we will give.' – LXX[Swete]

δώσομεν., '[we] will give.' – Brenton ABP

dabo, '[I] will give' – Vg[Colunga&Turrado]

In Genesis 34:11, the Hebrew text states that "I will give" (WLC) which refers to a singular subject, possibly the speaker, who is willing to give something. However, the Septuagint, a Greek translation of the Hebrew Bible, uses the first person plural "we will give" (LXXSwete) which implies that more than one person is involved in the giving. The Brenton ABP and VgColunga&Turrado also use first person singular form, indicating a single person giving something. This variation in the translations suggests that the original Hebrew text may have been open to different interpretations, and translators may have made different choices based on their understanding of the context and intended meaning.

Genesis 34:14

וַיֹּאמְרוּ אֲלֵיהֶם, *way-yō-mə-rū 'ă-lê-hem,*, 'And they said to them' – WLC

καὶ εἶπαν αὐτοῖς Συμεὼν καὶ Λευὶ οἱ ἀδελφοὶ Δείνας υἱοὶ δὲ Λείας, 'And Simeon and Levi the brothers of Dinah sons of Leah said to them' – LXX[Swete]

καὶ εἶπαν αὐτοῖς Συμεὼν καὶ Λευὶ οἱ ἀδελφοὶ Δείνας/Δίνας, 'And Simeon and Levi the brothers of Dinah said to them' – Brenton ABP

omitted – Vg[Colunga&Turrado]

The textual issue in Genesis 34:14 is related to the variations in the translations of the Hebrew text. The original Hebrew text states that "And they said to them" (way-yō-mə-rū 'ă-lê-hem). However, in the Septuagint, which is a Greek translation of the Hebrew Bible, the translation includes additional information about the speakers, stating that "Simeon and Levi, the brothers of Dinah, sons of Leah, said to them" (καὶ εἶπαν αὐτοῖς Συμεὼν καὶ Λευὶ οἱ ἀδελφοὶ Δείνας υἱοὶ δὲ Λείας). Similarly, the Brenton ABP, another Greek translation of the Bible, has a similar translation but omits the phrase "sons of Leah". The Latin translation of the Bible (VgColunga&Turrado) omits this information completely. This variation in the translations suggests that the original Hebrew text may have been open to interpretation, and translators may have added or omitted certain details to better convey the meaning in their own language.

Genesis 34:14

לְאִישׁ אֲשֶׁר־לוֹ עָרְלָה, *lə-'îš 'ă-šer- lōw 'ā-rə-lāh;*, 'to an uncircumcised man' – WLC

ἀνθρώπῳ ὃς ἔχει ἀκροβυστίαν·, 'to a man who has [a] foreskin' – LXX[Swete] Brenton ABP

homini incircumciso, 'to an uncircumcised man' – Vg[Colunga&Turrado]

In this passage, the Hebrew text of the WLC version uses the phrase "to an uncircumcised man" (lə-'îš 'ă-šer- lōw 'ā-rə-lāh) to describe the person to whom the brothers of Dinah are speaking. The Septuagint (LXXSwete) and Brenton ABP versions also use similar language, with the Septuagint using the phrase "to a man who has [a] foreskin" (ἀνθρώπῳ ὃς ἔχει ἀκροβυστίαν) and the Brenton ABP version using the phrase "to a man who has a foreskin." The Latin Vulgate (VgColunga&Turrado) version also uses similar language, with the phrase "to an uncircumcised man" (homini incircumciso). These variations in the translations indicate that the original Hebrew text was open to different interpretations, and translators have chosen different words or phrases to convey the meaning of the original text in their respective languages.

Genesis 49

Genesis 49:4

כִּי עָלִיתָ מִשְׁכְּבֵי אָבִיךָ, *kî 'ā-lî-tā miš-kə-bê 'ā-bî-kā;*, 'because you went up on the beds of [your] father') – WLC

ἀνέβης γὰρ ἐπὶ τὴν κοίτην τοῦ πατρός σου·, 'because you went up on the (marriage-)bed of your father;' – LXX[Swete]

ανέβης γαρ επί την κοίτην του πατρός σου, 'because you went up on the (marriage-)bed of your father' – ABP

quia ascendisti cubile patris tui – Vg[Clement] Vg[Colunga&Turrado]

Compare Leviticus 18:22; Leviticus 20:13.

The phrase "you went up on the beds of your father" in the Hebrew text of Genesis 49:4 (WLC) is referencing to the act of incest. The Septuagint (LXXSwete) and the Aquila, Symmachus, and Theodotion (ABP) translations use the phrase "went up on the (marriage-)bed of your father" to convey the same idea. The Latin translation, the Vulgate (VgClement VgColunga&Turrado) is similar, uses the phrase "ascendisti cubile patris tui" which also means you went up on the bed of your father. This passage is referencing to the act of incest and the translations convey this meaning in different ways.

Why Is It Important for Churchgoers and Pastors to Learn the Basics of Old Testament Textual Criticism?

Textual criticism is the study and analysis of the various written texts that make up the Bible. It involves comparing different manuscripts and versions of the Bible in order to determine the most accurate and authentic text. This is particularly important when studying the Old Testament, as the texts that make up the Old Testament have a long and complex history of transmission and preservation. Understanding the basics of Old Testament textual criticism is crucial for both churchgoers and pastors as it allows them to better understand the texts they are reading and interpreting, and to engage with the texts in a more informed and critical way.

One of the main reasons why it is important for churchgoers and pastors to learn the basics of Old Testament textual criticism is that it helps them to better understand the historical context and development of the texts they are reading. Textual criticism allows us to trace the evolution of a text over time, which can reveal important information about the historical context in which the text was written and the cultural and social influences that shaped it. For example, by studying the different versions of a text, we can gain insight into the theological and ideological perspectives of the different communities that produced and transmitted the text.

Another important reason why it is important for churchgoers and pastors to learn the basics of Old Testament textual criticism is that it can help them to identify and address potential issues and inconsistencies within the text. For example, by comparing different versions of a text, we can identify any variations or discrepancies in the text, and determine which version is most likely to be the original or most accurate. This can help to prevent misinterpretation or misapplication of the text.

Additionally, learning the basics of Old Testament textual criticism can also help churchgoers and pastors to better understand the relationship between the Old and New Testament. By understanding the historical context and development of the Old Testament texts, churchgoers and pastors can better understand how the New Testament writers understood and interacted with the Old Testament texts, which can aid in interpreting and understanding the New Testament.

Furthermore, knowing the basics of Old Testament textual criticism also helps pastors to better understand the historical context of the Old Testament text and thus be able to preach and teach from that context. It also helps churchgoers to be able to read the Old Testament text in context, and not to impose a 21st century understanding of the text.

Lastly, it is important for churchgoers and pastors to learn the basics of Old Testament textual criticism because it helps them to be better equipped to engage with critical scholarship and to be able to understand and respond to critical arguments and perspectives. This can help to deepen and enrich their understanding of the texts and to engage in more informed and productive conversations and discussions.

In conclusion, learning the basics of Old Testament textual criticism is an important step for both churchgoers and pastors in order to gain a deeper understanding of the texts they are reading and interpreting, and to engage with the texts in a more informed and critical way. This can help them to better understand the historical context and development of the texts, the literary structure and meaning of the texts, and to identify and address potential issues and inconsistencies within the text. Additionally, it can aid in interpreting and understanding the New Testament and better equipping them to engage with critical scholarship.

CHAPTER 12 The Importance of Textual Criticism

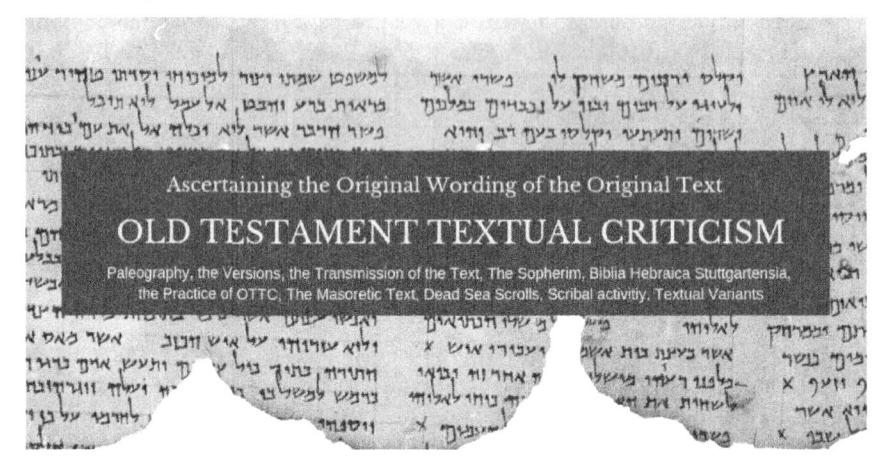

Ascertaining the Original Wording of the Original Text

OLD TESTAMENT TEXTUAL CRITICISM

Paleography, the Versions, the Transmission of the Text, The Sopherim, Biblia Hebraica Stuttgartensia, the Practice of OTTC, The Masoretic Text, Dead Sea Scrolls, Scribal activitly, Textual Variants

The Old Testament, also known as the Hebrew Bible, presents a unique and complex textual tradition. By studying and analyzing the various written texts that make up the Old Testament, we can gain a deeper understanding of the historical context and development of the texts, as well as the literary structure and meaning.

Textual criticism is the process of comparing different manuscripts and versions of the Bible in order to determine the most accurate and authentic text. This process allows us to trace the evolution of a text over time and gain insight into the historical context in which it was written, as well as the cultural and social influences that shaped it.

Additionally, by studying the different versions of a text, we can gain insight into the literary devices and techniques used by the authors, as well as the underlying themes and messages of the text. This can help to deepen our understanding of the texts and gain a deeper appreciation of their literary value.

It is important to note that textual criticism is not just a scholarly endeavor but is also integral to the church and its message. The goal of textual criticism is not to discover errors made in the transmission of the text, but to provide a reliable biblical text for practical use. This is the task that inspires the engagement of textual critics, as it enables the church to meet the living God through the Bible in a reliable way.

In order to understand the Old Testament and its message, it is essential for churchgoers and pastors to learn the basics of Old Testament textual criticism. This will enable them to engage with the text in a more informed and critical way, and to gain a deeper understanding of the historical context, literary structure and underlying themes of the texts. Additionally, by using textual criticism to determine the most accurate and authentic version of a text, churchgoers and pastors can be sure that they are reading and interpreting a reliable version of the Bible.

In conclusion, learning the basics of Old Testament textual criticism is crucial for both churchgoers and pastors as it allows them to better understand the texts they are reading and interpreting, and to engage with the texts in a more informed and critical way. It is not simply an historical undertaking, but has relevance for the present, and is an important aspect of the church's mission to provide reliable access to the Word of God.

Textual criticism is often viewed as a mere academic requirement within theological education, but it is much more than that. It requires the use of skills such as imagination, the ability to empathize with the text, and an intuitive understanding of variations in the text. It is, in fact, the gateway to exegesis and there is no other way around it. Its purpose is to open up the biblical text and unlock its meaning. Through a thorough analysis of the biblical text and a careful examination of available readings, textual criticism can reveal important theological issues that are hidden and require further exegetical consideration. Engaging in textual criticism is not a preoccupation with trivial matters but is highly beneficial. The literal and spiritual aspects of the text are not necessarily opposing, but rather they can be mutually necessary, particularly when God speaks to us through the Bible. This is why the study of textual criticism has genuine theological significance.

Christian Apologetics and Textual Criticism

Introduction

Old Testament Textual Criticism (OTTC) is a field of study that involves analyzing and comparing different versions of the Old Testament in order to determine the most accurate and authentic text. This process is crucial for understanding the historical context and development of the texts, as well as the literary structure and meaning. It is also of great importance to Christian Apologists, as it allows them to engage with the texts in a more informed and critical way, and to provide a solid defense of their faith.

Textual Criticism and the Defense of the Faith

One of the main advantages of OTTC for the Christian Apologist is that it allows them to provide a solid defense of their faith. By studying the different versions of a text, an apologist can gain insight into the historical context in which it was written and the cultural and social influences that shaped it. This can help to provide a more accurate understanding of the text and to defend against any accusations of mistranslation or misinterpretation.

For example, if an apologist is confronted with the accusation that the Bible is full of contradictions, they can use textual criticism to show that the apparent contradictions are actually the result of different authors writing in different historical contexts and using different literary devices and techniques. This in turn allows the apologist to present a more nuanced and accurate understanding of the text, and to defend against accusations of contradiction.

Additionally, by studying the different versions of a text, an apologist can gain insight into how the text has been transmitted and preserved over time. This can provide valuable information for understanding the historical context and development of the text, as well as the cultural and social influences that shaped it. For example, by comparing different versions of a text, an apologist can gain insight into the theological and ideological perspectives of the different communities that produced and transmitted the text.

Furthermore, textual criticism can help an apologist to better understand the literary structure and meaning of the texts they are reading. By comparing different versions of a text, an apologist can gain insight into the literary devices and techniques used by the authors, as well as the underlying themes and messages of the text. This can help to deepen an apologist's understanding of the texts and to gain a deeper appreciation of their literary value.

Moreover, textual criticism can also provide an apologist with a more reliable text, which can be used as a basis for defending their beliefs and engaging in theological discussions. This is because textual criticism allows us to identify and eliminate errors and variations that have been introduced into the text over time, which can provide a more accurate representation of the original text.

Old Testament textual criticism is a valuable tool for Christian apologetics, as it can help to provide a solid foundation for defending the authenticity and reliability of the Bible. By studying the different manuscripts and versions of the Old Testament, apologists can gain a deeper understanding of the historical context and development of the texts, as well as the literary structure and meaning. This can help to strengthen their arguments for the validity of the Bible as a source of divine revelation.

One key advantage of Old Testament textual criticism for Christian apologetics is that it can help to address objections and challenges to the authenticity and accuracy of the Bible. By carefully examining the different versions of a text and tracing its evolution over time, apologists can demonstrate the reliability of the text and refute claims of corruption or alteration. This can be especially important when addressing objections from skeptics or critics who may question the historical accuracy of the Bible or the authenticity of its texts.

Another advantage of Old Testament textual criticism for Christian apologetics is that it can help to deepen our understanding of the biblical texts and provide a clearer picture of the historical context in which they were written. This can be especially valuable when addressing theological or philosophical objections to the Bible, as it can help to provide a more nuanced and informed perspective on the texts.

In conclusion, Old Testament textual criticism is a valuable tool for Christian apologetics, as it can help to provide a solid foundation for defending the authenticity and reliability of the Bible. By studying the different manuscripts and versions of the Old Testament, apologists can gain a deeper understanding of the historical context and development of the texts, as well as the literary structure and meaning. This can help to strengthen their arguments for the validity of the Bible as a source of divine revelation and deepen our understanding of the biblical texts. Old Testament textual criticism can provide a valuable resource for Christian apologists as it allows them to better understand the texts they are reading and interpreting, and to engage with the texts in a more informed and critical way. It can provide insight into the historical context and development of the text, as well as the cultural and social influences that shaped it. Furthermore, it can help an apologist to better understand the literary structure and meaning of the texts and provide a more reliable text for defense and theological discussion.

Edward D. Andrews

GLOSSARY OF TECHNICAL TERMS

Aquila— Aquila was a Greek Jewish convert to Christianity who lived in the 2nd century CE. He is best known for creating a Greek translation of the Hebrew Bible, known as the Septuagint. This translation was intended to be more literal and accurate than the existing Septuagint version, which was considered by some to be too free in its translation. Aquila's version was widely used by early Christians, especially in the Eastern Roman Empire, and had a significant influence on the development of Christian theology.

Daughter Translation— A "daughter translation" is a term used to describe a translation of an ancient text that was made on the basis of a prior translation of the original text, rather than being a direct translation from the original language. An example of this would be the Old Latin, which was a translation of the Septuagint, a Greek translation of the Hebrew Bible, rather than being a translation directly from the Hebrew. This type of translation is also known as a "version." It is important to note that daughter translations can be less accurate than direct translations, as they may introduce errors or interpretive changes that were present in the prior translation.

Diplomatic Edition— A diplomatic edition is a type of critical edition that uses a single manuscript as the base text and records any variations or differences found in other manuscripts. This approach allows scholars to study the variations and variations within the manuscripts, as well as the specific characteristics of the base manuscript. Diplomatic editions are particularly useful for studying the evolution of a text over time and for understanding the transmission and preservation of a text. By comparing different versions of a text, scholars can gain insight into the historical context in which the text was written and the cultural and social influences that shaped it. Additionally, diplomatic editions can be used to study the literary structure and meaning of the text, providing a deeper understanding of the text and its literary value.

Dittography— It occurs when a scribe unintentionally copies the same letter or word twice in the same line or in consecutive lines. This error can be caused by a variety of factors, such as the scribe's fatigue or inattention, or a malfunction of the writing instrument. Dittography can occur in both handwritten and printed texts and can lead to confusion or misinterpretation of the text if not corrected. In the process of textual criticism, scholars use various methods to identify and correct dittographic errors in order to establish the most accurate and authentic text.

Documentary Approach—"Reasoned eclecticism" method in actual practice tends to give priority to internal evidence over external evidence. The documentary approach looks at all evidence but the primary weight of external evidence generally goes to the original language manuscripts, and the **Codex Leningrad B 19A** and the **Aleppo Codex** are almost always preferred. In Old Testament Textual Criticism, the Masoretic text is our starting point and should only be abandoned as a last resort. While it is true that the Masoretic Text is not perfect, there needs to be a heavy burden of proof if we are to go with an alternative reading. All of the evidence needs to be examined before concluding that a reading in the Masoretic Text is corrupt.

Eclectic Text—An Eclectic Text is a critical edition that is created by using the best readings from multiple available manuscripts, with the goal of recreating what is believed to be the original text. This method of textual criticism involves comparing different manuscripts and versions of a text and selecting the reading that appears to be the most authentic and accurate. The goal of creating an eclectic text is to create a text that is as close as possible to the original, and that reflects the original intent of the author. This method of textual criticism is often used when there are many different versions of a text, and when it is difficult to determine which version is the most authentic.

Editio Princeps— Editio princeps, also known as the first edition, refers to the first published critical edition of a text. This edition is considered the most authoritative and reliable version of the text, as it is based on the most accurate and authentic manuscripts available. The editio princeps is often considered the starting point for any future scholarly editions or translations of the text. It is produced by a team of textual scholars and experts who use their knowledge and skills in textual criticism to produce a critical edition that is as close as possible to the original text. The editio princeps serves as the foundation for all future studies of the text and is considered the standard version of the text.

Egyptian text family— The Egyptian text family is a group of Hebrew texts and versions that share significant similarities. This text family is characterized by certain linguistic and grammatical features, as well as specific textual readings that are unique to this group. The Septuagint, which is a Greek translation of the Hebrew Bible, is considered to be a part of the Egyptian text family. Additionally, some Hebrew manuscripts that were discovered among the Dead Sea Scrolls at Qumran also share many of the features of the Egyptian text family. These manuscripts, known as the

Qumran Hebrew texts, provide valuable insight into the textual history of the Hebrew Bible and the development of the Egyptian text family.

Haplography— Haplography is a type of scribal error that occurs when a scribe accidentally omits a letter(s) or a word(s) while writing or copying a text. This error can occur due to carelessness, fatigue, or other factors that may cause a scribe to miss a section of the text. Haplography can result in missing or duplicated words and letters, which can affect the meaning and interpretation of the text. It is a common problem in ancient manuscripts and can be difficult to detect and correct without the aid of textual criticism.

Hexapla—The Hexapla was a six-column work created by the early Christian theologian Origen. It contained the Hebrew text of the Old Testament, a Greek transliteration of the Hebrew, the revisions of the Greek translations made by Aquila, Symmachus, and Theodotion, as well as Origen's own revision of the Septuagint. The Hexapla was a tool for comparing and studying the different versions of the Old Testament in an effort to gain a deeper understanding of the text and its meanings. The Hexapla is considered a significant historical document for the study of Old Testament Textual Criticism and is an important source for understanding the development of early biblical translations.

Homoioarkton— Homoioarkton (also spelled "homoioteleuton") is a scribal error that occurs when a scribe accidentally omits elements of a text due to similar endings of words. This can happen when a scribe is copying a text and their eyes jump from one line to another, skipping over a portion of the text that is similar in structure or ending. This error can lead to missing words, phrases, or even entire sentences in the copied text. It is one of the common types of errors that can occur in the transmission of a text, and is often taken into account by textual critics when evaluating the reliability of a manuscript.

Homoioteleuton— Homoioteleuton is a type of scribal error that occurs when a scribe accidentally omits elements of a text because the endings of the words or phrases are similar. This can happen when a scribe is copying a text and their eyes accidentally skip over a section because the endings of the words or phrases are the same, causing them to miss a section of the text. This type of error is common in ancient manuscripts and is one of the reasons why textual criticism is important in understanding the original text. It is also a common reason for variations in different manuscripts of the same text.

INTRODUCTION TO THE TEXT OF THE OLD TESTAMENT

Kaige Recension— The Kaige Recension is an early revision of the Septuagint, the Greek translation of the Hebrew Bible, which aimed to bring the text into conformity with the protomasoretic text, which is an early version of the Masoretic text, the traditional Hebrew text of the Jewish scriptures. This revision is also referred to as proto-Theodotion, as it is believed to have been made by an editor named Theodotion or by a group of editors working in his tradition. The Kaige Recension is considered to be an important witness to the development of the Septuagint and provides valuable insight into the relationship between the Septuagint and the Masoretic text.

Ketiv (what is written)— Ketiv (what is written) refers to the text variant represented by the consonants that are written or printed in the text. In Hebrew manuscripts, the consonantal text is written without vowels. The vowels are supplied by the reader or scribe based on their knowledge of the language and traditional pronunciation. The ketiv text is considered the "written" or "original" text, while the text with the vowels added is called the "qere" (what is read). In Old Testament Textual Criticism, the ketiv text is the starting point for analysis and understanding the original text, while the qere text helps to understand how the text was traditionally read and understood.

Local Text— A local text is a text type, or group of texts, that share similar characteristics and are believed to have originated from a specific geographic location. This concept is often used in textual criticism to group together manuscripts or versions of a text that have similarities in language, style, or content. Scholars may use the idea of a local text to help identify the origin and development of a text, and to trace its transmission and evolution over time. Additionally, the study of local texts can also provide insight into the cultural and historical context in which a text was written, and can help to shed light on the social, religious, and literary influences that shaped it.

Masorah Finalis (final Masorah)— The Masorah Finalis, also known as the final Masorah, is a set of notations and annotations that were added to the text of the Hebrew Bible by the Masoretes. These notations were primarily used to ensure the accuracy and consistency of the text, and included information such as the number of times a specific word appears in the text, the number of verses in a book, and other similar details. The Masorah Finalis was typically printed at the end of each book of the Old Testament, and is considered an important tool for textual criticism and the study of the history and transmission of the Hebrew Bible.

Masorah Magna (large Masorah)— The Masorah Magna, also known as the "large Masorah," is a masoretic apparatus that provides verse references for the textual features noted in the Masorah Parva. This apparatus is typically found in critical editions of the Hebrew Bible, such as the Biblia Hebraica Stuttgartensia and the Biblia Hebraica Quinta. In these editions, the Masorah Magna is presented as a series of numbers that correspond to references in a separate volume, or in the case of Biblia Hebraica Quinta, the full references are included. The Masorah Magna is an important tool for scholars and students of the Hebrew Bible, as it helps to identify and understand the textual variations and features found in different manuscripts of the Bible.

Masorah Parva (small Masorah)— The Masorah Parva, also known as the "small Masorah," is a collection of notations and annotations that were added to the margins of the Masoretic Text by the Masoretes. These notations serve as a tool for preserving the accuracy of the text and for ensuring its proper transmission. They include information such as the number of times a particular spelling occurs, as well as other textual features that help to identify potential errors or variations in the text. The Masorah Parva is considered an essential aspect of Old Testament Textual Criticism as it helps scholars to better understand the historical development and transmission of the text. It is often used in conjunction with other critical tools, such as the Masorah Magna, to provide a more comprehensive understanding of the text. The Masorah Parva is a key element in the Biblia Hebraica Stuttgartensia and Biblia Hebraica Quinta editions of the Masoretic Text.

Masoretes— The Masoretes were a group of Jewish scholars who lived between the 6th and 10th centuries CE. They developed a system of vocalization, accentuation, and cantillation marks to indicate the traditional pronunciation and musical intonation of the Hebrew text. These marks were added to the consonantal text, which had been transmitted without any indication of vowels or stress. The Masoretes' work helped to preserve and transmit the traditional Hebrew text and played a critical role in the preservation of the Hebrew Bible. The two main groups of Masoretes were the Tiberian Masoretes, who worked in Tiberias, Israel, and the Babylonian Masoretes, who worked in Babylonia. The Tiberian system, which is considered more accurate and detailed, eventually became the standard system used in the production of Hebrew Bibles.

Masoretic Text— The Masoretic Text is the standard Hebrew text of the Old Testament that was transmitted and preserved by the Masoretes, Jewish scholars who lived during the 6th to 10th centuries AD. The Masoretes were responsible for devising a graphic system to represent the traditional vocalization, or pronunciation, of the Hebrew text. They also added diacritical marks to indicate the accentuation and cantillation of the text. The Masoretic Text is considered to be the most reliable and accurate version of the Hebrew Bible and is the basis for most modern translations of the Old Testament. It is characterized by its precise and consistent use of the Hebrew language, as well as its adherence to traditional Jewish interpretations of the text. The Masoretic Text is also referred to as the "Masora" or the "Masoretic Tradition."

Old Latin— The Old Latin is the earliest known translation of the Old Testament into Latin. It was made from the Septuagint, a Greek translation of the Hebrew Bible, rather than from the original Hebrew text. The Old Latin is considered to be a "daughter translation" because it was made on the basis of a prior translation of the original text. The Old Latin was widely used in the Western Church before the Jerome's Vulgate became the standard Latin Bible. The Old Latin is important for scholars of the Bible because it offers insight into the early transmission and interpretation of the biblical text in the Western Church. It also provides a valuable witness to the Septuagint, which was widely used in the early Church.

Palestinian Text Family— The Palestinian Text Family is a group of Hebrew texts and versions that share significant similarities. The Samaritan Pentateuch is one of the texts that belongs to this group and shares many of the features of the other texts in the Palestinian Text Family. The Palestinian Text Family is considered one of the major text families of the Old Testament and is thought to have originated in the region of Palestine, hence the name. The text of this family is characterized by shorter readings, a more consistent spelling, and a greater use of the divine name. This text family is considered to be more closely related to the Masoretic Text than the other main text family, the Alexandrian text family.

Pesher— Pesher is a Hebrew term used in the context of the Qumran community, a Jewish sect that lived in the area of the Dead Sea in the Second Temple period. A pesher is a type of commentary on an Old Testament book, in which the text is interpreted in light of the sect's beliefs and practices. The Qumran community produced many scrolls that contain pesharim, which are considered to be an important source of information about the sect's beliefs and practices. These pesharim reveal the community's understanding of the texts they interpreted, and provide insight into the sect's beliefs and practices, such as their eschatological expectations, their views on the end of time, their understanding of the nature of God and angels, and their views on the authority of the leaders of the community. They show that the community read these texts as prophetic texts and understood them as referring to the end of times and the coming of the Messiah.

Peshitta— The Peshitta is an ancient translation of the Old Testament into Syriac, a dialect of Aramaic spoken in the Middle East. It is considered the standard version of the Old Testament for the Syriac-speaking churches and is believed to have been translated from the Hebrew text in the 2nd century CE. It is notable for its adherence to the Hebrew text, and its translation is considered to be more literal and closer to the original Hebrew than other versions such as the Septuagint or the Targums. The Peshitta is also significant for its use in the liturgical and biblical studies of the Syrian Orthodox Church, the Assyrian Church of the East, and the Chaldean Catholic Church. It is considered an important witness to the text of the Old Testament and is used in textual criticism studies to help reconstruct the original text.

Proto-Lucian— This revision was named after the scholar Lucian of Antioch who is believed to have been involved in its creation. It was widely used in the Eastern Church and is considered to be one of the most important witnesses of the Septuagint text. The text of Proto-Lucian was characterized by a greater agreement with the Hebrew text than the original Septuagint, and it also included additional readings not found in the Septuagint. It is considered an important source for understanding the text-critical issues of the Septuagint and the relationship between the Septuagint and the Hebrew text.

Protomasoretic Text— The Protomasoretic Text refers to a specific family of Hebrew texts that were in circulation in the Second Temple period. These texts have the greatest representation in the biblical manuscripts found at the Qumran site, which were likely written and used by the Jewish sect known as the Essenes. The Protomasoretic Text is very similar to the consonantal text later preserved by the Masoretes, a group of Jewish scholars who devised a graphic system to represent the traditional vocalization of the Hebrew text, known as the Masoretic Text. This close relationship between the Protomasoretic Text and the Masoretic Text suggests that the Masoretes were likely influenced by the textual tradition represented in the Qumran manuscripts when they were developing their own system of vocalization and transmission of the Hebrew Bible.

Qere (what is read)— The Qere (also spelled "Kethibh" or "Ketib") is a text variant in the Masoretic Text of the Hebrew Bible represented by the vowels printed in the text, and the consonants printed in the margin. It represents the traditional vocalization of the Hebrew text as transmitted by the Masoretes, and it is often different from the consonantal text (Ketiv) written in the main text. The Qere is considered the correct reading, but the Ketiv is also included for reference, as it can provide insight into the history

INTRODUCTION TO THE TEXT OF THE OLD TESTAMENT

and development of the text. The use of Qere and Ketiv is an important aspect of Hebrew Textual Criticism and is used to study the transmission and preservation of the Hebrew Bible.

Recension— A recension is a deliberate revision of an ancient text or translation, usually done with the goal of standardizing or updating the text. It is distinct from a text type or family, which develops over time through the accumulation of scribal errors and other changes. This can include updating language, correcting errors, or making the text conform to certain religious or cultural standards. It is a process of making changes to the text to bring it to a certain level of accuracy.

Samaritan Pentateuch— The Samaritan Pentateuch is an edition of the first five books of the Hebrew Bible (also known as the Torah) that is preserved in the Paleo-Hebrew script by the Samaritan community. The Samaritans are a group of Jewish people who have a distinct religious tradition and history, separate from mainstream Judaism. The Samaritan Pentateuch is considered to be a unique version of the Hebrew text, with variations in wording, spelling, and punctuation compared to the Masoretic Text. It is considered to be a valuable resource for textual criticism and the study of the transmission of the biblical text. It is also considered to be a witness to the Palestinian Text Family, one of the main text types used in Old Testament Textual Criticism.

Septuagint— The Septuagint, often abbreviated as LXX, is a Greek translation of the Hebrew Bible. It is also known as the "translation of the seventy" because tradition holds that it was made by seventy Jewish scholars. The Septuagint was likely made in Alexandria, Egypt, between the 3rd and 1st centuries BCE, and it became the primary Bible of the Greek-speaking Jewish community, as well as the Bible of the early Christian Church. The Septuagint includes not only the books found in the Jewish canon of scripture but also additional books, called the "Apocrypha" or "Deuterocanonicals" which are not considered part of the Hebrew Bible. The Septuagint has had a significant impact on both Jewish and Christian tradition and has been used as a tool for understanding the meaning and context of the Hebrew Bible.

Symmachus— Symmachus is a reviser of the Septuagint, a Greek translation of the Old Testament. He is known to have lived in the late second century CE and is characterized by his good Greek style in his revisions of the Septuagint. He is one of the revisers whose work was included in Origen's Hexapla, which was a six-column work that contained the Hebrew text, Greek transliteration of the Hebrew, the revisions of Aquila, Symmachus, and Theodotion, as well as Origen's own revision of the Septuagint.

Syro-Hexapla— The Syro-Hexapla is a version of the Hexapla, which was a six-column work of Origen, that includes a Syriac translation of the fifth column of the Hexapla. The fifth column of the Hexapla is said to contain the symbols that Origen used to show differences between the Septuagint, which is a Greek translation of the Old Testament and the Hebrew text of his time. The Syro-Hexapla was made by Paul of Tella, who is believed to have been active in the 7th century. This version is said to have been used by later Syrian Christian scholars.

Targums— Targums are Aramaic translations or paraphrases of the Hebrew text of the Old Testament. They were initially passed down orally before being written down. They are known for their interpretive and explanatory nature, rather than being literal translations.

Textual Scholar— A textual scholar is an individual who specializes in the study of the texts of the Old or New Testament, specifically in the area of textual criticism. Textual criticism is the process of evaluating the different versions and manuscript traditions of a text in order to determine the original reading or the one that is most likely to be the original. This field of study involves analyzing the variations and errors that have been introduced into the texts over time and comparing different versions of the text in order to reconstruct the original version as closely as possible. Textual scholars use a variety of tools and techniques, including the study of linguistics, paleography, and historical context, in order to determine the most accurate version of the text. They may also use computer-assisted methods, such as statistical analysis, to aid in their research. Ultimately, the goal of textual scholarship is to provide a critical edition of the text that accurately represents the original wording and meaning of the text, and that can be used as a reliable source for scholars and researchers studying the text. The goal of Old or New Testament textual criticism has always been and should always be to determine the original reading or the one that is most likely to be the original.

Text Type— A text type is a grouping of texts and/or translations that share a significant number of common features. Text types are used in textual criticism to help scholars understand the relationships between different versions of a text, and to reconstruct the original text as closely as possible.

Theodotion— Theodotion was a Greek translator and reviser of the Septuagint, the Greek translation of the Hebrew Bible, in the second century CE. He is known for his "Theodotionic" recension, or revision, of the Greek text which aimed to correct and improve upon the Septuagint. Theodotion is believed to have used the kaige recension, an earlier revision of the Septuagint text, as a base for his own revision, but also made changes to the text that were more in line with the Hebrew Masoretic Text. His revision of

INTRODUCTION TO THE TEXT OF THE OLD TESTAMENT

the Septuagint text was widely used and accepted in early Christianity, and many of his readings were later incorporated into the Greek Orthodox Church's Bible. Theodotion's work had a significant impact on the development of the Septuagint and the understanding of the Hebrew Bible in early Christianity.

Transposition (metathesis)— A transposition, also known as metathesis, is a type of scribal error that occurs when the order of letters or words in a text is changed. This can happen when a scribe inadvertently reverses the order of letters or words while copying a text, or when a copyist is trying to correct an error in the text but ends up creating a new one. This type of error can result in changes to the meaning of a word or phrase, or even create new words or phrases that were not present in the original text. Transpositions are relatively common in ancient texts, particularly those that were copied by hand, and can make it difficult for textual scholars to determine the original reading of a text. However, the presence of transpositions can also provide valuable information about the transmission and evolution of a text over time.

Textual Critic: Textual criticism is a method of evaluating and comparing various manuscript witnesses to determine the original wording of a text. In the case of the Old Testament, textual criticism aims to reconstruct the autograph or the initial text of the Old Testament from which all existing copies originated. The textual critic uses a combination of mental and computer-based tools to decide between variant readings among the manuscripts.

Textual critics have different approaches and preferences when it comes to evaluating and comparing manuscript witnesses. Some prefer early manuscripts, which may have more difficult readings, as they believe that these readings are more likely to be closer to the original text. Others may prefer a specific manuscript, such as the Leningrad Codex, as they believe that it is one of the oldest and most complete manuscripts of the Hebrew Bible. Still, others may prefer to use versions, such as the Septuagint, as they believe that they can provide valuable insight into the text.

The process of textual criticism involves several steps, such as collecting and analyzing the evidence, applying rules and principles, and making a judgment about the original reading. The text critic must weigh the evidence in light of the rules and principles discussed above, as well as the text-critical context, such as the historical and literary background of the text.

Some of the principles that may be applied in Old Testament textual criticism include the principle of lectio difficilior potior, which states that the more difficult reading is more likely to be original, and the principle of lectio brevior potior, which states that the shorter reading is more likely to be original. Additionally, the textual critic may also use external sources such as the Septuagint, the Dead Sea Scrolls, and the Samaritan Pentateuch to aid in their decision making. The textual critic must also consider the context, style, and vocabulary of the passage in question, as well as any known scribal habits or tendencies that may have affected the transmission of the text. Ultimately, the textual critic must make a judgment about the most likely original reading based on all of the evidence collected and analyzed.

Textual Criticism: Textual Criticism of the Old Testament is a complex and nuanced field that requires a combination of both scientific and faith-based approaches. The goal of this field is to determine the original text of the Old Testament from the variant readings exhibited by extant manuscripts. To do this, scholars use a variety of tools, including statistics and computer processing, to compare and analyze the different readings.

One of the key challenges in Old Testament Textual Criticism is the fact that the original autograph is not extant, making it difficult at times to verify the accuracy of a particular reading of the reconstructed text. This has led to different schools of thought among scholars, with some preferring to rely on early manuscripts with more difficult readings, while others prefer to use a specific manuscript, such as the Leningrad Codex, or the versions.

Furthermore, many conservative theologians consider TC to be faith-based, as they believe that God has preserved His word among extant manuscripts. This view is reflected in the belief that conjectural emendation is unnecessary and unacceptable.

Despite these challenges, many critics have been able to reconstruct the original text of the Old Testament with a high degree of probability. This is achieved by using logic and the genealogical relationships between texts, along with other factors such as internal and external evidence. However, it is important to note that the results of TC are not always easy to verify and some decisions are based on a certain level of uncertainty.

In conclusion, Textual Criticism of the Old Testament is a challenging field that requires a combination of scientific and faith-based approaches. Although it is sometimes difficult to verify the accuracy of a particular reading of the reconstructed text, many scholars have been able to reconstruct the original text with a high degree of probability.

Variant Reading(s): A variant reading is a difference in wording or text found in multiple manuscripts of a certain text or document. These variations

INTRODUCTION TO THE TEXT OF THE OLD TESTAMENT

can occur due to errors made by scribes when copying the text, or because of intentional changes made by editors or translators.

Variation Unit: Variation units in Hebrew Old Testament textual criticism are sections of text that have variations in their readings between different manuscripts. These variations can include differences in spelling, word order, and even entire words or phrases. Setting the limits of a variation unit can be difficult and sometimes controversial, as some variant readings may affect others nearby.

It is important to distinguish between variation units and variant readings. A variation unit is the specific place in the text where manuscripts disagree, and each variation unit has at least two variant readings. For example, if two manuscripts have different readings for the same sentence, that sentence would be considered a variation unit, and the different readings would be considered variant readings.

Textual critics must carefully evaluate each variation unit to determine the original reading. They may use a variety of methods and principles, such as the principle that the shorter reading is more likely to be original, or the principle that the reading found in the oldest manuscripts is more likely to be original.

It should also be noted that the terms "manuscript" and "witness" may be used interchangeably in the context of Hebrew Old Testament textual criticism. A "witness" refers to the content of a given manuscript or fragment, while a "manuscript" refers to the physical document containing the witness. For example, one might say "the witness of the Leningrad Codex" to distinguish the content of that manuscript from others.

Edward D. Andrews

CHRISTIAN PUBLISHING HOUSE

SCRIBES AND SCRIPTURE

FROM SPOKEN WORDS TO SACRED TEXTS

INTRODUCTION-INTERMEDIATE
NEW TESTAMENT TEXTUAL STUDIES

EDWARD D. ANDREWS

THE BIBLE ON TRIAL

Examining the Evidence for Being Inspired, Inerrant, Authentic, and True

EDWARD D. ANDREWS

Edward D. Andrews

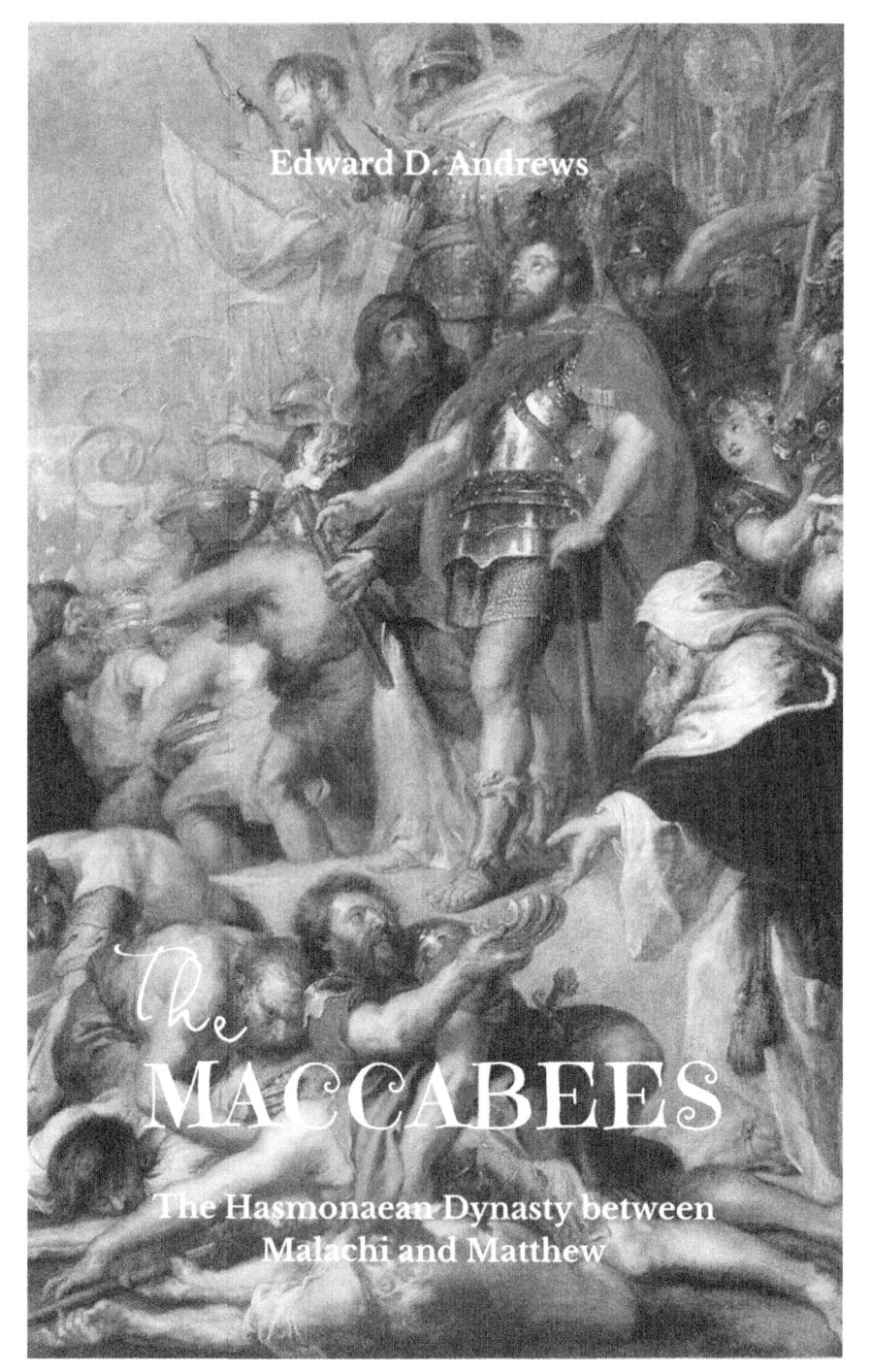

MACCABEES

The Hasmonaean Dynasty between Malachi and Matthew

BIBLIOGRAPHY

Abercrombie, John R. "Computer Assisted Alignment of the Greek and Hebrew Biblical Texts—Programming Background." *Textus* 11 (1984): 125–39.

Adler, William. "Computer Assisted Morphological Analysis of the Septuagint." *Textus* 11 (1984): 1–16.

Albrektson, Bertil. "Difficilior Lectio Probabilior: A Rule of Textual Criticism and Its Use in Old Testament Studies." *Oudtestamentische Studiën* 21 (1981): 5–18.

———. "Reflections on the Emergence of a Standard Text of the Hebrew Bible." In *Congress Volume: Göttingen 1977*, edited by Walther Zimmerli, 49–65. VTSup 29. Leiden: Brill, 1978.

Allen, James P. "Egyptian Language and Writing." In *ABD* 4:188–93.

Anderson, Robert T., and Terry Giles. *The Samaritan Pentateuch: An Introduction to Its Origin, History, and Significance for Biblical Studies*. Atlanta: SBL, 2012.

Archer, Gleason L., Jr. *A Survey of Old Testament Introduction*. 2nd ed. Chicago: Moody, 1974.

Baines, John. *Visual and Written Culture in Egypt*. Oxford: Oxford University Press, 2007.

Bar-Ilan, Meir. "Writing Materials." In *Encyclopedia of the Dead Sea Scrolls*, edited by Lawrence H. Schiffman and James C. VanderKam, 2:996–97. Oxford: Oxford University Press, 2000.

Barkay, Gabriel, Marilyn J. Lundberg, Andrew G. Vaughn, and Bruce Zuckerman. "The Amulets from Ketef Hinnom: A New Edition and Evaluation." *BASOR* 334 (May 2004): 41–71.

Barr, James. *Comparative Philology and the Text of the Old Testament*. 1968. Reprint, Winona Lake, IN: Eisenbrauns, 1987.

———. "Review of *Biblia Hebraica Stuttgartensia*, edited by Karl Elliger and Wilhelm Rudolph." *JSS* 25, no. 1 (1980): 98–105.

Barthélemy, Dominique, ed. *Critique textuelle de l'Ancien Testament*. 4 vols. to date. OBO 50. Göttingen: Vandenhoeck & Ruprecht, 1982–.

Beckwith, Roger T. *The Old Testament Canon of the New Testament Church and Its Background in Early Judaism.* Grand Rapids: Eerdmans; London: SPCK, 1985.

Ben-Hayyim, Zeev. "The Samaritan Vowel-System and Its Graphic Representation." *Archív orienta´lní* 22 (1954): 515–30.

Bentzen, Aage. *Introduction to the Old Testament.* Copenhagen: Gad, 1948.

Bibliorum Sacrorum Codex Vaticanus B. Bibliorum Sacrorum Graecus 1209. Bibiotheca Apostolica Vaticana. Rome: Istituto Poligrafico and Zecca dello Stato, 1999.

Borbone, P. G., ed. *The Pentateuch.* Vol. 1 of *Concordance*, which is part 5 of *The Old Testament in Syriac*. Leiden: Brill, 1997.

Bottéro, Jean. *Mesopotamia: Writing, Reasoning, and the Gods.* Translated by Zainab Bahrani and Marc van de Mieroop. Chicago: University of Chicago Press, 1992.

Breuer, Mordechai, and Yosef Oder, eds. *Jerusalem Crown: The Bible of the Hebrew University of Jerusalem.* Jerusalem: N. Ben-Zvi, 2000.

Brock, Sebastian P. *The Bible in the Syriac Tradition.* Gorgias Handbooks 7. Piscataway, NJ: Gorgias, 2006.

Brooke, Alan E., and Norman McLean, eds. *The Old Testament in Greek.* Vol. 1, pt. 4. Cambridge: Cambridge University Press, 1917.

Burrows, Millar. *The Dead Sea Scrolls.* New York: Viking, 1955.

Bush, Frederic W. *Ruth, Esther.* WBC 9. Waco: Word Books, 1996.

Campbell, Edward F., Jr. *Ruth: A New Translation, with Introduction, Notes, and Commentary.* AB 7. Garden City, NY: Doubleday, 1975.

Carbajosa, Ignacio. *The Character of the Syriac Version of Psalms.* Leiden: Brill, 2008.

Cargill, Robert. *Qumran through Real Time: A Virtual Reconstruction of Qumran and the Dead Sea Scrolls.* Piscataway, NJ: Gorgias, 2009.

Clarke, Ernest G., ed. *Targum Pseudo-Jonathan of the Pentateuch: Text and Concordance.* Hoboken, NJ: Ktav, 1984.

Cook, E. M. *A Glossary of Targum Onkelos according to Alexander Sperber's Edition.* Studies in the Aramaic Interpretation of Scripture 6. Leiden: Brill, 2008.

Cooper, Jerrold S. "Babylonian Beginnings: The Origin of the Cuneiform Writing System in Comparative Perspective." In *The First Writing: Script Invention as History and Process*, edited by Stephen D. Houston, 71–99. Cambridge: Cambridge University Press, 2004.

Cross, Frank M. *The Ancient Library of Qumran and Modern Biblical Studies*. Rev. ed. Garden City, NY: Anchor Books, 1961. Reprint, Grand Rapids: Baker, 1980.

———. "The Contribution of the Qumran Discoveries to the Study of the Biblical Text." *Israel Exploration Journal* 16 (1966): 81–95. Later published in Cross and Talmon, *Qumran and the History of the Biblical Text*.

———. *From Epic to Canon: History and Literature in Ancient Israel*. Baltimore: Johns Hopkins University Press, 1998.

———. "Problems of Method in the Textual Criticism of the Hebrew Bible." In *The Critical Study of Sacred Texts*, edited by Wendy Doniger O'Flaherty, 31–54. Berkeley: Graduate Theological Union, 1979.

Cross, Frank M., and Shemaryahu Talmon, eds. *Qumran and the History of the Biblical Text*. Cambridge, MA: Harvard University Press, 1975.

David, Clemens Joseph. *The Syriac Bible according to the Mosul Edition*. 3 vols. Piscataway, NJ: Gorgias, 2010.

Davies, Graham. "Some Uses of Writing in Ancient Israel in the Light of Recently Published Inscriptions." In *Writing and Ancient Near Eastern Society: Papers in Honour of Alan R. Millard*, edited by Piotr Bienkowski, Christopher Mee, and Elizabeth Slater, 155–74. New York: T&T Clark, 2005.

Deist, Ferdinand, and Walter K. Winckler. *Towards the Text of the Old Testament*. Pretoria: DR Church Bookseller, 1978.

Demsky, Aaron, and Meir Bar-Ilan. "Writing in Ancient Israel and Early Judaism." In Mulder, *Mikra*, 2–38.

Díaz Esteban, Fernando. "References to Ben Asher and Ben Naphtali in the Masorah Magna Written in the Margins of MS Leningrad B19a." *Textus* 6 (1968): 62–74.

Díez Macho, Alejandro, ed. *Neophyti 1: Targum Palestinense Ms. de la Biblioteca Vaticana*. 6 vols. Madrid: Consejo Superior de Investigaciones Científicas, 1968–79.

Díez Merino, L. "Targum Manuscripts and Critical Editions." In *The Aramaic Bible: Targums in Their Historical Context*, edited by D. R. G. Beattie and M. J. McNamara, 51–91. Sheffield: Sheffield Academic Press, 1994.

Diringer, David. *The Alphabet*. 3rd ed. London: Hutchison, 1968.

———. *Writing*. London: Thames & Hudson, 1962.

Dirksen, Peter B. "The Old Testament Peshitta." In Mulder, *Mikra*, 255–97.

Dotan, Aaron. "The Relative Chronology of Hebrew Vocalization and Accentuation." *Proceedings of the American Academy for Jewish Research* 48 (1981): 87–99.

Drijvers, Han J. W. "Edessa und das jüdische Christentum." In *East of Antioch: Studies in Early Syriac Christianity*, 4–33. London: Variorum Reprints, 1984.

Driver, Godfrey R. "Abbreviations in the Massoretic Text." *Textus* 1 (1960): 112–31.

———. "Once Again Abbreviations." *Textus* 4 (1964): 76–94.

Dyk, Janet W., and Percy S. F. van Keulen. *Language System, Translation Technique, and Textual Tradition in the Peshitta of Kings*. Leiden: Brill, 2013.

Edzard, Dietz Otto. *Sumerian Grammar*. Handbook of Oriental Studies 71. Leiden: Brill, 2003.

Elliger, Karl, and Wilhelm Rudolph, eds. *Biblia Hebraica Stuttgartensia*. Stuttgart: Deutsche Bibelgesellschaft, 1983.

Eshel, Esther, and Hanan Eshel. "Dating the Samaritan Pentateuch's Compilation in Light of the Qumran Biblical Scrolls." In *Emanuel: Studies in Hebrew Bible, Septuagint, and Dead Sea Scrolls in Honor of Emanuel Tov*, edited by Shalom Paul, 215–40. Boston: Brill, 2003.

Eshel, Hanan. *The Dead Sea Scrolls and the Hasmonean State*. Grand Rapids: Eerdmans, 2008.

Fernández Marcos, Natalio. *The Septuagint in Context: Introduction to the Greek Version of the Bible*. Translated by Wilfred G. E. Watson. Boston: Brill, 2001.

Field, F., ed. *Origenis Hexaplorum quae supersunt sive veterum interpretum graecorum in totum Vetus Testamentum fragmenta*. 2 vols. 1875. Reprint, Hildesheim: Olms, 1964.

Fishbane, Michael. *Biblical Interpretation in Ancient Israel*. Oxford: Clarendon, 1985.

Flesher, Paul V. M., and Bruce Chilton. *The Targums: A Critical Introduction*. Waco: Baylor University Press, 2011.

Fox, Michael V., ed. *Proverbs: An Eclectic Edition with Introduction and Textual Commentary*. HBCE 1. Atlanta: SBL Press, 2015.

Freedman, David Noel. "The Massoretic Text and the Qumran Scrolls: A Study in Orthography." In Cross and Talmon, *Qumran and the History of the Biblical Text*, 196–211.

Freedman, David Noel, James A. Sanders, Marilyn J. Lundberg, Astrid B. Beck, and Bruce E. Zuckerman, eds. *The Leningrad Codex: A Facsimile Edition*. Grand Rapids: Eerdmans, 1998.

Gall, August F. von, ed. *Der hebräische Pentateuch der Samaritaner*. 5 vols. 1914–18. Reprint, Berlin: Töpelmann, 1966.

Geisler, Norman L., and William E. Nix. *A General Introduction to the Bible*. Rev. ed. Chicago: Moody, 1986.

Ginsburg, Christian D. *Introduction to the Massoretico-Critical Edition of the Hebrew Bible*. London: Trinitarian Bible Society, 1897. Reprint, New York: Ktav, 1966.

Glenny, W. Edward. *Finding Meaning in the Text: Translation Technique and Theology in the Septuagint of Amos*. Leiden: Brill, 2009.

Goldwasser, Orly. "How the Alphabet Was Born from Hieroglyphs." *BAR* 36, no. 2 (2010): 43–44.

Gordis, Robert. *The Biblical Text in the Making: A Study of the Kethib-Qere*. Augmented ed. New York: Ktav, 1971.

Gordon, Cyrus H. *Ugaritic Textbook*. AnOr 38. Rome: Pontifical Biblical Institute Press, 1965.

Gordon, Robert P. "Foreword to the Reprinted Edition (1992)." In *The Bible in Aramaic*, edited by Alexander Sperber, 7–12. Leiden: Brill, 2004.

Goshen-Gottstein, Moshe H., ed. *The Aleppo Codex: Provided with Massoretic Notes and Pointed by Aaron Ben Asher; The Codex Considered Authoritative by Maimonides*. Winona Lake, IN: Eisenbrauns, 1976.

———. "The Aleppo Codex and the Rise of the Massoretic Bible Text." *BA* 42, no. 3 (1979): 145–63.

———, ed. *The Book of Isaiah*. HUBP 1. Jerusalem: Magnes, 1975.

———. "Hebrew Biblical Manuscripts." In Cross and Talmon, *Qumran and the History of the Biblical Text*, 42–89.

———. "The Rise of the Tiberian Bible Text." In *The Canon and Masorah of the Hebrew Bible*, edited by Sid Z. Leiman, 666–709. New York: Ktav, 1974.

Goshen-Gottstein, Moshe H., and Shemaryahu Talmon, eds. *The Book of Ezekiel*. HUBP 3. Jerusalem: Magnes, 2004.

Göttinger Akademie der Wissenschaften, ed. *Septuaginta: Vetus Testamentum graecum*. Göttingen: Vandenhoeck & Ruprecht, 1926–.

Grayzel, Solomon. *A History of the Jews*. Rev. ed. Philadelphia: Jewish Publication Society, 1968.

Greenberg, Moshe. "The Stabilization of the Text of the Hebrew Bible, Reviewed in the Light of the Biblical Materials from the Judean Desert." *Journal of the American Oriental Society* 76, no. 3 (1956): 157–67.

Haran, Menahem. "Book-Scrolls in Israel in Pre-exilic Times." *JSS* 33 (1982): 161–73.

———. "On the Diffusion of Literacy and Schools in Ancient Israel." In *Congress Volume: Jerusalem 1986*, edited by J. A. Emerton, 81–95. VTSup 40. Leiden: Brill, 1988.

Harrison, Roland K. *Introduction to the Old Testament*. Grand Rapids: Eerdmans, 1969.

Hatch, Edwin, and Henry A. Redpath. *A Concordance to the Septuagint and the Other Greek Versions of the Old Testament (Including the Apocryphal Books)*. 2nd ed. Grand Rapids: Baker, 1998.

Hayes, John L. *A Manual of Sumerian Grammar and Texts*. 2nd ed. Aids and Research Tools in Ancient Near Eastern Studies 5. Malibu: Udena, 2000.

Heater, Homer. "A Textual Note on Luke 3.33." *Journal for the Study of the New Testament* 28 (1986): 25–29.

Hendel, Ronald S. "Assessing the Text-Critical Theories of the Hebrew Bible after Qumran." In Lim and Collins, *Oxford Handbook*, 281–302.

Holmstedt, Robert D. *Ruth: A Handbook on the Hebrew Text*. Waco: Baylor University Press, 2010.

Hubbard, Robert L., Jr. *The Book of Ruth*. NICOT. Grand Rapids: Eerdmans, 1988.

Huehnergard, John. *A Grammar of Akkadian*. 2nd ed. Winona Lake, IN: Eisenbrauns, 2005.

Huehnergard, John, and Christopher Woods. "Akkadian and Eblaite." In *The Cambridge Encyclopedia of the World's Ancient Languages*, edited by Roger D. Woodard, 218–80. Cambridge: Cambridge University Press, 2004.

Hurvitz, Avi. "Ruth 2:7: 'A Midrashic Gloss'?" *Zeitschrift für die alttestamentliche Wissenschaft* 95, no. 1 (1983): 121–23.

International Organization for the Study of the Old Testament: Peshitta Institute, ed. *The Old Testament in Syriac according to the Peshitta Version*. Leiden: Brill, 1972–.

Iwasaki, Soichi. *Japanese*. Rev. ed. London Oriental and African Language Library 17. Philadelphia: John Benjamins, 2013.

———. "Japanese: Language Situation." In *Encyclopedia of Language and Linguistics*, edited by Keith Brown, 6:93–95. 2nd ed. Oxford: Elsevier, 2006.

Janzen, J. Gerald. *Studies in the Text of Jeremiah*. Harvard Semitic Monographs 6. Cambridge, MA: Harvard University Press, 1973.

Jastrow, Marcus. *A Dictionary of the Targumim, the Talmud Babli and Yerushalmi, and the Midrashic Literature*. 2 vols. 1903. Reprint, Peabody, MA: Hendrickson, 2006.

Jobes, Karen H., and Moisés Silva. *Invitation to the Septuagint*. 2nd ed. Grand Rapids: Baker Academic, 2015.

Johnson, Ricky L. "Bar-Kochba." In *HIBD*, 171.

Joüon, Paul. *Ruth: Commentaire philologique et exégétique*. Rome: Institut Biblique Pontifical, 1953.

Kahle, Paul E. *The Cairo Geniza*. 2nd ed. Oxford: Blackwell, 1959.

Kartveit, Magnar. *The Origin of the Samaritans*. Boston: Brill, 2009.

Kedar, Benjamin. "The Latin Translations." In Mulder, *Mikra*, 299–338.

Kedar-Kopfstein, Benjamin. "The Vulgate as a Translation: Some Semantic and Syntactical Aspects of Jerome's Version of the Hebrew Bible." PhD diss., Hebrew University of Jerusalem, 1968.

Kelley, Page H., Daniel S. Mynatt, and Timothy G. Crawford. *The Masorah of Biblia Hebraica Stuttgartensia*. Grand Rapids: Eerdmans, 1998.

Kennicott, Benjamin, ed. *Vetus Testamentum hebraicum cum variis lectionibus*. 2 vols. Oxford: Clarendon, 1776–80.

Kenyon, Frederic. *Our Bible and the Ancient Manuscripts*. 4th ed. New York: Harper, 1941.

Kidner, Derek. *Genesis*. Downers Grove, IL: InterVarsity, 1967.

Kittel, Rudolf, and Paul Kahle, eds. *Torah, Nevi'im ve-Ketubim: Biblia Hebraica*. Stuttgart: Privilegierte Württembergische Bibelanstalt, 1937, 1951.

Klein, Michael L. "Cairo Genizah Targum Texts: Old and New." In *The Aramaic Bible: Targums in Their Historical Context*, edited by D. R. G. Beattie and M. J. McNamara, 18–29. Sheffield: Sheffield Academic Press, 1994.

———. *The Fragment-Targums of the Pentateuch according to Their Extant Sources*. 2 vols. Analecta Biblica 76. Rome: Pontifical Biblical Institute Press, 1980.

———. *Genizah Manuscripts of Palestinian Targum to the Pentateuch*. Cincinnati: Hebrew Union College, 1986.

Klein, Ralph W. "Review of *The Israelite Samaritan Version of the Torah*." *Currents in Theology and Mission* 40, no. 6 (2013): 435–36.

———. *Textual Criticism of the Old Testament: From the Septuagint to Qumran*. Guides to Biblical Scholarship. Philadelphia: Fortress, 1974.

Lange, Armin. "The Textual Plurality of Jewish Scriptures in the Second Temple Period in Light of the Dead Sea Scrolls." In *Qumran and the Bible: Studying the Jewish and Christian Scriptures in Light of the Dead Sea Scrolls*, edited by Nora David and Armin Lange, 43–96. Leuven: Peeters, 2010.

Lemaire, André. "Writing and Writing Materials." In *ABD* 6:999–1008.

Leupold, Herbert C. *Exposition of Genesis*. Columbus, OH: Wartburg, 1942. Reprint, Grand Rapids: Baker, 1960.

Lim, Timothy H., and John J. Collins. "Introduction: Current Issues in Dead Sea Scrolls Research." In Lim and Collins, *Oxford Handbook*, 1–18.

———, eds. *The Oxford Handbook of the Dead Sea Scrolls*. New York: Oxford University Press, 2012.

Loewinger, D. S., ed. *Cairo Codex of the Bible*. Jerusalem: Makor, 1971.

Louw, Theo van der. *Transformations in the Septuagint: Towards an Interaction of Septuagint Studies and Translation Studies*. Leuven: Peeters, 2007.

Lundbom, Jack. *Jeremiah 1–20: A New Translation with Introduction and Commentary*. AB 21a. New York: Doubleday, 1999.

MacArthur, Elise V. "The Conception and Development of the Egyptian Writing System." In *Visible Language: Inventions of Writing in the Ancient Middle East and Beyond*, edited by Christopher Woods, 149–82. Chicago: Oriental Institute Museum Publications, 2010.

Maori, Yeshayahu. "Methodological Criteria for Distinguishing between Variant Vorlage and Exegesis in the Peshitta Pentateuch." In *The Peshitta as a Translation*, edited by P. B. Dirksen and Arie van der Kooij, 103–20. Leiden: Brill, 1995.

Margolis, Max L., and Alexander Marx. *A History of the Jewish People*. Philadelphia: Jewish Publication Society, 1934.

McCarter, P. Kyle, Jr. *Textual Criticism: Recovering the Text of the Hebrew Bible*. Guides to Biblical Scholarship. Philadelphia: Fortress, 1986.

McCarthy, Carmel. *The Tiqqune Sopherim and Other Theological Corrections in the Masoretic Text of the Old Testament*. OBO 36. Göttingen: Vandenhoeck & Ruprecht, 1981.

McNamara, Martin J., ed. *The Aramaic Bible: The Targums*. 22 vols. Collegeville, MN: Liturgical Press, 1987–2007.

Meyers, Eric M. "Khirbet Qumran and Its Environs." In Lim and Collins, *Oxford Handbook*, 21–45.

Millard, Alan R. "In Praise of Ancient Scribes." *BA* 45, no. 3 (1982): 143–53.

———. " 'Scriptio Continua' in Early Hebrew: Ancient Practice or Modern Surmise?" *JSS* 15 (1970): 2–15.

———. "Were Words Separated in Ancient Hebrew Writing?" *BRev* 8, no. 3 (1992): 44–47.

Minkoff, Harvey. "The Aleppo Codex—Ancient Bible from the Ashes." *BRev* 7, no. 4 (1991): 22–27, 38–40.

Moscati, Sabatino, et al. *An Introduction to the Comparative Grammar of the Semitic Languages*. Wiesbaden: Harrassowitz, 1969.

Mulder, Martin Jan, ed. *Mikra: Text, Translation, Reading & Interpretation of the Hebrew Bible in Ancient Judaism & Early Christianity*. 1988. Reprint, Peabody, MA: Hendrickson, 2004.

Muraoka, T., and J. F. Elwolde, eds. *Diggers at the Well: Proceedings of a Third International Symposium on the Hebrew of the Dead Sea Scrolls and Ben Sira*. Boston: Brill, 2000.

Naveh, Joseph. *Early History of the Alphabet: An Introduction to West Semitic Epigraphy and Paleography*. Jerusalem: Magnes, 1987.

Ofer, Yosef. "The Shattered Crown: The Aleppo Codex, 60 Years after the Riots." *BAR* 34, no. 5 (2008): 38–49.

Olofsson, Staffan. *The LXX Version: A Guide to the Translation Technique of the Septuagint*. Stockholm: Almqvist & Wiksell, 1990.

Pietersma, Albert, and Benjamin G. Wright, eds. *A New English Translation of the Septuagint*. Oxford: Oxford University Press, 2007.

Pontifical Abbey of St. Jerome-in-the-City, ed. *Biblia Sacra iuxta latinam Vulgatam versionem*. Rome: Vatican, 1926–.

Poole, J. B., and R. Reed. "The Preparation of Leather and Parchment by the Dead Sea Scrolls Community." *Technology and Culture* 3, no. 1 (1962): 10–14.

Powell, Barry. *Writing: Theory and History of the Technology of Civilization*. Malden, MA: Wiley-Blackwell, 2009.

Pummer, Reinhard. "The Samaritans and Their Pentateuch." In *The Pentateuch as Torah: New Models for Understanding Its Promulgation and Acceptance*, edited by Gary N. Knoppers and Bernard M. Levinson, 237–69. Winona Lake, IN: Eisenbrauns, 2007.

Quast, U., ed. *Ruth*. Vol. IV/3 of *Septuaginta: Vetus Testamentum graecum*. Göttingen: Vandenhoeck & Ruprecht, 2006.

Rabin, Chaim, Shemaryahu Talmon, and Emanuel Tov, eds. *The Book of Jeremiah*. HUBP 2. Jerusalem: Magnes, 1998.

Rahlfs, Alfred, and Robert Hanhart, eds. *Septuaginta: Id est Vetus Testamentum graece iuxta LXX interpretes*. Corr. ed. Stuttgart: Deutsche Bibelgesellschaft, 2006.

Roberts, Bleddyn J. *The Old Testament Text and Versions: The Hebrew Text in Transmission and the History of the Ancient Versions*. Cardiff: University of Wales Press, 1951.

Rollston, Christopher A. "Scribal Education in Ancient Israel: The Old Hebrew Epigraphic Evidence." *BASOR* 344 (November 2006): 47–74.

———. *Writing and Literacy in the World of Ancient Israel: Epigraphic Evidence from the Iron Age*. Atlanta: Society of Biblical Literature, 2010.

Rossi, Giovanni de, ed. *Variae lectiones Veteris Testamenti*. 4 vols. Parma: Regio, 1784–88.

Sabatier, P., ed. *Bibliorum sacrorum latinae versiones antiquae seu Vetus Italica.* Rheims, 1739–43; Paris, 1751.

Sadaqa, I. *Hatorah Haqedošah.* Holon: A. B. Institute of Samaritan Studies, 1998.

Sanderson, Judith E. "The Contributions of 4QpaleoExod[m] to Textual Criticism." *Revue de Qumran* 13 (1988): 547–60.

Sasson, Jack M. *Ruth: A New Translation with a Philological Commentary and a Formalist-Folklorist Interpretation.* Sheffield: Sheffield Academic Press, 1989.

Schenker, A., Y. A. P. Goldman, A. van der Kooij, G. J. Norton, S. Pisano, J. de Waard, and R. D. Weis, eds. *Biblia Hebraica Quinta.* Stuttgart: Deutsche Bibelgesellschaft, 2004–.

Scott, William R. *A Simplified Guide to BHS: Critical Apparatus, Masora, Accents, Unusual Letters & Other Markings.* Berkeley: BIBAL, 1987.

Smith, Payne R., and J. Payne Smith. *Compendious Syriac Dictionary: Founded upon the Thesaurus Syriacus of R. Payne Smith.* Winona Lake, IN: Eisenbrauns, 1998.

Snaith, Norman, ed. ספר תורה נביאים וכתובים [The Book of the Torah, Prophets, and Writings]. London: British and Foreign Bible Society, 1960.

Sokoloff, Michael. *A Syriac Lexicon: A Translation from the Latin, Correction, Expansion, and Update of C. Brockelmann's "Lexicon Syriacum."* Piscataway, NJ: Gorgias, 2009.

Sperber, Alexander, ed. *The Bible in Aramaic.* Leiden: Brill, 2004.

Stuart, Douglas. "Inerrancy and Textual Criticism." In *Inerrancy and Common Sense,* edited by Roger R. Nicole and J. Ramsey Michaels, 97–117. Grand Rapids: Baker, 1980.

Stuckenbruck, Loren T., and David Noel Freedman. "The Fragments of a Targum to Leviticus in Qumran Cave 4 (4Q156)." In *Targum and Scripture: Studies in Aramaic Translations and Interpretation in Memory of Ernest G. Clarke,* edited by Paul V. M. Flesher, 79–95. Leiden: Brill, 2002.

Syriac Bible: Reprint of the 1826 Edition of the Peshitta by S. Lee. [London]: United Bible Societies, 1979.

Tal, Abraham. "Divergent Traditions of the Samaritan Pentateuch as Reflected by Its Aramaic Targum." *Journal for the Aramaic Bible* 1, no. 2 (1999): 297–314.

Tallet, Pierre, and Gregory Marouard. "The Harbor of Khufu on the Red Sea Coast at Wadi al-Jarf, Egypt." *Near Eastern Archaeology* 77, no. 1 (2014): 4–14.

Talmon, Shemaryahu. "The Crystallization of the 'Canon of Hebrew Scriptures' in the Light of Biblical Scrolls from Qumran." In *The Bible as Book: The Hebrew Bible and the Judaean Desert Discoveries*, edited by Edward D. Herbert and Emanuel Tov, 5–20. New Castle, DE: Oak Knoll, 2002.

———. "The Old Testament Text." In *From the Beginnings to Jerome*, vol. 1 of *The Cambridge History of the Bible*, edited by Peter R. Ackroyd and Christopher F. Evans, 159–99. Cambridge: Cambridge University Press, 1970.

———. "The Paleo-Hebrew Alphabet and Biblical Text Criticism." In *Text and Canon of the Hebrew Bible: Collected Studies*, 125–70. Winona Lake, IN: Eisenbrauns, 2010.

———. "The Textual Study of the Bible—A New Outlook." In Cross and Talmon, *Qumran and the History of the Biblical Text*, 321–400.

———. "The Transmission History of the Text of the Hebrew Bible in the Light of Biblical Manuscripts from Qumran and Other Sites in the Judean Desert." In *The Dead Sea Scrolls: Fifty Years after Their Discovery; Proceedings of the Jerusalem Congress, July 20–25, 1997*, edited by Lawrence H. Schiffman, Emanuel Tov, and James C. VanderKam, 40–50. Jerusalem: Israel Exploration Society, 2000.

Taylor, Joan E. "The Classical Sources on the Essenes and the Scrolls Communities." In Lim and Collins, *Oxford Handbook*, 173–99.

Toury, Gideon. *Translation Studies and Beyond*. Philadelphia: John Benjamins, 1995.

Tov, Emanuel. *A Computerized Data Base for Septuagint Studies: The Parallel Aligned Text of the Greek and Hebrew Bible*. Journal of Northwest Semitic Languages Supplement Series 1. Stellenbosch: Journal of Northwest Semitic Languages, 1986.

———. "Correction Procedures in the Texts from the Judean Desert." In *The Provo International Conference on the Dead Sea Scrolls: Technological Innovations, New Texts, and Reformulated Issues*, edited by Donald W. Parry and Eugene Ulrich, 236–58. Leiden: Brill, 1999.

———. "Hebrew Biblical Manuscripts from the Judaean Desert: Their Contribution to Textual Criticism." *Journal of Jewish Studies* 39, no. 1 (1988): 5–37.

———. "A Modern Textual Outlook Based on the Qumran Scrolls." *Hebrew Union College Annual* 53 (1982): 11–27.

———. *The Parallel Aligned Hebrew-Aramaic and Greek Texts of Jewish Scripture.* Bellingham, WA: Lexham, 2003.

———. *Scribal Practices and Approaches Reflected in the Texts Found in the Judean Desert.* Leiden: Brill, 2004.

———. *The Text-Critical Use of the Septuagint in Biblical Research.* 3rd ed., revised and expanded. Winona Lake, IN: Eisenbrauns, 2015.

———. *Textual Criticism of the Hebrew Bible.* 3rd ed. Minneapolis: Fortress, 2012.

Tully, Eric J. *The Translation and the Translator of the Peshitta of Hosea.* Leiden: Brill, 2015.

Ulrich, Eugene. *The Dead Sea Scrolls and the Origins of the Bible.* Grand Rapids: Eerdmans, 1999.

———. "Methodological Reflections on Determining Scriptural Status." In *Rediscovering the Dead Sea Scrolls: An Assessment of Old and New Approaches and Methods,* edited by Maxine L. Grossman, 145–61. Grand Rapids: Eerdmans, 2010.

Vaux, Roland de. *Archaeology and the Dead Sea Scrolls.* Rev. ed. Schweich Lectures 1959. London: Oxford University Press, 1973.

Vercellone, C., ed. *Biblia Sacra Vulgatae editionis Sixti V. et Clementis VIII. Pontt. Maxx. iussu recognita atque edita.* Rome, 1861.

Vermes, Geza. *An Introduction to the Complete Dead Sea Scrolls.* Philadelphia: Fortress, 1999.

Waard, Jan de, P. B. Dirksen, Y. A. P. Goldman, R. Schäfer, and M. Sæbø, eds. *Biblia Hebraica Quinta.* Fasc. 18, *General Introduction and Megilloth.* Stuttgart: Deutsche Bibelgesellschaft, 2004.

Waltke, Bruce K. "The Aims of OT Textual Criticism." *Westminster Theological Journal* 51, no. 1 (1989): 93–108.

———. "Old Testament Textual Criticism." In *Holman Introduction to the Bible,* edited by David S. Dockery, Kenneth A. Mathews, and Robert Sloan. Nashville: Broadman, forthcoming.

———. "Samaritan Pentateuch." In *ABD* 5:932–40.

———. "The Textual Criticism of the Old Testament." In *The Expositor's Bible Commentary*, edited by Frank E. Gaebelein, 1:211–28. Grand Rapids: Zondervan, 1979.

———. "Textual Criticism of the Old Testament and Its Relation to Exegesis and Theology." In *NIDOTTE* 1:51–67.

Waltke, Bruce K., and Michael O'Connor. *An Introduction to Biblical Hebrew Syntax*. Winona Lake, IN: Eisenbrauns, 1990.

Wasserstein, Abraham, and David J. Wasserstein. *The Legend of the Septuagint: From Classical Antiquity to Today*. Cambridge: Cambridge University Press, 2006.

Weber, Robert, et al., eds. *Biblia Sacra iuxta Vulgatam Versionem*. Stuttgart: Deutsche Bibelgesellschaft, 2007.

Wegner, Paul. *A Student's Guide to Textual Criticism of the Bible*. Downers Grove, IL: InterVarsity, 2006.

Weil, Gérard E. *Massorah Gedolah iuxta Codicem Leningradensem B19a*. Vol. 1, *Catalogi*. Rome: Pontifical Biblical Institute Press, 1971.

Weingreen, Jacob. *Introduction to the Critical Study of the Text of the Hebrew Bible*. New York: Oxford University Press, 1982.

Weiser, Artur. *The Old Testament: Its Formation and Development*. Translated by Dorothea M. Barton. New York: Association Press, 1961.

Weitzman, Michael P. *The Syriac Version of the Old Testament: An Introduction*. Cambridge: Cambridge University Press, 1999.

Wilson, Penelope. *Sacred Signs: Hieroglyphs in Ancient Egypt*. Oxford: Oxford University Press, 2003.

Wise, Michael. "The Origins and History of the Teacher's Movement." In Lim and Collins, *Oxford Handbook*, 92–122.

Wonneberger, Reinhard. *Understanding BHS: A Manual for the Users of Biblia Hebraica Stuttgartensia*. Translated by Dwight R. Daniels. 2nd ed. Subsidia Biblica 8. Rome: Pontifical Biblical Institute Press, 1990.

Woods, Christopher. "The Earliest Mesopotamian Writing." In *Visible Language: Inventions of Writing in the Ancient Middle East and Beyond*, edited by Christopher Woods, 33–50. Chicago: Oriental Institute Museum Publications, 2010.

Woude, Adam S. van der. "Pluriformity and Uniformity: Reflections on the Transmission of the Text of the Old Testament." In *Sacred History and*

INTRODUCTION TO THE TEXT OF THE OLD TESTAMENT

Sacred Texts in Early Judaism: A Symposium in Honour of A. S. van der Woude, edited by J. N. Bremmer and F. García Martínez, 151–69. Kampen, Neth.: Kok Pharos, 1992.

Würthwein, Ernst. *The Text of the Old Testament: An Introduction to the Biblia Hebraica*. Translated by Erroll F. Rhodes. 3rd ed. revised and expanded by Alexander A. Fischer. Grand Rapids: Eerdmans, 2014.

Yardeni, Ada. *The Book of Hebrew Script: History, Palaeography, Script Styles, Calligraphy & Design*. New Castle, DE: Oak Knoll, 2002.

Yeivin, Israel. *Introduction to the Tiberian Masorah*. Translated and edited by E. John Revell. Masoretic Studies 5. Missoula, MT: Scholars Press, 1980.

Young, Ian. "The Stabilization of the Biblical Text in the Light of Qumran and Masada: A Challenge for Conventional Qumran Chronology?" *Dead Sea Discoveries* 9 (2002): 364–90.

Printed in Great Britain
by Amazon